BY WALLACE STEGNER

NOVELS
All the Little Live Things
A Shooting Star
Second Growth
The Big Rock Candy Mountain
Fire and Ice
On a Darkling Plain
The Potter's House
Remembering Laughter
Joe Hill
Angle of Repose

SHORT STORIES
The City of the Living
The Women on the Wall

NON-FICTION
The Uneasy Chair
Beyond the Hundredth Meridian
One Nation (with the Editors of *Look*)
The Gathering of Zion
Mormon Country
Wolf Willow
The Sound of Mountain Water

THE
Letters of Bernard DeVoto

THE
Letters of Bernard DeVoto

WALLACE STEGNER

1975

DOUBLEDAY & COMPANY, INC.
GARDEN CITY, NEW YORK

Library of Congress Cataloging in Publication Data

DeVoto, Bernard Augustine, 1897–1955.
  The letters of Bernard DeVoto.

    1. DeVoto, Bernard Augustine, 1897–1955—Correspondence. 2. Authors, American
—Correspondence, reminiscences, etc. I. Stegner, Wallace Earle, 1909–   ed.
PS3507.E867Z53   1975   818'.5'209[B]
ISBN 0-385-03706-6
Library of Congress Catalog Card Number 74–12715

[. . . .] I burst with creative criticism of America—I have at last found a kind of national self-consciousness. Not the mighty anvil-on-which-is-hammered-out-the-future-of-the-world. Still less the damned-bastard-parvenu-among-the-nations. But I have begun to see American history with some unity, with some perspective, with some meaning . . . to dare to think from cause to effect, from the past to the present and future, always with this new sense of yea-saying youth.

I do not commit the historic folly, from Washington Irving to Van Wyck Brooks, of hearing fiddles tuning up all over America. . . . But I have dared at last to believe that the Nation begins to emerge from adolescence into young manhood, that hereafter the colossal strength may begin to count for the better, as well as for the worse. That indeed we have come to say yea, at last.

And in the facts which alone can show whether we take the turn, or in the study of them, I shall, I think, spend my vigorous years. . . . I believe I have found something into which I may pour that arresting, God-awful emulsion that is I. . . .

Bernard DeVoto to Melville Smith, October 22, 1920

CONTENTS

INTRODUCTION

Dying of gangrene in the African bush, Hemingway's hero in "The Snows of Kilimanjaro" reflects that he has "sold vitality, in one form or other, all his life." That is what any thinker or doer does, what any writer of stature does. It is what Bernard DeVoto, one of the most vigorous of writers, did through a public career of more than thirty years.

He sold vitality where he could, for he had no private income or supportive family, and much of the time he had no professorship, editorship, or other salaried job. He sold it to *Redbook*, the *Post*, *Collier's*, *Harper's*, the *Saturday Review*, *Atlantic*, *Holiday*, *Ford Times*, *Fortune*, *Woman's Day*, and a hundred other places. He sold it under his own name and under the names of John August, Cady Hewes, Richard Dye, Fairley Blake, Frank Gilbert. He sold it to lyceums and lecture agents and women's clubs, sold it as history, criticism, pamphleteering essays, slick serials, serious novels, political and cultural reportage. In his productive lifetime he wrote twenty-one books, plus three that were not published, and nearly eight hundred and fifty magazine pieces. He edited two magazines (the *Harvard Graduates' Magazine* and the *Saturday Review of Literature*), each for about two years, and wrote the Easy Chair in *Harper's* for over twenty. He taught five years at Northwestern and seven at Harvard, and in middle life wrote to his friend Garrett Mattingly that he was slowing down badly—he couldn't seem to manage more than two full-time jobs at a time.

Vitality for sale. And for free. He gave it away with both hands to students, friends, colleagues, opponents, total strangers. The smallest expression of interest from readers stimulated him to response and sometimes to retort. Remembering his gift for controversy, one might be tempted to think of him as some sort of heat-seeking missile, except that he responded even more promptly to friendship, trouble, and human need than he did to hostility. The editors of *Harper's* said he collected underdogs the way a blue serge suit collects lint. A friend in trouble or in need could always count on his time— on whole generous nights and days of time that he did not really have to give. Having suffered most of his life from nervous depression, migraines, and blind panics, he could smell trouble in others, and he would put aside anything to try to help a friend with the horrors.

And not only friends. An unknown student who read one of his essays on education and wrote in asking wistful questions might get a three-thousand-word reply full of reassurance and wisdom. A correspondent moved to applause by one of his stout conservation pieces of the 1940s and 1950s was likely to find himself not only replied to but enlisted. Opponents who tried to brush away this troublesome fly found themselves entangled with a hornet, but any correspondent who indicated that he was willing to listen or argue was forthwith engaged in an educational exchange.

Young writers struggling with their tools found in him help, advice, warnings, and if they seemed to need it, correction, and if they seemed hopeless, blunt discouragement. Those who pitied themselves, feeling abused and victimized by a smug editorial world, got it between the eyes: nobody had asked them to be writers, nobody had guaranteed them a publisher and an audience. Any headway they made would have to be made against difficulties; that was not a conspiracy but a condition of the literary life.

One of the curious aspects of the public reputation of Bernard DeVoto, that contentious, outrageous, crosswise maverick of literature and opinion for whom *Time* always dragged out adjectives like "volcanic" and "angry," was the fact that behind this belligerent head-thumper more and more people came to recognize a champion of everything they believed in, and others discovered a tender, compassionate, patient, and understanding ally against the knocks and blows and injustices of life. Dozens of friends with emotional difficulties adopted him as a sort of lay healer. Dozens of total strangers wrote in from the far frontiers of his Easy Chair coverage and, by mail, did the same.

He was many things: antagonist of fashionable ideas, especially literary Marxism; guru of small-*d* democracy and champion of civil rights; cultural critic; political commentator; historian; novelist; patriot; and, as aforesaid, generous friend and exasperating enemy. Nobody took a neutral position on Benny DeVoto any more than he took a neutral position on anything or anyone. Even when he was abused by his correspondents and asked to do their work for them, he did not simply throw the letters away and ignore them. He blasted the writers for their presumption and bad manners. Away from his typewriter, Malcolm Cowley said of him, he was a pleasant and generous man. But how he did like to swing a shillelagh!

Vitality, given away as lavishly as it was sold. Like the western lumbermen and cattlemen whom he deplored and despised, he mined his resources ruthlessly and died of his own extractive excesses at the age of fifty-eight. He overworked himself; he ran tired all his life. Despite his never-suspended self-discipline and his control of his working life, he was as surely a sacrifice to literary Moloch as Hart Crane or Harry Crosby, contemporaries with whom he would not have enjoyed being compared. Led to the sacrifice, lowing at the skies, and all his silken flanks with garlands dressed? He would have had a pungent word for the notion. Nevertheless, he felt the literary dedication as surely as any of his aesthetic or Marxist contemporaries. He started out wanting to be a literary artist and ended as a historian, a public defender, a voice of the national conscience. And he killed himself carrying out the terms of his dedication; he ran out of the vitality that had been his resource.

I have recorded his life and the curve of his ideas in *The Uneasy Chair*. This volume of his letters—148 selected from many thousands—is an attempt to let him speak for himself, in those private moods of affection, generosity, fatigue, excitement, irony, indignation, argument, rebuttal, and blunt repudiation that accompanied his public life.

The unconscious, he said in *The World of Fiction*, is not *below* the conscious, as the common spatial metaphor would have it, but fused with it. "The Mississippi of the mind is always below the mouth of the Missouri." Something of the same sort applies here: private and public lives have flowed together and are not quite separable. The public life was notable for its controversies—with Van Wyck Brooks and the young intellectuals, with the literary Marxists, with Sinclair Lewis, with the censors, with the assembled art critics, with the departments of literature and the academic historians and the Southern revisionists, with the stockmen and the landgrabbers and the Corps of Engineers—and the controversies overflow into the correspondence. His private expressions of opinion and his public, published statements are part of the same flow. But also the correspondence reveals, more clearly than any of the essays and books, the private life that is often uneasy, scared, sometimes close to panic, deeply attached to friends and to certain saving rituals of friendship and to certain loved places.

In selecting from the mass of his letters I have tried to follow his own historical method of the "test-boring"—what he called synecdoche, the part for the whole, samples. The letters selected are arranged not according to chronology, but under nine topical heads, so that letters on the same general subject may be read together. Because DeVoto was articulate to a degree, and moreover wrote many of his letters late at night when fatigue or a couple of nightcap highballs had encouraged prolixity, I have reluctantly availed myself of the editorial privilege and have cut out matter that seemed irrelevant or verbose or repetitive. Material likely to be hurtful to living persons I have sometimes cut; sometimes I have simply left names blank. All omissions are indicated by four periods of ellipsis enclosed in brackets, to distinguish them from the unbracketed elliptical periods that DeVoto sometimes used as a mark of punctuation.

I have corrected obvious typographical and spelling errors without calling attention to them; have supplied, within brackets, occasional words obliterated or unreadable in the originals; have normalized punctuation and spelling to conform to DeVoto's own general practice, which was both good and consistent; have provided headnotes where some context or explanation seemed called for; and have identified in footnotes names not likely to be recognized by the ordinarily intelligent and aware reader of the 1970s.

The letters from which the present volume is selected are all in the Stanford University Library. After long pondering, I have decided not to reprint any of the letters addressed to Kate Sterne, the tubercular shut-in with whom DeVoto kept up an intimate correspondence for eleven years, though they never met. The situation, actually, is more striking than any of the letters, which were meant to buck up the invalid, and which embroider on fact and go to extreme lengths in portraiture, especially of people whom De-Voto disliked or whose ideas he disapproved. I have used much material from these letters in *The Uneasy Chair*; but DeVoto would not himself have printed them, or a selection from them, verbatim, and I see no reason why I should.

Los Altos Hills, California
August 25, 1974

ONE
Self-Scrutiny

The two years following his graduation from Harvard in 1920 Bernard De-Voto spent in his hometown of Ogden, Utah, trying to write a novel, falling in love and out again and in again, suffering depression and panic, and pawing over his own guts in an agony of indecision and self-doubt. Yet even from the depths of a nervous breakdown he was capable of occasional outbursts of euphoria, confidence, and vision such as the fragment that serves as an epigraph for this volume.

Rescued from Ogden when his Harvard friend and teacher Dean Russell LeBaron Briggs found him an instructorship at Northwestern, DeVoto was rescued neither from self-doubt nor from his passionate desire to be a writer. The writing career began with publication of his first novel, The Crooked Mile, in 1924; proceeded through several years of journalism and book-reviewing; began to move when H. L. Mencken discovered him and opened The American Mercury to his essays; and was going full speed when DeVoto quit Northwestern in the fall of 1927 and went back to Cambridge to live and write.

The first four letters in this section show him recovering, by degrees, from his nervous breakdown. Those to Robert S. Forsythe and Miss Burke were written as aids to people studying his biography and career. They have some of the self-consciousness of a man being modest and offhand for the press, and some of the excessive confidence of a man to whom confidence is a new acquaintance. And two letters, those to Robert C. Elliott and Jarvis Thurston, represent DeVoto's explanation and expiation of the brashness that marked his literary beginnings. He never got over treating fairly gingerly the "God-awful emulsion" that was himself, but he came to understand the chemistry of the emulsion very well.

TO MELVILLE SMITH

September 25, 1922

Dear Melville,

Facts first. I have been here for a week, after two weeks with the Haglers in Springfield.[1] I am employed as an instructor in English at Northwestern University. For all the time before that I was in Ogden, except for a couple of weeks on a ranch in Idaho.

You speak, in your latest letter, a great deal of inhibitions. Perhaps you can understand, with that word as a guide, just what has caused the almost, but I hope not quite, unpardonable silence which has given you such anxiety. Oh, just God, I am glad that it was anxiety . . . I must be explicit, and the very things I must say make me shudder. About fourteen months ago I had a sort of nervous breakdown. From that time my life has been wholly unlike anything you know about me, a vivid nightmare of morbidity, fears, inhibitions, compulsions, neuroses. I will harrow neither you nor myself with details of them, but among them was the one that kept me from writing to you. Think not to you only. I wrote to no one, not to Dean Briggs[2] nor Hurlbut,[3] not to Gordon King,[4] not to the very people who had got me my years of Cambridge—except one. I did write to Clarissa Hagler,[5] for she needed my letters, and I think that the knowledge that some one needed me was about all that kept me sane, if I was, am, sane. Clarissa I did write to, at the expense of what terror and pain I hope she never discovers. I don't know—it may be that, if or when the mists clear away, I shall marry her. I hope so. She, and another woman, one in Ogden, have become about all the dignity of existence—my ideas of which have undergone rather comprehensive changes.

I grasped at the offer of this position. I am here not to teach English but to make myself over from the debris that remains. It is a job, you can understand, of size, pain, and effort. I am confident that I can make it success-

---

[1] Parents of another Harvard friend, Kent Hagler, who had died mysteriously in Paris in the fall of 1920.
[2] His Harvard writing teacher.
[3] Byron Hurlbut, another Harvard writing teacher and friend.
[4] A close Harvard friend, for whom DeVoto's first son was named.
[5] Sister of Kent Hagler.

ful, but I do not minimize the labor and heartbreak that it means, and I beg you not to.

Isn't that sufficient? I don't want to spend any more time or thought on what has been the matter, though if I have not convinced you, I will send you some interesting evidence. Is it not enough that I have spent months in hell?

In utter candidness, believe me, I may say that I have had the thought of you with me even in hell. Your letters came; they touched me to the heart; I tried to answer them; and I was plunged into deeper misery. Count it a victory for me that I write tonight. There are some things a man must do alone, some places into which he can take no one. Do not think that I dramatize myself. When I see you I shall have things to tell—things like Doré's Dante.

But I have it in my heart to reproach you. I should have understood if you had forsaken me utterly, believing that my love was not worth even the chagrin of misconception. In France that would have been the intelligent thing to do . . . and I shall not forget that you did not do it. One man out of a thousand would have kept faith, and you were the one. Only, faith did falter, didn't it? And it was yours, not mine. From first to last, I have had no doubt of you, nor of your affection. I have not now, and I trust that you will have none hereafter. You remain then nearest to me of all flesh. I count it one chief part of the future—the future alone has any reality to me—that it ought to hold somewhere another meeting with you. Some things, not many, are good.

Right now, there is no more to say. By the time I learn whether you have received this and what effect it has on you I may be able to write as I used to. It may be, too, that I shall have a better typewriter than this, which seems to have sand in its esophagus. Because I have written of things in cold blood, don't imagine that they are not hot in the veins, and don't think that my ultimate re-creation is yet within sight.

One word still. You seem to be in the Menckenian mood toward America, what with your flings at repression, legislated morality, and prohibited paganism. I am not sure that you aren't making a grave error of judgment, and the whole American intellectual hierarchy with you. Art, my statistical mind tells me, has always been under the ban of respectability, not here only but everywhere else. I think of the greatest age of dramatic writing in any country, and remember that the theaters were forbidden London, and that Marlowe, Fletcher, and Shakespeare wrote for production on the banks of the river, out of the jurisdiction of the city, coming midway between the brothels and the bear-pits. Have not the greatest always been under one ban or another? Is not art itself the resolution of the force of unlimited freedom opposed by that of complete repression or legality?

And if the worst of what you say be true, as it is not, what is the difference? Take this country of ours, of mine at least, with its hundred million of people, every one a member of the human race, albeit of a lower species. Repressions, censorship, cramped, fear-ridden lives. Even so. There is your marble; you are not concerned with why or how; you are to carve it into your statue. It is idle, trivial, to mourn that these people are not like some other. Thank the gods for novelty, for uniqueness. Here is ugliness, apparent everywhere—build with it. Here are beauties, no less genuine for being strange—build with them. Here is a whole continent stuffed with living things. Put your tongue in your pocket and get to work with them.

Do not persuade yourself that art is greater than life; that the greatest art is as worthy as the meanest life. Gravest of all, do not think that art can be separated from life for one second's existence in itself. Make music. Make music of the elevated, of the billboards, of the vaudeville, of the baseball games, of the gasoline air, of the river stinks, of the garbage cans, the slums, of every blatant and vulgar monstrosity of this civilization. Incredibly vulgar it may be, offensive, repellent, hideous, intolerable. Nevertheless it is alive; and while it is, your duty is to make art of it. . . . And America, alive, is the future.

That is almost worthy of immortalization on Christmas postcards. You have my heart.

TO BYRON HURLBUT

December 1922

Dear Mr. Hurlbut:

My shame is swallowed up because it is now intolerable to go longer without writing to you, telling you about myself, endeavoring in some way to explain what has kept me silent—hidden, for it was hiding. Perhaps—much as I dread to think so—perhaps you have forgotten who I am. If you have, please think for a few minutes about one Bernard DeVoto. See whether after a while a nebulous memory doesn't bubble up, of one who was eternally doing and saying the wrong thing, appearing at precisely the wrong moment, blundering into the most absurd speeches, ideas, and impulses possible to man. That memory, if fixed, will finally present me to you. Gauche as it will be, I shall be very happy if it does appear.

There isn't any justification. But there is an explanation. For eighteen months—to be explicit—I have been, rather *was*, something between a seventh and an eighth of a man. Nervous breakdown, followed by a prolonged neurotic depression. I shall not enumerate the fears and compulsions, nor the months of self-abomination and despair. If one is insane and conscious of insanity at the same time, this side of hell, I was. The only thing I need mention is the positive inhibition of all communication with any one who had been part of the life which I came to associate with the youth of the world, with a golden age of innocence and happiness. I wrote to no one. If I have lost your friendship, so have I that of more than a few others. There was some sort of wall between me and my friends. Please believe that. Believe that, though the thought of you has probably been in my mind every day and has grown infinitely dear, I could not write. There was a finality about it like a sentence on Judgment Day. That's all I shall say about it— and I shouldn't say that, for it shames me, and I have sworn a mighty oath never to talk about those months—and I shall not talk about it again.

I am rather well out of it now. During the early part of it I had managed to keep in touch with Dean Briggs, and I think that it must have been through him—I have never learned—that late last summer I got the offer of an instructorship here at Northwestern. It reached me while I was vainly trying to work myself into health at a ranch in the Idaho desert. I came east, if this be east, in September, and since then I have been getting back within sight of normality. The college is pleasant and the work easy—and the delight of talking to intelligent people again nearly as welcome as the return of self-mastery.

I don't plan beyond tomorrow's breakfast, but Evanston is certainly only a stop on the way east. As soon as I can, I shall go back to New England. That is where I belong, or at least where my quietest dreams are set. Cambridge and the winter Yard, evenings at your house, the Symphony, talk about a half dozen fireplaces, twilights over the Charles—these things have lined the darkest hours I ever spent with a half-intolerable beauty of reminiscence. I think, and for over two years have thought, of the hillsides at Barre and at Ayer and Shirley as I saw them in the summers, of Saturday walks past Waltham or Lexington, of summer afternoons down Brattle Street or Mt. Vernon Street, of the shadows in the Widener stacks with the light of my stall in them—the stall you got for me—and wherever I am I feel a quiet assurance that one day I shall come back to them as to my own place.

I haven't, I say, any plans at all. But in another year or two I shall be able to spend another year in study. It may be that after that I can get into some pleasanter part of journalistic work; or if not, certainly some New England college not too far from the North Station will find room for me when A.M. is added to my name. I shall work with you—if you will have me. You will not care whether or not I am profoundly ignorant of Old Frisian or the Icelandic derivations of the root ge-wesen. And the 18th Century becomes more and more a haven for my fancy [. . . .]

Oh yes. In the West, as one of the many successive and ineffectual barriers against myself I did much work in frontier history. When I am able to get it all together it will make a formidable ton.

And the urge remains. The worst of all has been my utter loss of belief in myself, but somehow I have managed to retain the curious conviction that I must write fiction and as the mists thin I come back to it. The novel that was to astonish a satiated world came to an abrupt end eighteen months ago, but in Evanston I have written fifty thousand words. Intolerably dull— but it is satisfying just to have written it and the end is far off.

You will at least let me know that you have received this. And you will understand and pardon the affront of my long silence. Please, too, when you see Dean Briggs, explain to him what happened to me. Mine is a wintry and thwarted heart, but you and he are at the core of it and I may in no wise phrase all that you mean to me. Tell him that I will presently write to him.

And let Mrs. Hurlbut have my regards—and please think well of me.

Yours,

TO BYRON HURLBUT

May or June 1923

Dear Mr. Hurlbut:

I have much to tell you, much to ask. When I wrote you last December, I told you of the trouble that had oppressed me for two years. The winter that followed my letter was full of attempts to master it, and I can now write you that they have proved successful. I am master of myself. I have conquered the depression, regained supremacy over my body, and brought my mind back to where it ought to be. I am surprised to find my nature deeper and more sympathetic: I think that I understand life far better because of my experience, and I know myself.

Well . . . I could analyze the past two years in thousands of words, but I shan't. I want to tell you the more important things that have happened to me, and to ask your advice. Curiously, I have always been asking you to advise me—do you remember that our friendship began with a question of undergraduate ethics? And there is no one else in the world that I want to consult now. I know that you will give me the time, however pressed you may be, when you hear my problems. Please, though, let it be confidential.

First, then, my plans for the summer. About the fifteenth of June I expect to go north—either to Michigan or to Wisconsin[1]—to some quiet,

1 It turned out to be Washington Island, in Lake Michigan.

cool place on the lake and there I intend to write until September. All year, in the face of discouragement and depression that were more than once despair, I have kept at work on my novel—a little at a time, until now it needs only a month of uninterrupted work. I shall finish the novel and then work it over into the best possible shape so that it will be ready to submit to publishers in September. I have no idea how good it is, and can get no good criticism here. I am afraid that the marks of disease are on it, traces of the neurotic despair in which parts of it were written, but I know too that parts of it are genuine and beautiful and I count much on being able to round it off and unify it in revision.

Put that down as the first fact, that I shall have a novel in September. Meanwhile I shall be writing short stories too, a half dozen I hope during the summer. These I shall try to sell to the magazines. If I can sell just one to the S.E.P., most of my uncertainties will disappear. I am not counting on that, just hoping. I have never tried to write for publication, but I think that I am now far enough along to try. I have not yet put myself to a test that I did not pass—if the last one has taken two years. I remember how I was assured beforehand that I could never make good at Harvard, in the army, as a teacher, and that I made good in all three. So, unfamiliar and dubious as the idea is, I begin writing for publication with confidence if not assurance.

In September I can come back to Northwestern. The college will pay me $1700, and I can add $500 to that by teaching one night a week in the school of commerce. If the summer is not successful, that is what I shall do.

Now. Sometime between the first of September and the first of February, I shall be married.[2] That is the reason for all this detail. I had better tell you about my fiancée, Helen MacVicar, whom I met last year in the startling relation of teacher-pupil. She is very young, she has the subtlest mind I have ever known, and it was because I was in love with her that I was able to pull through the year and bring it to a successful and even, professionally, a triumphant end. I want you to realize that, Mr. Hurlbut. I came here last fall with no motive left for living, with the thought of suicide not out of my mind, waking or sleeping, for a moment. Only some irony of despair ever brought me here, and only the idea of giving the gods a good battle kept me going till I met her. I think that, without realizing it, I must have been in love with her from the first. I know that from the middle of October, when I began to know her intimately, the knowledge of this arrogant splendor of youth, this fine steel-sharp flame of living showed me that after all it was my vision, not the world, that was wrong—and I found the first pleasure I had had in two years in bringing to her the things that she had wanted. A girl from the hideous copper country of Calumet, a girl who played César Franck and the subtler Strauss, who read and thought as intuitively as I, who wrote prose far more sensitive than mine, and who brought to life that ancient

2 They were married very shortly after this letter, in June.

ache and hunger of beauty that, at my best, I had had. Well, I think that my first afternoon with her decided the course of my year [. . . .]

Wouldn't it be the worst kind of folly for us to delay? Helen is the focus of my life. She is courage, faith, certainty. And—God help me—by some miracle I mean the same to her. We want from life only hard work and each other. We are poor, unknown, insignificant; yet the very fierceness of the joy with which we realize that we are is proof enough that we shan't always be. We want to begin living together—*living together*—both words set in black-face capitals. Poverty and obscurity are precisely what we want, for they will make us share life and work. We are resolved to be married soon. The summer is a concession to—not to necessity—to proof. Not more than half the winter will be added to the concession [. . . .]

At the worst: If I sell no manuscripts we will come back here, be married, live in the tiniest apartment we can get. I will teach at Northwestern another year and write all year, write as long as necessary to get my work accepted.

At the best: If I sell enough manuscripts, we will come to New England —I don't know where, near Wellesley, near Ayer, near Barre, or somewhere in New Hampshire—and live quietly in some little town while we write together, and while I find some position that will provide a small salary—in Boston, I assume [. . . .]

Now I know as well as you do the limitations of Boston, yet there are magazines there, and publishers, and there are no castes in the mind—and my mind is as deep a certainty as I have. I believe that if I have resources enough to run me for some months I can find a place. Modesty has never been a vice of mine—I am wholly confident of my ability to make good when I get the chance. My mind is as good as there is, and it has the sort of subtlety and discipline that publishers and magazines need [. . . .]

Yours faithfully,

TO MELVILLE SMITH

March 8, 1925

Dear Melville:

[. . . .] It has been no lack of desire that has kept me from writing to you. Even now an instinct, supported by a vague geography, warns me that 159 East 33rd Street on my envelope will carry it off somewhere among the wholesalers of dry goods and cosmetics and that your true address is in the neighborhood of 12th Street or else somewhere to the northward of 205th.

I have no assurance that you are either living or teaching on 33rd. . . . No, I have wanted to be in touch with you, have promised myself—and Avis,[1] who has glowed to the mythology I have spun out of my long friendship with you—a summer with you somewhere along the coast. I still do, but I grow timid with age, and I am no longer confident that we shall ever again neighbor under one roof.

No lack of desire, Melville, only lack of your address [. . . .]

And further, Melville, I have been busy, to you incredibly busy. Consider, I must first earn a living: by teaching full time at Evanston and by going into the city twice a week to teach there. Living, even the bohemian squalor of our life, is very high in Evanston. And then, in what is left of the week, I must lead a full time literary life—for Avis and I are both determined that the unpleasant necessity of teaching shall not hamper the very slow, the very minute beginnings of another career. For instance, this week. Two nights were, of course, wholly wasted teaching downtown. Five others went to the novel which is now coming on toward the end of the first draft and which is promised for delivery sometime between June 1 and July 1— between now and then it must be finished, revised, and re-revised. There are the seven nights. Meanwhile I have read themes and exercises for three classes and lectured two or three times apiece to four. And, packed in between, I have completed the revision of my chapter in *The Taming of Ten Cities*[2] which is to be published in the fall, and have got it off to the agent who, I fervently hope, will be able to sell it for magazine publication before the book comes out. And, in this same week, I have made vague gestures toward a publicity article about me which is to appear in a western magazine. And I have written two reviews for the local sheet, two more for the Chicago *Post*, and one for Canby's *Review*. Or, rather, I shall write the last as soon as I sign my name to this letter.

That is a fair sample, no exceptional week. The average would show more reviews. To be sure I haven't money for the luxurious delights of the theater and the symphony—I have been once to both since September, though I have managed to send Avis more often—but even if I had it, I could not go. What time have I for any indulgence, even letters? This week, no doubt, I shall receive a wail from Gordon King, he being the other friend I have, Melville, complaining that I have not answered his letter of six weeks ago and, what is more heinous, have not commented on the ms. of a play he sent me at the same time. . . . This Evanston life is very pleasant, I am happier far than I have ever been before, but I lead it under a great pressure,

[1] Helen Avis MacVicar, who shortly after her marriage to DeVoto began to go by her middle name.
[2] Edited by Duncan Aikman, the book appeared as *The Taming of the Frontier*. DeVoto's contribution was a scalding portrait of Ogden called "Ogden: The Underwriters of Salvation."

a pressure which gives me no time for either thought or humanity and which prevents me from doing my best work at anything. It must continue as far toward eternity as it takes me to establish a public that will support me. That does not use up so much time as it would seem, for if ever my royalties amount in a lump to two thousand dollars, or if ever my ideas of good short stories coincide that far with public taste, we shall cut loose and go hoboing in a mild way. That is all I ache for, since I have no doubt of the ultimate outcome, and till it comes I suffer gladly the extreme boredom and low-caste of teaching.

I was in debt, of course, when we were married and the proverbial first year so added to the debt that it is only now that we begin to see free air ahead. Actually, I contemplate, with the coming of next month's check, the purchase of the first suit I have had in three years. But it has all been delightful. Avis is far too young and I am not yet so far gone in age for us to think of ourselves as married. We contribute neither dignity nor solemnity to the commonwealth. We are only two people who like living together and do so without much reference to the proprieties. I wish you could share our life for a while; its inconsequence, its delightful disreputability would enchant you.

The Crooked Mile[3] got a most flattering critical reception, but for the most part the public shied from it. The royalties, due within the month, will clear our debts and take us west for the summer, where Avis has never yet been exhibited to my father. They will not materially contribute to our ease thereafter, though I suppose it will have a small sale for a while. Meanwhile the new novel[4] is a gamble. I have no way of judging it; it seems to me quite idiotic; but Avis thinks it better than the first. If you want the first, by the way, you must buy it. I tried to send you one last fall, but I have none left. You might contribute twenty cents to my comfort.

By the summer of 1926 we ought to be somewhat easier. That is the summer, God and you willing, I propose to spend within reach of you. There is a great deal to talk over, including one long story not to be confided to paper which I think will amuse you. Can you contemplate the prospect without a shudder? Of course, you might come to Chicago. It seems to me that every musician in the city is wealthier than a bank director. Why should you not provide yourself with ease by ministering to the culture aspirations of the prairies? I don't know of any reason.

Meanwhile, I suggest that you look up Gordon King, 323 West 22nd Street. You will like him.

Is this amends?

I expect acknowledgment of this soon—to prove that it really *is* your address. And please don't be dignified with me, Melville, I don't really merit it.

---

[3] DeVoto's first novel, published by Minton, Balch and Co. in the fall of 1924.
[4] After many tentative titles, it appeared as *The Chariot of Fire* (Macmillan, 1926).

TO ROBERT S. FORSYTHE

Forsythe, once a colleague at Northwestern,
had moved to the University of North
Dakota. Later he settled at the Newbery
Library in Chicago. At the time of this
letter he was writing a little biographical
and critical booklet about DeVoto which
Macmillan would publish in conjunction
with DeVoto's third novel, The House
of Sun-Goes-Down.

October 6, 1927

Dear Prof:

A headache, one of the sequelae of that accursed coryza, having made my projected evening on the Comstock Lode impossible, I try to make at least some gain for God by addressing my biographer, though the movement of my mind, barely discernible from that of a mud-dab, will probably bore you so that you cry aloud.

What do you mean, data? I guess you'd better send me a questionnaire. You tell me what you want to know and I'll see that you learn it, though I may asterisk the more actionable portions. The subject of this sketch was born at Ogden, Utah, January 11, 1897. I don't know what else happened in history on that solemn day. Ancestry mayhap? Well, my Pa's Pa came to this country, I think from Milan, though there are also Genoa and Florence connections—it ain't important—some time before the Civil War, I don't know when. The yarn is—I do not vouch for it—that his wife, who was a DeRosa of the ancient house, was the daughter of a count or something of the sort and that the marriage with my Grampa, who came from a military family (what was a military family in Italy, at that time?) was sanctioned only on the condition that the pair would remove themselves permanently from the fatherland which she was disgracing by mingling her seed with that of a commoner. So runs my Aunt's account, but if God ever made a fool, she's it—though she was several years older than my Dad, and so knew more of their parents. Anyway, the old man seems to have had plenty of money, and he made more here—running commission houses along the Mississippi and Ohio. He lived at various times at St. Louis, Cairo, and Cincinnati. He seems to have been (1) a royal old soak, and (2) a realist. In support of the second, I offer this anecdote, about the only one my dad ever told me about him. When a rebel raid got to Covington (I've never investigated which one—weren't there two?) and the burghers of Cincinnati were subjected to an impromptu draft to dig fortifications and man them, the old man decided that he didn't care for glory. He hid out on them. But there were rumors running about that he was a rebel sympathizer (and, I suspect, that he had been making a penny or two selling supplies down the river) and they sent out a provost guard to apprehend him. After some days, or nights, he crept in for food and they nabbed him in the clothes closet clad in one of his wife's dresses.

Anyway he and his wife died when my dad was very young—I'd say 1867 or thereabout—and my dad and his sister were confided to the church, he being sent to Notre Dame, which ran an infants' department in those days, and she to St. Mary's nearby. There was a considerable estate. My dad lost it all in a Boom in the west. He first went West with my Aunt and the Mother Superior of the order of Holy Cross nuns, when she went to Utah to establish St. Mary's Academy in Salt Lake City. Some day I'll write a dissertation on the attitude of the Mormons and the Catholics to each other— very interesting. He never got away again. My aunt did well for herself, marrying V. H. Coffman, Sheridan's surgeon-in-chief in Texas after the war and practically that during the war, who went to Omaha, made a vast reputation for himself as a doctor and several millions out of advancing real estate values.

My dad has the finest mind I've ever known. Hanging around Notre Dame so long, he naturally acquired everything in the way of a degree they issued—M.A., M.S., B.A., B.S., LLB. It was before the Ph.D. reached the middle west, and I never understood why or how he was able to acquire so many seemingly self-cancelling degrees, but he did for I've got the diplomas, and though I don't read much of the Latin I do know that they are real sheepskin—and I'll be damned forever if mine is. Dad is, really, a genius, about the only one I've ever known. He had a strong artistic strain, painted well, and when a French artist (I've a slight hunch it was Puvis de Chavannes, but have never investigated) came to paint murals in the chapel at N.D., Dad became his protégé and helped on them. He wanted to be a painter but my aunt and the Mother Superior promptly killed that—for, I blush to confess it, there are Catholic puritans, and my aunt had a gentility complex. Then he wanted to go to Columbia and study law, but the two of them killed that. He was, and is, a mathematical wizard, sorcerer, necromancer. He taught math at N.D. for a year or so, and I've thought that that was the life he should have kept to, failing the others, for he would have enjoyed the quiet and the intellectual surroundings and would have made a great, though captious, teacher. I have a letter from the chief of the Bureau of Standards, saying that he (Dad) taught him all the math he knows. For years

15

engineers came to him from all over the West to have their insoluble problems solved for them. I've seen him clear up, in less than an hour, a maze of miscalculations that had stalled the whole engineering force of a transcontinental railroad for thirty days. He must have earned a million dollars in expert's fees in his time—and never charged a cent of it. He's that way. He threw away one-third of the Silver King mine (Sunrise Queen) because he thought there should be honor in national politics, the damned idiot. He located one of the richest Portland cement deposits in the country (for he is also a mineralogist and assayer) but he never went to the trouble of doing anything about it, and he has cursed the men who did for thieves, all his life —for he is very bitter and a complete misanthrope, and he believes that it is dishonorable for one to make money where he has scorned to do so. All the other abstractors in Utah are corrupt, you understand, because he is still charging the fees he set in 1900. He charges the Sugar Trust precisely the same fee he charges some meek little widow who wants a deed drawn up, with the difference that he will send the Trust a bill, five or six years after the statute of limitations has operated on the account.

Well, when he had blown the family pile in boom lands, he went to work for the UP. I never knew just what he did. He was a train dispatcher, I think. He acquired, during the strikes of the early Nineties, a conception of laborers and labor unions that accords with his conceptions of all other people. After a while he became an abstractor of title and has remained one ever since—a tragic waste of such gifts as his, but inevitable when you consider the defeatist philosophy he breathes out at every pore. It is impossible for me to tell you how good a land-expert he is. Well, you are a learned man and you can imagine how learned a man can get to be, such a man as my dad, in the insanely complex land-titles of the West, with their Spanish grants, a dozen different kinds of U.S. patents, squatters' rights belatedly recognized by courts, and above all the mining law in its half-Spanish, half-Vigilante intricacy. He has had, from the first, magnificent offers from land companies, banks, etc., all over the West and especially in California, but he has been almost psychopathically resolved to stay on the scene of his failure, surrounded by people he hates, no equal of his ever appearing there. He could have been Land Commissioner of every state in the West, or, if he did not have a compulsion to insult everyone he talks to, of the national government. No big bank on the coast, including the Federal Farm Loan bank, will accept any abstract to any land in Weber County unless it has been passed on by him—in fact, none in the State that involves anything but straight-from-patent stuff. Knowledge of this fiendishly intricate and exact science, I'm sure, has been the one solace of his years.

If you can imagine a combination of Heyst, in Conrad's *Victory*, and the Swift who wrote about the Yahoos, you've got the secret philosophy of my dad. I mean, his life has been a terrible tragedy, with my mother the one good thing in it, and he is the bitterest man I've ever known. All men are fools, liars, and knaves, infinitely petty, infinitely noisome, and nothing in life is worth a damn. His experience has been just that, in ways it would take me too long to describe here. He himself has the finest honor I've ever known, and he has kept it clean at the expense of all the friendships he never formed. . . . And yet he is also the kindest man that ever lived. He has been poor all his life not because he didn't make a lot of money (though not one one-thousandth of what he might) but because he has kept alive literally scores of people, broken down whores, old desert rats that are quite mad, my mother's enormous family, beggars, poor people, God knows whom. He would give his shirt to anyone, and has many times, and many people have exploited his benevolence. In another way, he is a gentleman of the old school, ferociously upright, reactionary, a lover of the classics (which he reads in the original to this day), an unreconstructed states rights Democrat who hated Bryan but voted for him, who despised Roosevelt and who belongs exactly and completely in that simpler day when there were men and principles in politics. He played a considerable part in the early Democracy in Utah, and especially in the Liberal Party that freed Ogden from the Mormons (see DeVoto, Bernard, "Ogden: The Underwriters of Salvation" in Aikman, Duncan, *The Taming of the Frontier*).

My maternal grandfather[1] was, as a young man, converted to Mormonism in, I think, Liverpool, though it may have been London. He was a laborer in a linseed-oil mill. He and his newly acquired wife came to this country in one of the Emigration Companies organized by the colonization dept. of the church. He landed in Boston where he went to work as foreman of a linseed mill in Charlestown. Later, he went to Brooklyn in the same capacity and there my mother was born, the second child and oldest girl of a family of seven children. Five other daughters followed her. Soon there was talk of drafting soldiers instead of getting them as volunteers and if my granddad had been more bellicose than he was he wouldn't have found any encouragement among the Mormons, who frankly sympathized with the South but weren't going to shed any of their blood for either side. His journal merely says that there was no sense in staying east any longer, especially when he could make sure of not being drafted by going West. (The church encouraged its converts, you understand, to stay east a while and pick up a stake before going to Zion.) Well, my mother was born in 1861 and was something over a year old when her oldest sister was born in Wyoming in the bed of an emigrant wagon. Sam—his name was Samuel G. Dye, but he didn't have anything in common with Sam Bingham[2]—knew nothing about farming, and I may say that damn few Mormon converts of that day ever

---

[1] DeVoto wrote an affectionate portrait of him in "Jonathan Dyer, Frontiersman" (reprinted in *Forays and Rebuttals* as "The Life of Jonathan Dyer").
[2] A character in *The House of Sun-Goes-Down*.

did, but after letting him drive a freight wagon for some months, the Church directed him to go to Uintah, in Weber Valley, eight miles south of Ogden, and buy a farm from one of the brothers there. He did so and there he stayed till a year or so before he died in 1925. He obeyed the church in all things but one and believed in it till his dying day. He was a perfect peasant, submissive, unimaginative, stolid, industrious, faithful, thorough. His wife was far finer stuff—the true frontier woman, a type I haven't tried my hand on yet, though I've approached it in some ways with Mrs. Yancey.[3] All that I'm proud of in my maternal inheritance, and I'm really proud of that whereas I merely accept the paternal (and larger) inheritance, was due to her. The one disobedience in granddad's life came when the Bishop of the Uintah ward, seeing that the old man was now sufficiently prosperous to provide each child with a covering though not with underwear or shoes, told him to take a second wife. The old man got out the horse pistol and drove the bishop off the place, and the subject was not brought up again. But that's the real lowdown on polygamy, Prof, on this gilded Oriental luxury and vice we read about. Oriental luxury, hell, it was damned poverty.

The poverty of those days simply cannot be imagined today. The kids never had shoes. The only plaything I ever heard them tell about was an old scoop in which they used to coast down the hills in wintertime. There was no school—my mother was the only one who got any schooling and she did it by working out in Ogden—there was not the slightest comfort in the house, not even bare necessities for years. Everyone worked his head off, kids and all. The railroad buzzed through in '69 and improved matters somewhat by hiring the old man as a teamster. I don't go into that life here, though it's tremendously fascinating. Don't identify the Dyes with the Binghams, for at least four of the Dyes had real stuff in them. Some day I'm going to make a novel about them.

Nor need I dwell on the long and important story of my mother's ill health, though that too makes a novel. She was a widow with one child when Dad married her in Ogden, 1895 I believe. She was keeping a rooming-house and supporting two or three of her sisters, who were trying to be dressmakers etc. Their married life was really noble, which is a word that sits strangely on my lips, and the only happy thing in the life of either one. She lived to be very proud of me, for, of course, a boy in Harvard who was also a lieutenant in the army symbolized dizzy grandeurs to her. She always thought that the poverty in which my dad supported her was the wildest kind of affluence. It was, to her. She died in 1919, after a long siege of the sequelae of influenza, and what her death did to me, though interesting to a psychiatrist, does not interest a biographer.

None of my progenitors appears in any of my books, as such. Whether

[3] The leathery heroine of a number of DeVoto's early short stories.

they have colored them or not, you can judge better than I. The farm at Blaine in the early *CM*, though not in the later book, is an idealized version of my grandfather's farm as I remembered it from my childhood. The situation is literal to the last syllable.

TO ROBERT C. ELLIOT

DeVoto's first published work was a pair of articles denouncing the cultural and intellectual deficiencies of his hometown of Ogden and his home state of Utah. Five years later, Utah was still seething with resentment, and Robert Elliott, an editor of the Salt Lake Telegram, *wrote DeVoto challenging him to back his criticisms with specifics. The letter below was his reply, written for Elliott's private consumption only; the public reply that DeVoto promises was never written. But years later, in May 1943, he wrote to Jarvis Thurston, an ex-Utahn, the letter which immediately follows this, in which he substantially modifies his early violence. The Thurston letter was printed in the* Rocky Mountain Review *and later in the Mormon journal* Improvement Era, *but did little to soften the anger that Utahns and especially Mormon Utahns felt against DeVoto. The name of Utah's most prominent writer is still spelled in his home state with three letters, M.U.D.*

November 4, 1930

Dear Mr. Elliott:

I must ask you to regard this letter as purely a private communication and must insist on your not publishing any part of it. Later I will write an extended answer to your questions, which you may publish in the *Telegram* or put to any other use that pleases you. Here, however, I desire to speak personally and so cannot allow you to print what I have to say.

You say, "Tell us explicitly how it may be done,"—that is how Utah can be made to produce fine literature. This seems to me a naive request. There are no recipes for the production of good literature, and no community can add a cubit to its literary stature by taking thought. Any formula or prescription that I, or anyone else, might give you would be utter nonsense. There is no specific for art. I can, however, mention a few characteristics of life in Utah which seem to me to inhibit the growth of literature there, and which in my opinion must be obviated before writers or artists of any kind can flourish there.

Let me begin with my own experience and your remarks about me. The first, foremost, and indispensable condition for art is a society intelligent enough, or educated enough, or sophisticated enough, to permit the free play of intelligence. This requires that ideas of any kind, however offensive to anyone, be discussed purely as ideas. It means intelligent interest in ideas as ideas. It means sincere insistence on the right of your most violent opponent to express himself on any subject even if it be violent denunciation of your ideas. It means a society eagerly interested in the interplay and mutual interaction of ideas. And what is more immediate to my theme, it means the assumption that an idea is no less sincere for being contrary to what oneself believes. Specifically it means that when I express ideas about Utah which differ from those which you hold, you are displaying an offensive form of the obscurantism which prevents the growth of literature, when you assume that they are not honest and sincere opinions but are dictated by what you speak of as mercenary in one place and as immediate cash value in another.

Parenthetically I may say that your allegation is by far the decentest that has been made against me in Utah. I do not object to your particular form of assumption about me, since it is only impersonally insulting, but my collection of letters from Utah, now numbering over six hundred (hardly a fifth of them signed), contains a much more obnoxious obscurantism. I have been called a thief, a coward, a moral leper, a homosexualist, a defaulter, an adulterer, a sensualist, and every other opprobrious and obscene term that the resentment of Utah could devise. The natural impulse of uneducated and Philistine people is to denounce as some form of immoralist any person whose ideas differ from their own. Until some change in this habit of mind occurs, no artistic progress is possible in Utah.

Let me answer your allegation before I go on. I do not remember how much I received for my first article on Utah in the *Mercury*, but it could not have been more than $125.00. The second, I happen to remember, paid me $190.00. Is it your honest opinion that a man whose fee from such magazines as the *Saturday Evening Post* is considerably in excess of ten times this price will write for such magazines as the *Mercury* unless he has something to say and believes in it? Prices apart, why assume, in any event, that the motive is mercenary? Why not do yourself the credit of assuming that your opponent is as sincere as you? More than that, why scrutinize the motive at all? An idea is true or false, or partly true and partly false. What has the motive behind its expression to do with its truth? The way to oppose an idea is to scrutinize and analyze it for truth, not to attack the moral character and veracity, or the mercenary motives of the man who utters it. If the idea is true, it makes no difference what sort of man utters it or what his motives are. If it is false, your job as antagonist is to point out its falsity. If it is a mixture of truth and falsehood, your job is to determine the amount of each. True or false, it must be opposed by ideas, not by insulting accusations about its author.

The first step toward the naturalization of polite letters in Utah must necessarily be an increase in the ability of Utahns to stand criticism. They must learn that the man who honestly points out what seem to him defects in their civilization is not necessarily a murderer or an adulterer. They must learn to deal with ideas as ideas, not as a means of personal defamation. They must learn the necessity of upholding the right of anyone to say what he pleases. Freedom of thought and speech is the first essential of the intellectual life, and until it becomes possible in Utah any attempts to improve the status of literature must necessarily fail.

Another essential is the stringent development of self-criticism. This is especially necessary in the production of literature, even more than in the allied arts. There is a very definite provincialism in the West, by no means confined to Utah but characteristic of it. Let any native tenth-rater, however stupid and inept, write anything, however tawdry, and the West will pronounce it a masterpiece merely because a Westerner did it. This is a trait of undeveloped or unsophisticated societies, and a perfect suffocation of art. When Utah is able to forget the question of a writer's birthplace and to concentrate on the worth of what he writes, literature will look up in Utah. If a Utahn produces first-rate art, let us accept him as an artist, a cosmopolitan. Let us not praise him as a home-town boy. If a Utahn produces something silly and worthless, let us call it silly and worthless and not excuse him as a home-town boy who must be encouraged. The best way to encourage good art is to denounce bad art. And of all places for denunciation to begin, the best place is home.

Again, ability in criticism must develop before there can be progress in literature. Utah must raise its standards and increase its knowledge. In my own case three novels, each one of them the product of the most intense work I am capable of (two of them, incidentally, about Utah—a fact which you seem unaware of) fell into the void with hardly a sound from Utah, whereas every trivial and commonplace yarn I publish in the *Saturday Evening Post* is received with yells of delight from my former companions in the state. That is one aspect of what I mean. I find another aspect in your editorial. You link such ephemeral and fourth-rate people as Riley and Nicholson with first-rate artists like Tarkington and Cather. You join such a pretentious sentimentalist as Ruth Stuart with a fine artist like Cable. You throw the ephemeral Page into a serious discussion which includes names like Robert Frost. You join O'Neill and Marc Connelly in one sentence, which is equivalent to joining Shakespeare and Ella Wheeler Wilcox. And you call a tenth-rate bit of fiction by Vardis Fisher a classic. This is a woeful lack of discrimination. It springs from enthusiasm about the literature of the West and things near your heart, but enthusiasm and optimism are no substitutes for critical judgment, and a *sine qua non* for the development of literature is a critical standard that will distinguish the ephemeral from the permanent, the trivial from the significant.

I may even say, again purely for your ears, that the opinion of Edgar Lee Masters[1] is hardly important. Precisely as Utah must give up believing that all adverse criticisms of it are the work of devils, so it must give up the idea that all flattering criticisms are the work of angels or of geniuses.

With the other side of your polemic I am heartily and wholly in accord. In Utah and in the Western experience generally there is latent an almost untouched treasury for the artist. I will say more about this when I write a public answer to your editorial and letter. I have, of course, published far more on that side of the ledger than on the other—a fact of which you and my other Utah antagonists seem completely ignorant. So far as I have a public personality, it consists almost wholly in arguing in behalf of American themes and in particular of Western themes. I remember to have received from Utah not one word of recognition of what I have written in celebration of the West, and in what you print about me there is no hint of it. Yet my reputation in the East is almost wholly that of an enthusiastic upholder of Western civilization. It seems to me demonstrated that the West does not read me except when I grow violent about the West, and then it decides that I probably beat my wife, or in your case that I make untold sums from such cautious and canny people as Alfred Knopf and Henry Mencken.

If after reading this letter your desire still holds I will write an article of three or four thousand words on the subject you propose and give it to the *Telegram* with my compliments. I cannot do so until some time after the middle of December. I have at last snatched a couple of months free from my manifold activities and must devote them to finishing my life of Mark Twain. Sometime between December 15 and January 15, however, I will write you such an article, if you still want me to. It must necessarily be impersonal, since I do not care to discuss my private experiences in print. Let me know if, after this frank reply, you care to have me do it.

Sincerely yours,

[1] Masters had advised aspiring artists to go to Utah instead of to Paris.

TO JARVIS THURSTON

May 24, 1943

Dear Mr. Thurston:

I have long intended to thank you for your understanding and uniformly generous reviews of my stuff and defense of me generally in Ogden. I am once more in debt to you now for an excellent and unquestionably over-kind review of my new book.[1] But what finally pricks me out of amiable intention into action is not that review but a clipping which I take to be from Frank Francis' column in which he quotes you. I gather that Frank had said something about me in his column previously but, if he did, my clipping bureau missed it. Well, you bring up the question of those two early articles of mine and I'm in a mood to make a statement about them. I make it to you, to show you how I feel and think about them today, for your private information. If at any time you care to quote any part, or all, of what I say, you have my full permission to do so. But I am not interested in your doing so: I am making an explanation to a man whom I recognize as a supporter of mine in my home town.

Many years have passed since I would have attempted any justification whatever of those two articles. They were ignorant, brash, prejudiced, malicious, and, what is worst of all, irresponsible. They were absolutely in the *Mercury* mood of illegitimate and dishonest attack. They represented the only occasions in my career when I yielded to that mood. I have spent practically all my literary life attacking other manifestations of that mood, and I have always regarded my yielding to it on those occasions as an offense which can be neither justified nor palliated.

There was, and doubtless remains, much in the life and culture of Utah which could be legitimately criticized. Some of the things I said in those articles made points which would have been legitimate criticism if I had said them fairly and objectively—and if the entire mood and atmosphere of the articles had not been atrociously offensive. It was, and doubtless remains, thoroughly possible to oppose some of the tendencies and manifestations of civilization in Utah on reasonable, empirical grounds. But that consideration is irrelevant, since my criticism and opposition were embodied in a lot of prejudice, irresponsible humor, and a general yanking out of shirttails and setting them on fire.

I cannot now remember whether I realized as much when I was writing. Certainly I realized it soon afterward. I believe that everything I have written about Utah and the Mormon Church ever since has been fair-minded and objective. I go farther than that: I think that everything I have

[1] *The Year of Decision 1846.*

written about them since those articles has been informed by a basic sympathy. But again, that does not matter . . . except that very little I have since written about them has been taken into account by the people who go on denouncing me.

Why did I write them, and write them as I did? Well, for one thing I was a young buck, intoxicated with the newly achieved privilege of publication, full of wild and yeasty irreverence, and obviously gifted at burlesque and extravaganza. (That last, I may say parenthetically, is an embarrassing, occasionally dangerous gift. It has recurrently thrown me throughout my career and even now sometimes prods me into writing passages which react against the serious intention of my work. We have been told that a sense of humor is fatal to a career in politics. It is a handicap to any career in literature and an extremely serious handicap to a career in social criticism. It has joined with a habit of using concrete words to keep my stature in contemporary letters considerably smaller than it probably would have been if I had expressed myself solemnly and abstractly. In beautiful letters, the light touch is dangerous.) For another thing, I was, if a cocky young fool, also an over-sensitive young fool—and I had, or thought I had, been widely snooted and derided in Utah for presuming to desire a career as a writer. Ogden, Utah generally, is a far more sophisticated, far more cultivated society now than it was when I was growing up there. In my adolescence I was certainly the only person in the state, male of female, who aspired to such a career. The fact that such an ambition is now fairly common there and is treated as a matter of course is a sign, not that I was wrong and the attitude toward me right, but that the local culture has progressed in thirty-odd years. At any rate, I was widely treated as a fool on the one hand, for it must be foolish of me to suppose that I could ever be a writer, and as a kind of pansy on the other hand, for obviously only the epicene would aspire to a career so obviously trivial and even sissy as that of writer. I was, I repeat, widely snooted and derided on just those grounds. Now unquestionably I exaggerated this, but unquestionably also it existed. The attitude was not, at that time, confined to Utah; it was characteristic of provincial America everywhere although I think it was more evident in Utah than in most places, for Utah was nearer than most places to the pioneer society in which literary activity has always been considered foolish and sissy. I resented it violently—much more than I should have resented it if I had been older, wiser, more cultivated myself, or more sophisticated. So I reacted against it when I came to write those articles. In some degree they were acts of self-vindication, in some degree acts of revenge.

Later on, I deeply regretted having written them. I do not regret them now. I conceive that the damage they did to Utah was nil—was wholly non-existent. (In all those years of the *Mercury*'s slam-bang, indiscriminate derision of American life, was any attack on any community written that is now remembered in the community attacked, save only mine? I doubt it. An antiquarian, a historian of that period, I am familiar with most of those attacks and as I go about the country I inquire about them. I never find anyone except antiquarians and historians who remembers them. And most of those people do not remember them at first hand but have encountered them in research.) They did Utah no harm and they did me much good. For one thing they succeeded in rousing a historian's conscience in me, so that I have never again written anything without knowing what I was talking about. But what is much more important, they have enabled me to understand that period, the youth and young manhood of my own generation, as I should never have been able to understand it if I had not both written and repented them. They were absolutely and altogether of my literary generation. The revolt against the home town and the dishonest attack on it are type-specimens, absolute stigmata, of the period. My own career in letters has been in absolute opposition to the main literary current of my time. From my second novel on to my present book and the one now in manuscript, I have set myself to oppose the ideas, concepts, theories, sentiments, and superstitions of the official literature of the United States between the two wars. If I have any significance as a writer, it derives entirely from that fact. And that fact in turn rests, intellectually, on two realizations: my realization of what I had done in writing those articles and my realization of what Van Wyck Brooks had done in evolving and elaborating his system of thinking about American culture. I could not have understood my literary generation, and certainly could not have taken a stand in opposition to it, without either experience.

So much for my part. Let me add what I believe to be true about the reception of those articles in Utah and their subsequent reputation there.

We cannot imagine those articles being written today: the world has changed too much. Mutatis mutandis, granting the idioms and sentiments of this later time, if the equivalent of those articles were to be published today, they would, I think, cause considerably less stir and offense in Utah. The state has grown more sophisticated, it has come to understand more what intellectual and literary discussion are, it has become at least a little more tolerant. More people are accustomed to the play and interchange and expression of ideas. Ideas are more likely to be received as ideas, not epithets, not insults, not imputations of dishonor. The booster state of mind, which in the West of the 1920s was the equivalent of the vigilante state of mind of earlier days, has lapsed considerably. If I or someone else were to say the same things today, in today's idioms, there would be a lot less fuss.

And yet it is true, I think, that Utah, and especially the Mormon culture, is extremely sensitive and intolerant to criticism and even to difference of opinion in which there is no criticism whatever. That is probably true of the West in general, as distinguished from other sections, even the

25

South, but it is more true of Utah and the Mormons than of the rest of the West. I have been, not surprised, but exceedingly interested to see the old patterns repeated in the comments I get, in correspondence mostly, about my current book. There can be no question whatever that that book contains the most sympathetic treatment of the Mormons ever published by a Gentile. Any dispassionate mind need only compare it with, say, Linn or Werner. It is packed full of the most flagrant and even fulsome praise of the Mormons, condemnation of their oppressors, admiration of their achievements, sympathy with their suffering, patient exposition of their point of view. Yet I receive a steady stream of vilification on the old, familiar grounds (you're a liar, you're a mobocrat, you're a homosexual, you're a publicity seeker, you're a cheap sensationalist, you're a defiler of the prophet and an author of filthy pornography, etc.), the Deseret Book Company holds up its order until it determines whether the book is sanitary or should be burnt by the public hangman (and how it made up its mind I haven't bothered to investigate), and somebody to me unknown sends my publisher a copy of a radio script which discusses the book purely in terms of those two old articles, as if there were nothing else in it. Except for you, nobody in the state reviews the book. Except for three or four people, and they friends of mine mostly, everyone who writes to me damns me for having blasphemed the religion of which, it is repeatedly pointed out, my mother was a communicant.

Now in the first place I think it is true, as you say in Frank Francis' column, that most of these people who are so sore at me have not read the articles. They know my name as that of a son of a bitch who once wrote a lot of damned lies about Utah, and that relieves them of any obligation to know either what those damned lies were or what the present book is. But in the second place, it is lugubriously true that the orthodox Mormon mind cannot tolerate any objective treatment of Mormon history whatever. All treatment of the Mormons must completely accept the Mormon doctrinal, metaphysical, and supernatural assumptions. If it does not accept them, then it is ipso facto prejudiced, unjust, and libelous. All Mormon actions have always been pure and sanitary; all criticism of them has always been evil and mendacious. Who is not for them is against them. That is why the fact that I have presented the Mormons to the readers of American history more sympathetically and with a more careful exposition of their relationships to their time than anyone had done before me goes without recognition in the abuse heaped on me. It is enough that I do not accept the Mormon assumptions. This is what I have sometimes called the Mormon inferiority complex. Something of the sort is, of course, a part of all religious orthodoxy. Yet it is perfectly possible for any writer to handle any other religion in America objectively and to be answered objectively in turn. It is not possible of the Mormons, and that is further evidence of their cultural lag.

All this makes no difference to me. I have no desire for Mormon praise and no need of Mormon approval. Neither do I desire the people of my home town to pay me any respect whatever. It certainly matters nothing to them that I have become a writer and, as one, have frequently written about the West. I should rather have them friendly toward me than otherwise, but I have become so thoroughly a part of a different society that I am fundamentally indifferent. I dislike it when I get a letter of fulsome praise from some Ogdenite who has seen my name in the papers and is impressed by the publicity without giving a damn for the work and, most likely, without having read it. To the same degree, I dislike it when I get a letter full of equally ignorant abuse. I should like to know that there are a few people in Utah who like me, without reference to my work, and a few who like my work, without reference to me. And I should like those who dislike my work to dislike it with reference to the work itself, not with reference to idiocies I committed long ago, which they may know, besides, only by hearsay.

When one is young and idiotic there may be some ambition to be known as a final authority, an important writer, a man of distinction and publicity or even fame. It doesn't last: one matures. One comes to understand that what counts is the honesty and thoroughness of the work. I should find it hard to state exactly what my ambition as a mature man is. It would run something like this: to do good work, to do work in which I may take some satisfaction and my friends some pleasure; at the utmost, as Frost once said of Robinson, to put something on the record that will not easily be dislodged.

All this doubtless sounds vague and inconclusive. Some weeks ago I came down with a streptococcus infection, the most serious illness I can remember having had, and my mind has lacked teeth ever since. I began with some notion of expressing my thanks to you and my feeling that you read me with much more understanding and sympathy than most writers get from most readers, and that in a very warming way you are a friend of mine.

Sincerely yours,

TO A MISS BURKE

The letter that follows was written in
response to an inquiry from a graduate
student at the University of Wisconsin who

*was contemplating a dissertation on DeVoto
as a literary critic. The dissertation does
not seem to have been completed.*

March 27, 1944

Dear Miss Burke:

My secretary is laid up and you will have to take my typing, which is as inaccurate as a *New Republic* lead. Moreover, your thesis topic seems to me tolerably footless. I should never have approved it when I was a teacher. However, your letter makes a serious request and I am undertaking to answer it seriously—always something of a strain on me when literary criticism is being discussed. So seriously that I'm mailing you a copy of Mattingly's book,[1] which you should know is an advertising brochure, and a copy of a new book which, I hope to God, represents my last flirtation with criticism.[2] I set up a demand in return; send me a copy of your thesis when it's finished. If it's a long one, send me the typist's bill.

You should also be told that Mattingly is a friend of mine, just about my best friend. Discount what he says. He is a Renaissance historian and the biographer of Catherine of Aragon but is now in the Navy, teaching intelligence officers something far too secret for me to know about. He was up here over the weekend and took a pleasant and alcoholic plunge into theories of history and criticism. After six drinks I became a monument signalizing the end of Renaissance thought and also the Thucydides of American nationalism. It would be wise not to adopt that ground in your thesis.

Nothing much has ever been written about me and there is nothing much to write beyond what is said in *Who's Who.* Back in the days when the literary were talking about the forthcoming communist revolution in the United States, various devoted souls took me to pieces as a black Fascist in the *New Masses,* the *Daily Worker,* etc. I don't remember who or when. Edmund Wilson, who was still under no contract to be interesting; who had not yet become one of us pros or undertaken to fill Kip Fadiman's shoes, did the same in the *New Republic,* about 1937 I think.[3] There's a reply to him in *Minority Report,* written in part while I was running the *SRL.*[4] *Current Biography* had a biographical piece about me, some seventy-five percent accurate, in, I see, September 1943. Another friend of mine, Catherine Drinker Bowen, has kidded herself for several years that she is

[1] Garrett Mattingly, *Bernard DeVoto: A Preliminary Appraisal* (Little, Brown, 1938). Like Forsythe, Mattingly had been a colleague at Northwestern. At the time of his death he was professor of history at Columbia.
[2] The book was *The Literary Fallacy,* which within two weeks of this letter would precipitate a furious attack by Sinclair Lewis, "Fools, Liars, and Mr. DeVoto," *Saturday Review of Literature* 27 (April 8, 1944).
[3] "Complaints: II, Bernard DeVoto," *New Republic* 89 (February 3, 1937).
[4] "Autobiography: or As Some Call It, Literary Criticism."

writing something about me, but I don't think that even she believes it, certainly I don't.[5]

I have not too much respect for the practice of literary criticism, very little for any of its methods, and practically none at all for its absolute and systematic branches. Necessarily, then, I am not comfortable when called a critic. I do not regard much of what I have written as literary criticism. Much of it is social history and much is analysis of thought, and both departments frequently work with literature as data, but few of my judgments are aesthetic and, I hope to God, none of them are absolute, deduced, or arbitrary. I never think of myself as a critic and so, you can see, the entire effort of your thesis seems to me a misconception. However. . . .

"Autobiography: or As Some Call It, Literary Criticism," in *Minority Report* and "Mark Twain and the Limits of Criticism" in *Forays and Rebuttals* state such principles as I stand by. A good many other essays in those books apply them, and you will find them applied in the book I am sending you, an advance copy of *The Literary Fallacy*, which will be published, I think, April 18. I see no point in repeating here what I have said there. I told Wilson that I am an empiricist, a pluralist, and a relativist, and if you like words and categories, those will do. Let me try to put it in another way.

No mind is ever of one piece, simple, consistent, or even coherent. Put it this way: I have always been allergic to the point of complete intolerance to abstract thinking, deductive reasoning, and systematic logic. My mind is the exact antithesis of, and completely antipathetic to, a mind like Lewis Mumford's, for example, or Thorstein Veblen's (whom I knew), or Stuart Chase's. All my life I have consoled myself in lugubrious moments by reading men like them—they can heal all wounds in my soul and restore any self-esteem I may have had beaten out of me. It is a low and malicious taste, I have no doubt, but there it is. All my life I have been congenial with people who work with concrete things or concrete thoughts, and all my life I have quarreled with people who work with abstractions, generalizations, or systems. I get along well with novelists and painters, not critics; with historians, not philosophers; with scientists, not systematists. I admire all kinds of skill and so I admire even skill at systematic logic—but wryly, and I'm afraid never in public. Robert Frost has been a deep friend of mine, so has Archie MacLeish, so have other poets; a dozen of my friends are novelists, a dozen others historians, and I have had dozens of scientific friends all my life. But I have never got along with a critic and though, for my sins, I have had to associate with a lot of philosophers, I can't say that I have ever been intimate with one. Or for that matter a sociologist or any academic psychologists.

[5] Mrs. Bowen wrote nothing about DeVoto during his lifetime. After his death she published "The Historian" in Bowen, Mirrielees, Schlesinger, and Stegner, *Four Portraits and One Subject: Bernard DeVoto* (Houghton Mifflin, 1963).

Harry Murray, an academic psychologist, has been quarreling with me for years, whereas I have been friends for years with at least half a dozen psycho-analysts. You see, it's the concrete thing, the living thing that I go for, and the abstraction from it that repels me.

I was first a protégé and then for twenty years a friend of Lawrence J. Henderson, the biochemist. Hans Zinsser, the bacteriologist, was certainly one of the deepest of my friends and for many years, and you will find me in his two literary ventures, both by name and as the unnamed literary person he sets up as a straw man to knock over for his own fun.[6] Hans was a romantic from head to heels, and so was the opposite of my pedestrian and humdrum self, but he was not a romantic scientist. I suppose that these two men may have had a considerable effect in shaping my mind— certainly Henderson did, and for years it was a very painful process. I learned skepticism, empiricism, the limited concept and the limited result from both of them. But, of course, I should never have been congenial with them, or with such men as Pete Bridgman, the physicist, or Larry Kubie, the psycho-analyst, if I had not something of the same cast of mind. You must understand, I had no set intention, ever, of becoming a writer— it was just one of those things, it happened as the line of least resistance, and in great part because I was too old to take the medical training I had expected, when the last war finished, and likewise too much in debt.[7]

Well, that's the clue, if there is a clue. Anyway, since long before I wrote *Mark Twain's America*, I have undertaken to oppose absolutes and systems in thought. I have sometimes opposed them in literary thinking, but more often in social and political thinking, where they are far more dangerous. Two things have always been quite clear to me, that uncontrolled thinking is essentially totalitarian in effect and that the kind of thinking I trusted, and the standards it necessarily enforced on me, put me out of touch with the literature of my own generation, if not usually antagonistic to it. Since I did not think too highly of that literature, I have not minded. And, though I would not say this in public, I have had a certain satisfaction in seeing literary gents come round to the positions which they raised hell with me for standing on just a little earlier. My ideas about at least American history and American culture are now fashionable as all hell, but they weren't fashionable twenty years ago, or ten, or five. You will find me being very snooty about this fact in the new book. Excuse it—I am sufficiently tainted with the literary point of view to be an exhibitionist.

So much for the exalted attitudes of criticism. On a humbler level, I am interested in the techniques and the psychologies of the arts, and necessarily

[6] In *Rats, Lice, and History* and in *As I Remember Him*.
[7] DeVoto made this statement many times, and seems to have convinced himself that it was true. From the evidence of his Harvard record, he was never anything but single-mindedly literary. Compare his letter to Jarvis Thurston with its report of Ogden's scorn for a man who wanted to be a writer.

therefore of literature. I certainly rank skill higher than it deserves, and have frequently outrageously overvalued second-rate stuff on the simple ground that it was superbly done. I respect fiction in particular, and poetry almost as much, just about in proportion as it may be psychological—but I am not using that word as professors of English use it. I revere wisdom, and especially the wisdom of the heart, the knowledge of how people feel, how they behave, what makes them feel and behave as they do. Again, you see, the concrete thing, the living thing. As a matter of fact, I don't know [above] three professors of English who [know] the first damn thing about fiction or psychology in those terms. Professors of English too are abstractionists.

I dislike amateurs, esthetes, dilettantes. I dislike coteries. I dislike literary attitudes and those who take them. I dislike people who think that literature is important, and especially those who think that it is an equivalent of or a substitute for experience. But, hell, if you've read my books, you've observed all that, and all the above, including the obvious fact that I'm something of a Freudian.

I have, I honestly believe, no literary attitudes of my own—but you must decide that for yourself, or ask Matt. I have a considerable pride—that of a professional writer. I take an obvious satisfaction in being able to write with some measure of authority on matters so diverse as the Shakers or the Oneida Community, T. S. Eliot or Ezra Pound, the Union Pacific Railroad, the Oedipus Complex, the fur trade, geopolitics, and the technology of the factory system—while at the same time supporting myself almost exclusively by writing popular fiction. It may not be known to you that I am John August.[8] The chaste Wisconsin library probably does not have his books, but you will find them in a lending library. My spread is from such publications as *The Psycho-analytical Quarterly* to *Woman's Day*.

I don't know what else there is to say except that my best book is certainly *We Accept with Pleasure*, which you have not read. You would have to read it twice, possibly three times, to understand why.

If you read it, it might reveal something about the other side of your inquiry. Frankly, my child, when you want to know about me as a man, I don't know what to say. Dicky Quintana of your English department was a friend of mine when we were undergraduates, but I've spent only half an hour with him in all the years since, and I hear he is very superior about me now. Better not ask him, maybe. I don't think there's anyone at Wisconsin who knows me any better. It's hard enough for me to be solemn about myself as a writer, you mustn't expect me to be solemn about my per-

[8] The nom de plume of John August was invented in 1926, either by DeVoto himself or by H. L. Mencken, to disguise authorship of an article called "Sex and the Co-Ed." The article was never published. In 1938 DeVoto revived the pseudonym to keep his popular magazine fiction separate from his serious work. In all, John August wrote five *Collier's* serials, four of which were published also as novels.

sonality. Lots of people like me, lots hate me like hell, I'm not a congenital grouch, I'm not a drunkard, and my wife has not divorced me—I talk far too much and far too late at night—I work hard and read everything—I like good tobacco, good liquor, and a good job. But if you are going to deal with literary matters, you must get firmly in mind, as the foundation of your entire edifice, that writers are damned dull, the dullest people on earth, and that what they are does not matter in the least, it matters even less than what they write. My advice to you, unasked I grant you, is to get the hell out of the study of literature and take up history, where you are certain to find interest and, it may be, even profit. Both of which you assuredly will never find in an English department.

Sincerely yours,

TWO
Education

Throughout his mature life, from the time when he began to publish essays on education, literature, and history in the *American Mercury* and *Harper's*, in the mid-1920s, DeVoto received letters from people asking his advice on where to get a liberal education, how to write, how to read a book or mix a martini, how to reconcile the claims of personal freedom and social responsibility. The very positiveness of his published opinions led the uncertain and bewildered to him. He answered them, invariably and courteously, often at great length if their inquiries struck him as honest and earnest, occasionally with brusqueness if he thought them vicious or inclined to take advantage. Some of his replies were essentially essays, and indeed did now and then form the base for future articles. Quite apart from his opinions, which might be called radically middlist, commonsensical, civil libertarian, and pragmatic, his letters are commonly marked by a scrupulous kindness to the seeker. He was extravagantly generous with his time and energy to people whose only claim on him was their need or their trouble. Which is to say that even when he was not teaching, he was a born teacher. He accepted the responsibility that his published articles and books threw upon him.

TO A MR. COLLIER

March 15, 1928

My dear Mr. Collier:

I cannot ignore the obvious urgency and earnestness of your appeal, and yet I cannot in any degree answer you satisfactorily. For you express yourself far too generally and too impetuously for me to know precisely what you want or, even, precisely what state of mind you are in or hope to achieve. I can only try to deduce as much as possible from your letter, without any means of controlling or correcting my deductions.

Let me say, then, that you seem to have done too little thinking about the problems you ask me to solve. You ask me flatly, "Where can I get a good cultural education?" That is—you will pardon me—more than a little naive. It is clearly an unanswerable question, for the answer is, in one aspect, "Nowhere," in another aspect, "Almost anywhere," and in a third aspect, "My dear sir, that entirely depends on you, who and what you are and what you desire to be." Perhaps the best answer is still another one, "What is 'a good cultural education'?" . . . A "good cultural education" is not, of course, an entity: it is not something that can be bought and sold over a counter. That is obvious enough. Perhaps you have not realized that it is equally obvious that a "good cultural education" is not something that can be attained by mental discipline and coordination, as one obtains grace or strength by gymnastic exertions. I think, in fact, that part of your present bewilderment comes from your failure to realize that simple fact. You tend to believe that if you only go to the right place, do the right things, perform the right routine, take the right courses under the right instructors, and devote the right amount of time to the right road—some happy day you will be educated.

Believe me, it is not that simple. If it were, there would be sanity in the democratic belief that we can educate everybody. But education is not a process, nor a formula. It is not, in any particular, comparable to the elaboration of a chemical body or the integration of a mathematical series. I distrust all metaphors and analogies,[1] but if a figure of speech will help

---

[1] This is perhaps the wildest statement that even Bernard DeVoto ever made. He never thought except in analogy and metaphor, he could not argue without them, he got most of his illuminations from them. Here, he was probably reflecting the influence of L. J. Henderson, with whom he had renewed acquaintance in the fall of 1927 after a lapse of seven years.

you see education more clearly, let me compare it to the polishing and correcting of a lens, to the end that shaped glass may transmit more light, transmit it in lines more nearly straight, with less distortion, less ocular illusion, and greater fidelity to the natural objects on which it is trained . . . Education, I would have that metaphor say, is the correction of an individual mind so that it may more clearly perceive and more exactly interpret the reality of the objective world and of society. And—perhaps because of my own idiosyncrasies—I should prefer to interpolate the adjective "present" before the noun "reality" in that sentence.

If I am right in my understanding of education, it follows, then, that the problem of education is indissolubly linked with the problem of character. The lens will never be better than the limitations of the glass it is shaped from. And if that is true, then the course of any given effort for education should be controlled and directed by the personal individuality of the one who is being educated. I cannot attempt to prescribe for anyone by mail. I have tried to prescribe specifically for very few young people, and when I have done so it has been on the basis of intimate, personal study of them.

But, lest such an answer as I have given you prove disappointing to you and dampening to your obvious enthusiasm, perhaps I can give you a few generalizations that may help you. Certainly, I can answer specifically one or two of your questions.

Let me say then that your willingness to make "a trip to the farthest corners of the earth" need not necessarily be called upon. Please understand this simple principle: the philology of the word "education," with rare felicity, exactly expresses the process—it is e-duco, a leading-out of that which is within. For some minds, for some purposes, unquestionably Oxford or the Sorbonne, or such cities as London, Berlin, Paris, and New York, would be more effective environments for the process. For others, unquestionably Harvard or Columbia (or, just as unquestionably Union Theological, or West Kansas Baptist Seminary) would be more effective environments, looking toward true education, than the University of Michigan. For some minds, any college or any metropolis would be poison. And in general, any place that has a library, a laboratory, and a backyard is just as good for education as any other place on earth.

It happens that I am fairly well acquainted with the U of Michigan. Now, God knows, I am no frantic admirer of it, and God knows, too, I am aware of its pretentiousness and its empty showiness and its more than occasional idiocy. But don't forget that those epithets do not tell the whole story about Michigan, or that they apply to all other colleges as well. And, what is particularly important, don't forget that a college may have all those limitations and still be a splendid instrument for the education of a mind that is determined to utilize that college's capacities and possibilities. True,

if I had a son about to go to college in America I would send him to
Harvard or, for secondary choices, Columbia or Brown or even Wisconsin—
but to deny that Michigan may be the avenue to a genuine education
would be folly. Do not abandon it in the expectation of finding the earthly
paradise at some other college. The Utopia of education, like all other
Utopias, exists only in daydreams: this is a faulty world and wise men
adapt their actions to its limitations. Do not, in any event, abandon
Michigan until you are convinced, by actual trial, that the ends you desire to
accomplish cannot be achieved there.

You ask about the New School for Social Research. I can tell you that
it has a brilliant faculty and that it is suffused with an atmosphere of
genuine intellectual freedom and activity. That sounds enormously attrac-
tive. But there are other sides to the picture. It is not a place for anyone
under thirty. And, what is more vital, it is not a place for the type of mind
that, in my private opinion, the seeker after truth must have. It is not, I
mean, a place of dispassionate inquiry. It is dedicated to the, perhaps
praiseworthy, effort of ameliorating social conditions. If, eventually, you
believe that social conditions, the social complex, can be in any way
changed by writing books, passing laws or enumerating causes of prostitution
or labor disputes, then by all means go there. For you will be happy in the
company of like-minded people. But you will not be educated, in the sense
of which I have written, or capable of education.

No, my dear boy, the problem of education is at once far simpler
and far more complex than you think. Get mastery of your tools. Get that
while you are still of college age—and then spend the rest of your life
getting education. You must realize that: there will never be any definite
Commencement Day in the intellectual life, there will never be any given
day when you may feel that you are educated. Education, I repeat, is not
an entity. It is simply—growth.

What do I mean by your tools? Well, first French and German. They
are indispensable, the sine qua non. Not a speaking but a reading knowledge
of them. Save for the departments of education and sociology, the modern
language departments, I know, are everywhere the weakest in the colleges.
You will waste time, you will fumble badly in the courses in French and
German you can get at Michigan, but at least they can teach you to read.
Next, mathematics, if you have the kind of mind that is adapted to mathematical thinking. If you haven't, don't waste time studying math, but if
you have, study as much of it as possible, four, six, eight courses—till your
mind begins to work naturally in the mathematical phase, till you think
about the discrete phenomena of experience in terms of calculus, integration,
descriptive geometry, and the theory of probability. Third, all the science
you can cram into yourself. Any science, but especially biology (first),
physics (second, if you can understand it), and chemistry. Every hour that

you spend in the laboratory, any laboratory, will repay you ten thousand times—in knowledge of the world, in wisdom, in the habit of thinking about objective reality in the terms of the best, the scientific, approach to it. The sciences are, in fact, the greatest good that the colleges offer—for everything else in education the determined individual can get for himself, alone if need be, but laboratories he cannot have, and they are vital. Fourth, something that will a little train you in the perception of objective or subjective rhythms: drawing and design if you have some skill with pencil or crayon, or harmony and counterpoint if you have some grounding in music—but do not expect much from courses in these subjects, for in the nature of things they can give anyone only a little. Fifth, but only if you have been troubled by religious questions, something that will acquaint you with the history of religions and especially of primitive religion.

Those are your tools. The rest is living, observing, analyzing, and above all, reading. You must read enormously, encyclopaedically. The educated man is the reading man. What shall you read? Everything. The intelligence yearns for every field. But especially, history and literature. I do not say which is the more important, which the greater: in my mind they are indissoluble . . . Understand, I am not recommending courses in literature or history. For the most part, such are a waste of time. Master your tools— and then employ them in omnivorous reading.

One sentence in your letter suggests that you are on the brink of a great error. You say that you will probably "major in English or Rhetoric." (The University of Michigan's quaint conceptions linger in that "Rhetoric.") Well, I have been a Professor of English, and I say to you: you can get it better by yourself.[2] And that is especially true of Michigan—you have a department of English which, in a profession overrun with asses, is extraordinarily asinine. You will do me the grace of not repeating that judgment to anyone, but it is true. But the best of English Professors, and there are many very good ones, live a nonessential life. The books exist for anyone to read, and the man who is capable of being educated needs no help with them.

Similarly, even more emphatically, avoid the departments of philosophy, economics, sociology, and psychology. The first is amusing but immaterial intellectual horseplay, a polite chess. The other three, in the present state of knowledge, are downright dangerous: the man who teaches any of them, knowing the truth about it, is a charlatan or a quack, and the man who teaches it not knowing but believing is a fool.

One thing more, this about yourself. You are, of course, utterly unknown to me. But I tell you, whoever and whatever you are, as a college

[2] Despite this opinion, expressed shortly after his escape from Northwestern, DeVoto went back to teaching the moment Harvard asked him to in the fall of 1929, and he did not teach tools, he taught English.

man you must make your choice. You cannot have both the show and the substance. If you are a fraternity man, if you are an "activity" man, if you desire to be either, then you will no doubt enjoy college and will probably have a happy life, but you will not be educated.

Now, I am a very busy person, and a very tired person. I cannot put my time at the disposal of others, and I must willy-nilly set a limit on my correspondence. But I am willing to help young people if I can. If your letter to me came out of anything but impulse, and if my answer to it suggests questions that you would like me to discuss at greater length, I will freely do so. You must, however, tell me more about yourself—you neglected to tell me even your age, let alone your interests, ambitions, and early environment. Do so, if you write again—but briefly and impersonally. I cannot promise to write more than once more, but that, at least, I will do if you feel that I can help you.

Sincerely yours,

TO RALEIGH BLAKE

1929[?]

I wish you had written to me at greater length telling me more about your likes and dislikes, your ambitions, your expectations, and your natural abilities and disabilities. I can't hope to do much more than suggest to you a few generalizations that apply to most people who are beginning college.

About Northwestern first. When one has watched the colleges as long as I have, one realizes that the best education, and indeed the only education possible, is self education. That is possible at almost any college, certainly at Northwestern, and one might look at certain handicaps that North W puts in the way of the students as so many benefits, as stimulants to the attainment of education. Still, I hope that you will not decide on NW if you find it decently possible to go elsewhere. This for a number of reasons. To begin with, there are neighboring colleges that are distinctly better from nearly every point of view, Wis., Ill., Minn., Mich., Chi. But what is more important, if you were at NW you would be too near home. I don't like that for anyone. In the first place, a young man of college age should be without the supervision of his parents. He must accustom himself to making his own decisions, directing his own actions, and choosing his own goals, and directing his efforts toward them—and to accepting the consequences. In any given choice, he must be at once free and willing to make up his mind without reference to anyone but himself, and he must be far enough from home to escape the natural wish of his parents to share the choice, and his own natural wish to share the responsibility. Again, he must be able to enter completely into the life of his college and his companions: he must not be subject to either his duties or his affections at home. And again, the farther he is from home, the more strange and various people he will meet, and the more widely he will be able to enter, imaginatively, the life around him.

Those are generalizations. I suggest that, since you aren't going to college this fall, you defer for a while the choice of your college. Your point of view will change considerably during the next year, and many things may happen that will conceivably be of importance to your decision.

Let me now take up more personal questions. You say that you have not been a good student in New Trier. Well, that isn't of much importance. What is of importance is your cause of failure to be a good student. You want to be one when you go to college—else why go there?—and if you can understand yourself and the problems of education sufficiently well to avoid making the same mistake hereafter that will be a great gain for you. I cannot, of course, at this distant short acquaintance pretend to be accurate about you. But perhaps I can give you something to think about. I'm going to begin with your attitude toward your teachers.

First, let us assume that your attitude toward them is wrong. We'll take the other point of view in a minute—but you must understand that the first step in education is the willingness to be corrected if one is wrong, in fact not mere willingness, but passionate eagerness. What is a scientist? A man who exercises every possible effort to prove himself wrong in every step he takes and rejoices if, at the end of a lifetime's work, he can prove that everything he did in that time was erroneous. You say that you have sat in classes and acted bored, that the teachers seemed to be dummies, that the material was cut and dried and formal. You are afraid that the atmosphere in college will be similarly irksome, that the teachers will be cut and dried old fogies, incapable of original thought.

My dear boy, the world is under no obligation to entrance you. There was no thought of pleasing you when it was created. The difference between any two of us is so slight that ten feet of darkness annihilate it, so immaterial that the notion there is any at all may well be an illusion. From the distance of half a mile, or fifty years, what is the difference between Raleigh Blake and Bernard DeVoto, or between either of them and a Chicago gangster, or between either of them and an Australian Bushman who has no more than forty words at his command, and has never learned to make a fire? Very little. Very very little if there is any at all. I mean to suggest merely that the world looks with equal indifference on us all. It presents itself to you and whether you find it a magical drama or whether you find it an intolerably dull tale is equally indifferent to the world, which goes about its cycle without reference to your pleasure or ennui. There is nothing interesting or dull in any subject you have studied or will ever study. The interest and dullness inhere in you, and in studies as in most other things, you will get out of them what you bring, and no more. Bring to Mathematics no more interest, curiosity and will to explore than, in my time, I have brought to it, and you will never be able to balance a check book with more self assurance than I have at the job. Bring to Mathematics the fierce curiosity and will of a Newton or Einstein and you will very considerably alter the appearance of the world with them.

Your job is not to go into a class room and dare the teacher to make his subject as dramatic as the last reel of a movie. Neither he nor the subject is under any obligation to be vivid to you. The subject's obligation is merely to display before you a set of facts or theories or observations that the experience of many men has made available and that you have decided may have some bearing on your life, either as preparation for something else or as data in themselves. The teacher's obligation is merely to help you to understand and master them. Now, if the subject is merely a means to an end, a preparation for something else, you are being very foolish if you stop to consider whether or not it is interesting, if you let the notion of "being interesting" enter your mind at all. It is a step toward an end, an end that you have foreseen and chosen—either of your own thought or because you have been willing to trust the wider experience of others. If you are taking the subject as an end in itself, to familiarize yourself with its material and to put its data to the use of immediate knowledge, then how foolish it is to complain that it has not been made interesting for you. Do you see?

Let me give you an example from my own education—which I assure you, is continuing from day to day, though I am six months past my 32nd birthday. . . . For five years I have been studying the life and work and times of Mark Twain. The end of this study is to achieve as complete an understanding of Mark Twain as is possible, so that I may write a book about him. That has immediately necessitated a comprehensive study of life in the primitive Missouri where he was born. Do you think that latter study was interesting? Well, try sometime reading say a hundred thousand pages of county histories, intolerably dull accounts of lumber rafted down the Mississippi, the number of tons of hay produced in Clay county in 1841, the destruction in the flood of 1857, the amount of malaria in Arkansas in years that cannot possibly be of importance to any one any more, tons of statistics, oceans of births and deaths, millions of lies. Well, I have had to spend months at this sort of thing, and months more at much duller stuff, till my mind was sodden, and my whole impulse was to quit the job and take up book keeping as an employment full of thrills and excitement.

That sort of thing is tolerable when one gets usable material from it. But what of it when day after day produces only this fact: there is nothing here? Dull? It is the abysmal nadir of ennui. But, don't you see? It is essential to the larger purpose, the understanding of Mark Twain, which I assure you, is breathlessly fascinating. Was it my business to complain that the material was dull, cut and dried, unoriginal? Such a complaint would be as irrelevant as to object to a sheet of music because it wasn't printed in green ink on pink paper. My job was to do that work, to go through the material and report the results. And the result "there is nothing here" is just as important as if every line of print carried an important fact hitherto unknown about Mark Twain. Before, neither I nor anyone else could say what that material was worth. Afterward, I *knew*. Do you see the fable?

Now as to teachers. Is it not presumptuous for you to judge them and find them wanting? A high school teacher is a very humble person, scholastically, compared to such a scholar as Professor Michaelson or Professor Kittredge. But, with young people, he does a job they could never do. And whatever his training and his personal defects, he knows more about the subject he is teaching than the students in his classes. I don't think it is very mature to say "Lo, here is a very dull fellow, a thickwitted zany indeed; go to, I will not learn in his class—I'll show the beggar he can't get dull with me." That's a childish response—a boy of eight quitting a game of follow-the-leader because he isn't satisfied with the way the leader jumps the fences or crawls thru drainage pipes. A much more intelligent response would be: Lord what a dull fellow. (If you're sure he is dull)— Well, I'll learn what I can from him, and then get out of his way.

And now I'm going to tell you something about the way our minds work, especially when we're at the age you now have. We are born with a furious necessity of dominating others, of being first in everything, of showing our superiority to everyone else. Psychologists call this the ego urge. Our ego frantically requires us to be always asserting and proving this superiority to everyone else. The urge reaches its greatest intensity about your present age. After that the world has tamed us so that we begin to be satisfied with superiority in one thing, then with leadership in it, then with competence in it, and finally with mere normal functioning at it. This declaration is called growing up, or attaining wisdom, or what you will. But pending that final stage, the mind plays tricks on us. Daily experience proves to us that there are hundreds of things that we do less well than others do them, that can never be superiorities of ours. Now, the mind won't accept that idea, finding it intolerable that we, WE, should be in anything inferior to anyone. So the mind begins to discover unsuspected causes that bore on that only apparently disastrous result. We could have won that race if only we hadn't pulled that tendon last week; we could have scored that touchdown if only we hadn't developed a headache. We could

44

have beaten out Joe in the rivalry to take Mary to the dance, if only we hadn't been convinced that we didn't really want to take her. We could have been first in the Ancient History test instead of a dumb little dimwit like John Smith if only the teacher hadn't been so dull that we lost interest in the whole subject. The mind has a really terrifying power. Have you ever seen athletes pale with headache or actually vomiting from acute nausea before a contest? They were going into the contest resolved to do their very best. The contest meant so much to them that they would do their very utmost . . . so much that the idea of defeat, of failure, was actually intolerable. But deep down in their minds, suppressed or never even consciously felt, is either the knowledge that someone else is better than they, or the fear that someone may be. Out of that fear springs the headache or the nausea. They could not live at peace with themselves after defeat if the reluctant mind had to acknowledge that it had crossed swords with an actual superior. The thought is intolerable. So sickness came upon them. Then if they were defeated, there was a perfect explanation for the eyes of the world, and much much more for the eyes of the mind. I don't expect you to see now that a great part of the dullness of your teachers has been the unconscious fear in the back of your mind that you wouldn't be distinguished in their classes. But very certainly a great part has been.

This has all been in my experience, and I have had to work through to a realization that honesty with oneself is the best thing in life, that to know the truth about oneself is infinitely finer than to luxuriate in the false consolations of the ego-urge. I think that every intelligent person works through the same experiences to the same conclusion.

Let me now turn to the other assumption that you are right in calling your teachers dull. I can at once partially confirm it by my observations in the class room at NW. There is no question, if my experience is valid, that the students that came to us from New Trier were, as a group, more inadequately prepared than those from other high schools in the Chicago area. So that my prepossession is that you were in part right about the teachers, and I add to that, knowing your mother, and having your letter to judge by, the further assurance that you are an intelligent chap and likely to be right about them.

Well, what if they were dull? What if the teachers you will have in college prove dull, old fogey-ish, cut and dried? Are you going to sulk like a small boy and refuse to use them? The world is full of dull people—there are many to whom you will be dull to the verge of intolerability—and you'll have to live with them as best you can. And these particular people, the teachers, are the material offered to you with which to get an education. They are the tools you must use in order to master the larger tools that comprise an education. An education, remember, is not something you can buy like an automobile, or earn like a merit badge in the Boy Scouts. It is merely a certain expertness in the use of certain tools, the languages, mathematics, the historical method, the scientific method, and so on. If you are to lead an intelligent life, do intelligent work, enjoy intelligent society, then you must get that expertness, that skill. Well, the teachers are tools. Some of them are good tools, some of them bad tools, more merely indifferent. The wise man of course wants, for any given job, the best tools he can get. But he doesn't throw up a job and quit when he only has a two dollar saw to cut planks with while there are forty dollar saws on the market. If getting from one place to another is the whole desideratum, then a 1911 is fully as good as a 1928 Rolls. Some day I hope you will read the life of Pasteur. No man who ever lived did more to revolutionize the outer world and the world of the intellect—he was a very great genius and he actually changed the conditions of life and our understanding of it. When you read his biography, observe his materials that comprised his laboratory. A little room in a barn. A few cans to hold solutions, a simple microscope so faulty that the veterinary who takes care of my dog would throw it away, a handful of candles and an oil lamp, some glasses such as my mother used for jellies (which by the way she was able to preserve because of what Pasteur discovered). Not much, is it? The dark room I have brought into the woods so that I can develop pictures is complicated and expensive compared to it. You probably have a more complicated outfit to take care of the family radio. But simple as the tools were, they sufficed him for his experiments with ferments—and those led to what one might soundly consider the greatest discovery of all time. Later, Pasteur had one of the finest laboratories ever made up until then, and in it he made magnificent discoveries; but he never again equaled the first one, which was made with tools we could buy today in Woolworth's. Or read about the rural family physician, Koch, who in his own kitchen, in hours when he wasn't spraying tonsils, revolutionized the science of bacteriology. Or Count Rumford, who laid the foundation of modern physics with this equipment: a team of horses, a barrel of water, and an auger.

It isn't the tools that count: It's the skill you develop with them. Not the teachers, but the use you make of them. You want the best you can get of course, and therefore you want to go to the best college open to you. But what happens once you get there depends entirely on you. Any teacher on earth will bore you, and any subject, if you are willing to be bored, if you inwardly challenge him to interest you. But if you are wise, if you really want to get out of life the pleasures and compensations that an education can afford you, you will disregard the teacher except as a tool. Find out what larger tools you want. Take the courses that will make them available to you. And then use the minor tool, the teacher, to the full extent of your ability. I assure you that you won't anywhere find many college teachers who are actually unfit for their jobs. You may, of course, but if you think you have, be at first suspicious of your own judgment—always a desirable habit of mind to cultivate—and consider that experts that know rather more about it than you have passed on his fitness. If you become finally convinced that he is unfit, then drop him cold, without reproaching him or feeling superior, and move your efforts elsewhere, to some place where they can be made fruitful. Don't for God's sake pride yourself on having exposed a bore—that is perhaps the easiest accomplishment in the world, and nothing to be proud of.

It might be illuminating now and then to frame to yourself the picture of you in the teacher's mind. Teaching, you know, is hard work. I've held a variety of jobs, many of them calling for great physical labor. But none ever took such energy out of me, not a fourteen hour day in a hay field, not sixteen hours in a saddle roping nervous steers or marching all day with sixty pounds of field equipment and fourteen of rifle, as three class sessions of one hour each. A teacher is always at the limit of his strength—and he isn't particularly inspired to do his best for a student when he realizes, as he always does, that that student who knows less than nothing about the subject being taught, is sitting inert before him, gently warmed by a specious feeling of superiority, and damning him because he isn't being brilliant.

. . . . The conclusion of all this is that you're probably wrong, most of the time, about teachers and subjects being dull, and that, even if you're right, the fact of their dullness has nothing to do with the question of education. No pleasure in the world has quite the adventurousness of learning. But if you are to enjoy it, you must have first the desire to learn. After that, you must have the courage to learn, and that includes the willingness to be rigorously stern with yourself. You must be prepared to sacrifice all of your self esteem and all of the protective devices with which the mind ministers to its own comfort. You must learn to be humble, which means to count the proved fact, the real thing, that entity that *is*, as worth far more than any bearing it may have on yourself or your ideas or your prejudices or your emotions or your affections. And you must be prepared to sacrifice, in order to attain the fact whatever it may cost. The truth, we have been told, maketh alive. I think it does make alive those who are daring enough, and hardy enough to seek it out. But I know that it kills the less fit who purposely or accidentally get in its way—which is why most people should never set out for it. The pursuit of truth—or the similitude that in an illusory world seems to be the truth—is the most splendid adventure open to us. But in order to undertake it one must first be a man.

There are doubtless many things that I should discuss specifically. I will, if you will suggest which ones you would like me to. Don't hesitate to. You are not likely to say anything that will seem ridiculous. And don't consider my time. I have always plenty of time for such discussions as these.

As for athletics—I should advise you either to do no more than will

47

suffice to keep you in good health and can be made enjoyable, or, if you want to adopt the pseudo-professional career of college athlete, to go to a small college such as Wabash. In the Big Ten you would probably not be a success anyway—that time has passed when the genuine amateur can be an athlete in the universities, which employ professionals, trained in the rolling mills, frankly as publicity-gatherers. And the mere effort of trying to keep up with the competition of Slovak professionals would strain you unbearably, rob athletics of all pleasure, and certainly frustrate your efforts to get, incidentally, an education. The small colleges remain on an amateur basis: you could be in one of them, at one time an athlete, a student, and a gentleman. In the Big Ten that is quite impossible.

But of course I ought to tell you my own opinion. I attribute no value to it beyond my own point of view. It is this: college athletics are the diversions of boys, the intellectually immature, the retarded. And college students should be men.

TO CATHERINE DRINKER BOWEN

1935

Dear Kitty:
This ought to be the right time to write to you, for I've just heard Gladys Swarthout singing that grand old tomato *Mon coeur s'ouvre à ton* etc., and it may be catsup to you but it's great stuff to Papa for there was a contralto in Ogden, Utah, in the fragrant yesterdays who had prematurely gray hair and a lively eye and eloquent calves and she would warble that number in a way to open the heart of many a man more hardboiled than I am. But her mother had a bad heart in a convenient way and would begin to breathe cyanotically whenever I came up the front steps, so it seemed best not to follow that line any farther and we never did get to the shearing scenes. But I forget that a musical Bourbon is the worst kind of snob there is and you begin to breathe unevenly, as of swollen turbinates, whenever any simple pleasure like singing is mentioned. Thereby crushing the spring violet in my soul that would trade all the Prousts and Joyces, yes and all the Tschaikowskis in the world for balance enough to roar Gunga Din in the same key throughout. You have no idea how the humbler folk live, my dear. Did I tune in on Kubelik last night? I did not. I said Kubelik is for my betters, Kitty maybe has temporarily overcome her shrinking and at this minute is in the kitchen listening. So I spun the dial till I found—what? Till I found Uncle Jasper and His Hillbilly Octet singing She'll Be Comin' Round the

48

Mountain. Then I was happy. Happy as any man can be who has spent a quarter century wishing he could sing She'll Be Comin' Round the Mountain and never got there.

Yes, and don't ask me why the hell I haven't written to you. The dual life I lead has damn near broken me open. To begin with, the *Post* has been rejecting me right and left, and I think I'm on the verge of the ultimate humiliation that anyone in our profession, dear, can suffer—rejection by *Liberty*. I've been writing all hours of the day and night. And if that, plus imminent bankruptcy and eviction, isn't enough, damn if I haven't run out of material in my Harvard course on From Dreiser to Dada with B. DeVoto. For six weeks I've been just ten minutes ahead of that class, and if you think it's an easy life reading Evelyn Scott while shaving and writing lecture notes on Ezra Pound while waiting for the morning coffee & cigarette to take effect, I wish you'd come up here and take over some of my leisure for me. What the hell do I know about Ezra Pound? Exactly nothing—or rather, exactly enough to keep talking at a moderate rate from seven minutes past two till the clock strikes three. How much did I know about him at this time yesterday? Just one lone & far from pregnant fact: that he was born in Hailey, Idaho, 275 miles north of Ogden, Utah. And Pound is just one day in this course, my dear, just 53 minutes of concentrated information and offhand but, by contrast, brilliant criticism. 53 minutes of Pound being over, I can then go out and prepare 53 minutes apiece on T. S. Eliot, Ernest Hemingway, Wm. Faulkner, Archie MacLeish, Hart Crane, Thomas Wolfe—and have you splashed your way through any thousand pages in *Of Time and the River?*—and so on until God sends Reading Period and I can put on my old pants again.

But you know what the answer is—the Message that the old Professor would have written long ago if it were possible to write letters while driving the Pontiac fifty miles an hour in order not to cheat the undergraduates of two minutes of Ezra Pound—and what he now undertakes to write. It's this, space, new paragraph, message, to-wit:

Forget all the other books,[1] forget my book, forget all the books that agents & publishers have held up to you. Get them out of your mind. And don't listen to anybody, especially a publisher, who pours advice & suggestions into your ear. Sit down & write that book the way you want to. The way the idea first hit you. Be as anecdotal as you like, write yourself into it as much as you have an urge to. You will certainly color with your personality & style every book you write. That's okay. It's a swell personality & a swell style. Go ahead. The main thing is to get it down on paper somehow, anyhow. We can begin to get critical about it then, as critical as you like. You won't really know what kind of book you're writing until it's in first

[1] Mrs. Bowen was writing *Beloved Friend*, a biography of Tschaikowski. She had shown DeVoto parts of the manuscript at the Breadloaf Writers' Conference during the summer.

draft. Then you can look at it and see. Then you can tell whether any of the parts have to be shrunk or stretched, whether the edges need sandpapering, whether you've let too much of your back hair get into the argument. Then, if you like, I can read it for you. I don't know, & never have, why you profess to find my judgment so valuable, but God forbid I should do anything to dispel the pleasantest delusion I've ever encountered. Say the word and I'll come down & go over your first draft with you—at Merion, if you're there, at Hebron, if you're there. Or throw it in your reticule & bring it up here and we'll put the level & calipers on it here. . . . But my point is, don't let the commiserating and unctuous suggestions of friends, agents, publishers & music critics deter you in any way from writing it the way you want to, the way you feel about it, the way the book writes itself in your mind & nerves. That's the way the book should be written. Go ahead & write it.

And the more Kitty Bowen you put into it the better it will be. Type that off fifty times and if you can get it by heart. Paste up a copy over your desk. No, don't type it. Write it in longhand so you don't have to study it out. . . .

TO WHEELER TIPPETT

February 4, 1946

Dear Mr. Tippett:

As you well realize no one can say anything that will help you solve your dilemma. If dilemmas are ever solved in this world, they are solved from within. You have got to follow your own deepest impulse and there is no assurance that it will lead you right. My own feeling is that it is always best to fight back, to swim against the current, to make an effort against whatever odds rather than surrender. Conrad says something about immersing oneself in the destructive element and by the labor of one's hands and feet forcing it to bear one up. I believe that one achieves an irreducible dignity by doing so. In terms of my personality it would seem preferable not to retire into contemplation but to do what one can in the world of human relationships however frustrated or corrupt or evil human relationships may be.

At the same time I have no answer or comment to make to anyone who sincerely decides that the religious life offers him the best chance for happiness or self-fulfillment. If you judiciously decide that it does, not being driven to that decision by fear or despair, then obviously you should act upon it. I suggest merely that you first make sure whether you have not resources of stoicism and courage within yourself and whether you have not some capacity to work upon the objective world to some satisfaction, say as a teacher.

Sincerely yours,

TO MARK SAXTON

*The Breadloaf Writers' Conference, on
whose staff DeVoto served each summer
from 1932 through 1939, and in five
subsequent summers, was the institution
which DeVoto loved above all others except
Harvard. Until a quarrel with Robert Frost
produced strains that first troubled him and
then led him to stay away, he felt that
Breadloaf was the best club he ever
belonged to, a place where he could relax
from controversy and be companion,
teacher, pundit. He thought its teaching
was the best he ever saw done anywhere,
and said so repeatedly in print. In the way
that* Harper's *and for a while the* Saturday
Review of Literature *were above the
factionalism of critical and political schools,
he felt that Breadloaf was above the
faddishness and coterie-making of the
literary. Especially after he was not
promoted at Harvard, he found there the
lectern and podium that were an abiding
part of his essential spiritual machinery.
This letter was written after the 1947
session.*

September 18, 1947

Dear Mark:

[. . . .] What you say about my performance on campus makes highly gratifying reading but is much too generous. The three of us[1] did by a good deal the best job on fiction that has been done in the eleven sessions I've graced, and I'm confident the best that has been done there, but it was team-

[1] DeVoto, Helen Everitt, and William Sloane are listed as the fiction team in 1947. Saxton, then an editor at William Sloane Associates, may have substituted for Sloane.

work that did it. We demonstrated the superiority of the T-formation to the single wingback, and I got an aesthetic satisfaction from the running plays. It was a cooperative endeavor that teaching ought to be and damn seldom is . . . You are at least right in this, that I have always liked teaching. When you come to write that obit for Fred Melcher,[2] recollect that one of the biggest of the conflicts that have made my inner life as picturesque as the Valley of Dry Bones is the one between teaching and writing. Jim Conant,[3] who resolved it without solving it, sacrificed the useful part of me and certainly did nothing much for beautiful letters. On the other hand, he came closer to making me a whole man than I was ever likely to be under the elms. But there appears to be no answer to teaching, anyway. I think we demonstrate at Breadloaf that pros do it best and in no field are there enough pros to go round and in some there aren't any at all. Best write our God-damn books, I suppose. It will take the moral effort of my life to get me back to mine.

B L, as may have occurred to you, is the damnedest place. My own hangover has persisted up to now. The bloody membrane of personalities, about which I unfortunately know even more than Bill does, oppressed me there and does still. I went only under duress and it about used up my margin of safety. At the same time, the experience of working with friends at a common job is damn near inestimable. An original thinker—let's call him Red Lewis—once remarked that writing is a lonely occupation. What he should have said is that a man who is at once bright enough and ass enough to be a writer is also sensitive enough about his personal deficiencies to long for functional justification as part of an institution. I suppose that's why so uncomfortable, vexatious, and emotionally exhausting a place as B L becomes so memorable to us as experience looked back on [. . . .]

Yours,

TO LEWIS U. HANKE[4]

March 15, 1948

Dear Louie:

I will probably be in Cambridge when you get here. Phone me and come over for dinner or at least a drink. There is, however, a chance that I may be in New York and so I briefly outline my opinions on the subject.

[2] Editor of *Publisher's Weekly*.
[3] President James Bryant Conant, of Harvard, had made the ultimate decision not to promote DeVoto in Harvard's English Department.
[4] Historian, then head of the Hispanic Institute at the Library of Congress.

I have always supposed that the more knowledge a writer had the better for him and have always advised young aspirant writers to complete their college course if they had the price as a preliminary to anything else. I have always supposed, too, that the kind of knowledge they got in courses was just about the most useless on tap in the colleges, that they could get a better knowledge of literature for themselves for sheer love of reading it, and that they could profitably employ their time in college on other courses. I have always thought it was best for them to follow their own bent in choosing those other courses but with my own predilections I have always recommended history and the natural sciences. They seem to me to give more guidance to both human experience and the modern world than anything else.

The teaching of writing in college, or for that matter anywhere else, is a complex and mostly unsatisfactory business. See a piece by me in the Easy Chair for last November[5] and one by Wally Stegner in a *Saturday Review* of not more than four weeks ago.[6] At college age not much can be done but something can be and at any rate a serious young person can be brought to see some of the personal and artistic problems that lie ahead of him and under expert criticism can by trial and error learn the beginnings of some of the fundamentals. I believe on the basis of all my experience and observation that except in the occasional case of a highly intuitive man like Dean Briggs, only people who are themselves experienced writers can give anybody even this minimum. I am glad to say that the situation has changed greatly since you and I were in college, when English departments assumed that anybody could teach composition and so usually gave the courses in it to people who they knew could not teach anything else. In the last few years a recognition that writers make the best teachers of writing has spread fairly widely and there must now be a dozen colleges where writers of considerable skill and experience give courses in writing. The best ones of course are those who add to professional experience an ability to analyze it and so communicate intellectually what they know in their integrated skill. Stegner mentions a number of teachers in his article and you can easily find out where there are others. I would have to see you in person and discuss Peter as an individual before I should care to make a recommendation myself.

I think you should labor to make him understand, though you will find it difficult, that practice in writing is the least important thing that a person who wants to be a writer needs at his present age. It is, in fact, not altogether a necessity but to some extent a self-indulgence. It does keep a young person's interest alive and gives him more pleasure perhaps than he is likely to get out of other courses. (That is what makes teaching it so much fun

[5] "Breadloaf Writers' Conference," *Harper's* 195 (November 1947).
[6] A slight error. The article he had in mind was "New Climates for the Writer," *New York Times Book Review*, March 7, 1948.

for the teacher.) Nevertheless the important thing is to develop and train his mind generally, equip it with the tools for getting further knowledge, and fill it with such knowledge as he can get in college. In the end, what makes a writer is knowledge and understanding and wisdom and we hope that college can make something of a start toward them. At any rate, college is the thing no one gets a chance to get in later life. The real apprenticeship in writing itself cannot really begin until one is older than college graduates usually are. It is a hard and difficult apprenticeship and it requires at least a little maturity before it can even be begun. By chance, my next Easy Chair, which will be out at the end of this month,[7] deals with this subject and you might read it and have Peter do the same.

This is the basis of what I will say to you in greater detail if we meet, as I hope we can. It will be very nice to see you and I am only sorry that Kate is not coming with you.

Yours,

[7] The Easy Chair, *Harper's* 196 (April 1948), is a rumination on writing and reading.

THREE

The Mark Twain Estate
and the Limits of Patience

DeVoto's associations with the literary works and personality of Mark Twain were varied, profound, and of long duration. His first real public notice came with *Mark Twain's America,* which defended Mark Twain against the spoiled-artist theories of Van Wyck Brooks, and he went on defending Mark Twain against a variety of at-first-unlikely-looking enemies, including Mark Twain's biographer and literary executor, Albert Bigelow Paine, his daughter Clara Gabrilowitsch, and Thomas Chamberlain, the lawyer for the Mark Twain Estate. There is evidence that he adopted Mark Twain as the first of his several surrogate fathers, for in the early 1930s, coming out of a post-analytical storm, he remarked to his helper Henry Reck that he was not only feeling better but writing better "now that I'm no longer trying to be Mark Twain."

Admiration, with DeVoto, was usually conceived as attack and defense. His whole involvement with Mark Twain was controversial, beginning with his vigorous—in the opinion of many, over-vigorous—public attack on the ideas of Brooks. When he was not granted access to the papers under Paine's control, he attacked Paine. When he thought Clara's concern for her father's reputation was leading her into bowdlerization and suppression, he resisted Clara. When he took over the Mark Twain Papers, largely through the influence of Harper and Brothers, in 1938, he immediately began to find suppressions and omissions in Paine's editing. And when Charles Lark, the first lawyer for the Mark Twain Estate, was replaced by Thomas Chamberlain, DeVoto swiftly found that Chamberlain too was, in effect if not in intent, an enemy. When he resigned from the curatorship of the Mark Twain Papers in 1946, DeVoto did so partly because he simply could not get along with Chamberlain, and partly because he could no longer afford the unpaid time that the Papers demanded. But also, one guesses, he could contemplate resigning as Mark Twain's public defender because he had won most of the battles. Between 1932, when he published *Mark Twain's America,* and 1946, when he turned over the Papers to Dixon Wecter, he had had a significant part in enlarging and deepening and solidifying Mark Twain's reputation as one of the greatest, and certainly the most American, of our writers. If he had not disposed of the Brooks thesis, he had seriously weakened it, and a whole new generation of scholars and readers had grown up who followed the DeVoto line, not that of Brooks. One suspects that he could leave the curatorship of the Papers because he was no longer interested in a subject with no fights left in it.

His considered views of Mark Twain's career, and his interpretation of specific works, ought to be consulted in his books, not only *Mark Twain's America* but those which he put together out of the Papers or derived from study of the Papers: *Mark Twain in Eruption* (1940), *Mark Twain at Work* (1942), and *Letters from the Earth* (1962). The letters published here report principally DeVoto's personal relations, as he worked through the Papers, with Paine, Clara, Chamberlain, Harper and Brothers, and certain reviewers and correspondents. They demonstrate his willingness to carry on the war on any front that opened, and to carry it on with a crustiness and a pungency of phrase reminiscent of Mark Twain's own public commentary.

*When he first began to work on a book
about Mark Twain, DeVoto wrote to Paine
asking certain questions and requesting
permission to see the Papers. Neither that
letter nor Paine's reply seems to have been
preserved. This present letter, dated
September 27, 1928, is DeVoto's reply to
Paine's rejection of his request.*

*As he reported in his "Foreword to
Robert S. Forsythe" in* Mark Twain's
America, *his questions and request had not
been entirely disingenuous. He called them
"a species of blackmail." He thought that
Paine must have misread some of the
Papers, and the only way to find out was
somehow to make him grant permission to
check the documents. Paine, according to
DeVoto, replied that the papers were Mark
Twain's "refuse," containing nothing of
value that he had not already made use of
in his biography and in the* Autobiography
and Notebooks. *According to DeVoto, he
said that no more books need to be written
about Mark Twain.*

*Paine and the Estate's lawyer, Charles
Lark, read those remarks in the Foreword
to* Mark Twain's America *and were furious.
They hinted a slander suit unless DeVoto
produced the letter he purported to be
quoting. DeVoto does not seem to have
produced it, but by November 4, 1932,
Paine had cooled off. "Hell, let it go," he
said. At that point neither he nor Lark
could possibly have foreseen that DeVoto's
ironic offer, "Public benevolence constrains*

*me to offer the Estate my services," would
turn out to be prophecy, and that shortly
after Paine's death DeVoto would be
appointed curator and editor of the Papers.*

September 27, 1928

Dear Mr. Paine:

I am reluctant to intrude again on your time, but, since you feel unable to give me the information I asked for, I should like to know whether you will permit me, in my book, to quote freely from your Biography of Mark Twain. As I indicated in the preface I sent you, I am accepting it wholly, and shall want occasionally to quote from it. I should like to do so with your permission and good will . . . Incidentally, I am much more familiar with it than you seem to think. I have read it entire five times in the last three years, in addition to two earlier, uncritical readings, and have followed it page by page in my detailed study. I wrote to you for further information about Grant's *Memoirs* not because I didn't know what you said about the writing of them but because what you said had been challenged by Burton Rascoe and because I hoped to be able to add any documentary evidence you might have to my own rebuttal of him. There has never been in my own mind, apart from a momentary suspicion not occasioned by your book, any idea that Mark Twain had anything to do with the writing of the *Memoirs*. Only, when the question has been raised, however unjustifiably, it seems to me obligatory to notice and answer it.

I am therefore very sorry that you do not feel the matter important. And I am sorrier still that you will say nothing more about the Bret Harte incident. I quite understand your point of view: you did the job once and for all in the way that seemed best. This is the only point where I have ventured to disagree with you, believing that the matter was of public importance. I still believe that it is, and so I shall assemble as much relevant material as I can. I shall, for instance, publish the following from *The Letters and Journals of Thomas Wentworth Higginson*, under date of July 31, 1905, at Dublin, New Hampshire: "Evening, Dined . . . with Mr. and Miss Clemens . . . An interesting talk . . . after dinner. [Dots in the original.] Clemens lent three thousand dollars in all to Bret Harte when he first came East, though knowing him to be laden with California debts already. When H. asked him for two hundred and fifty dollars, he proffered five hundred dollars. One man to whom BH owed three thousand dollars for loans wrote him on his birthday, sending all his notes back, and B wrote one of the most brutal letters he ever saw."

I cannot postpone my book for five or ten years. I am under contract, and have already delayed more than a year past the promised time—wholly in an effort to make it as thorough as possible. It is the only work of criticism

I am ever likely to undertake, and for that reason alone I want to get it done as soon as possible. May I venture to say, in all humility, that I seem better acquainted than you with the spread of Brooks's doctrines? Instead of fading from the public mind, they seem to me to be intensifying. They are now working into histories of literature and even into college courses—which, however one may ignore them as unimportant, are at least fertile ground for the widespread propagation of error. There is probably no way of convincing you that I am anything but a presumptuous young squirt with a good journalistic sense of the publicity to be had from writing about Mark Twain. Nevertheless, I do not quite measure up to that judgment: the preface that I sent you told the whole truth about the origin of my book, and about my desire to combat Brooks in public. That is why I sent it to you: It would have been easy enough to delete the sentence which suggested that I dissented from some of your critical judgments and which, I observe, you have marked in the margin.

I am, however, genuinely grateful to you for writing to me. I hope, too, that you will freely, and explicitly, give me permission to quote from your book. I am accepting it as the final authority in everything except critical opinion: to reject your authority there seems to me in no way impertinent. Literary opinion is never infallible and can never be final—and since I have grown up in a later and changed America, and so have necessarily a different point of view, I cannot believe that I am lacking in honesty, in respect for you, or in literary legitimacy by presenting, publicly, the significance of Mark Twain's work as I see it.

Faithfully yours,

TO MARK VAN DOREN

Having walked out into Main Street with his guns buckled on, DeVoto replied to any fire that came at him from the corners of saloons and the windows of the newspaper office. He was wise enough to know that an author who challenges a reviewer in print stands to lose more than he can possibly gain; but he was not willing to let the reviewer himself go unanswered. Van Doren's review of Mark Twain's America *appeared in* The Nation *for October 19,*

1932. In the DeVoto correspondence at Stanford University there are two Van Doren letters, dated October 23 and November 20, 1932, defending his review, suggesting that DeVoto's bumptiousness had stimulated him to resistance, and remarking on the irony of his defending Brooks, with whom he disagreed as much as DeVoto did.

October 17, 1932

Dear Mr. Van Doren:

I must ask leave to bore you dreadfully over some pages. It happens that a half-dozen reviews of my book, *Mark Twain's America*, seem to me to have misrepresented it, and that I select yours to examine in detail. I shall make no reply to the others. The authors of some of them seem to me to have no authority to pass judgment on the book. The authors of the rest interest me so little that I do not care what they say. You, however, have a position of unquestionable authority, and I happen to respect your mind. So I ask your patience while I examine your review and describe what seems to me its misrepresentation. I risk a further offense by deciding that, since you have authority in its field, your misrepresentation cannot be the result of either ignorance or accident.

Let me make clear that I do not question any of your opinions about the book's merits or success or failure. Nor do I question any judgment of me or my motives that you derive from my book—though, having in part written it to exhibit the folly of deriving psychological theories from literary works, I cannot believe that any you may form about me will be realistic. I shall argue one or two matters with you, but as opinion only and with no conviction that argument is important. My principal point raises a question of fact and of a reviewer's responsibility toward fact.

I begin with the fourth paragraph of your review where, after you have diagnosed what it amuses you to call my anger and loudness, you assert that I am wrong when I say I have no theory about Mark Twain. I cannot believe that you misunderstand the method used in my book. I find it equally hard to believe that an elementary difference between two ways of thinking is unknown to you, or that you intend to quibble about mere words. The method my book objects to is the derivation of conclusions *a priori*—the deductive method, if you will, specifically the psycho-analytical method of Mr. Brooks. That is the method of theory, and I am quite sure that my definition of it is both accurate and clear. It has proved accurate and clear enough to be satisfactorily reported by men whose intelligence is unquestionable. The method of my book is exactly the opposite. It is to assemble all the facts I can find that relate to Mark Twain's books—if you want to substitute the word "data" for the word "facts," I do not object—and then to state the conclusions they indicate. It is, if you will, the inductive method. There is an irreconcilable difference between the *a priori* method, the theory, and the empirical method, the conclusion from data. I think that my method succeeds—I should not have published the book if I didn't think so. But—here enters the question of a reviewer's integrity—though you are certainly free to decide that it fails, are you free to misrepresent my book by describing its method as similar to the one it attacks, when in fact it is not similar? I cannot believe that you misunderstood so elementary a difference. But if you didn't, does not this paragraph avoid the reviewer's obligation to describe fairly the book he is reporting on?

The next paragraph. "I doubt very much whether the America he describes . . . would recognize itself in his pages." I do not fully understand that. It appears to be a cautiously phrased declaration that I am wrong about the frontier. But just how and where? When you tell a historian—permit me to call myself one for the moment—that he is wrong, you must specify the nature and extent of his error, or your accusation will be meaningless. In my book I make no unsupported statement about what I describe as Mr. Brooks', Mr. Mumford's, or Mr. Frank's mistakes. I quote or summarize what they actually say and then set against their statements a bulk of "data" which allows the reader to compare them with the facts. That is the only way in which accusations of error can be given responsibility. You make no effort to identify my errors; you say I am wrong and let it go at that. Unless one assumes your infallibility, as I see no reason to do, your accusation is irresponsible.

Were the readers of the *Nation*, I among them, supposed to regard your review as a report of my book for which you accepted responsibility? Then point out to me the facts, the "data," about America in my book that are erroneous.

The paragraph goes on, in support of your assertion, with misrepresentation that cannot possibly be inadvertent. You say that I knew "the wilder aspects of frontier life—the brawling, the bawdry (you rather make a point of the bawdry, but just where do I?), the dances and the songs, the tall tales and the merry ones." You immediately add, "But that this was America is, I submit, a theory . . ." No possible wrenching of words will make your two sentences anything but an assertion that I say this was America. If you have read my book and if your phrase "wilder aspects" is to be taken as meaning what it says, then you very seriously misrepresent what the book says. I do not say that you misrepresent it from malice—I avoid subjective interpretations— I here assert that you falsify its obvious intention and its actual content.

Did you read the second chapter, the fourth chapter, the fifth, seventh, tenth and twelfth chapters? I must assume that you did—how otherwise would you have ventured to review it? But if you did, then you read a constant insistence on qualities of frontier life as different as possible from the "wilder aspects." You read about music, the jubilees, the hymns, the theater and the concert hall and the minstrel stage. You read about a pleasant rural society and its schools, churches, quilting and fanning bees, the developing social organization—its constant attempts at decent human intercourse. You read my repeated declaration that the frontier had leisure and peace and quiet as well as energy and turbulence. You read my tiresomely repeated description of various idyllic "aspects" of the frontier, my long analysis of the beauty and freedom of frontier life as they are reflected in Mark Twain's books. Furthermore, you knew when you wrote the review that this effort to present hitherto disregarded and specifically denied "aspects" of the frontier, not "the wilder aspects," was the principal effort of my book. I presume to write that last sentence as a statement of fact on the basis of an induction: everyone with whom I have been able to talk about the book and two hundred reviewers recognize it as the principal effort. Your review makes no mention of that effort, but specifically and by implication denies that it is made. I repeat: you are entitled to any opinion about my book that you may care to express but if there are standards of critical integrity, you are not entitled to falsify it.

I use such words as "misrepresent" and "falsify" with complete deliberation. Only an explanation of the discrepancies I here point out can convince me that I am wrong in using them.

Your next paragraph. I do not understand your argument very well here, and your statement that "the only thing that can answer a theory consciously held is another theory consciously held" seems to me mere nonsense. But I do understand that you believe my book "open on every side." Yes? Are my facts, my "data" subject to overthrow? One interpretation of your sentence would be that you think they are. If they are, then the book certainly fails, as you say it does. But which "data" are subject to overthrow, and why do you not overthrow them? You say I am wrong but you do not show wherein I am wrong. Your assertion is irresponsible until you do. Make the effort, point out where my "data" err, designate those which are mistaken or unrepresentative. If you do, I will modify the book in later editions, for I respect data more than you do. If you prove unable to do so, then this part of the review is another misrepresentation.

"His data . . . actually support the contention of 'The Ordeal' that something better had been possible." This is said unequivocally as a statement of fact. Well, which data? Better than what? Data I supply, you say, prove me wrong. Name them, point them out, specify page and line, or quote the words that phrase them. Until you do, your assertion is frivolous— the reviewer's cheap dismissal of authority on his unsupported statement. And "better" than *Huck Finn*, do you mean? "Better" than the passages I have called the best things in American fiction? The data I use to prove *Huckleberry Finn* the best of our native literature really prove against these very data, that better stuff than *Huckleberry Finn* was possible? I cannot see in this notion of yours anything but uncontrolled theorizing, and I shall be unable to see anything else in it until you point out which of my data support it. I accept it as a revelation of your sentiments, but it is irrelevant in a discussion of my book.

"And his proof that the pioneer democrat thought pretty regularly about sex. . . ." Another falsification. There is no such proof, no such assertion or suggestion in my book. Here I deny as flatly as possibly what you say: you are distorting my book in a manner that nothing can excuse. If you can support your statement, please do so at once in a letter to me. But if you can't support it, then this is one more serious misrepresentation. If your desire was to report to your readers what I said about sex on the frontier, then you should have reported it correctly. You should have said that I opposed to the idea that sexual repression characterized frontier life a certain number of facts, "data," and drew two conclusions from them. One conclusion was that the sexual customs of the frontier were freer than those of the seaboard. The other conclusion was that "the relations of men and women remained the relations of men and women" on the frontier—an assertion that they were normal relations. I nowhere said or suggested that "the pioneer democrat thought pretty regularly about sex." Your obligation was to report correctly what I said before you began to argue about it. I cannot see that you fulfilled the obligation by attributing to me almost the exact opposite of what appears in my book.

I do not raise the question of criticism. The standards of criticism, I believe, would have required you to examine the content of my refutation instead of dismissing it in epithet. They would have required you to appraise the method I offer in substitution for the one I attack—to pass judgment on "data" you dismiss. They would have required you to tell readers that I examine Mark Twain's books in relation to my "data" and then to appraise what I say about his books. They would have required you to discuss the validity of my appraisal of Mark Twain—in short, to criticize the results I reach. Instead, you announced that you agree with Mr. Brooks. You are certainly entitled to agree with him, but, I think, you are not entitled to offer a distortion of my book in support of your agreement. But I am concerned solely with that distortion, not with what you might have said. I have made herein certain assertions that you have misrepresented my book. So, this question: are my assertions true?

The convention that forbids a writer to reply in print to a reviewer is, I think, a healthy one. At least it is one I do not care to violate. But it does not proscribe a private answer and this is one. This is an effort to hold you to accountability for what you have said in public about my book. My conclusion has been stated: for motives I do not venture to guess about, you deliberately misrepresented my book to the *Nation*'s readers. I do not know whether you will care to answer me. If you do, and if it appears that I owe you a retraction, I will make one. Otherwise, consider that this letter offers you, uncalled for, my opinion about the value of your judgment of my book.

Very truly yours,

TO A MR. MORDELL

February 10, 1933[?]

Dear Mr. Mordell:

My notes are stored but I think you will find the account of Whittier's new pants in *The Early Years of the Saturday Club* and, as I remember it, also in various histories of the *Atlantic Monthly*.

I'm afraid I must take issue with several things you say. It is a matter of indifference to me what label is affixed to the method of my book, though as a former college teacher I feel that you cannot have read many college theses if you find one in *Mark Twain's America*. Buckle I have never read and so can't judge how relevant your allusion is, and I read Taine so many years ago that all I can remember is a mass of turgid French that ended by boring me. But the principles of history to which I adhere and which I tried to make govern my book are contained in Chapters 1, 4, 5, 8, & 10 of Vilfredo Pareto's *Traité de Sociologie Générale*. I have described and debated them so often that I can only refer you to those chapters, especially the 4th and 5th, "Les Théories Qui Dépassent l'Expérience" & "Les Théories Pseudo-Scientifiques," for evidence that my influences are twentieth century and the dialectic behind them sound. But you are mistaken if you think I am incompetent at psychoanalysis. I have studied it for—well, my first article on it was written in 1916, and I claim to be letter-perfect in all the principal writers and works and fairly well acquainted with most of the minor ones. Simply, as I said in *Harper's* and in my book, I cannot convince myself that it is a fact-finding instrument in history or biography.

May I call your attention to two things in your letter to me? You say that I "unaware" used psychoanalysis when I "correctly criticized Mark Twain for ignoring the whoring that went on in the Mississippi boats." Excuse me, I did not criticize him at all. I stated the fact descriptively, precisely as I stated the fact that he was a pilot on those boats and went out sounding on the ice. That he did or didn't ignore the whoring is completely indifferent to me. My effort is wholly descriptive, to establish the exterior facts about him—in this instance in opposition to mis-statements of Brooks —and I am content to leave the interior facts, if any, to people who believe in their ability to establish them, as I do not. . . . Again, you say "every superstition owes its rise to a phobia, a compulsion, a complex." Suppose you were called upon to prove that assertion? How would you do it? *Every* superstition? Have you examined them all? Has anyone? Are the facts about their origin always recoverable? Has no one ever acquired a superstition by accident? By imitation? Are none of them spontaneously generated? Are none of them fashion? Are none of them rational interpretations of ignorance, of inferior or incomplete knowledge, of misinformation? Are none of them mere matters of formal cult, unrelated to emotion or experience? How do you know? What data have you that bears on their origin? How do you prove the point? [. . . .] I am well acquainted with the literature of psycho-analysis and I know that, finally, your belief in that origin of superstition rests on dogma. You would prove your statement by reference to the canons of Freud. I do not criticize that proof nor do I question your logic in holding to it. I merely say that my book was written from a different point of view.

I find it extremely difficult to convince people that my primary, in fact my sole interest in it was to establish what objective facts I could. Those that I succeeded in establishing did, I believe, make impossible Brooks's subjective interpretation. Anyone may now use my facts as the basis of another subjective interpretation. That's as may be and I'm not interested one way or the other. My only point is: any interpretation hereafter that ignores my facts, and any objective ones that may be added to them, will be wrong. You do not charge me with being wrong in fact but only in method. I can only say: point out to me where my facts are wrong. No one has done it yet. When someone does I will cheerfully modify whatever is necessary, in succeeding editions.

Well, to quote Mark, it is difference of opinion that makes horse races. Thanks for writing to me and especially for writing so generously.

Sincerely yours,

TO CATHERINE DRINKER BOWEN

1934

Well, you are a darling, Kitty, and I love you extravagantly and I'm damned glad you like *M T's A*—nor have I had so much praise in my time that I curl at the edges when some comes my way. I think it's a pretty good book. God knows it's an honest one—though, honesty being the one literary virtue that's available to everyone, that doesn't raise it out of the lower magnitudes at one stroke. It will be a better one, of course, when I get around to revising it. In the Light of Eternity, I mean, cutting out most of the controversial stuff. I deliberately wrote it that way, intending to cut it out later. The point was: the Brooks-Frank-Mumford-Lewisohn system was the most important critical idea about American life that my generation produced, and the most cockeyed, and no one had ever challenged it, and for the sake of the decencies, the record, and the future, someone had to challenge it. So I did. The result was to make a lot of mess on the floor, spatter blood and marrow on the walls, and give portions of the book a distinct resemblance to an abattoir, but it had to be done. The literary are such swine, Kitty—here's a whole new generation of critics assuming my stuff precisely as the earlier swine assumed Brooks's. Well, some day, if people ever buy enough of my books to enable me to write them, I'll bring out a revised edition, simply ignoring my opponents and writing for the future [. . . .][1]

TO CLARA GABRILOWITSCH

DeVoto's first effort as curator and editor of the Mark Twain Papers was to assemble into a book certain unpublished manuscripts that had been passed over or withheld by Paine. These he quickly put together as Letters from the Earth, *so titled from the longest and most important of the manuscripts. But Clara Gabrilowitsch, disturbed by a current pamphlet purporting to prove Mark Twain was anti-Semitic, and fearing that some passages in the book might be construed as showing him either anti-Semitic or anti-God, vetoed the publication. DeVoto, true to his role as Mark Twain's defender, was diligently destroying*

[1] He never made those revisions.

the anti-Semitic charges in an article, "Mark Twain about the Jews," Jewish Frontier *(May 1939), at the time when Clara voiced her fears. But he was unable to break down her objections to* Letters from the Earth, *and the book remained in Harper's safe until it was finally published in 1962, seven years after DeVoto's death.*

The other jobs DeVoto foresaw when he took over the Papers were a book of autobiographical fragments not used by Paine, and a volume of letters. The autobiographical scraps appeared as Mark Twain in Eruption *(1940). The volume of letters was never completed.*

April 3, 1939

Dear Madame Gabrilowitsch:

I have seen this vile leaflet and, in fact, I arranged last week to expose and rebut it in a magazine called *The Jewish Frontier*, which I shall do as soon as I get back to Cambridge.

I understand what you say about "Letters from the Earth" and, of course, should not think of appealing from your decision. I think, however, that, as you say, it would be best for us to talk the whole problem over before you make your decision final. I am not sure that the effect would be what you anticipate, if the "Letters" should be published. I think it might even be the opposite of your anticipation. But let us talk this out at length in May.

Meanwhile, it is of the utmost importance, for the various plans of publication, for me to know whether you dislike the rest of the manuscript as well. Is it only "Letters from the Earth" you object to? Is the rest of the book as now made up acceptable? If so, I had better get to work at once and find something to take the place of the "Letters"—though that has been the principal item in my conception of the book. If not, then I had better tell Harper's at once so that they can halt their plans for publicity and publication. I sincerely hope that the rest of the manuscript is not distasteful to you, for I think that America very much needs that book and I am sure that it would have a warm and grateful reception.

Please let me know at Cambridge—776 Widener Library—what you think.

Sincerely yours,

TO CHARLES TRESSLER LARK

April 10, 1939

Dear Mr. Lark:

Another serious problem has arisen. I don't know whether, in my consternation at Mrs. Gabrilowitsch's letter about our book, I told you that I had had an earlier letter from her. But I did. She said that she had at last found the chest of manuscripts which she had previously thought of as destroyed during a siege of housecleaning. The manuscripts, she said, were some that either Mark Twain or Paine, or both, had decided should be destroyed. She thought, however, that she had better submit them to my judgment and so was sending them on to me. They were waiting for me when I got back from New York.

And I'm stunned. There is considerable duplication since some of them are typed as well as in manuscript, but the total additional bulk of material must be at least six thousand pages. And even with only a couple of days' survey of them I can see that they make a good deal of the work I've been doing this year useless, since it will have to be done over in the light of this new material;[1] that they supply extremely important information and clear up a lot of mysteries that had been troubling me; and that they raise a whole series of new problems.

In the first place, I don't see why these manuscripts were to be destroyed if many of those in the material turned over to me were to be kept. In fact, many of these are parts of the manuscripts I've been working on. I can see no possible explanation of this splitting up of manuscripts. It appears to have been done either by chance or in haste or in ignorance.

In the second place, I don't see why any manuscripts were to be destroyed and I want to raise the question with you whether these should be. I don't know whether any of them will justify publication—I can't possibly know that till I've read them all—but a thorough study of them will be necessary both for the sake of our books and for the sake of any other books that any scholar may ever write about Mark hereafter, if the Papers are turned over to any library or foundation. And even supposing that not a single one

---

[1] As curator of the Papers, DeVoto had the task of supervising the cataloging of the vast hodgepodge of manuscripts and of typing a large portion of them. Primarily for this purpose, the Estate supplied him with secretary and typists and met his small bills for expenses. As curator he received no salary, though before he was appointed custodian he had made a survey of the papers for a fee of $1,000.

of these proves to be worth publishing as a whole, it is practically certain that portions and extracts will prove to be publishable.

In the third place, even if they are ultimately to be destroyed—and I hope they won't be—still it is only good business, from our point of view and that of Harper's, to study them minutely before doing anything else about them or even about our projected books. And I don't see how this can be done except on the same basis we've been working on. And that means more expense.

As I told you, I have counted on letting Reck[2] go about the first of June, putting Mrs. Chapman[3] to work this summer on the notebooks, and letting her carry the whole burden next year, the letters, the private papers, the preparation of our projected books for private publication, etc. But that program will be quite impracticable if this new material is to be handled with even the decent minimum of intelligence and business sense—and even if the ultimate decision is to destroy it. I could have saved you much money and saved myself much time and wasted effort if only I had had these papers with the rest of them last September.

Well, at the very least I will have to devote two months of my own time to the new manuscripts—whatever happens to them, whatever your decision is. And, whatever that decision, I think that we should at least get them, or the relevant parts of them, typed for our own use and reference as our publishing program goes on. That means, I think, that Reck should be kept on all through the summer. Just what part of these manuscripts must be typed will depend on two things: your decision as to the ultimate disposition of them and my judgment, after I have studied them, as to their relevance to our whole program. But I imagine that there will be at least a summer's work for Reck in them. In any event there will also be an enormous amount of additional work for Mrs. Chapman—the greater part of which could have been saved if we had had these manuscripts from the beginning. When you and Mr. Langdon[4] and I got together late last fall, we agreed that it would be desirable to keep her at work all through next year. Well, this new development makes it absolutely inevitable.

There is also the problem of my work, but that is adjustable and need not trouble us now.

But the long-range view had better be talked out sometime this spring. I have already told you that the *Notebooks* will have to be done over—that

2 Henry Reck, who after graduation from Dartmouth spent several years as general factotum in the DeVoto house in Lincoln, Massachusetts. In 1938 he became one of the typists of Mark Twain manuscripts. Still later, after service in the Navy, he was an assistant to Samuel Eliot Morison. At the time of his death in 1974 he was teaching American history at CCNY.
3 Rosamond Chapman, DeVoto's secretary, whom he moved into the job as secretary of the Mark Twain Papers.
4 Jervis Langdon, one of the trustees of the Mark Twain Estate.

the present volume is inferior and even misrepresentative and that a far better volume can, and should, be made up. It will soon be necessary to face the problem of the letters, which so far we have held in abeyance. I am continually getting unpublished letters (copies of them, I mean, from collectors). There are a number of collections in libraries, copies of which we shall have to have—nearly two hundred here at Harvard, the Hutton letters at Princeton, about twenty at the New York Public Library, etc. And there are a great many unpublished ones in the Papers. It has been my intention to put Mrs. Chapman to work on them next year, as soon as she has got the notebooks in shape. (It is absolutely essential to get the notebooks typed. They are in pencil, mostly, and we have to refer to them constantly and so must anyone who works on the Papers hereafter, and we must have a typescript to work from when we bring out the enlarged edition.) Well, we must soon determine just how to publish them. Harper's have been opposed to doing the whole job over again—bringing out a new three-volume edition in place of the present two-volume one, with the new letters inserted in the proper places. Yet there is no other intelligent, useful or potentially profitable way to do the job. A volume of random, unrelated, new letters, with great gaps between and constant editorial references to other letters not before the reader's eyes would be grotesque and would fall flat. Whereas an intelligently done job with the new letters so marked and inserted in the proper places will have a double audience waiting for it. What dismays Harper's is the expense. But I have talked to George Macy of the Limited Editions Club, who now owns the Nonesuch Press and has recently brought out the enormous, complete edition of Charles Dickens' letters—a project at least twice the size of ours. He would be glad to make a limited edition of our three-volume set, sell it at a huge price to his subscribers, and turn over the plates to Harper's for the trade edition. If Harper's don't want to take the risk, here is a way out for them.

There is also another project which we must talk out. It is too lengthy for me to write about, but if we get together on the above paragraph I can explain it then.

I will keep the new manuscripts wholly separate from the others till I learn what your decision on the various questions I have asked is. I think I had better buy another filing case for them—we shall eventually need it for the others, even if the new ones are destroyed. But please let me have at least a tentative opinion on them as soon as possible.

I am, of course, still up in the air about "Letters from the Earth." As you know, Mrs. Gabrilowitsch's objection is one I was totally unprepared for. I thought I had foreseen every possible objection but I hadn't foreseen the suspicion of anti-Semitism. So far as I'm concerned, it seems altogether unrealistic and groundless. And I can't make out where it leaves our book. I have not heard from her yet and still don't know whether she also objects to the rest of the book. I have been forced to tell Saxton[5] that he must hold up his plans until May. And I hope you will read the typescript as soon as possible and let me know what you think and send it on to Mr. Langdon for his opinion. I myself doubt the wisdom of publishing the book with its most important single item left out. I'm not confident that the rest of the book will have sufficient pull in itself, and I am quite sure that there is nothing in the Papers which I could substitute for "Letters from the Earth" that would really take its place. I was prepared to sacrifice two of the "Letters" if the decision of the Estate should be that they were too nearly obscene—though in my best judgment they are not—but I am not sure that we can get out the book at all if the "Letters" must be left out altogether.

Please let me hear from you in as much detail as possible as soon as you conveniently can. I'm stymied about our book and I'm bewildered by all this new material.

Sincerely yours,

TO WILLIAM BRIGGS

Letters from the Earth had been put away unpublished, and another book, which Harper's wanted to call Mark Twain in Eruption, *had been submitted by DeVoto and approved by* Harper's, *when DeVoto and Arthur Schlesinger, Jr., took a trip West together in the summer of 1940. On returning, DeVoto found that Clara had again raised objections and that Harper's had yielded to them.*

July 11, 1940

Dear Mr. Briggs:

After reading the various letters you sent me, I can see nothing for me to do but to dissociate myself from the whole enterprise. I do not do so at once because I want to talk to Mr. Lark first—I want to cause him as little embarrassment as possible, having had the greatest consideration and co-

[5] Eugene Saxton, of Harper's. As Mark Twain's publishers, Harper's exercised considerable influence on the editing of the Papers, though ultimate decisions were made by the Estate or, more accurately, by Clara.

operation from him. I telephoned his office a few minutes ago but found that he is out of town until Monday. I will get in touch with him then.

The next question is, how can I cause you people the least trouble? I can't let my name go on a book that has been altered after I finished it. Any further alteration in this one will not only violate my judgment of what makes a good book but will reduce the careful statements of the Introduction to a mockery. So you will have to leave the Introduction out and carefully abstain from presenting me as the editor. Furthermore, I have been extensively advertised as the editor, in your catalogue and publicity. So there will have to be some kind of statement. I'll go as far with you as I can, but I shall want it clearly said that I do not assume responsibility for the editing and that the book as published has not been prepared by me.

You'd better see what kind of statement you can get together. Send it to me for okay before you give it out. But as for me, there is no reason why I should lose any more time on a footless and timorous enterprise, why I need take irresponsible insults from Mrs. Gabrilowitsch, or why I should further compromise with my own critical standards in trying to meet the capricious requirements I have so far had to deal with in a continuing succession.

I'm not making any kicks about you people. That was another book. But I can't stultify my own good sense any further.

Sincerely yours,

TO EUGENE SAXTON

July 11, 1940

Dear Gene:

I write this to you rather than add it to my letter to Briggs on the chance that he may want to send my letter to Mrs. Gabrilowitsch, as a kind of leverage. My guess is that it won't do any good, but if he wants to try, let him go ahead.

I'm quite clear in what I say to him: I will not let my name be attached to a book that departs from the text I am responsible for, and I won't make any changes in the text serious enough to cover what, apparently, she wants. I had no objection to the changes in the Introduction you wanted, and I would conceivably agree to leaving out a whole section, say the Rockefeller section. But I would want to fight for that section, and if anything I have submitted is only partly published, then I get out. I worked hard to make the best book possible out of the unpublished autobiography, and I brought to bear on the job the longest study and the most intimate knowledge of Mark Twain available anywhere. I made it my job to see the book from the publisher's point of view as well as the editor's, and I called on whatever capacity I may have as an editor and as a critic. And no one has more respect for Mark Twain than I have, and I do not need instruction in good taste from his daughter. In short, you people originally proposed me for the job because you thought I was the best man to do it, and I did it as well as I know how. You have never found me unreasonable, but the margin for adjustment in a question like this is necessarily small. I'm willing to discuss that margin but once it's exhausted I can only, in respect of my own intelligence, say: the job is done, take it or leave it.

My own guess is that you'll never get a satisfactory or even a publishable book while she is still alive. If Lark will crack down on her—as he has done sometimes before—then maybe you will. But if he won't, then you won't. The book as it stands now is wholly without offense to anyone but her. She apparently wants her father presented in accordance with her picture of him. I suppose nobody can reasonably object to that. But it will necessarily prevent the publication of a truthful book about him or even, in modern terms, an interesting one. The book you've got is plenty interesting. But it won't be when she is through with it.

There has been a lot of publicity about my editing this stuff. You can readily understand that, since there has been, I will have to make it plain that I'm not responsible for the ultimate product. I'll do my best to make it inoffensive and it can come from you people first, if you want to have it that way, but it will also have to be quite clear.

As for the other projects we had tentatively lined up, the hell with them. I've lost an enormous amount of time already. I'm not disposed to lose any more.

I'm going to telephone Lark on Monday, when he'll be back in his office. If you've got any notions before I do, telephone me here on Friday.

Yours,

TO CHARLES TRESSLER LARK

July 27, 1940

Dear Mr. Lark:

I have not been working on the Autobiography because neither the original typescript nor the carbon copy has been returned to me, and because it is impossible for me to do anything to it, even after one of the copies is sent back, until I know completely and specifically what you people want me to do to it.

Harper's were willing to publish it as it stood, asking me to leave out of the Introduction certain remarks about Mr. Paine's editing of the two earlier volumes of Autobiography. I had put in those remarks not, as Mrs. Gabrilowitsch supposes, to decry Mr. Paine but to secure Harper's, the Estate, and Mark Twain himself from the accusations which, I foresee, will be made when the book appears. It is necessary to bear in mind that Mr. Paine's editing was capricious, arbitrary, and sometimes incomprehensible. There are passages in our book which he elided from the middle of passages which he published. There are other passages which he partly published not in the Autobiography but in other books of Mark Twain's and in his own Biography. There are other passages which he used in his Biography as alleged conversations with Mark Twain, and still other passages which he wove into his text as his own, without benefit of quotation marks. It may be squeamish on my part to pay attention to what qualified critics and scholars will say about these things, but they are certain to discuss them. I tried in my Introduction to draw their teeth and to set the model for what they would say by making as complete an explanation as possible. However, I was not greatly troubled by Harper's proposal to leave out the explanation. I agreed, Harper's were satisfied, and when I left for the West both they and I assumed that the book would be published as it stood.

I am not greatly concerned about such changes as you propose in your letter and mentioned to me over the phone. They are unimportant and small in bulk. I have no doubt that we could fix them up in an hour and alter my Introduction to fit. I do not share your belief that anyone would bring suit—I think it altogether impossible—but I am quite willing to go over the manuscript and bring it into accord with your specifications.

As for Mrs. Gabrilowitsch's objections, which are the cause of the present impasse, I do not understand them and, so far as I do understand them, I can only say that they leave us without a publishable book. What is left would bore the general reader, bring down the derision of scholars and critics on us, and impair Mark Twain's reputation.

Mr. Briggs has sent me copies of Mrs. Gabrilowitsch's letters to him and to Mr. Langdon. Some of her objections seem inconsistent with others, but there is no doubt that they add up to what she herself calls "insurmountable objections" to the book I prepared. In order to prepare it I carefully winnowed all the unpublished Autobiography, and then worked hard to arrange and edit what I had selected for publication. In my judgment the text I prepared is all that is worth publishing of the unpublished Autobiography. In my judgment, further, if the text as I prepared it is seriously cut down in bulk or if the things which appeared to me most interesting in it are deleted, then we shall be left with a book that is not worth publishing.

In the face of that, it seems idle to discuss her objections in detail, but, for your information, I point out the effect of some of them.

Mrs. Gabrilowitsch says she is "not willing to have people attacked whose relatives are still living." There is no appeal from that, and on that basis half or more than half of our book is suppressed. My own feeling is that there is only one passage in the book (since I deliberately edited the one about Mrs. Aldrich) that would cause the kind of pain she has in mind, the one about Bret Harte. I left out of that a passage in the original which seemed to me too personal for inclusion, and what is left goes no farther in criticism of Harte, or in attack on him, than what has been said by many critics, literary historians, and other autobiographers. The whole burden of Mark Twain's judgment is conceded in, for instance, George Stewart's life of Harte. What Mark Twain says seems to me not only magnificently interesting and not only charmingly illuminative of Mark Twain himself, but also of the utmost value for the history of literature. It seems to me that, quite apart from the interest of the passage itself, there is a certain public obligation to publish it. The truth about our literary past is part of the common wealth of American culture.

I should make the same point about the passages that deal with Carnegie, the Rockefellers, Roosevelt, and other public figures. Historical figures are in the public domain, and Mark Twain is in that domain also. What a great man says about them is important to the nation, and the free criticism of leaders of public life is one of the essential mechanisms of democracy. I should say that our book would, at this moment, be a considerable service to America. But there are more practical things to say. These passages have been withheld so long that they cannot possibly offend anyone. Far more violent criticism of them all is in the ordinary reading of everyone, and what Mark says about them is interesting not because it is a new kind of criticism, which it isn't, but because of the individuality, color, personality, and magnificent style Mark imparts to it. Still more practically, what he says is so richly humorous that most people will take the laugh and ignore the barb . . . With all of this Harper's were in complete agreement when I talked to them last April.

Mrs. Gabrilowitsch says that this part of the book is repetitious and boresome. That is a matter for empirical test. I did not think it so and neither did Harper's. Their judgment as publishers was that it was interesting —they wanted to publish it.

She says that the reader of the book is "drowned in an avalanche of critical poisons that give false testimony to the character of Mark Twain." Well, after all Mark Twain wrote it. It is harmonious with much that is in the published *Autobiography* and much more that I have not proposed to publish, and it is not, in sheer space, disproportionate to the rest of the book . . . When I put it in the book, I did so because it seemed to me interesting. In fact, fascinating. Furthermore, on the basis of what Mark published in his lifetime, what Mr. Paine published after his death, and what remains unpublished in the Papers, it seems to me quite true to the character of Mark Twain. Clearly, he was not out of his mind when he wrote it and the mood is so common and so voluminous that it must be taken as a fundamental part of him. For my part, it is one of the greatest parts of him, and I am confident that countless others think the same, on the basis of what has already been published.

Mrs. Gabrilowitsch objects to the attack on religion. I think she misconceives it and is wrong about its probable effects, and I think further that our principal question should be, Is this true to Mark Twain?—and I think it is. But I have no desire to argue against her.

She says that "the entire Webster attack[1] must be discarded." I think that Mr. Webster's son would not be offended by it, but her decision is flat and there is no appeal from it. But by now a good deal more than half of our book is gone. She then says "Why would it not spare Mr. DeVoto a lot of work and trouble if he *asked* the trustees or me about certain people before he does all his type-copying, etc." It happens that I described this particular passage to both you and Harper's and asked you whether [it ought to be used. You said] "put it in and then we'll see about it."

There is no point in my replying to the various epithets which Mrs. Gabrilowitsch applies to me in her letters to Mr. Briggs and Mr. Langdon. I was instructed to prepare what seemed to me the most interesting book it was possible to prepare from the unpublished manuscript. I did so, wrote an Introduction to it as I was asked to by both you and Harper's, and sent off the typescript. But, for your information, I will comment on one paragraph of the objections she makes to my part of the job. She says:

> "Mr. DeVoto uses a certain acrimonious tone in his notes and general remarks about Father that give the impression of a very large chip on the shoulder—or a desire to inflate his own intellectual reputation by brilliant adverse criticism. For instance what does he mean by the note 'Mark Twain always confused the Immaculate Conception with the Virgin Birth of Christ'? Also consider the tone in his note about Snodgrass, Page 212. And his insinuations in connection with the Bliss Publishing Co., that Father was overreaching his rights in pecuniary settlements, etc., etc."

(1) The note about the Immaculate Conception and the Virgin Birth means exactly what it says. They are two separate and distinct doctrines. The Immaculate Conception deals with the birth of Mary, the Virgin Birth deals with the birth of Christ. Mark Twain did confuse them consistently throughout his career, speaking of the Immaculate Conception when he meant the

[1] The reference is to Charles Webster, Mark Twain's onetime partner in the publishing business.

Virgin Birth. He so confuses them in the passage to which the note is attached. It is attached to that passage for a simple reason: to prevent people from objecting to it. When I alluded to this passage in the *Saturday Review of Literature* two years ago, in the article which you approved, I received several letters of complaint and explanation from prelates of the Catholic Church. I put the note in to anticipate such letters and to mollify the potential writers of them. Such a note is obligatory on an editor.

(2) The Snodgrass note is factual. Mr. Paine had already annotated that passage in the unpublished typescript: I substituted a note which I considered better than his. One was necessary, as Mr. Paine apparently understood, because the passage might conceivably be libelous unless the editorial explanation was made. I called your attention to this passage and this note when I turned over the typescript to you. You commended the note, saying that it covered our position, made the necessary explanation, and protected us against suit. The facts are on record in a number of places, notably in Charles Honce's edition of *The Adventures of Thomas Jefferson Snodgrass*.

(3) The note on Bliss was made for the same purpose. Mr. Paine says much what I say in his discussion of the matter in the Biography. I felt that it ought to be repeated in our text, both for our protection and for the information of the reader.

This, in explanation of three specific complaints. I have no desire to comment on Mrs. Gabrilowitsch's personal remarks about me. Conceivably I was asked by the Estate and Harper's to do this job because I was thought to be the person best qualified to do it, and certainly you people and Harper's have the right to reject the work I have done. I was told to prepare a book that I thought would be true to Mark Twain, interesting, and salable. I think that the book I have prepared is just that, that it will interest many people and bring about a renewed interest in Mark Twain, and that it will sell well and enlarge the market for his other books. I think that it is particularly salable, as well as particularly valuable, at the present time. I have repeatedly called to your attention the parts that would get preferential publicity during the present campaign. But I have been over all this, and much more, with you before and there is no point in repeating it here.

There remains the question of what to do about the book. I suppose that we ought to get together over the manuscript, you, Harper's, and I. I can't do that for a month or six weeks. Furthermore, I doubt if we can cut the manuscript to accord with Mrs. Gabrilowitsch's desires and come out with a book that Harper's will be willing to publish, or one that I would be willing to recommend to them or to you. I'm willing to try but I see no chance of success.

If we did succeed in cutting the book, two considerations would remain. At best I should have to write another Introduction, for all the careful statement of editorial method and responsibility made in the present one would be ridiculous in the light of the cuts. But I probably couldn't accept the editorial responsibility for the resulting book, anyway. There are certain standards of editorial integrity which Mrs. Gabrilowitsch ignores but which I can't ignore. If the proposed cuts go beyond them, then I shall have to get out of the picture. I am willing to do anything I can to help you bring the book to the shape you want. But if that end-product doesn't agree with my ideas of what it ought to be, then we will omit my introduction and notes and leave my name off the title-page. That ought to satisfy everyone. You will have your book and I won't be subjected to assault in the reviews.

In spite of Mrs. Gabrilowitsch's objections to me, I suppose it would be absurd to turn over the rest of the job of arranging the Papers to someone else. You would lose more than two years of work. It will take, I think, only till next June to complete the job. Unless I hear otherwise from you, I will go on with that. It is besides almost altogether Mrs. Chapman's job now, under my direction.

Please telephone me, or at least write to me on the day you get this, what you think of what I say here and what it is advisable to do. I do not see how I can arrange to come to New York to go over the manuscript for at least another month. If you see any hope of working it out, however, I will do my utmost to arrange to come.

When I telephoned to you, you agreed to pay Mrs. Chapman $80 a month instead of $65, and to send her a check for $165, to cover her last month and her vacation. It hasn't come yet, and neither has the $130 you owe me, for payment of thirteen weeks' wages to Reck. Reck, by the way, has another job in prospect, which is convenient, since there are only three or four weeks more work for him to do.

I trust that you understand that I am grateful to you for your kindness and cooperation. Nothing I say here is meant to express anything more than my opinion, as a scholar and a literary critic, of the best kind of book for us to publish.

Sincerely yours,

TO CLARA GABRILOWITSCH

September 11, 1940

Dear Mrs. Gabrilowitsch:

Mr. Lark and Mr. Langdon have probably described to you the decisions made at our recent conference in New York. Proofs of the book should reach you soon: my information is that it is now being set up. Before you read them I want to express my point of view in this complicated matter as freely and frankly as I can. Please understand that I do so not with any desire to oppose your point of view or question either the authority or the validity of your judgments, but to speak as a literary man who is deeply reverent toward Mark Twain, is trying to live up to his conception of an editor's standards and obligations, and feels fairly confident of his ability to appraise the values and forecast the opinions of the current literary scene.

The manuscript which I prepared seemed quite unexceptionable to Harper's. They did not anticipate that anyone's feelings would be hurt or that any undesirable emotions would be stirred up by its publication. They are seasoned and realistic men; I suggest to you that their opinion was pretty objective. Certainly, I anticipated none, except possibly to the passage relating to Bret Harte, to which I will return in a moment. I had carefully edited the passage relating to Mrs. Aldrich so as to remove the unquestionable offense and preserve both the humor and the literary history. There were a number of passages small parts of which seemed to me to verge on libel but since they concerned no one now alive and since, also, they seemed to me to have public and historical importance, I left them in. My idea was to consult with Mr. Lark and, if I could not convince him that libel suits were unlikely, to modify them just as far as he might require me to but no farther. Apart from these the manuscript was edited just about as far as I could bring myself to edit it. I had already done to it about as much as my conception of the duty of an editor would permit.

At the conference we cut out the passage on God entirely, in complete obedience to your wishes. That cost me no pang. It was the least interesting part of the book, I thought, and it added little to what was already in print over Mark Twain's signature. You will find, however, that we have modified only details in the other portions. And, frankly, I fought, cursed, and pleaded over each change. As it is, I feel that I have seriously compromised with my own standards—and Mark Twain's also—in changing the text as much as we have done. Your father, I am confident, would have been furious. And I think he would have been justified.

For, try as I will to find palliations, I cannot escape from the fact that Mark Twain wrote this book, wrote it deliberately and carefully, revised it over and over till it said precisely what he wanted said, and made it the central effort of his life for a period of several years. On these things he intended to stand. He wanted to say them, he intended to publish them, he would face eternity and the opinions of posterity with his name signed and underscored on the page that printed them. They were a matured, well-considered, long-deliberated, and rigorously revised book. Called upon to edit this book—remember, I did not ask to do this job but was asked and, honored as I felt and glad as I was to do it, I nevertheless did it at the sacrifice of plans for books of my own—called upon to edit it, I have felt from the beginning that I must not edit Mark Twain's intent. At our conference I expressed to Mr. Lark and Mr. Langdon my feeling that they were trustees not of Mark Twain's estate alone but of his intentions as well. I felt that there was on them as on me the obligation to further his intent to the utmost limit of our ability to do so—to circumvent it only with the greatest caution or reluctance, and only in regard to special, urgent considerations.

That your objections rest on what seem to you special and urgent considerations I am completely aware. And yet, with the greatest gravity, I must express my belief that you are over-anxious and therefore mistaken. Your heaviest fear is that the book will add to the hate now loose in the world and play into the hands of the forces that you and I, and Mark Twain equally, oppose with all our strength. I do not for a moment believe that it will, I believe quite the contrary. But even if I did not, I should still be constrained to feel that suppressing the deliberate intent of a great American writer would be in itself an act of darkness, an act of the other side, a kind of miniature burning of the books. It is to be said, no matter what the content of this book, that in America, thank God, we are still free to state and discuss, to criticize and object, to illuminate counsel—and to learn from our great men. Publishing what Mark Twain has to say about the figures and standards of his time is an act in the service of truth, and if that particular kind of act in the service of truth is becoming increasingly impossible elsewhere in the world, we are all the more constrained to hold by it and facilitate it in America.

But nearly forty years have passed since Mark Twain wrote these things. In that time many other people have drawn the picture he draws. We are accustomed to it, it is widely accepted, we have adapted to it and learned from it. He has little to say about the plutocracy that has not been said by others and accepted by nearly everyone. The special value of what he says is not in the novelty of what he describes but the color and vividness his personality gives it, and above all the vigor and splendor of his prose. There is no new ammunition here for the common enemy—the same ammunition, if it is worth anything to the enemy, which I doubt, is and long has been available in hundreds of books. But there is here the final judgment of one of our great men on his time and some of the actors in it. That seems to me to have an immortal value, for American life and American culture, and as such, I think, it is our duty to our time to publish it.

As for certain special instances, I think some sensitiveness in you makes you find a far greater offense than anyone else is likely to. Again, Harper's are specialists in these things; they are quite as eager as you to preserve Mark Twain from accusation, though their motive is the lowly commercial one. Well, it seems to Harper's, and I agree with them, that time has taken the sting out of these personalities. Specifically, there can no longer be any offense in the remarks about Carnegie, John D. Rockefeller, Sr., Senator Clark, the various publishers, and so on. The passages about Webster which you dislike seem to me so charmingly wrapped in an obvious burlesque that no one can be hurt—and I am quite sure that Mark Twain calculated precisely that effect. He counted on the gusto of exaggeration, which takes the reader into his confidence with a wide and enjoyable wink, to take the personal sting out, to focus enjoyment on Mark Twain himself, not on the butt of his humor. That goes for practically everything else in the book—and I ask you to remember that the reader, who will usually be familiar with Mark Twain, counts on that very thing as part of his own delight, he comes to it with a specific anticipation. The passage about Bret Harte, and to a certain extent the one about Aldrich, rests on a different basis. I have cut out of the Aldrich one a passage which I think no one would want to see in print while Bailey Aldrich is still alive, and I omitted one whole section of the Harte dictations because it seemed to me needlessly harsh on Harte's daughter and irrelevant to the portrait of Harte. But certainly the rest of the Harte chapters and to a lesser extent the Aldrich chapters are a vital part of our literary history, of our cultural heritage, and I feel strongly that our obligation is to publish them—we are in a sense custodians and trustees of the truth on behalf of the public. Furthermore, the portrait of Harte drawn here is attested by many other portraits of him. Biographies and even his own letters verify the details and are far more savage in bulk. So that if anyone should be pained by this portrait it cannot possibly be a new pain but, so to speak, in the public domain. Finally, this passage reveals that the break between Mark Twain and Harte did not originate in Mark Twain's jealousy, as some writers have alleged. For that reason alone, if there were no others, I should feel that we are under obligation to publish it.

And so on, all the way through. I think that your fears are unjustified.

And finally I cannot forget that no man ever labored harder or more passionately than Mark Twain for the right of writers to say their say, for the freedom of literature. Wherever the subject comes up in his work, his prose gets white hot. In a sense, we are suppressing his freedom, we are venturing to impose on him a limitation he angrily repudiated many times, we are, really, forbidding him to publish work that he intended to be published, work that he labored over as deliberately and as carefully as anything in the whole range of his books. Once more, this is not a happy time to arrogate that responsibility to ourselves.

That's my case. I have felt that I must put it to you, as my obligation to Mark Twain and even to you. You will at least allow it the weight of sincerity, coming from a man who has spent a good many years and much labor in the study and praise of Mark Twain.

Sincerely yours,

83

TO WILLIAM BRIGGS

September 27, 1940

Dear Mr. Briggs:

I have never supposed that titles counted for much, and I think they count for less than usual in this case, since Mark Twain's name will sell the book. But in that case, why not be candid? The word "Papers" misrepresents the whole enterprise and is doubly unfortunate in that it suggests a radically different content from what the reader will find in the book. My own feeling is, as it has been from the first, that the title page ought to state clearly and unequivocally that this book is made up from the unpublished Autobiography. However, I have no estate in the title: if you people think that you've arrived at the best one, go ahead.

Mrs. Gabrilowitsch has the right to omit that passage about Rockefeller. I think that it's a silly, a footless omission and that it deprives the reader of a characteristic Mark Twain blast which would not offend anyone, but if she says omit it, that's that. On the other hand, it further twists my carefully phrased introduction out of line with the truth. I can keep my mouth shut unless called upon to deliver. If any prominent reviewer takes me to task, I'll have to admit that the text has been changed further than I say.

In my time I've had my style improved by college freshmen and some of the damnedest people and I imagine I can take improvement still. You have my authority to change "exasperating" to "annoying" on Galley 3. On Galley 4A she has a point, though not the one she makes. *The editorial changes must be admitted.* I hope to God you people realize that I'm protecting you in admitting them, as I can't seem to make her understand that I'm protecting both Mark Twain and the Estate. But we need not drag Bret Harte's daughter in. So telescope the last two sentences of that paragraph into the following: "The omitted passage, quoting the usual newspaper headlines, rakes up a distressing episode which was intended to add to the portrait of Harte but it is irrelevant."

The other two passages she has marked, on Galleys 3A and 6, must, I'm afraid, stand as I wrote them. Stet OK. You have my permission to use any kind of language you like in denouncing me to her or explaining the wild and murderous moods that sometimes obscure my judgment. But the reason for both of those passages will be crystal clear to every student of Mark Twain, and it is to students and historians of literature that I, as editor, owe my strongest obligation. I am doing my best, under pressure, to give the editing of Mark Twain the decent responsibility it has never had before. Mrs. Gabrilowitsch does not see that need, but since all she alleges against these passages is that they are boring, I think she can consent to a little boredom on behalf of fair dealing with the public.

We can't get to work on the index until we begin to get page proofs. So far we've had only galleys, the last of which will go back to you on Monday.

I feel easier about this book, since reading your letters and the inclosures, but a habitual pessimism restrains me from thinking we are in the clear yet. I have already bent so far back from my conception of an editor's duties that I can't take much more. For the love of God, let me know as you get further word.

Sincerely yours,

TO LEWIS GANNETT

June 10, 1942

Dear Gannett:

I'm glad to have you turn back to my earlier Mark Twain book in a discussion of the new one,[1] as few are bothering to do, but I plead mildly that if you had gone a little farther with it you would have found an answer to one of your own questions. What I proceed to say here is not argument —I'm not interested any more in arguing about Mark Twain—but merely to set forth for you where I stand on your two questions, pessimism and sex, at the present stage of my grace and enlightenment.

You are quite right in saying that the fatalism and misanthropy of *What Is Man?* go far back in Mark's earlier work. I said so myself, very loudly, in *M.T.'s America*, and traced the strains back through all his stuff to the pieces he turned out as a newspaperman in California. In *Mark Twain at Work*, as in the earlier book, I point out that *Huckleberry Finn* is charged with a high-voltage philosophical pessimism. Historically speaking, it is almost true that the literature of pessimism—on an adult level and with any mature literary skill—in America begins with Mark Twain. I imagine that Dixon Wecter will take that stand in a book he's writing about Mark Twain, Ambrose Bierce, and Henry Adams. It is not quite true, for the literature of pessimism in America really begins with Melville. There are holes in that

---

[1] That is, turning back to *Mark Twain's America* for light on the recently published *Mark Twain at Work*.

statement, too, but it's the best that can be made. The literature of pessimism certainly did not begin with Poe or Hawthorne.

From his earliest stuff on, fatalism and misanthropy do keep cropping out in Mark's stuff. The trouble is that they are shouted down by a far more copious, more continuous, far louder, far more heartfelt first-half-of-the-nineteenth-century strain of rampant optimism. If one wants to get solemn about the least solemn of writers, one can—as I have done—see in Mark Twain's work the nineteenth century in America becoming aware that some of its assumptions have been proved wrong, and that there are limits to what democracy can be or achieve. That, in my opinion, is one of the reasons why *Huck Finn* is a great book. It is a thoroughly undeluded statement of the cruelty and spiritual squalor of the human race and at the same time it makes an affirmation of human heroism, through Jim, and of human decency, through Huck. It is a resolution of two conflicting strains in Mark's feelings. The nineteenth century is the great age of the world, the American nation is the greatest nation in history, we are a free and mighty people who can and will do everything, progress is the first article of the Constitution, ours is an imperial culture and we are bringing in an era of universal freedom, comfort, and happiness. And so on. It is simply frivolous to ignore this or to try to depreciate it: there it is on eight out of ten pages he ever wrote.

Nevertheless, it would be idiotic to say that Mark was actually a misanthrope or believed in philosophical pessimism or held to the sentiments of *What Is Man?* before the events which I deal with in the last essay of the new book.[2] The strain was there, as it is present in every man of sense, but it was held in healthy equilibrium by the exuberant, unfettered happiness of his personal life and the altogether fantastic success of his literary career. Mark believed nothing basically evil of a world in which his career could happen. He said so frequently even in his last years, when he was also saying that men were bacteria and God was the kin of fiends. (Incidentally, I formally challenge you to find any moderately rigorous statement of either of the two main notions of *What Is Man?* anywhere in his work earlier than 1895. Don't take up the challenge. It can't be found.) Nothing could be fundamentally wrong with a world in which it was possible for Sam Clemens to become Mark Twain. Any little imperfection that might be observed was certain to be erased by American energy and industry, the rising standard of living, his brothers the workingmen, and the nineteenth century overthrow of unreason. Pessimism, misanthropy, doubt of the nineteenth century, or anything else of that sort was never more than a passing mood down to the time when his own calamities broke over him.

Then why *What Is Man?* I wrote the last essay in my book to explain why. The pessimistic strain had always been in him, but it had been held in

[2] "The Symbols of Despair," in which DeVoto developed his theory of the agonized composition of *The Mysterious Stranger*.

an intelligent equilibrium, it had been a minor strain. Now, as the result of his own misfortunes, it became an obsession. The evidence is overwhelming —far more in bulk and in relevance than I had room to describe.

Here a couple of incidental remarks. I don't apologize for psycho-analyzing Mark's stuff. I never had any objection to literary psychoanalysis so long as it was done by someone who knew something about psycho-analysis, was fenced round by common sense, and was clearly understood to be mainly speculative. I did violently object to Brooks's psychoanalysis, which didn't meet a single one of those requirements.

Brooks's book about Mark Twain was and remains silly. He knew ex-tremely little about Mark and even less about the America out of which he came. I think that Brooks now thinks just about as I do, in regard to that book. At least he has taken it back chapter by chapter in his later books. All except his notion that *Huck Finn* is a boy's book and the product of an im-mature mind. I certainly call that notion silly, and my hunch is that you do too.

On your second question, sex. Certainly the dilemma you propose is easily disposed of—it doesn't amount to much. Was sexual exuberance and frankness lacking in the society of Mark's boyhood, or did Mark ignore, repress, avoid, or inhibit his realization of it? You and I both know enough about that bucolic, recently frontier society to know that its sexual mores were as free as possible. "Here lies the body of Charlotte Maginity. To the age of thirteen she kept her virginity. Damn good record for this vicinity." That epitaph belongs, I think, to the 60's but it describes Hannibal during the 40's perfectly. And certainly my exposition of the southwestern humor from which Mark's humor stemmed (see *M.T.'s. A*, 43–46, and a good many other passages) and the exposition of other critics, notably Frank Meine and Walter Blair, shows that there was no avoidance or censorship of sex in the literary tradition which Mark brought to its highest expression. Neither society nor literature in those parts was in the least "puritanical."

That's what makes Brooks's analysis so damned cockeyed. He was right in believing that Mark's avoidance of sex (though he seems to think Mark avoided it in the flesh and only alleges that Livy kept him from using some strong words, in literature) required explaining. It certainly does. But in order to explain it he fell back on the preposterous discovery that a society which was extremely free in its sexual habits was repressive and prohibitory. He fell back, that is, on pure and shrieking nonsense.

My stand is this: we are faced with an individual problem, we have to treat it precisely as we'd treat such a problem among our friends. Our own generation has not been notably puritanical and yet it has contained some persons who were inhibited, either personally or in what they wrote.

Some negatives first. If it wasn't the social milieu, neither was it Mark's mother. She was no Aunt Polly. I've got some of her letters. She was a warm and loving person. If there was a stern, reticent figure in that family, it was Mark's father. Certainly it wasn't Livy. The inhibition was formed long before Mark met her and my best judgment is—and I've got some evidence —that the bond between them was as ardent in the flesh as it clearly was in the spirit.

Now, the inhibition of sex in Mark's books is striking. It's more complete than in any other principal figure of our literature. As I point out in my new book, there is no sexual relationship anywhere in all his work, no sexual motivation, no recognition of sex anywhere except in the single fact of Roxy's son in *Pudd'nhead Wilson*. Compared to Mark's novels, those of James and Howells are pornographic in their insistence on the relationships between the sexes. Moreover there are practically no allusions to sex. When you look at it squarely, you realize that this is an amazing fact. No one, not I even and certainly not Brooks, has ever pointed out how amazing it is.

Moreover, the unpublished evidence all points in the same direction. There are few explosions, even, of the kind that every writer I ever heard of occasionally makes. There is 1601—written when he was forty-one. I have two other pieces in much the same mood, one unfinished, both written at a much later time. One notebook, of the 90's, contains several pages which seem to be notes on snappy stories he's heard lately. There are a couple of explicitly sexual sneers at Whitelaw Reid, when Mark is pretty mad. There are a dozen and a half sexual expressions, or curt allusions, in letters—but the letters which so troubled Howells that he could neither bear to keep them nor to burn them up would not make a nun blush. There are a couple of loathesomely coy stories in unpublished portions of the *Autobiography*, timorous and sniggering, one about a pure, sweet, little girl (and sometime somebody is going to say that Mark expended a hell of a lot of suspicious adoration on little girls) who couldn't possibly understand the implications for adults of something she was saying. There are several passages, one of them very long, in the unfinished stuff that [carry] on the *What Is Man?* line in his last two or three years—written at white heat, Mark denouncing God and Christianity and punching both in the nose with indecencies that obviously scare him more than they rouse his anger.

And that's absolutely all. Now, at present, I don't undertake to explain the staggering facts. I do say, however, that when I fall down and break my leg, it is not that a repressive society has left my son's marble on the floor, and when one of my friends crashes in a breakdown because his sex is all twisted, I don't allege that the United States is an unworthy culture. The explanation of such facts as these is to be sought exclusively in individual psychology. And I'm enough of a Freudian to believe that it is to be sought so far back in childhood that there is no possible chance of ever arriving at it. It's beyond me, it's a job for a real psychoanalyst. And that's exactly what

I propose to do with it. I have an agreement with Lawrence Kubie[3] that, if it's ever possible to take up the pursuits of peace again, the two of us will do what can be done with this question.

As a devout Freudian, however, I'm willing to tell you some of the things that strike me as significant. To-wit.

Mark did not marry until he was thirty-five. Then he married a woman who had been—and later became again—a complete invalid. If that isn't a "permissive" marriage, I never heard of one. He hankered after the society of his tenth year all his life long—and here add all the analysis of his boyhood that I have written in various places. He never drew a living picture of a girl past the age of puberty or of a woman of an age when it is still possible to desire her. (Exception: Joan of Arc. A virgin. And, earlier, I should have pointed out that Huck has no mother and his father is killed, that Tom has no parents at all, that there are exceedingly few people anywhere in the books who can possibly fornicate. What happens when the lovers try to get married in *Huck Finn?* Where is Jim's wife? Who fall in love anywhere, except pre-pubic boys?) Moreover, in his notebooks are many suggestions for stories, and in the Papers are many stories finished and unfinished, which hinge on the exchange of sex, on girls trained by their fathers to behave like men or forced by circumstances or urged by their own desire to wear men's clothes, or of boys or men masquerading as women or forced by circumstance or enemies to wear women's clothes or to live women's lives. There are a striking and, I think, significant number of these, and some of them get pretty involved, psychologically . . . As one of Hemingway's scared blowhards once put it, "It is dangerous to be a man." So damned dangerous, in fact, that Mark sometimes wondered whether he really were one and sometimes did his damnedest to escape being thought one.

In short, somewhere down deep in him, he was scared as hell of sex. That is the fact that needs explaining. At present, I don't undertake to explain it.

Well, you brought this on—suffer it decently. And, in closing, here's a tip freely and generously offered to you. If you want to cause me—or any other student of Mark Twain—some real trouble, sometime inquire just why Mark got so mixed up with God. There, if you like, is a problem that needs expounding.

Yours,

---

[3] He and Dr. Lawrence Kubie had many discussions of the relationship between art and psychiatry—discussions that developed into stiff arguments. Several years after this letter, Kubie proposed a continuing seminar composed of writers and psychiatrists, and DeVoto enthusiastically agreed, but the seminar never developed.

TO THOMAS CHAMBERLAIN

Near the end of 1943 Clara Gabrilowitsch,
now Clara Samoussoud, removed Charles
Lark as lawyer for the Estate and replaced
him with Thomas Chamberlain, a maritime
lawyer with no experience in literary matters
and—DeVoto quickly decided—no
understanding of them. One of his first acts
was to indicate that DeVoto must ask
permission to make use of any unpublished
material in the Papers. Later he created
difficulty by insisting that all materials
published from the Papers must be
copyrighted in the name of the Estate, and
the Estate credited by the publication in
which they appeared. The normal, and
much simpler, procedure was to have these
materials copyrighted along with the entire
magazine's contents, and then to have
copyright assigned to the Estate. And
finally, either caution or procrastination led
Chamberlain to delay so long on specific
matters that opportunities for publicity
and profit were lost. It took three years for
Chamberlain's methods to drive
DeVoto finally out of the Mark Twain
business. It took less than three weeks to
exhaust his patience.

December 17, 1943

Dear Mr. Chamberlain:

You are a lawyer. I am a man of letters. The Mark Twain Company and the Estate of Samuel Clemens are certainly a business. They are, however, a business which depends absolutely on, and in fact consists almost exclusively of, the intelligent handling of literary affairs, of a literary reputation, and of literary procedure. My value to the Estate is that I am an expert in such matters. I have had no trouble of any kind with the Estate since I first got to work on the papers. I have had no trouble with Harper's. Neither the Estate nor Harper's has ever lost a dime through me. To the contrary, both have profited considerably from my work.

You and I will, I trust, get along as amiably and effectively as Mr. Lark and I did. But you must bear in mind that, as a writer, a scholar, and an editor, my career depends on my integrity. No allegation of dishonesty, sharp practice, or intent to profit at anyone else's expense has ever been made against me. If you can assume that I will conduct myself hereafter on that basis, then I am willing to continue, but I do not care to be under constant scrutiny and I refuse to be under suspicion. If I cannot continue on the basis of the last five years, if you propose to hold me to a series of legalities, then I must ask you to do either of two things. Either draw up once and for all a strict statement of what you expect of me and what conditions you are putting on me, so that I can submit it to my own lawyer and either agree or refuse and think no more about it, or else consider this my resignation, notify me that you are accepting it, and authorize me to arrange the return of the Mark Twain material in my possession to you forthwith.

Mr. Hoyns's[1] memory is not altogether accurate. Part of what he says, in the statement, is absurd.

For your information, I am one of the editors of *Harper's Magazine*, I expect to continue to be, my relations with Harper and Brothers are friendly and of many years' duration, all the officers of the firm are friends of mine, and finally I am and long have been their Mark Twain expert. They consult me in regard to every publishing project that concerns Mark Twain—have done so within the last two weeks. No permission to quote unpublished material could come to their office without being referred to me at once. If, under the paragraph in Mr. Lark's letter which you mention, I should ask permission to quote Mark Twain material, they would have no one but me to pass on it.

Now, the paragraph in question, according to which I am to be given permission to quote unpublished material is part, and by far the largest part, of my compensation for more than five years of editorial work on the Mark Twain papers and editorial and literary advice to the Estate. If you will consult the statement I dictated in your office, in fact if you will read the paragraph in Mr. Lark's letter, you will see that this permission is not intended, and is not understood by anyone, to cover the publication of books, articles, or even pages made up of Mark Twain's work. It is intended to cover the use, in original books by me, of purely illustrative material. It means that if I revise either of my two books about Mark Twain, or if I write further books about him, I am free to *quote* material from the unpublished papers in support of what I say.

[1] Henry Hoyns, Chairman of the Board of Harper's.

If Mr. Hoyns does not know that I would never try to profit at the expense of Harper's, every other member of the firm knows it. And Mr. Hoyns knows that, if I should ever ask permission under that letter from Mr. Lark, the material I should want to use would be of such a kind that Harper's could not possibly publish it and would not be interested in publishing it. It would be illustrative material exclusively. It would be, for instance, a few lines from a notebook here, a letter there, a paragraph or two from a fragment of manuscript somewhere else. It would have no meaning and no value except as part of my text, the text which I myself had written. Published by itself, or published in anything which Harper's publish or might want to publish, it would be not only meaningless but chaotic.

Mr. Hoyns also knows, and I have clearly stated to you, that I am engaged, by understanding between the Estate and Harper's, in the preparation of books made up of material by Mark Twain, books which Harper's are to publish. For instance, the letters I described to you, the enlarged edition of the notebook, volumes of stories, etc., as well as various other books never so clearly envisaged but suggested by various members of Harper's, including Mr. Hoyns. In such projects I am working as an agent of the Estate and of Harper's. Mr. Hoyns knows, and you should clearly understand, that these books and all other books to be made up of Mark Twain material are clearly covered by the existing contracts between the Estate and Harper's. He knows, and you should clearly understand, that such books have nothing in common with books which I myself have written or might write about Mark Twain—books in which any unpublished material would be occasional and fragmentary, unpublishable of itself, and amounting to only a few pages all told.

He also knows, and you can easily ascertain, that I have three times asked for, and received, permission to insert such material in work of mine, twice at the instigation of the Limited Editions Club, once on my own initiative. The Limited Editions Club asked me to prepare editions of *Tom Sawyer* and *Huckleberry Finn*. I did so and I put into each of them small bits of unpublished material. For this material the Limited Editions Club asked permission; it also paid for it. There was no trouble, and in each instance I myself arranged to have the copyright transferred to Harper's. I also, by full and free permission of Harper's as well as Mr. Lark, put other unpublished material into my *Mark Twain at Work*, and arranged for the transfer of copyright to Harper's, who now hold it. Please note that I received no royalties whatever on that book; it was a scholarly book, nonprofitmaking. In fact, I offered it to Harper's, pro forma, and pro forma they turned it down.

Now, I understand and have understood through the five years during which I have worked on the Mark Twain papers:

That I must ask permission from the Estate and from Harper's to publish in my books anything that is in the unpublished papers.

Note, however, that I also understand, and have understood for five years, and have worked for the Estate in the clear understanding, fully talked out among Mr. Lark, Mr. Langdon, Harper's, and myself:

That such request would be granted on my making it;

That it covered everything and anything I might want to quote;

That both Harper's and the Estate would regard me as being entitled to publish anything I might want to and would make no objection whatever and ask no fee;

That the only exception would be in case I might want to publish something so seriously improper as to damage Mark Twain's reputation (if such material should exist and if I could be conceived as wanting to publish it);

That, in such an event, we would amiably refer the difference of opinion to impartial and qualified parties for decision.

That is and has been my understanding. More simply: I understand that, in consideration of five years work on the Mark Twain papers, I have the right, on request, to publish in my own critical books about him any material whatever I may find in the papers, subject always to my discretion as editor.

That is putting it flatly—which happens when people try to be legal. Hoyns knows, Lark knows, the literary world knows, and you ought to know, that I would never make any improper request, and I would never in any event make any request whatever to which you and Harper's could not agree.

However, you must also bear in mind that I have done an enormous amount of expert work for the Estate for which I have had no compensation whatever. My compensation for that work was intended, from the beginning, to be precisely that permission to quote. (Incidentally, I do not now contemplate ever making use of it—I have moved into a wholly different field of literary activity.) If the occasion should arise, if I should desire to revise my present books about Mark Twain or to write a new one, and if you should refuse permission to quote, then I should certainly request compensation in money for the work I have done. I should do the same if Harper's refused permission to quote, and my claim would necessarily be against the Estate, not Harper's, since the work was done for the Estate.

It would then be necessary to set a value on that work. In the last ten years my income from writing has never fallen below twenty thousand dollars a year. I am an expert on Mark Twain; without egotism I can claim to be the leading expert. I am a writer of established reputation, as is testified by my position on the Writers War Board, the Council of the Writers' Guild, and various other responsible or honorary bodies. In fact, Mr. Lark, Harper's, and I agreed that I should have to charge more than the Estate could afford to pay, that I could not afford to work for anything the Estate could pay, when we made our original arrangement.

93

This is, however, wildly and absurdly legalistic. It would never occur to me to make trouble for the Estate or for Harper's, to try to profit at the expense of either, or to do anything whatever that either would disapprove. I have served the Estate for five years in a good many ways, without expecting payment, without causing any trouble or embarrassment, without infringing on its rights. I am a decent man, a writer held in decent estimation by the public, a responsible scholar, and a lover of Mark Twain—as well as a friend and editor of Harper & Brothers.

Now, either treat me on that basis or else state clearly what basis you expect to treat me on, or, finally, permit me to resign.

Sincerely yours,

TO THOMAS CHAMBERLAIN

January 12, 1944

The copies of *What Is Man?* which I have are numbered 150 and 191. The latter, at a cursory glance, looks imperfect but I have had no chance to examine it. It was my intention to add them to the material in my Harvard study, since I have had, heretofore, to use Harvard's copy, which can be used only in the Treasure Room. I may, however, mail them to you. I will return to this in a moment.

Harvard has no insurance on the Mark Twain manuscripts in my study and assumes no responsibility whatever for them. They are, however, subject to the same safeguards as Harvard's own collections, many millions of dollars worth of manuscripts and many millions of dollars worth of rare books. No one can get into my study except Mrs. Breed[1] and me, unless a duplicate key has been made unknown to me. Mrs. Chapman and two other people have had such keys at various times but all have been returned. In my opinion there is no point in insuring them. They cannot be stolen or burned and they cannot be damaged except as they may be damaged in use, and since the important ones have been typed they are not used.

You have aroused my legal impulses and I want to repeat that I have not checked the list which Mrs. Chapman sent you.[2] I assume it to be both accurate and, as far as it goes (subject to what I have told you before), complete, but until I have checked it I must necessarily say there is always a possibility that it is inaccurate, incomplete, or even in some respects false. Since I did not make it I must decline to be responsible for it till I have checked it.

---

[1] Elaine Breed, who had replaced Rosamond Chapman as secretary-assistant.
[2] Chamberlain had asked for a complete checklist of all the Mark Twain Papers, an absurdity in view of the mass of single pages, memos, invitations, cards, and other chaotic or worthless material. Chamberlain's apparent motive was to get a clear idea of the market value of each piece of paper.

Mrs. Breed writes me that she does not care, and has not really got time, to check and complete the inventory. I suppose that that puts it up to me. I can probably do it—with the aid of a stenographer—in a few days and I will do so on my first visit to Cambridge, in fact, I will arrange to stay there long enough to do so within a month or so.

Meanwhile, let me recapitulate some things which you must bear in mind about the manuscripts:

1. We have very few complete manuscripts, very few manuscripts of books which have been published, and very few signed manuscripts.

2. Some of the manuscripts we have, notably the *Mysterious Stranger* (though not even I can always tell which parts of this can be called final and authentic), are probably very valuable in a financial sense. I mean, a few could probably be sold for handsome sums. Many others are of some—but usually inconsiderable—financial value. I mean—a few could be sold for, say, $100; rather more for, say $25 to $50; a good many for say, $5.00 to $25.00. In my opinion, this class of manuscripts are worth more to the Estate in the collection, for the use they can be put to and the light they cast on Mark Twain, than their sale could possibly be. Finally, the great bulk of the manuscripts have only such value as is given them by the fact that they are in Mark's handwriting. At best this is not much; it would become less or even vanish if they were offered for sale. And many of them are of no value (financial value, I mean) whatever. In addition we have a mass of stuff which can only be called rubbish. Once an inventory and appraisal have been made, I shall ask leave to destroy much of this last, or, alternatively, give some of it away to people who may value its association with Mark Twain. (What, for instance? Well, we have blank contract forms, menus of banquets, invitations to Clara's wedding, visiting cards of Mrs. Clemens, etc., etc., etc.)

Unquestionably our most valuable (financially) items are the notebooks, which I described to you and Mr. Swain.

I think it important for you to understand that most of our manuscripts are fragmentary, incomplete, and usually unfinished. At least 85%, possibly 90%, must be so described. And well over 50% are trivial—brief, uninteresting, haphazard. Please bear that in mind. To the editor, the biographer, the critic, the student of Mark Twain or of American literature they are almost indescribably important and valuable as a collection, but as business assets the overwhelming bulk of them are worthless or nearly worthless.

Furthermore, I must ask you in all seriousness, and I trust with all courtesy, not to let Mr. Swain and Mr. Retz impose on you, as Trustee, their point of view as sellers of books and manuscripts too far. They make profits from the turnover of such stuff as ours—never forget that. Mr. Swain is a charming gentleman and has already in the past shown me and the Estate much kindness and done us much service, but I confess some of the things he said the other day horrified me.

Let me give you example of what I mean. If you were to offer to give me any manuscript in our collection that I might choose, I would not choose any of the notebooks, which at auction would bring high prices, or *The Mysterious Stranger*, which, at a guess, may be worth $5,000. I should choose, as by far the most valuable, a few pages of notes for the writing of *Huckleberry Finn*, which at auction might bring $75 or $100. Any true student or lover of Mark Twain, I think, would do the same—for they are infinitely valuable. They are priceless, to an understanding of him. And, in the long view, this $100 manuscript will put more profit in the Estate's bank account than *The Mysterious Stranger*.

I think I will venture to keep in the reference books the copy of Cyril Clemen's book which I took. You have 200, about, in that case. None of them is worth 5¢.

Finally, one very important caution. Mark Twain—and one essay in my *Mark Twain at Work* discusses this—very often wrote a number of versions of a given book. The reasons are much too long and complex for me to repeat here. Everyone knows that to some extent, but I have a far better idea than anyone else how often he did and to what extent and in what instances. But even I do not know all the cases. Now, make a hypothetical case. There is a Mark Twain book called, say, *Life in Hannibal*. (There isn't.) We have, let us assume, a manuscript of it, or part of a manuscript. Mr. Retz or Mr. Swain knows of no other manuscript—why should he? So he values it at $1000. But two years from now my researchers reveal that a collector named Jones in San Francisco has a manuscript of *Life in Hannibal*, a part of a manuscript. What happens to Mr. Swain's $1000 valuation? In the first place both our manuscript and Mr. Jones' drop in value, for neither is unique, as both were believed to be. Well, one may be worth $500 and one $50, and nothing but the most patient study by me (or some other authority) can determine which. I (or some other authority) must—with enormous difficulty —determine which was written first, which is nearer to the published book, which casts more light on Mark Twain, which has the most interesting changes and deletions, which shows most relation to his other books, etc., etc., etc., and it may be that Mr. Jones will deny me access to his manuscript. So what becomes of our asset which we thought was worth $1000?

I have angered you before this. I trust it will not anger you when I say that, in my opinion, you must, in order to do your job as Trustee, carefully read all Mark Twain's books, all the collections that have been made of his early work, Paine's biography, my two books, and a considerable list of critical works. Thus it is discouraging that you do not know *What Is Man?* The edition you saw was issued anonymously in the year given. Much later an edition was brought out with Mark Twain's name on the title page. *There are many differences between them.* Furthermore (see the 3rd essay in my *Mark Twain at Work*) Mark wrote a large number of other dialogues, some complete, some unfinished, which he meant to be a part of *What Is Man?* but for various reasons did not put in it. A number of these are in our stuff and I believe (though I would have to check) that we have the manuscript of the 1906 edition.

Now what gives the 1906 edition its financial value is its rarity plus the fact that it was anonymous. But the vast interest of our unpublished stuff gives it far higher value to the student, though it has only a slight money value. *What Is Man?* has little literary value. The 1906 edition has considerable collector's value. Our stuff has great biographical and critical value.

Now, my wife, who in my absence from Cambridge opens my mail in order to determine what to forward, added a note to your letter, "Better resign—all you're going to get from now on is headaches." Again, I want to speak frankly but without offense. I have had a great many headaches in five years of being the Mark Twain editor. I anticipate more. I want to keep them at the minimum. And it is quite true that I am under strong temptation to quit—I am paid nothing, I do a lot of work, much of the work I do is of an annoying, detailed, routine kind and distasteful to me. But I consider that I must string along for the time being. It will simplify matters if I make a general statement about the assets of the Estate, as I see them.

Over the years, it seems to me, by far the greatest asset is the sale of Mark Twain's books and of such subsidiary rights in them as movie, radio, etc. Compared with this, the value of our collection is slight, even if you realize $100,000 from it (as you wouldn't). Our main job is what may be called institutional advertising—the spread of discussion of Mark Twain in order to maintain and increase the sale of his books. Thus, if I were to go on and complete the edition of letters and make the edition of notebooks as our original plan called for, both books would sell well and go on selling. Both would make 10 to 20 thousand dollars in themselves. But far more important would be the fact that they would lead old readers to buy Mark's books and create new readers who would also buy them. You have made $8,000 in royalties from *Mark Twain in Eruption*, which I edited, and in the end will make twice that. But in the end also you will make four times $8,000 from the sale of Mark Twain's books which would not have been sold except for the stimulation of old readers and the creation of new readers by *Mark Twain in Eruption*.

Similarly with the books I have written and may yet write—and the books which other qualified students may write about Mark Twain, the institutional advertising which such books will create will be of great and in fact indispensable value. In fact, if Mark Twain is to go on selling, he must go on being discussed, and if he is to be discussed books about him, especially controversial books, must continue to be written.

That is the one prime reason for keeping our collection together as a unit—so that I and other qualified students can use it for the writing of books about Mark Twain. (Paine never understood this simple fact; Lark has always

97

understood it.) It is also the prime reason why the Estate must have me or someone like me on the job—a qualified editor who knows Mark Twain thoroughly and knows the publishing business and the literary world. There are several publishing ventures and revisions which must be undertaken very soon and when you have settled into your job I will propose them—I have already discussed some of them with Harper's.

I apologize for writing by hand; it is late and the hotel stenographer has gone off duty. Please have a typist copy this and send me a carbon for my files.

I shall be at the Hay-Adams House from the 13th to the 18th, but it is impossible to guarantee any Washington address very long. You can always address me, for forwarding, at Cambridge.

Sincerely yours,

TO A MR. CORNWALL

May 25, 1945

Dear Mr. Cornwall:

There is an assumption in your letter which I can not permit to pass unchallenged. I want to make it quite clear that my introduction to *Mark Twain in Eruption* describes in exact detail the only changes I have ever made in any Mark Twain manuscript. I was directed and I wanted for my own part to make an interesting book out of a confused manuscript, which was quite unpublishable as it stood because of its arrangement and because of the presence of ferociously dull material. I did precisely what the introduction clearly says I did. I left out a lot of trivial talk about newspaper headlines, the frequency with which Mark washed his hair, what his secretary reported about the bright sayings of children, and similar topics of a positively lethal tiresomeness. I then rearranged the good stuff that was left so that it had the sequence and coherence which Mark's method of dictating had completely denied it.

In one instance, which is mentioned and described on Pages XI and XII, I left out a large part of a dictation for other reasons than dullness. My reasons are stated quite clearly in the introduction. To begin with, I had in Mark Twain's own handwriting on the typescript itself prohibition forbidding anyone to publish any part of the dictation before 1971. The right to publish unquestionably belonged to the Estate whose agent I was. The Estate agreed to ignore Mark's prohibition provided I would leave out a certain ill-tempered and quite untrue passage, publication of which would unnecessarily wound and offend the son of the person whom the passage was about.

I was the more willing to agree because I had been able to establish that the passage in question was quite false. I see no reason why anyone, even a great writer, and even a dead great writer, should be permitted to lie in print about anyone who cannot answer back.

I cannot imagine where you get the idea that I altered or smoothed out Mark Twain's opinions or his language in any way. No editor of integrity would ever dream of doing so, and I certainly never dreamed of doing so, or would do so. When exterior reasons justify such alterations in the text as those I have just described, it is the plain duty of any editor to account for them quite clearly as I did in my introduction. If this is not satisfactory, let me add to you personally that there is no change whatever in Mark's language and that no passage was left out of *Mark Twain in Eruption* because it touched on religion or on any other subject. I mean to say as clearly as possible that no effort has been made by me, by the Estate, or by Harper's to suppress or in any way alter or weaken any part of Mark Twain's autobiography, of which *Mark Twain in Eruption* is a part, on religious or moral grounds. No change whatever has been made except those mentioned in my introduction and again summarized for you here.

Nor can I, as one who has studied Mark Twain for over twenty years, understand why you believe that Mark's religious ideas were particularly violent or profound. For the most part, what he had to say about religion was based on his boyhood conception of frontier evangelism, and practically all he ever said was on an adolescent level. He seems to have been fixed, to have been arrested at the level of Ingersoll from whom many of his notions were doubtless derived. Even in the books published toward the end of his life, he was still ferociously rebelling against outworn religious dogmas which nobody of any intelligence or sophistication had believed for fully fifty years. He never was a particularly profound thinker about anything, but I have always thought it more than a little ridiculous for him to go on fulminating like a high school boy about matters which no longer bothered anybody except high school boys.

Sincerely yours,

TO WILLIAM BRIGGS

On January 10, 1946, DeVoto wrote to Dr. Howard Raper, the author of Man against Pain, *telling him about two Mark Twain fragments dealing with Mark Twain's treatment, under anesthetic, by a Hartford*

*dentist. On February 4 he sent Dr. Raper
the sketches. From then until May they
were in correspondence about the interest
of the pieces as bearing on the history of
anesthetics, and through Dr. Raper, DeVoto
proposed to publish them in some medical
journal. On March 23 he wrote that he was
starting on the tedious rigmarole of
permissions. On October 4, more than six
months after starting these negotiations, he
wrote to Chamberlain blowing up about the
delay, and three days after that he wrote
his I-wash-my-hands-of-it letter to Briggs.*

October 7, 1946

Dear Bill:

No, I'm sorry. Your own letter contains the complete rebuttal. I cleared those pieces with McGregor[1] in early May. I sent them with an explanatory letter to Chamberlain on May 21. So he writes to Harper's about them on July 9. And I'm told in the middle of the summer that it can go over till fall so that we can talk it over. I'm damned if I will. We have had innumerable such consultations and they all come to the same thing in the end. I'm not going to sit in on any more of them or waste any more of my time working out a system that has been worked out fifty times. To hell with it.

And this time, as earlier in the year, the God damned nonsense has cost Harper's and the Mark Twain Estate thousands of dollars of free publicity, publicity that cannot possibly be bought—and now won't be got at all. There was no reason why either McGregor or Chamberlain had to read those pieces at all. Both Harper's and the Estate turn to me for advice when something comes up and both act on my advice—it's in order to get good advice that they call on me. But every single God-damned time I have tried to initiate something on my own behalf—using the same judgment that Harper's and the Estate call on (but incidentally never pay a cent for)—since Chamberlain took over, I have got stalled for months in the same morass of delay, vagueness, and red tape.

Look, I know the Mark Twain papers—neither Harper's nor Chamberlain does. I know publishing and the literary world and literary opportunity—Chamberlain doesn't. I'm the only complete expert on Mark Twain. I'm the one you both come to for advice. But I can't take advantage of my knowledge *on your behalf and the Estate's* because what I propose has to go through a process that never yet has taken less than six months. It ought to take no more than the time needed to get a letter from Boston to New York and a reply back in the next day's mail.

[1] Frank S. McGregor, president of Harper's.

I repeat, it costs you money. Plenty of money. Why in hell couldn't I have been told yes, go ahead, publish those anesthesia fragments without anyone's reading them? I told McGregor that Harper's wouldn't want to publish them—I know, I'm a Harper's editor—that no literary sheet would want to publish them, and I know, I've edited a literary sheet—that no one would want to publish them *except the people who, by hard labor and at my own expense and without compensation I had found.* I knew—for Christ's sake, if you're willing to take my judgment on the innumerable Mark Twain matters you submit to me, if the Estate is willing to take it on the matters it submits to me, why couldn't it be taken in this one? But, okay, Chamberlain has to read them. God knows why—God knows, in fact, if he has read them yet. Why couldn't he read them and tell me to go ahead? If he had told me before I left here on June 10—twenty-two days after I sent them to him—next week you'd be getting thousands of dollars of front page publicity that you won't get because he didn't. God Almighty, Bill, every manuscript that comes into the office of *Harper's Magazine* is read and returned in less than ten days.

This is what I had worked hard to set up and this is what you—and the Estate—lost out on because you simply would not accept the judgment that is always the one you think the best available when you initiate something. Here are these two fragmentary Mark Twain manuscripts on the discovery of anesthesia—the next week Boston and the entire medical world are celebrating the discovery of anesthesia. It will be in all the papers, it's a great day in the history of civilization, it's the greatest centennial of this year which is packed full of centennials, the entire world is interested in it, all the newspapers and journals of opinion and medical journals will be discussing it. And I had it set up so that, right at the time, this month, now, two medical journals would be running previously unpublished Mark Twain manuscripts on the discovery of anesthesia. And I had it fixed so that the world authority, Dr. Howard Raper, the author of last year's best-selling and very brilliant book, *The Conquest of Pain,*[2] would be editing and presenting them. All that remained was to put it on the press association wires next week and there we'd be.

It makes me so damn mad I can't see straight. Go out and try to buy that publicity for Mark Twain and see where you'll get. And I'd fixed it up —there it was. Now you won't get a line of it. Simply because something that had been settled fifty times before, and always settled in the same way, had to be settled once more.

Nobody else would publish those pieces—they aren't worth publishing. I told McGregor so and I told Chamberlain so. I know—if I don't know, for God's sake what do you refer Mark Twain matters to me for? But I had it fixed so that they would be published in circumstances that would have

2 He means *Man against Pain.*

focused the attention of hundreds of thousands of people on them. Was that worth doing or wasn't it?

The same identical God-damned thing happened last winter. I suddenly see that Winston Churchill is coming to the United States. I have about two weeks to move round in—less than that, for the time to spring it was not anytime during his stay but the day he hit New York. So I fix it up to get Mark Twain on every press service and on half, no, five-sixths, of the front pages of America. There's an unpublished account—a few hundred words—of a meeting between Mark Twain and Churchill just after the Boer War. Nobody would ever publish it for itself, but in those circumstances it was irresistible. I set it up—*American Notes and Queries* to run the piece in full and me to give the news bureaus a quotation and a summary. Thousands of dollars worth of publicity that can't be bought. What happened? It got bogged down in the damned idiotic red tape. To this day it hasn't been settled, I haven't got the green light—and now I don't want it, for Churchill isn't here and those few hundred words are altogether worthless.

Figure out for yourself how much Harper's and the Estate lost from those two episodes alone this year.

Well, I'm through with it. I phoned Chamberlain a couple of weeks back and told him I wanted to get out—give up the papers—throw over the program. When I was in New York I told McGregor that I'd stay on till we could get the letters published. Damned if I want to, and the more I think of it the more convinced I am that I won't. Letters, enlarged notebook, proposed anthology, proposed volume of short quotations—to hell with them. I've wasted a hell of a large part of eight years and I don't want to waste any more of my time. For one thing, elsewhere, on other subjects, I can get my opinion valued, I can get some discretionary power to act on it. For another, elsewhere I can get my time paid for. Let Harper's and the Estate find somebody else who can qualify as a Mark Twain expert—and is willing to on the terms I've had.

I simply will not go through that discussion of what to publish and how to publish again. We all know what to publish and what not to publish. We all know what the routine is. We all know what the principles are and what the method is and what values have to be consulted. Nuts. If you and the Estate want any more of my Mark Twain knowledge, you'll damn well have to find some way of not wasting my time and paralyzing my endeavors. I have made you both thousands of dollars and never yet lost you a dime. Try to get someone else who can qualify to do the same in less than ten years of full time work—that you'll have to pay for. And when you've got him, for God's sake act on what he says, and act on it in something less than six months.

Yours,

FOUR

Controversies, Squabbles, Disagreements

To Lewis Gannett, March 29, 1936
To Lewis Gannett, April 6, 1936
To Robert Hillyer, November 13, 1936
To a former student, September 18, 1941
To Dorothy Thompson, December 11, 1942
To Robert Frost, June 7, 1943
To Van Wyck Brooks, August 2, 1943
To Malcolm Cowley, April 15, 1944
To Malcolm Cowley, April 22, 1944
To Winfield Townley Scott, April 29, 1944
To Norman Cousins, May 8, 1944
To a Mr. Alfonte, May 9, 1944
To Norman Cousins, May 19, 1944
To Malcolm Cowley, June 1, 1944
To Paul Kneeland, June 9, 1945
To Herbert Evison, December 3, 1948
To the editor of the New York *Herald Tribune*, January 3, 1949
To a Mr. Sabin, February 3, 1949
To Alfred Barr, March 16, 1949
To Holger Cahill, April 11, 1949
To Lloyd Goodrich, April 21, 1949
To Holger Cahill, June 24, 1949
To E. B. Loomis, March 13, 1950

A good part of DeVoto's correspondence, like a good part of his published writings, could be classified as controversy. He had strong opinions and a pungent way of expressing them, and he was completely unawed by—in fact felt challenged by—lofty reputations. Sometimes, as in his famous disagreement with Van Wyck Brooks, he was never directly replied to, and no reconciliation of opinions or personalities ever took place, though Brooks did revise *The Ordeal of Mark Twain*, partly on the basis of DeVoto's criticisms, and DeVoto intended but never actually made a revised edition of *Mark Twain's America*, removing or softening the personal attack on Brooks. In other cases, as in his exchange with Malcolm Cowley over *The Literary Fallacy* and that with Holger Cahill over the state of art criticism, a dispute that began fairly hotly worked toward adjustment and mutual respect.

Ideas mattered intensely to DeVoto, and his characteristic way of dealing with them was by impetuous attack or defense. But if he found that he had overstated himself, he was willing to eat crow. His principal weakness as a controversialist—and there have been few more formidable controversialists in our literary history—was that he did not understand that words like "fool" and "stupid" might be taken personally. And with certain ideas, such as the Brooks-Mumford-Frank "misrepresentation," as he thought it, of America, and the glib assumptions of the literary Left, and the repressive dogmas of the authoritarian and censorious, he never made peace. He never made friends with their advocates. As he said, he saw no reason for praising or liking a man who had been wrong for years, when he finally arrived at the position that men of sense and integrity had occupied all along.

TO LEWIS GANNETT

Gannett, daily book reviewer for the New York Herald Tribune, *took exception in his column to DeVoto's Easy Chair, "Another Consociate Family,"* Harper's *172 (April 1936), in which DeVoto had ridiculed progressive educational experiments in general, and Black Mountain College in particular. The DeVoto essay, precipitated by a Louis Adamic article in praise of Black Mountain, was part of a deliberate campaign against the literary and leftist intellectuals. The outcome of the exchange with Gannett was an indication of how quickly DeVoto calmed down if his opponent came back purring instead of roaring.*

March 29, 1936

Dear Mr. Gannett:

I have never met Louis Adamic. I should be glad to do so, though I don't get to New York very often and though I don't see what bearing an introduction to him would have on my opinions about Black Mountain or "experimental" education in general.

But I take exception to a phrase in your note and, with less feeling than I have a right to, to one in your *Herald Tribune* remarks about my Easy Chair article. If I am less entitled to object to the latter, since a reviewer is working in the public interest, I am the more moved to because, as a reviewer, you have the privilege of saying anything you like about me in complete safety, since I have no public forum for a reply. The privilege should make you careful. You ought to make sure that you know what you're talking about.

You say in your column that if I "looked deeper into the effect those passing schools, and the earlier communities, had on thousands of lives," I should "be less snooty and more intelligently critical." And you say in your note to me, which is certainly not in the public interest, that one third of my remarks are "sheer ignorant boorishness." That is an insolent phrase: the kind of insult that is deliberate, not inadvertent. I do not see just how it is called for, but the adjective fits in with what you say in your column. Now, opinion is one thing, and you are as free as possible to differ from my opinions and to denounce them as much as you like. But ignorance is quite another thing. My guess is that I know more about the experimental sects, communities and colleges than you do, that I have gone more deeply into them than you have, and that I have investigated their effects on more lives than you have looked into. My opinions may be wrong but they are based on experience and prolonged study, and I doubt that yours are. I think that I know more about these matters than you do, by a damned sight. Are you willing to match up with me?

I have been a college teacher for twelve years. How much college teaching have you done? I have steadily read and reflected on and sometimes reviewed the books and reports of the theorists and experimenters in education. How closely have you followed them? Part of my professional routine is to keep in touch with the projects of such places as Mena, Rollins, Olivet, Antioch, Sarah Lawrence, Bennington, etc., and I have visited many of them and been exposed to the arguments of them all. How much do you know about such places? I have published about a dozen articles on the subject of college education, several of which have been widely reprinted and one of which has become something of a classic.[1] How much have you written about college education?

As for the sects and communities. I grew up in Utah. I experienced one experimental society—certainly the most successful and in many ways the most radical of all—in the most intimate way possible over a period of twenty years. This started me reading Mormonism, and reading Mormonism soon required me to read deeply in all the others as well. I am an acknowledged authority on Mormonism. I was asked to write the articles on Joseph Smith and Brigham Young for the D.A.B., and if you will read the latter when it comes out (the former is too short to show much) you will have an index to the depth of my study. An article of mine, "The Centennial of Mormonism," is listed in the bibliographies as the authoritative summary; it will be reprinted in a revised and enlarged version next fall. I imagine that most American historians would say that I know what I'm talking about in regard to Mormonism, and the greater part of them would accept me as the leading authority.

But no one can know anything about one sect without studying them all. I have studied in great detail the Shakers, the Millerites, the Oneida Community, Hopedale, Icaria, Fruitlands and Brook Farm. I am familiar

[1] "The Co-Eds: the Hope of Liberal Education," *Harper's* 155 (September 1927). Reprinted as "The Co-Eds: God Bless Them," in *Forays and Rebuttals*.

with the history and the general publications of all the rest—several dozen in all. I have read, I imagine, all the twentieth century studies that have been made of them. My guess is that I have devoted more study to every one of them than you have to the whole field. I give a graduate course at Harvard in the Literature of the Frontier[2] in which the experimental sects and societies are a primary objective. For the last six years I have been reading for a book[3] which specifically undertakes to appraise the part they have played in the development of American culture . . . All right, how widely have you read in this literature? When you call me ignorant of the communities, just what gives your judgment weight?

Or make it simpler: I said in the Easy Chair that Adamic's summary of Rice's ideas reminded me of the *Dial* and the *Harbinger*, of Alcott, Brownson and Ripley. Have you read enough of any of these five to know whether I am right or wrong? If you haven't, is your opinion in the matter worth a damn?

Well, what is boorishness? The word is subjective, and I might call its indiscriminate use, together with "braggart" and "bully" and other nouns you have pinned on me in public, rather boorish. But subjective is subjective —I am interested not in your epithet but in your accusation. You are not content to take issue with my opinions; you question the legitimacy of my having them. I don't know what your opinions about the sects and communities are; they may be good, indifferent or cockeyed but they are not in print and I have no reason to suppose that you are entitled to any. That is exactly what, in the face of your insulting phrase, I want to know. Are you? How much do you know about the communities? How many lives have you investigated?

Or is this just another case of a reviewer pressed for time and shooting his mouth off about a subject he is ignorant of? I've been there, I review books too, and I take full advantage of the convention of infallibility. But I take care not to accuse anyone of ignorance except in fields that I know something about. God forbid that I should instruct you, but you might meditate that principle before you again jeer at me in a public place where I have no come-back. Your next jeer may be as ignorant as this one.

Sincerely yours,

---

[2] DeVoto's summary of his competence in the communal sects is essentially true, but this statement is not. Though he says in his statement to the Harvard Committee, pp. 221ff., that his course in Frontier Literature "was actually scheduled for 1936–37," the only courses he was actually teaching—had ever taught—at Harvard were a writing course and a course in contemporary American literature. This is an instance of his tendency to overclaim authority, to be accurate in general and excessive in corroborative detail. Here there was surely no need. Every historian at Harvard would have freely testified to his knowledge of the sects.

[3] Apparently a reference to *The Year of Decision 1846*, which did not appear until 1943, but which was begun at least as early as May 1933.

TO LEWIS GANNETT

April 6, 1936

Dear Mr. Gannett:

Sure, but "ignorant" is something else. Call me a thief, call me a low-brow, call me a Republican and it's O.K., but my neuroses rise up when I'm called ignorant. Reflect: my public career is based on a simple and repetitious formula, "He doesn't know what he's talking about." My God, suppose you were to print in your column an allegation that John Chamberlain had never read Sumner. That Mencken was corresponding secretary of B.P.O.E. That Dietrich had varicose veins. That you'd seen Villard in the Century Club wearing a Landon button.

Well, so far as I can see there is only one thing to do. If I remember my Thackeray—do you not divine it, embrasson nous.

But hell, I've just riveted myself still more tightly to the established order and climbed forever out of the class of you lowly who travel in Fords—I've bought, Lee Hartman[1] cooperating, a Buick and driven it to the Cape. Last summer was sacrificed to the literary life and it looks as if this will have to be too. My western trip has now no status outside of fantasy and if I ever follow you to the high plains and the Rockies, it will be when the world has grown amenable. But there are plenty of roads in these parts. I don't carry on controversies past the time mud dries in Vermont. I'll give you one more enthusiast in the June *Harper's*—J. A. Etzler, whom Thoreau reviewed—but that's positively the last one till it's time for Prestone again. My simple mysticism is that no one can be alarmed about the Americans while traveling cross-country in an automobile, and if that makes me a Republican, have it your own way. . . . I suspect that I'm temperamentally with the Thoreaus and against the Etzlers and nothing can be done about it. It all depends on the ones you choose. Don't forget that one conspicuous product of Brook Farm was C. A. Dana. If you brought him within gunshot of an idealism, he didn't need a gun. Maybe that also happens—maybe the communities also produce subversive cynics. Brigham Young invented most of the devices that Hitler has found useful, and Brigham was head of a perfected society of just men made perfect. The trouble with the saintly is that they don't see the lice for the glory of God, and though no Puritan, I think we should move against the lice. . . . Well, it's a date, the first time I get to New York.

Yours,

[1] Editor of *Harper's Magazine*.

TO ROBERT HILLYER

Hillyer had published in the Saturday
Review of Literature *in early October 1936
a poem in rhymed couplets entitled "A
Letter to the Editor." It began, "Time
brings us, Benny, to our middle years," and
attacked the symbolists, the proletarians,
the Marxists, and other literary enemies,
wishing with Caligula that they all had one
throat and he a knife. In reply, Granville
Hicks submitted the "Letter to Robert
Hillyer" spoken of below, in which he
attacked not only Hillyer but DeVoto,
Frost, and the whole Breadloaf crowd. After
DeVoto rejected it for anything but the
Letters column, Hicks let it lie fallow until
the publication of Hillyer's poem in a
volume entitled* A Letter to Robert Frost
and Others. *Then he printed the less
abusive parts of it in the* New Republic *of
October 20, 1937.*

November 13, 1936

Dear Robert:

Ten days ago I received a long reply in couplets to your "Letter" by
Granville Hicks. They are pretty bad couplets as poetry and compose a really
scabrous attack on you and on me too. You probably know Hicks and so can
guess the content, and, as I did, the intention. I felt that he was trying to
push me and the magazine into a position from which he and his pink play-
mates could profit. My feeling was that any publication of the couplets
could do neither you nor me any harm, because they are so obviously angry
and vituperative. I therefore sent them back to him, saying that, if he was
submitting them for publication, I must decline them on the ground that
they were pretty bad poetry, but that, if he was submitting them as a comment, or an answer to your satire, I would be willing to run them on my correspondence page, provided he would reduce them to reasonable compass.

I have not heard from him since, and really did not expect to. My best

111

guess is that he will run them entire in his own house organ, *The New Masses*. If he sends them back to my correspondence page, I will run them if I think he makes sufficient of an ass of himself, or handle the situation otherwise, according to expedients that suggest themselves to me. This is merely to let you know what he has done and to prepare you for a possible appearance of his stuff in the *Masses*.

Yours,

TO A FORMER STUDENT

September 18, 1941

Dear W.[1]

My point was quite simple: I didn't want to get involved in the irrelevant offensive-defensive state of mind I've seen you produce over other things. Over, among them, my failure to make use of you at the *Saturday Review*. I was operating under a time-limit there, had to improve the sheet as fast as I could, in fact faster than I could, and felt that I could use only the best and most experienced reviewers for everything except the most unimportant books. Such a policy excluded you as a youngster and had nothing to do with either your personality or your talents, but, because among the literary nothing is ever private, my friends were presently carrying to me reports that I had a grudge against you. I can take a lot of that sort of thing but I don't want to take any more of it than I have to.

You now jump to the conclusion that I'm going to bring in an unfavorable judgment on your article—which is precisely the pattern I'm talking about. I haven't read it yet—it arrived when I'd begun a rush job on a novel by a friend of mine which is preparing for the press—and I probably won't till the week-end. But I'm not going to bring in an unfavorable judgment. If it needs further work on it, I'm going to say so. If it needs doing over, I'm going to say so. I know in advance that it needs cutting down, but beyond that I don't know anything. I'll do anything I can to see that it gets into print. Only, if I have to advise a major operation, I don't want my friends to learn that the advice proceeds out of either spite or jealousy, for it won't.

My further point, I freely admit, is none of my damned business. At the same time, whether or not you believe it, it rests on the fact that I've always

[1] I have expunged the name of the addressee for obvious reasons. He has had a distinguished career, and is in need of no such instructive scolding now, perhaps because DeVoto as a friend told him some home truths in 1941. There is a further poignancy in this letter, in that the home truths DeVoto told his young friend were truths very like what some of DeVoto's friends might have told *him*. He himself often increased the heat of his opposition by his vehemence.

been well-disposed to you and want to see you get ahead. It's this: you habitually have too big a chip on your shoulder and you too easily feel and express contempt for people who have done nothing in particular to deserve it. I twice went to bat for you at Harvard and both times had to face an irrelevant obstinacy that rested on the fact that you had talked unwisely and too often about some of my colleagues. You keep remarking to me about motives of, say, Morrison, Perry Miller, and Murdock which I know they haven't got. They're white men or there aren't any white men. They have no grudge against you, and especially they don't cherish a grudge and wait for some opportunity to express it. You have some picture of bellicosity that does not correspond to the facts; something in you impels you to repel attacks on you that aren't made. I am as intimate with Ted Morrison as any man alive and I know for certain that he had no such feeling toward you as your letter alleges. Why should he? I frankly doubt whether Louis Untermeyer was gunning for you, as you think. I can only conclude that your attitude toward them is exaggerated, unreal, and defensive. You look for trouble where none is to be expected. You find slights where none are intended. So when you go out to avenge them, people fight back.

Thus your taking young W away from Bread Loaf was interpreted as a deliberate affront, the kind of revenge I'm talking about. Since I was laid up at the time, and since, further, I exchanged no conversation with the kid at any time, I don't pretend to know. I do know that, whether or not you had anything to do with it, he acted like an adolescent, or like a horse's ass, in leaving. How good a poet he may be, how much talent and promise he may have, I don't know. But he came there with all the auspices in his favor. Morrison, his sponsor, dipped into next year's funds to pay his expenses. The little printer was promptly set to work setting up his pamphlet. Untermeyer got to work on him. Various others undertook to interest two different publishers in his stuff. The best will in the world was expended on him and, if he's got some stuff, he could have shortened his portage by several years. The sum may be trivial, he may have felt that Bread Loaf was absurd and that these people were making a pompous and absurd effort that should properly be classified with the uplift, or with whatever the literary young are despising this year. And he may have been right. But decent people were going out of their way to treat him as decently as they knew how, and it was up to him to be decent in return. He wasn't. Drunk or sober, he subjected them to an unjustified, an indecent affront. On my way out of Bread Loaf I heard him saying that he felt like a rat, and that was OK with me.

My point is that there was no preliminary knife-whetting for you before you came to Bread Loaf but that W's behavior was, rightly or wrongly, attributed to you. That being so, people felt that you were committing an act of psychological revenge—and revenge for something that had not occurred. I don't know whether they were right or crazy, but the surface appearance seemed to justify them.

I've got reason to know that you've had a lot of tough breaks and have had to take some stiff jolts on the chin. I've never felt that Harvard looked good in divorce—though even there I think that Durand and others could have saved you if you hadn't done too much talking in the meantime—people will, you must realize, get their backs up when called fools. But I think that some of the breaks have been worse than they would have been if you hadn't added to them an element that was not there in reality. It gets into your mind that people are hostile to you when they really aren't. That embarrasses other people and eventually embarrasses you.

That's all I meant—or mean.

Yours,

TO DOROTHY THOMPSON

When, toward the end of 1942, Dorothy Thompson announced that she was selling her house and buying war bonds with the money, because we as a nation and she as an individual lived too luxurious lives, and were being defeated in war by the Japanese, who lived on a cupful of rice a day, and the Germans, who had been malnourished all through their childhood, DeVoto rebuked her in an Easy Chair, "Wait a Minute, Dorothy," in the December 1942 Harper's. He reminded her of columns in which she had sketched a most materialistic future for the have-not peoples, and asked why, if materialism was the hope of the have-nots, it was the doom of the haves. He commented on the luxury of her house and advised her to get off her knees: materialism was what all the world wanted, and what our civilization had begun to give it. It was false and puritan to deplore it. Moreover, morale in wartime did not depend on grim self-punishment, as she suggested. Miss Thompson replied by letter, objecting, and elicited the following, approximately the length of DeVoto's original essay.

December 11, 1942

Dear Dorothy:

I've got out your original piece and mine, and have re-read them. I didn't save the *Look* piece[1] last summer and didn't have it when I wrote. We should always check our quotations and I should have checked my photographs. As a result of not checking them I seem to have misrepresented you by one or more sofas and a number of lamps and hangings which I thought I remembered. If you want public reparation for that, I'll provide it at the first convenient opportunity, but I can't see that I misrepresented either you or your article beyond those items. I didn't misrepresent you in them, really, since they composed a generalized symbol of comfortable and even luxurious living, which was germane to the point I set out to make.

Certainly I was using the *argumentum ad hominem*. It was obviously my job to do so. When I read your column on the false standards of American culture which had led us to the edge of the abyss and may well shove us over it, on the vile worship of material goals, my mind recurred irresistibly to the job in *Look*. I imagine a good many other minds did too. My first job— I'm a working journalist too, my dear, and specifically an analyst of ideas— was to pin that house down as one fixed point in the discussion I proposed to conduct. That house was evidence. I couldn't go beyond the published facts; there it was, as you'd say, on the record. (I'm a softie, though, and if my piece had not been on the press when your fire occurred, I would have killed it.) The photographs certainly showed a hell of a lot of comfortable goods, gadgets, and fixings—vile material goods—and I can't say that your explanation that it is all waste-saving and functional changes my point any. The fact remains that a four-story house in the East Forties, furnished with indirect lighting, equipped with labor-saving devices, and staffed by two servants plus a cleaning woman once a week—well, it represents something altogether beyond the expectation of the ordinary Americans whom you were reviling for basely desiring just such a house. I don't envy you the house: I own a big one myself, sanctified by the earlier ownership of another ornament of literature, and I live there in great comfort, in comfort far beyond my deserts and, like yours, well out of the reach of most people. And I don't begrudge you your house, and wouldn't if it were ten times as luxurious. I'm damned glad you've got so good a place to live in. I wish more people had and I devoutly hope that more people will have.

I made a perfectly valid point about your house, as part of a bigger point. I called your attention and the attention of as much of your audience as might belong to mine to the highly relevant fact that your scorn of material ambition was conducted from a happy financial estate which could take for granted as ordinary working and living conditions, as mere appendages of

[1] A picture story on Miss Thompson's residence and working quarters.

personality, a complex of things, of goods, which for the people you were denouncing can only be matters of wish, dream, and ambition. I said and repeat that that fact considerably weakens your assault on them. I said and repeat that there is nothing evil in desiring material things. I said and repeat that comfortable houses, mechanical gadgets, fine furniture, silk stockings, cosmetics, and the other things you inveighed against are all bound up in the native conception of "the good life," that it is not an evil conception, that it is a good conception, and that you yourself usually know consciously that it is and always know unconsciously, for that's the way you act . . . I could have carried the *tu quoque* a lot farther and still been legitimate. You wrote some columns once about your kid and how the medical profession had failed to diagnose him correctly and what a fine job a school in (as I remember it) Arizona had done for him. That's perfectly swell, and with a difficult kid of my own I've sometimes wanted to talk that school over with you. But I point out to you that the whole episode is indissolubly a part of the state of mind, ambitions, and ideals that arouse your ire when the ordinary American aspires to two green vegetables and two desserts, sound teeth, and a number of other excellent things. It isn't the advertising business and it isn't Thorstein Veblen's theory of conspicuous waste that makes people want those things. It's the human desire—and the human need—to live well, to give the kids a good start, keep healthy and keep the kids healthy, to enjoy the capacities of the human body for experiencing pleasure, and to free the kids' bodies to a less twisted, less frustrated or handicapped capacity for experiencing pleasure than ours have had. It's the desire to get those infected tonsils out. It's the desire to send the kid to that school in Arizona. Why send him to Arizona? Well, you sent your kid there to give him a better chance, but you seem to think that John Doe is either a brainless victim of some advertising bastard or else he's a bastard himself. John Doe aspires to send his kid to school in Arizona for snobbish or business reasons, to keep up with the Joneses or to get ahead and slip something over. Nuts. He wants the kid to go there so that he'll get more out of life than I did. And that's no evil ambition.

I don't know why you object to my saying you're highly paid. You certainly are. You're paid and you're highly paid. You're paid by society. You—and I too—are in fact paid a hell of a lot more than can be justified, than we're worth, except on the basis of what remains of an economic organization that permits us to earn more or less what we can by the sedulous use of our talents. Take it at the first and easiest step: what fraction of your present income would you be making if you were doing the same job for OWI or in some other branch of the government? But I was lumping you with other highly paid journalists—I'm one, myself—and pointing out that it's comparatively easy, at twenty-five thousand a year and upwards, to rebuke people who make two thousand a year for worshipping the golden calf. Also fallacious. The virtues which that piece of yours was recommending are virtues that do not exist and can't be afforded below a certain income.

All that, however, is the minor point. In your letter you don't say much about the main one. Nevertheless, with whatever insistence and impudence, I proceed to Set You Right.

In the first place, I acknowledge that I know you do not regularly and systematically hold to the ideas which you expressed in the piece I objected to. You meant them when you wrote it [but] for the most part you are on the other side, and everybody is permitted a fair amount of temporarily changing sides and a reasonable amount of sheer inconsistency. In the second place, for the most part, or at least for a workable fifty-one percent of the time, you and I are on the same side of the fence. (I have an advantage in arguing with you, for I read you regularly whereas you don't read me.) I am fully as far to the left as you are in belief, and I dare say even farther, but I am a hell of a lot farther to the right in expectation, which makes me a hell of a lot less impatient with the generality of mankind, and specifically of Americans. I string along with you in a good deal of what you say. But I note some recurrent things which seem to me to be clichés and fallacies. My job, as I see it, is to dissect clichés and ventilate fallacies wherever I encounter them. And especially among my allies.

Well, I think that you sometimes fall into the cliché which is the occupational disease of intellectuals and literary people. That in so generously desiring to improve the people's lot that, irked by the slowness of the people or by their frivolity or stupidity, they are willing to improve that lot by force. Nobody knows better than you that if certain financial interests and linkages in this country are a potential source of fascism, so are certain high-minded, wholly selfless, altogether dedicated liberal philosophers in, or seeking to be in, high places. Ordinarily you would do your damnedest to avoid giving them aid and comfort. Nevertheless, and I wonder you didn't see it, you were playing their game when you made the series of accusations which I called Puritanical. It simply is not true that we have made our civilization anarchic, false, and tawdry. You know damned well, usually, that it is not true. You are simply playing the enemy's, the domestic enemy's, game when you say so. That's a dangerous state of mind, permanent or transitory, wherever it occurs.

Furthermore, I accuse you of sometimes succumbing to two fallacies, fallacies which, again, are endemic among intellectuals and literary people. The greater one does not involve the point we are now debating and I pass it by, saying merely (I said so in print once but you missed that) that you are wrong as hell about the Civil War and seriously wrong about the nature and course of the industrial developments that followed it. The other one does involve our present point, and I accuse you of sometimes accepting an unreal, literary, highly fictitious characterization and simplification of the 1920s in America. In your letter you wonder if I "mean to say that our business civilization is perfection and our society a paragon and that all that has been written about it in" the four magazines I hurled at you is hooey. I don't, and you are yielding to a literary way of thinking when you wonder if I do. (Though I will say that in a quarter of a century the *New Republic* has tried to be wrong about everything all the time with a soul-stirring resolution that seems superhuman to a comparatively weak-willed man like me, and has come closer to succeeding than God usually permits anyone to do.) On the other hand, you frequently write as if you were repudiating the Twenties altogether. I know you aren't but I know also that the main current of fashionable intellectual analysis all around us does repudiate it altogether. One of the tragedies of that era was the separation from its experience of its literary and critical interpreters; their present successors have adopted their descriptions and have piled on top of them ignorances and misunderstandings of their own, and one of the great dangers we face is that that mass of clotted ignorance and arrogance may become the basis of belief and action hereafter. I know that and when I see the fallacy I hit it, even when I see it in you, my dear, as it was certainly present in the piece I went after.

What the literary forget is that a composite literary representation of American life by Mencken, Red Lewis, John Dos Passos, Bill Faulkner, and Tom Wolfe is not the sum of American experience in the Twenties. What you ignore is the tremendous cultural, economic, social, human achievements of that tragic decade. When you think of the Twenties you tend to think of a fictitious cliché—you think of what you call "business civilization" and so disregard a large part of business and most of civilization. You think of economic imbalances and malpractices, not all of them America's fault, of a complex of financial errors and crimes, of related things which assisted in producing the downfall, and of a lot of practically unrelated abuses of mere taste which happen to offend you, or happened to offend a lot of literary people whose ideas for the moment you are uncritically willing to substitute for your own. You leave out of account a hell of a lot which it is your professional obligation not to leave out of account, and you say "the hell with business civilization." You disregard things which vitiate the things you say. Not to mention the really majestic social and cultural achievements of business itself during the Twenties—and they exist in open view—you leave out of account, well, how's this, a magnificent spread and remodeling of the entire educational system from primary to professional schools which made American education enormously better than it had ever been before, enormous advances in public health, more genuine progress in medicine than had ever occurred anywhere in any ten years of the world's history, comparable progress in all kinds of laboratory and theoretical science, four times as much progress in applied science, enormous inroads on such persistent problems as rural decadence and the conservation of natural resources, a vast beautification of the countryside, a vast lightening and improvement of the ordinary circumstances that surround the lives of ordinary people.[2]

2 He is prestating the case he made in the Patten Lectures at the University of Indiana in 1943, and published in 1944 as *The Literary Fallacy.*

You leave out of account the labors of hundreds of thousands of solid men and hundreds of great men, not one of them ever in the least a part of or touched by the things which you so arrogantly attribute to them. You leave out of account the vast mass of ordinary citizens who were not in the least vile or tawdry or false or anarchic but only did their best to live decently and bring up their families. You leave out of account yourself, and the aspiring minds you respect—who were part of the Twenties. You forget that the vision of better things which you have became a possible vision during the Twenties, that the implements which may some day effect it were forged by the Twenties and had never existed before. You forget that the people on whose behalf you held that vision are, precisely, the people who composed the Twenties. You forget that the American democracy we are so vocally approving now is, precisely, the American mob the literary were denouncing half an hour ago—and whom you are denouncing when you write pieces like the one I went after. You forget that, much as you may want to achieve for our society, there is one absolute law and condition: that it can be worked with only in its own terms.

And I say that, in your position, you are not permitted to forget these things or to leave them out of account.

I say there are two ways of looking at the literature whose gross errors you sometimes accept. It can be looked at as a pleasant, entertaining, brilliant species of parlor game, in which case it can be accepted on its own terms and not brought seriously to bear on the problems of our civilization. Or it can be looked at as a serious factor in a serious effort to orient ourselves in the world, in which case the final judgment that has to be passed on it is that, between wars, American literature occupied itself chiefly with lying about America. I say further that if we are to have any success in the job ahead of us now, we cannot make our judgments and plot out our course of action on gross errors and flat lies. Specifically, we cannot face the future on the basis of your simple description of our last quarter century as anarchic, false, and tawdry. It was not: the description is false.

You are now corrected. In a lifetime of controversy I have never convinced anyone and have no expectation of convincing you now. But I lived through the Twenties and worked decently and with as much enlightenment as was vouchsafed me; so did you; so did most people. Wherefore I will not permit you to slander your own knowledge without making a protest. I read somewhere that you grew up in a parsonage. I would wish that the religion you came to rebel against had been Catholic and not Protestant. There might have clung to you vestiges of a warmer charity for both the strivings and failures of imperfect man.

Yours,

TO ROBERT FROST

---

*One of the most intense relationships of
DeVoto's life, and ultimately one of the
saddest, was with Robert Frost. The two
met at Breadloaf in the late summer of
1935, met again at Amherst that fall, met
again in Florida that winter and became
fast friends and mutual admirers. DeVoto
felt that Frost was "the greatest living
American"; Frost in turn wrote DeVoto in
November 1936 that "you and I without
collusion have arrived at so nearly the same
conclusions about life and America that I
can't seem to figure out how we came to
vote different tickets at the lost election.
. . . I can't get over my not having realized
you were on earth. You don't know your
own power."*
    *But the friendship and mutual
admiration that was born at the Miami
Winter Institute of Literature, grew quickly
during the next spring when Frost delivered
the Norton Lectures at Harvard, and was
consolidated during two summers at
Breadloaf, came to a sudden chill during
the Breadloaf session of 1938. Whether his
disenchantment with Frost derived from his
own imagination or whether it had actual
justification in Frost's actions, DeVoto
never again looked upon "the greatest
living American" without dark suspicions.
The "quarrel" came to a head when they
were both lecturing at the University of
Indiana in the spring of 1943, and when
DeVoto later heard rumors of remarks that
Frost had made about him in Bloomington*

he wrote the note below, which was, on his
part at least, the final ending of their
friendship. The entire course of their
relationship is traced in The Uneasy Chair,
and also in Lawrance Thompson's Robert
Frost: The Years of Triumph *and* Selected
Letters of Robert Frost.

June 7, 1943

Dear Robert,

Various remarks you made about me in Bloomington have been faithfully reported to me. I find myself not liking one of them, one which you
have been making for a number of years in various parts of the country. It
is reported to me from Bloomington by one of the eight faculty men at the
dinner where you made it in words which he says are exactly or substantially
yours, as follows:

"DeVoto, you know, has been under the care of a psychiatrist, who has
told him that I am not good for him, that if he is ever to succeed, he must
not cultivate my company: I am too strong for him and have a bad effect on
him. . . ."

Another guest at the dinner separately reports you in almost exactly the
same words. Over a period of some years various friends and acquaintances
of mine have reported your saying the same thing, or variants of it, in a good
many places.

The statement is altogether false. No part of it is true. I think you know
that. What satisfaction you get from circulating a false and damaging statement about me I don't know or care, but I have made no earlier protest out
of respect to years of friendship with you. I have decided, however, that I no
longer care to submit to it. I do not want to hear of your making that statement again in public or in private. Please see to it that I do not have to act
any farther in the matter than thus calling it to your attention.

Yours,

TO VAN WYCK BROOKS

At the time when Brooks sent DeVoto an
invitation to participate in a literary panel
on peace, DeVoto had been Brooks's
self-appointed opponent for over a decade,

since the publication of Mark Twain's
America *in 1932. He was about to challenge
Brooks's ideas a second time in* The Literary
Fallacy, *and had already delivered the
Patten Lectures at the University of Indiana
which were the core of that book.
Consequently the letter from Brooks, who
had never personally replied to the robust
criticism of his* Ordeal of Mark Twain, *put
DeVoto in an embarrassing position. He
still disapproved of Brooks's ideas, including
the idea for the symposium to which Brooks
now invited him. But he could not help
knowing, from the friends they had in
common, that Brooks was a gentle and
likable man who would probably disarm him
if they met. The reply he wrote to the
invitation was awkward but honest.*

August 2, 1943

Dear Mr. Brooks:

I appreciate your invitation and have thought about it carefully, but I end by deciding that I had better not accept it. I expect to be in Washington on September 9, half-way through a special job. I could let it go at that and spare you some annoyance and myself some embarrassment. But I want to answer your letter with the same seriousness that prompted it and so I go on, I hope not offensively.

In the first place, I think I should not contribute anything to the small group you are calling together. I could argue with you amiably, I believe, though God seems to have put me together according to a formula which keeps me in opposition to your ideas, and others whom you name would similarly have my respect. Thus, though I have vigorously attacked various stands and books of Cowley's, I have always respected his ideas while rejecting them and have liked him personally. But still others you name are, if I understand their writing, so remote from the ways of thinking I trust that it would be idle for me to sit down and try to talk things over with them. I should be estopped in advance from taking them seriously, I should add nothing to a discussion in which they took part, and I should be wasting not only their time and yours and mine but that of the group as a body trying to reach sensible conclusions.

That, however, is unimportant: it is the larger purpose that runs head-on into my disbelief. The truth is, I am constrained to doubt the utility not only of your smaller meeting but of such projects as the Conference itself.

The list of those who have convoked it is studded with names I respect, some of them friends of mine, many others my allies or at least supporters of the general ideas I hold. But I believe profoundly that their meeting together cannot accomplish anything toward the end in view. It will enhance their feeling of unity and it will produce much intelligent and enjoyable talk; it may clarify their ideas and, perhaps, enable them to write more pertinently and effectively. But it seems to me that the "intellectual and spiritual bases for enduring peace" are not to be sought in or furthered by meetings of writers and intellectuals. It seems to me that writers and intellectuals who hope to do something about those bases, if they attend any meetings at all, ought to attend the meetings of people who are concerned with them *effectively*; meetings, say, of political parties, labor unions, business men, war veterans and others through whom the energies of peace, whether intellectual or spiritual, will find expression. I believe that writers and intellectuals isolate and insulate themselves too much from the reservoirs of energy, and convocations of writers and intellectuals have always seemed to me ineffective, and not only ineffective but unrealistic, and not only unrealistic but irresponsibly frivolous. I hope that I say this without arrogance—in an effort to show you why I should not be able to take part in such discussions with belief.

Finally, I should feel some constraint in your presence. I have recently sent to the printer the manuscript of some lectures I delivered last spring, and in the course of them I again attack your books. The attack is certainly sincere and, I believe, thoroughly respectful. It is conducted, I think, solely as part of the warfare of ideas. But I am a weak vessel and before this have abandoned stands which I ought to have maintained because I found that so-and-so was a good fellow and it seemed a shame to contend with him. I resisted impulses of Hans Zinsser's—he had much the same role in my life, I believe, that he had in yours—to bring us together so that we might iron out our differences, because it seemed to me important that the edge of difference ought not to be dulled by any discovery that it was pleasant to spend an evening talking and drinking together. So now. There are issues between us. They seem to me fundamental in the cause for which the Conference is called. They have to be argued out. Unquestionably it is weak-willed of me, but I am essentially a genial soul with little backbone and I am afraid that a familiar consequence would follow once more: that I should begin to find persuasive reasons why I ought to suppress or at least modify what amounts to a statement of belief—oh, Brooks is a nice chap, he's had as hard a life as the rest of us, in the larger sense we're all working toward the same end, and why make such a fuss? In my own efforts to define the intellectual and spiritual bases for an enduring peace—not an important effort but all I have—that would amount to a catastrophe.

Sincerely yours,

TO MALCOLM COWLEY

Publication of a chapter from The Literary
Fallacy *in the* Saturday Review of
Literature *of April 8, 1944, provoked a
furious reply from Sinclair Lewis, who was
an old acquaintance and a sort of friend but
who, as one of the writers of the twenties
disparaged in* The Literary Fallacy, *as the
husband of Dorothy Thompson, who had
been publicly rebuked by DeVoto, and as a
close friend of Van Wyck Brooks's, had a
threefold grievance. His attack ("Fools,
Liars, and Mr. DeVoto") was so personal
and vituperative that Malcolm Cowley,
reviewing* The Literary Fallacy *for the* New
Republic, *wrote DeVoto to explain in
advance that his unfavorable reaction to the
book had nothing personal in it. An
antagonist who stood to his guns but did not
respond to vehemence with vehemence
always disarmed DeVoto, and here, as in his
epistolary bouts with Lewis Gannett and
with the assembled art critics, what began
as dispute ended in good feeling.*
    *Years after DeVoto's death, in a letter
of May 6, 1973, Cowley wrote me, "Did I
tell you the sequel to our brush over* The
Literary Fallacy (*which was in turn the
sequel to another brush, over* Exile's Return,
*with Benny writing the meanest review I
ever received of any book I dared to
publish*)? *Anyhow, at one time I projected a
collection of the Davy Crockett Almanacs
and asked Benny's help. Help? He poured it
forth generously and even had me around to
the Century for an evening during which,*

*having nothing new to fight about, we
relapsed into silences. Amicable silences. In
his last years, when he was doing those
wunnerful ecological pieces for the Easy
Chair, I thought he was an admirable
character. But he did love to swing a
shillelagh."*

*He did indeed. But more often than
not, it was ideas that infuriated him, not
people. With people he had a predisposition
to be friendly.*

April 15, 1944

Dear Cowley:

That shows how my luck runs. If you had had to deal with a less obviously gentle nature than mine, you might well have brought in a finding of a dogged, perhaps dedicated application of a point of view in spite of all hell, commendable to anyone and worthy of imitation by the young, but with me it's only a half-suppressed wish to be Robert Hillyer. There are those who could resent that.

I file lesser exceptions:[1] not two years at the University of Utah but one, not Philistine but, as I have been pointing out all these years, Populist, and certainly not academic but just professional, since no college will hire me to more than visit it and all literary scholars and all but a handful of historical scholars who speak of me at all speak biliously. But you commit one error which works out so close to libel that I could demand a recantation. I have worked hard to make "Ogden" and "Utah" a single hyphenated noun in all literary minds, and here you are wilfully if not maliciously depriving me of my cosmopolitan heritage and relegating me to Salt Lake City. The next time I get you in my sights, I am going to attribute you to Mauch Chunk.

As for the principal charge, I might submit an alternative hypothesis: that maybe I am one of a small, dwindling number who take literature so seriously that they ask it to be serious and proceed to prophesy against it when it fails to be. I might support the hypothesis with the observation that the only other person around Boston sufficiently concerned about the dignity of literature to make a fight for it is a man, perhaps the only person alive, who takes literary ideas seriously enough to hate mine.[2] And in support of the thesis of my book I might point out that there has been a notable lack

1 To a short biographical and critical piece that Cowley published in the *New Republic* the week before his scheduled review of *The Literary Fallacy.*
2 F. O. Matthiessen.

of writers hereabout hurrying to back us up.[3] To the generality of New England writers neither their civil rights nor the dignity of their calling is worth even the effort it takes to write a letter to a newspaper.

But I don't submit that hypothesis, I submit an even simpler one. Maybe within the terms announced in my first chapter what I say in the following chapters about the literature of the 1920s is true, in part or even as a whole. I hope you are testing that hypothesis at least in part next week.

Those things aside, is it not time to begin splitting the MacArthur vote? If I presently launch a Wainwright for President boom, I shall expect the support of your journal.

Yours,

TO MALCOLM COWLEY

April 22, 1944

Dear Cowley:

I was in New York all week and return to find my house parting at the seams with correspondence about my book and the SRL's excerpt from it, Red Lewis's piece, and the *Strange Fruit* episode. That last comes to its first climax on Wednesday—there has lately been a slight suggestion that the cops are getting coony and may take the one really dirty course open to them, dismiss the charges against us—and necessarily gets precedence over everything else. When I get a chance, I'd like to answer your letter and comment on your review at some length. I am, of course, a long-winded bird and will probably inflict more on you than you ever bargained for. Meanwhile let me thank you for both the letter and the review.

As for the latter, I would agree with a good deal more than half of what you say down to the conclusion, which is I suppose the issue between us. Some of the things you allege to be weaknesses in my position certainly are weaknesses and there are others you pass over—sometime somebody is going to ask me to review a book of mine and whoever does will get a genuine exposé by a man who knows all the breaches in the wall, or maybe I should say all the holes in the cheese. But I leave you finally and fundamentally where you say that we get what the times were by adding up the various shafts that various writers have sunk into it. (Excuse the imprecision. I read the review at the Harvard Club, came home last night, and have not been

[3] In the *Strange Fruit* case, in which Matthiessen, a longtime literary enemy, was associated. In deference to the uneasy alliance in which he found himself, Matthiessen canceled his intention to blast *The Literary Fallacy* in *The Nation*.

out to a newsstand yet. When I try to answer you at length, I'll have your piece in front of me.) That's precisely what I deny. It seems to me, and this is the point of my book, that the writers I was talking about sank their shafts in too small, too restricted, and too unrepresentative an area. Certainly the plumbing industry thinks that bathtubs are the measure of civilization, which leaves criticism the duty of pointing out that they really aren't. So I point out that literary experience isn't the measure, either.

I owe you a considerable debt for stating in public what the book is about. So far, in the stuff that has come in, only Harry Hansen, apart from you, has done that. It's unfortunate, from my point of view, that the discussion has moved away from the thesis to the individual judgments—and, I'd maintain, has separated them from the context. It's only silly of, for instance, Gannett to maintain that when I talk about Powell, medicine, and the like I'm showing off how much I know and calling people's attention to the fact that so and so knows less than I do. What I'm saying is, look, this kind of experience is one of a good many kinds that the boys failed altogether to sink their shafts into, and until they take this and other vital kinds of experience into account, what they say is necessarily wrong. That's my thesis.

Now consider this, and please don't think I'm kidding. I honestly think that the book is good-natured and soft-spoken. I intended everything I said about individual writers to be considered in the light of the reservations and qualifications which I thought were made sufficiently clear in the opening statement. Especially I intended it to be clear that I was deliberately and openly talking about one aspect only of any given writer—in my eyes the most important aspect, of course, but one which I conceded to be only a part, and frequently only a very small part, of the man's work. However, let's let that go until I write at, God help us, greater length—all I want to say now is that I don't think I'm strident, angry, or unjust. At least, the mood I thought I was writing in was that of a chemist analyzing something for a particular chemical, quite unconcerned with the beauty of the product.

I did know about Brooks's breakdown. I faced that question long ago. I had written about half of my first Mark Twain book when I learned about it. Nothing in the world appeals so directly to my emotions as nervous trouble. I scouted around and found out that Hans Zinsser was an intimate friend of Brooks's. I went to him and said, look here, I'm writing such and such a book, saying such and such things—told him the whole argument and all the points I intended to make, reading him some of the passages I had written. I offered to do either of two things, drop the book entirely or rewrite it centering the argument on someone else and leaving Brooks entirely unmentioned, if he thought that it would have a bad effect on Brooks, wound him personally, or affect his future. It was the first time I had met Hans and one of the most profound friendships of my life began that day.

Hans first said that he did not think my book would have a bad effect on Brooks, that if it had any effect at all he thought it would be a good one. Then he turned to and preached. He said, you damned young fool, this is your book isn't it? you mean and believe what you say, don't you? then what in hell do you mean by taking into account anything except what you conceive to be the truth? He laid into me as few ever have, and I went away and took up my stand at the passages of Jordan. Ever since then I have tried to concentrate on the idea, whether Brooks's or anyone else's, and to disregard the personality of its begetter, along with its psychological origins.

Incidentally, in what I said in the book about *Arrowsmith* I was paraphrasing Zinsser. Or, more accurately, my ideas about science in general and about bacteriology in particular, are in great part the result of years of intimacy with him. (Also with L. J. Henderson, Pete Bridgman, and a lot of lesser lights. I suppose I have had more intimate associates among scientists, especially medical researchers, than among any other species. Tie this up, if you like, with my own frustration. I didn't become a writer by first intention. All through Harvard until the war I was aiming at psychiatry. The war cost me what I have always regarded as my career.[1]) Specifically, I remember one phrase of Hans's. You remember Arrowsmith's prayer. Hans picked it up one evening and read it aloud. He said, "That makes me want to puke—how about you?"

As for your letter, all I'll say now is this: you may not realize it but you issue a dangerous invitation. In effect you're calling on me to write another book. At the moment that is probably actionable under some war statute. When I write at, as we say, length, I'll tell you about a couple of books I've thrown away.

                                                                    Yours,

TO WINFIELD TOWNLEY SCOTT[2]

                                                                    April 29, 1944
Dear Scott:

Compared to some of the blockbusters that have been falling on me, your dissent is mild, sweet and perfumed with mignonette. Although I was adjudged not to be a criminal Thursday, I am still far too involved with the

---

[1] This statement, as indicated on p. 30, does not seem to be true. Neither his Harvard record nor his correspondence nor the reminiscences of people who knew him in the Harvard years indicates any medical intention. Nevertheless, there was a spoiled medic in him, as well as a spoiled psychiatrist, and he did seek the company of scientists and doctors; and when he inserted some surgical scenes in his novel *Mountain Time* (1947), he had numerous letters from doctors and doctors' wives praising the accuracy of his medical fiction.
[2] Then literary editor of the Providence *Journal*.

Strange Fruit episode to reply to you at length. I will, however, say something about your two principal questions.

My fifth chapter is not written to assert the superiority of scientific knowledge over any other kind or to maintain that the United States in either of the periods touched upon in it was Utopia. I merely say—here are various kinds of endeavor and experience which were unquestionably fine, virtuous and in the best sense of the word cultural but which nevertheless are left altogether out of account in the appraisals I have been dealing with. Since they are left out of account, it seems to me that the appraisals are to that additional extent unsound. Since they did exist and were what I say they were, our civilization was better and healthier than the appraisals made out.

Your next question follows directly. Beginning on page 153 and continuing down to the last paragraph on page 164, I rapidly outline matters which must be taken into account in order to explain the nation and its moods in the 1920s. It seems to me that you, in common with practically everyone else who has reviewed the book, ignore that passage altogether. It is heaved straight at you as if to say—here, these things are the true explanation of the data with which the critics I have denounced were trying to work. I should have indeed been foolish, more foolish than I think I am, and certainly less expert at controversy, if I had said or anywhere assumed that there was nothing wrong with American life during the 1920s. What I have tried to do is to denounce errors and particularly errors which seemed to me superficial and even idiotic, and to open avenues of approach which will in the end produce valid judgments and useful results. I also call your attention to the fact that I say repeatedly that sometimes I am forced to deal with aspects of a writer's work which may be only minor aspects. I am pursuing what seems to me the cardinal error. Obviously it differs in extent and intensity from writer to writer and from book to book. I am making a qualitative analysis, so to speak, and not a quantitative one.

The more thoroughgoing and exhaustive study which you call for certainly needs to be written. That is not my business, for I have other things to do. What I hoped to do was merely to roll a boulder into the garden sufficiently big and sufficiently heavy to remain in the way of anyone who approaches the ultimate job. There it is and whoever does attempt a more conclusive study will have to deal with it. It will warn him to be more thorough, more profound, wiser, more honest, and more knowledgeful than the boys I am dealing with.

Now you can do something for me. You seem at once sympathetic to me and objective toward the controversy—a description which does not fit many of my adversaries. I did not suppose that the boys would take the book lying down and was prepared for exactly what has occurred (except Red's piece,[3]

[3] Sinclair Lewis's "Fools, Liars, and Mr. DeVoto," about which at this time a furious controversy was raging, DeVoto's friends and enemies both pitching in to flood the *Saturday Review of Literature* with letters and comments.

for which I am eternally grateful, since it goes far toward establishing my thesis for me). But I was not prepared for the accusation that the book is written in an angry state of mind. I am honestly surprised by the accusation and honestly do not believe it is. It seems to me cool, reserved, qualified, and tranquil in tone. I think perhaps I was unduly rough on Geismar, but it seems to me that everything else in the book is said reasonably quietly. What I wish you would do is to comment on this impression of mine and point out specific passages which are angry and extreme if you find such. I mean, do this in a letter to me, not in your sheet. I am not making any public rejoinder to anyone. I have said my piece and it is now the boys' turn to say theirs. I privately agree with what you say in your letter about my overrating Brooks's books. His mind seems to me effeminate, soft, and diabetic—with a sugar content altogether intolerable. For purposes of analysis I had to take him far more seriously than in reality I do. Through twenty years I have hoped to center such an analysis as this book makes on Lewis Mumford, but it is only when I am out of touch with his books that the idea seems possible. As soon as you approach his books you see that he has nothing that can possibly be described as a mind or a philosophy and that what he substitutes for them is at once too invertebrate and too slippery to be held long enough for even the briefest analysis [. . . .]

Yours,

TO NORMAN COUSINS

DeVoto had elected not to reply to Lewis's attack, because he felt that Lewis had not addressed himself to the ideas at issue, but had instead made illegitimately personal remarks about DeVoto's motives, personality, and appearance. When the letters page of the Saturday Review *continued to print letters with similarly personal comments in them, he wrote Norman Cousins to protest. Cousins replied, essentially, that the letters run were statistically more for him than against him. DeVoto in turn replied that he was not objecting to numbers, or even to adverse criticism, but to the nature of the criticism. In the end, he blamed Cousins at least as much as Lewis for what he thought a foul*

blow, and some of his more personal
letters, as for instance his December 4,
1950 letter to Garrett Mattingly, speak
slightingly of Cousins's intelligence and
integrity. This was unfair and unfortunate.
Cousins himself, reviewing The Uneasy
Chair *in* Saturday Review/World, *April 6,*
1974, reported his own awkward position as
a young editor forced to try to contain the
Lewis fury, and his regret at the way the
controversy developed.

May 8, 1944

Dear Cousins:

This is not for publication. Don't publish any part of it and don't allude to it in print.

When I talked to you in New York a couple of weeks ago I understood your position to be this: in the situation that had arisen you conceived that the most equitable solution was to permit Red Lewis to make a personal attack on me, but you nevertheless regretted the personalities and would have preferred to conduct the discussion of my book on the basis of its ideas only. You will remember that, in this understanding, I made no protest beyond formally telling you why I thought Red's article should not have been published.

I cannot see wherein such a position requires you to go on publishing further personal attacks on me, as you have done on the letters page in two issues since Red's original piece. Granting your conviction that you had to let Red say his say, what requires you to run serial personal abuse of me? Neither freedom of expression nor frank and full literary discussion is at stake on your letters page. What appears there is entirely up to you. You are under no ethical or journalistic obligation to publish anything at all there. Still less are you under any obligation to publish illegitimately personal remarks about me. There comes a point where every editor must remember that freedom of speech is a guarantee of protection to the speaker, not a compulsion on the editor. It seems to me that that point has been reached and passed in the *Review*. I continue to believe that the publication of Red's piece debased literary discussion. But whether it did or not, the continued publication of personal attacks on me does increasingly debase such discussion. I ask you to put a stop to it. Publish anything you like about my book, its ideas, its judgments, or its conclusions, but stop permitting correspondents to make personal slurs on me.

In the current issue, for instance, Melville Cane's couplet is entirely illegitimate. In the first place, there is no way in which I or anyone who accepts my critical thesis could reply to it. In the second place, it is made in an

131

area entirely outside the issues raised by my book. If it is not a personal slur on me, if it is legitimate literary discussion, then there is no validity whatever in any literary criticism. If my book is to be answered by saying that I am jealous of the writers it deals with, then any review of any book in your columns and any critical judgment expressed on your editorial page is to be rebutted with the same accusation, as you know quite well. By what principle of free speech or open literary discussion do you give it your editorial okay?

Now look at the second paragraph of the letter by Charles Raddock—a name, by the way, which does not appear in the New York phone directory. What in hell do you mean by permitting a correspondent to speak of my "maniacal ravings"? Granting that you felt obliged to let Red use similarly intemperate language about me, what is your obligation to let any casual bystander use it? Granting your correspondent's right to express such ideas, what is your obligation to let him express them in the *Review*? Of your own certain knowledge you know that there are no ravings in my book and that I am not a maniac. Neither Henry Canby nor George Stevens nor I ever permitted anyone to use such language in the *Review*, and I say quite soberly that I believe I am the only writer ever attacked personally in its columns. You permit the personal attack to go on week by week. Just why?

I call your attention to the further fact that no such abusive phraseology as "maniacal ravings" appears anywhere in my book.

Your correspondent goes on to say that I am not creative enough to be a novelist or scholarly enough to be a historian. When you permit him to say so, you stultify yourself and your predecessors. The *Review* took my four novels quite seriously when they were published. On another page of this same issue there is an editorial suggestion that a book of mine may well have deserved the Pulitzer Prize in history. Which is the responsible attitude, or are both attitudes irresponsible? But quite apart from that question, is the way to rebut what I say in my book to allege that I lack creativeness and scholarship? Must not the rebuttal instead be made *ad hoc*, with specific reference to statements made in the book? Your correspondent's letter is altogether outside the bounds of legitimate controversy: it should never have been published. My book nowhere makes any judgment on the motives of the men I was writing about. It deals exclusively with what they wrote. What have my motives, real or alleged by a correspondent, got to do with the truth or falsity of what I said? By what principle of literary discussion do you sanction correspondents to attack my motives instead of my book?

To sum up, no attack on the ideas of my book, however violent, will draw any protest from me, but I call on you to give no further editorial sanction to libellous and abusive attacks on me personally. Controversy is good journalism but if you are unable to hold the controversy to the issues raised by my book, then bring it to an end.

Finally, you have by now put me in an extremely embarrassing position. When Amy[1] asked me two weeks ago to do certain reviews, I could only say that I thought it improper to do so at present. On Friday Henry[2] asked me to write a piece for the forthcoming anniversary number. Because of my long friendship with and loyalty to Henry, and because I once edited the *Review*, I certainly ought to say yes. But I cannot see how it is possible for the *Review*, without making itself ridiculous, to publish both stuff by me and stuff which attacks me personally. And I cannot see how I could retain my self-respect and still write for a magazine which regards personal attacks on me as legitimate journalism.

Sincerely yours,

TO A MR. ALFONTE

May 9, 1944

Dear Mr. Alfonte:

Usually I do not answer intemperate and denunciatory letters. But yours roused an echo in my mind and set me searching through my books for a passage it dimly reminded me of. I have just found the passage and I am going to quote part of it to you.

"There was a little revolt of one against the process of education at Vanderbilt University in the spring of 1891. The rebel was the son of a clergyman in Georgia, densely shocked when a professor gave him translations from Haeckel and a classmate advised him to read the perfumed insufficiency of Ernest Renan's life of Jesus. Rebellion carried him through a quarrel with a young instructor and into the office of the chancellor, a Virginian gentleman named Landon Cabell Garland. The boy stammered out expostulations; biology, agnosticism and the sinfulness of the French language bubbled together in his head and, being a Georgian, he had committed an oration before the old mathematician said in his thin, aged drawl: 'Men never amount to much until they outgrow their fathers' notions, sir.' . . ."

The passage begins the chapter called "The Unholy Host" in Thomas Beer's *Mauve Decade*. You would find it profitable, I think, to read the whole chapter, even the whole book.

For your letter dismays me. It dismays me as a former college teacher, as a former officer of the United States Army, and as a student of American culture. By one of the pleasant coincidences that make a writer's life amusing, I received in the same mail with your letter another one which says almost

[1] Amy Loveman, book review editor of the *Saturday Review*.
[2] Henry Seidel Canby, the founder and first editor, whom DeVoto succeeded in 1936.

the same things in very much the same language, and the other letter also is postmarked "West Point." But that West Point is one I had never heard of before, West Point, Kentucky, and the letter is by a boy who says that he is fifteen years old and a junior in high school. I can understand his state of mind but I cannot understand yours. You must be an intelligent young man or you could never have got so far as the Academy, but you have let anger, bigotry, and provincialism temporarily short-circuit your intelligence and betray you into a very stupid act. An act not only stupid but of a highly dangerous kind.

In the first place, at your age and the present state of your education you should be able to examine and discuss ideas, even ideas you dislike, objectively, impersonally, with detachment and a cool mind. In the second place, you should be able to recognize irony when you read it. The current Easy Chair[3] says exactly the opposite of what you have taken it to say. And, whatever it says, you have responded to it not as an educated man but as an unstable and bad-tempered child. That does not speak too happily about your mind or about your future success in accepting the responsibility of commanding troops.

I send you back your letter. I think it would be well, purely as a step in your education, for you to take the letter and the Easy Chair you have made an oration about to some older, cooler mind, perhaps to one of your instructors, and talk them over.

Sincerely yours,

TO NORMAN COUSINS

May 19, 1944

Dear Cousins:

You mistake my complaint. If you had filled your "Letters" page with unfavorable comment on my book and had published no favorable comment whatever, you would have had no kick from me. I am not interested in a plebiscite and I don't give a damn how the vote goes. Long before the book was published I expected it to be attacked vigorously and no doubt violently. I don't care how many letters attacking the book you may publish hereafter, and I don't care whether or not you publish any defending it. Even if I did care, I should hold my peace on the principle that so long as the letters in question are about the book, it is none of my business what you publish or whether you publish anything.

[3] An account of the Boston booksellers' censorship of *Strange Fruit*.

My letter to you the other day was not a protest against letters unfavorable to the book, and I have not counted and do not care what the score is pro and con. I was protesting against what seemed to me, and still seems to me, illegitimate personal abuse. I think I am sufficiently objective to dislike and protest personal abuse in a literary magazine, no matter whom it is directed against. If someone were to write in, for instance, saying something to the effect that Lewis is well-known to be a dipsomaniac and must have been drunk when writing his piece, or saying that for ten or fifteen years he has written undiluted tripe and must have been writing this time out of spleen, envy, malice, or whatever—in such a case I should say that the letter ought to end in the waste basket. I merely maintain that there is literary discussion and there is personal abuse, that they are not the same thing, and that whereas one is legitimate, the other is not.

It is, of course, perfectly possible to guess that Lewis's piece set the tone for the others you mention, that the discussion of the book would have been more objective if Red had been more objective. I do not raise that question, however, and I have no desire to hold either you or him responsible for what anyone else does.

As for my having primed the pump,[1] you can go through my book with a fine-tooth comb and find no personalities whatever in it. It is certainly a forthright stand expressed as vigorously as I am capable of expressing anything. I expected and continue to expect it to be answered just as vigorously. I cannot see, however, that vigor of intellectual argument requires or licenses anyone to assert that I am jealous, envious, or malicious, or that the book is composed of maniacal ravings, or that I am without imagination or scholarship. When you go on the air and talk about the peace settlement this principle is obviously clear to you. I cannot see why it isn't clear in the present case. If I am wrong about, for instance, Brooks, then the way to answer what I said about him is *ad hoc*. A correspondent of the *Review* who points out any error of fact, any misrepresentation of what Brooks has said, any misinterpretation of his text, any defect in my logic, or any gap in the case I make against him—any such correspondent will be legitimately replying to my book. Anybody who says instead that I wish to God I were as good as Brooks and that wish explains what I say will not be replying legitimately. I get the same type of argument on the *Strange Fruit* case. Christian Fronters write in accusing me of wanting to debauch pure Catholic girls. Southern orators write in asking if I want my daughter to marry a Negro. Both arguments seem to me at once irrelevant and illegitimate. For the decent dignity of literature I think similar ones should be kept out of literary criticism.

[1] Cousins had suggested that DeVoto invited intemperate criticism by the intemperateness of his book. Cowley too, among others, thought the tone "angry." Quite evidently DeVoto was not aware of having been especially forceful, or at least personal, though friends of Brooks's might well have thought otherwise.

Precisely that may be an over-sensitiveness about Mr. Raddock's name. I wondered if it were an alias. Every day I get anonymous and pseudonymous letters about *Strange Fruit*. I am beginning to get some about *The Literary Fallacy*. I do not like them and I am glad that Mr. Raddock's was not what I took it to be.

Sincerely yours,

TO MALCOLM COWLEY

June 1, 1944

Dear Mr. Cowley:

I learn that your dinner is to be June 28. The trouble is that on June 20 I'm taking my family to the shore, at precisely the most inaccessible spot on Cape Ann.[1] That would be no bar to our getting together if there were gasoline, but the train service to Gloucester is not all it should be and the bus service from there on is not only vile but unpredictable as well. What makes it worse, the telephone company took out all phones during the winter and will restore none of them. If we're going to meet then, we'll have to calculate with a slide rule, days ahead.

I'm coming to New York Sunday, June 4, and will stay over Monday and take the Owl home that night. I suppose you won't be in the city on Sunday. Will you be there Monday? If so, will you stay in and have dinner with me? I'm signed up for lunch and up to seven o'clock, but won't you make any arrangements for dinner and the evening? Send me a postcard or leave word at the Harvard Club, where I'll be staying, and if you can come, I'd like you to. If you can't, I'll try to tear a hole out of the middle of the afternoon, if you can see me then.

I have it in mind that I was going to write you a long exegesis. My impulse faded after you decided that I am making war on writers and literature whereas Archie and the others[2] aren't. I'm not, and I think you ought to know I'm not. You quoted[3] a paragraph about the correspondence between the description of American culture in the literature I was talking about and the description of it in the geopolitical and other political literature in Germany. You say I leave the reader to infer that a variety of American

[1] For a number of summers DeVoto and his family occupied a cottage on the Ames estate at Annisquam.
[2] Both Archibald MacLeish ("The Irresponsibles") and Van Wyck Brooks ("On Literature Today") had been led by crisis patriotism into attacking the writers of the twenties, for reasons that looked superficially like DeVoto's, but that he declared erroneous.
[3] In Cowley's review of *The Literary Fallacy*, *New Republic*, April 24, 1944.

writers were originally responsible for the German plans against us, etc. Excuse me, but I don't—read the paragraph again. I certainly do say that the geopoliticians and the general staff used that description as data. That's a matter of fact—not of opinion. The publications of the Geopolitical Institute and a lot of lesser stuff, including Spengler, do in fact analyze and describe American culture, life, and ideals in precisely the way I'm talking about. I can cite it to you by the barrel. Later on, you say, "It was Hitler, not Haushofer or Spengler, who determined German policy . . ." I don't say that Spengler did, though he had a strong influence on Haushofer, especially his stuff later than *The Decline of the West.* I do say that Haushofer worked absolutely in cooperation with the General Staff, that he perfectly expresses the General Staff's ideas, and that the General Staff can't be ruled out of the picture as easily as you rule it out. Neither of us can know, but I believe that the General Staff made the plans for the war, both the general and the specific plans, determined its date, and had primary charge of it down to the split over the attack on Russia.

I say that one of the mistakes the General Staff made was in taking the 1920s literary description of America at face value, as data. "Criminally responsible"—hell. All I say is the boys were wrong. As for making war on writers and literature, hell again. Does my obligation to defend freedom of speech and the dignity of literature require me to keep my mouth shut, suppress my own opinions about literature and refrain from pointing out what I take to be its mistakes? I'm literature too—are you making war on me when you say I'm wrong? Are you part of a black-hearted reaction that intends to hack and stab in an underhanded way and entertain your subscribers at the same time? Balls. Neither am I.

However, let's argue this out in person. If you can have dinner with me Monday—or Sunday, either, for that matter—send word to the Harvard Club. If not, let's appoint another time.

Sincerely yours,

TO PAUL KNEELAND

One of the things that made DeVoto most intemperate in his language was the suggestion that his language was sometimes intemperate. It was one of his quarrels with Time, *which habitually described him as*

"volcanic." Here he lights on a Boston
reporter who, he thought, was after "color"
at the expense of truth.

June 9, 1945

Dear Mr. Kneeland:

I was not going to say anything to you about the interview; but since you asked for comment I see no reason why I shouldn't supply it. From your point of view the sensationalism which you put into it doubtless is a success; but from my own point of view it is not only bad, it is misrepresentation. It is such a thorough and deliberate misrepresentation that since this is the third or fourth time something of the sort has happened with a Boston paper, your net result is that I am not going to submit to any more Boston interviews.

I pass over the inaccuracy of your background material which you worked up from some carelessly used source and then attributed to me. I pass up also the god-awful language which you put into my mouth, which you seem to think is clever, and which only in small part corresponds to the meaning of what I said to you. I pass these over altogether although I was taught that the job of an interviewer was first to get his facts right and then to write the interview in such a way that it didn't distort what the man interviewed had said.

My real objection to the interview goes beyond its inaccuracy and distortion. My opinions and my expression of them are no more violent than yours or anyone else's. I talked to you quite tranquilly, did not use superlatives, made proper qualifications and reservations, and in no way behaved according to your trite and quite false adjectives, verbs, etc. Such expressions as "bomb blast," "word-slinging," "pin-point bombing," "sockeroo sentence structure," "sizzling and seething," "eruptive" have no correspondence to what I said or to anything of mine you may have read. They are idiotic and, furthermore, they are not your own. You have simply picked up the language of *Time* which I mentioned to you, and which you specifically said, as you left my house, did not in the least correspond to what you had seen there.

There is no point in my protesting all this, but it harmonizes with earlier Boston interviews and points a moral. Apparently Boston interviewers are not bothered by inaccuracy or misrepresentation so long as they can get sensational results. I do not propose to let you or any other Boston newspaperman misrepresent or lampoon me any longer. You can tell the City Desk that interviews with me are out for good.

Sincerely yours,

TO HERBERT EVISON

Like many another man who had done work
for the government (he was then a member
of the Advisory Board for National Parks,
Historical Sites, Buildings, and Monuments,
working with the Secretary of the Interior),
DeVoto ran into the red tape of the
bureaucracy and the infuriating
incomprehensibility of its forms. Unlike
most of us, he rebelled, as in this note to an
official of the National Park Service.

December 3, 1948

Dear Mr. Evison:

It is precisely this situation that is going to get me out of all government service for all time and eternity. I could not possibly furnish any of the information you say is necessary except white copies from the book of Requests for Transportation originally sent to me and these concerning only the one-way trip from Boston to Washington. I have run into the same situation with the State Department in regard to my two weeks in Denver as a delegate to the Conservation Conference. It is not only maddening to try to supply these details, it is quite impossible. The blank itself is unreadable and the system of accounting idiotic beyond the conception of intelligent men. I am not even going to try to solve the puzzle. I will make the United States a present of my expenses as well as my time on both of those expeditions into the public service, but if the United States wants my services any more it can damn well send a car for me.

Sincerely yours,

TO THE EDITOR
OF THE NEW YORK *HERALD TRIBUNE*

DeVoto's fur trade book, Across the Wide
Missouri, *was stimulated by, and eventually*

contained, many watercolors by the Baltimore artist Alfred Jacob Miller, who had accompanied Sir William Drummond Stewart into the West in 1837. In writing his book, DeVoto had to instruct himself in the early painters of the West, including George Catlin. He was much helped by Dr. Robert Taft, a chemist at the University of Kansas, but little helped, as he felt, by the museums and art critics and art historians. His Appendix, "First Illustrators of the West," was a pioneering study, and remained the best, as well as the most provocative, until publication of Taft's Artists and Illustrators of the Old West; 1850–1900, *in 1953.*

In the New York Herald Tribune Books *for December 19, 1948, DeVoto reviewed Lloyd Haberly's* Pursuit of the Horizon, *a biography of George Catlin, and expressed his unfavorable judgment not only of Haberly's book but of much of Catlin's art. In reply, five museum directors and art critics signed a letter to the* Herald Tribune *defending Catlin as an artist and suggesting that DeVoto had no qualifications to have an opinion. They were Alfred Barr, of the Museum of Modern Art, Lloyd Goodrich, of the Whitney Museum, J. I. H. Baur, of the Brooklyn Museum, Dorothy Miller, of the Museum of Modern Art, and Holger Cahill, once director of the Federal Art Project—what amounted to the united art establishment.*

The confrontation was of the kind that DeVoto relished—himself against the solid front of official art criticism. Baur, Barr, and Miss Miller were quickly eliminated as opponents, and he settled down to deal with Cahill and Goodrich, who were more inclined to argue. With Cahill especially he went through a long examination of the status of Catlin scholarship and many

questions that touched it only peripherally.
He ended by admitting that he had been
wrong in some respects and expressing
gratitude to his instructor. By the letter of
June 24, 1949, after half a year of argument,
he is addressing Cahill in terms of real
friendliness. Later still they were allies in
the fight against the McCarthy witch hunts.
The best answer to a DeVoto left to the
body seems to have been a right counter to
the head.

The exchange begins with DeVoto's
letter to the Herald Tribune *in reply to the*
letter of the art critics. Or perhaps it begins
much earlier, with a footnote in Across the
Wide Missouri—*a challenging footnote that*
may well have smoldered in the mind of one
or more of the art critics: "There is no
dependable study of Bodmer. There is, in
fact, no such thing as systematic scholarship
in the history of American painting. Apart
from a small handful of books dealing with
individual artists there is no scholarship at
all. . . ."

January 3, 1949

Dear Sir:

Coarse, untutored persons who invade the monopoly of art criticism are always promptly set right but I hardly dared hope for such a list of twelve point heads as those who have written to you about Mr. Lloyd Haberly's book about George Catlin. Their joint letter has so much richness in it that I hardly know which aspect to reply to. Perhaps it is best to welcome them and their museums belatedly to what their letter calls "contemporary art scholarship." When I began to work on Catlin no scholarship whatever had been shown by these gentlemen or their museums about Catlin or indeed any other early painter of Indians and so far as I am aware none has yet been shown. The museum whose name Mr. Goodrich signs under his own hung three Catlin pictures in the 1945 exhibition called "The Hudson River School." They were not only dreadfully bad but so far below Catlin's average achievement that I had to protest in *Across the Wide Missouri* and suggest that an artist is really "entitled to be judged by his best work rather than his worst." In 1943 Mr. Barr's museum hung four Catlins of which only one was decently representative; the other three did him a serious injustice. For both exhibitions the paintings had obviously been picked at random. I found

141

and still find it impossible to believe that those who selected them had any acquaintance with the bulk of Catlin's work in the National Museum, the American Museum of Natural History, and elsewhere. I am one of the coarse and untutored but I must express my doubt that anyone at either museum or any of the other people who signed the letter to you are sufficiently well acquainted with Catlin to be qualified to express any opinion about him, apart from the perfumed infallibility of any art critic rebuking those who speak from outside the sanctuary.

I work in a field where the word scholarship is used seriously. To a serious scholar what the catalogs of the two exhibitions I have mentioned said about Catlin—even granting the inability of the average art critic to grapple with history at all—is merely funny, or would be if it were not so saddening in its revelation. If as the letter to you says contemporary art scholarship has caught up with Catlin, why does it not publish some of its results? Meanwhile, it is a precious thing that these people have put in print that Catlin "was a great painter of Indians." Now if they and their museums will inquire a little into other painters of Indians perhaps it will not be necessary for us uncircumcised to do their work for them.

Sincerely yours,

TO A MR. SABIN[1]

February 3, 1949

Dear Mr. Sabin:

My real offense was not that I expressed unfavorable opinions about Catlin but that I expressed opinions about painting, which a layman is not permitted to do. Art criticism is as tight a monopoly as any in the world and the consecrated never permit the vulgar to practice it unrebuked. Of the five people who signed that letter to the *Herald Tribune* none has given any public evidence that he knows anything whatever about Catlin and I doubt that any does. What makes the situation all the more amusing is that there is practically no such thing as historical scholarship in writing by art critics about American art. Of that five, Goodrich is an excellent biographer but neither he nor any of the others has any real sense of history or what historical scholarship ought to be.

Haberly's biography of Catlin is much worse than I said. It is a thoroughly preposterous job and should never have been published. For-

---

[1] Probably Edwin Sabin, a writer of historical Western books for boys, who seems to have commented on the critics' letter or DeVoto's reply.

tunately two other biographies of him are on the stocks. Both will be much better but I am afraid that neither will be as good as it ought to be for one is by an ethnologist who is irritated by Catlin's having wasted time as a painter and the other by an orthodox historian in whose ability to deal with artistic questions I have no profound faith.

It is good to hear from you and I take advantage of the opportunity to express again my enormous indebtedness.

Sincerely yours,

TO ALFRED BARR

March 16, 1949

Dear Mr. Barr:

I do not suppose that I take correction any more gracefully than the next man but I do try to take it. I was not able until a week or so ago to take the time to look up what you and your associates call "contemporary art scholarship concerning Catlin." My bibliography was complete up through 1945 and I have been unable to find anything since then that seems to matter much. Will you send me a list of references to look up.

Sincerely yours,

TO HOLGER CAHILL

April 11, 1949

Dear Mr. Cahill:

The simple truth is that I am caught between natural annoyance and an honest desire to repair my ignorance and correct my judgments if they are wrong. Five of you people sign a public letter about me, leading up to the announcement that "Mr. DeVoto will regret his statements when he has had time to familiarize himself with contemporary art scholarship concerning Catlin." When I wrote my book my bibliography on Catlin was, I have every reason to believe, complete to March 1, 1946. That is, as an experienced researcher I had sought out and studied everything written about Catlin up to that time. In addition to this, I had spent a very long time looking at and forming opinions about practically all the Catlin paintings, drawings, and prints in the United States besides making an exhaustive study of Catlin's ethnology, and so far as it affected my book, his biography as well. I had, and still have, no reason to suppose that I had missed anything important or that I had failed to qualify myself to say what I did about him.

When five leading art critics tell me that I will regret my statements if only I will acquaint myself with the results of art scholarship, I am naturally interested. I wrote to Mr. Barr, asking him approximately what I asked Mr. Goodrich in the letter which he passed on to you. He replied that he was unable to bring my bibliography up to date but had joined some colleagues in differing from me in my "qualitative judgment of Catlin as an artist." That seemed to me a very different thing from your common accusation that I was ignorant. I thereupon wrote to Mr. Goodrich, who passed my letter on to you without answering it. Now you tell me that "any differences I might have with you . . . would be differences of opinion." This again seems to me wholly different from accusing me of ignorance. Meanwhile Mr. Baur has published a short piece in the Bulletin of the Brooklyn Museum in which his principal reliance is my Appendix on Catlin but in which he makes a number of errors which, however insufficient my scholarship may be, I at least know enough not to have made.

What am I to think? Differences in opinion, and especially in esthetic opinion, are of no particular moment to any historian. He recognizes their validity and expects them. Assertions that he does not know what he is talking about, however, are something else. There will be later editions of my book and if the scholarship you speak of can repair errors I have made or correct misjudgments, I want to know where I can find it so that I can make use of it. On the other hand, if there is no such scholarship, it seems to me that you people should have attacked my judgments on entirely different grounds than the ones you chose.

Sincerely yours,

TO LLOYD GOODRICH

April 21, 1949

Dear Mr. Goodrich:

I am going to disagree with you sharply, so let me say at the beginning that I have the highest possible regard for your work. Your books on Homer and Eakins are on my shelves, and I have read your book on Blakelock and as well a good deal of your occasional writing. Without considering that I have any special right to speak, I think your books the best in American art

144

criticism and I may add that you are one of the few critics who write about American art who have a historical sense. Furthermore, I make no pretense that I have ever studied any artist as thoroughly as you have studied many and I should never set up my opinion against yours in fields about which you are entitled to speak—though if the question were one exclusively of individual taste I should not hesitate to do so even there.

Nevertheless I take issue with you both over the original letter you people wrote to the *Herald Tribune* and in much of what you say in your letter to me.

To begin with, I think that if the phrase "contemporary art scholarship concerning Catlin" does not describe your objection to my review, you ought not to have signed the letter without saying that it did not. To go on with Catlin, the criticisms I made in my review roughly agree with common criticisms made of him during his lifetime, which as a historian I took care to consult and which I can cite to you voluminously, and with those made of him during the twentieth century so far as there are any. I have found no one of any pretense to authority who ever considered him "one of our great native painters," on any except ethnological grounds, and since the future is an open field I am certainly entitled to believe that no one ever will. Both the critics of his time and his fellow painters said approximately what I did of him—you will find this developed at proper length in my appendix, "The First Illustrators of the West" in my *Across the Wide Missouri*, where I did not have to work under the space limitations of a review. What is more to the point, I am by no means convinced that a thorough study of his painting by anyone will justify what you say in the first paragraph of your letter to me, whereas I am convinced of two things: that it will substantiate what I have said about him at least as an informed personal opinion, and that it will prove what Haberly said about him excessive to the verge of absurdity.

You would not, of course, have to make anywhere near as long a study of Catlin's paintings as I did in order to speak authoritatively about them. You will forgive me, however, if I obstinately continue to believe that you have not as yet studied them thoroughly enough. Your membership on the Smithsonian Art Commission does not necessarily mean that you have spent long hours studying the canvases stored in the museum's top garret, and your letter contains implicit evidence that you have not done what is necessary before you can speak authoritatively on what I have done, that is compare Catlin's paintings with those by contemporaries of his who painted Western Indians.

I am afraid, too, that what I said about the institutions of the signers of the original letter will have to stand and the paragraph on your second page does not make me change my mind. All the artists you name except Seth Eastman are irrelevant to the point at issue, and you are as wrong as it is possible to be when you say that Seth Eastman was quite unknown until your exhibition of 1935. I cannot remember a time when I, for instance, did not know him, and the reasons which made him known to me have always made him known to such students of early Western painting as there have been, to all historians of the West, and to all ethnologists. The simple fact that he illustrated Schoolcraft's big work has kept him alive, for everybody who works with either Indians or the frontier knows Schoolcraft. I first saw the Eastman paintings in the committee room of the House Committee on Indian Affairs at least 20 years ago and historians have talked about him for a generation. The standard discussion of his work was published in 1932 by the institution of whose art commission you are a member. I believe that the Whitney Museum did not have space to hang the three canvases by Alfred Jacob Miller that the catalogue of the show lists, though I grant you that the Art Institute did hang them. But your catalogue note contains unpardonable errors and the simple fact is that it was I, a historian, who introduced Miller, one of Catlin's immediate contemporaries and direct rivals, to the public and who did all the scholarly work on him that the five of you and your institutions should have done before saying in print that I did not know what I was talking about. It was the art department and the art museum of the University of Michigan that did the conclusive work on John Mix Stanley, and it was David I. Bushnell, Jr., an ethnologist, who did the pioneering work on him. It was the Bureau of American Ethnology that did the work on Friedrich Kurz. It was the Indiana Historical Society that did the work on George Winter. It was the Missouri Historical Society and an art museum certainly provincial from your point of view that did the work on Charles Wimar. As for systematic study of the whole field of early painting on the Western frontier, absolutely all that has been done is that by Dr. Taft, the chemist I mentioned, and none of you signers and none of the institutions you represent have so far done any at all. None of you or your institutions have done any work on Catlin comparable to that published as an appendix in my book, and I remain entirely skeptical of your qualifications even to pass judgment on my work, still less to dismiss it as cavalierly as you did. The first paragraph of your letter to me strengthens my skepticism.

A touch of farce is added to the situation by Dr. Baur's "After Catlin" in the fall Bulletin of the Brooklyn Museum. Not only does he speak of my appendix as "a good discussion of the roles of Bodmer, Miller, and Catlin" and not only does this particular footnote clearly rest on me and Dr. Taft, but the body of his article contains both a number of errors which I know too much to make and also implicit evidence that his acquaintance with Catlin's work is superficial and incomplete. There is no point in enlarging on this, though if you care to know what the errors are and why I use the words superficial and incomplete, I will be glad to tell you. To make the farce even more pointed, he confines his evidence for Darley's having been influenced by Catlin to the illustrations in Catlin's book (surely Catlin is not being a good draughtsman in those illustrations, he is not even being as good a one as he is in his paintings), whereas if he had gone only a little farther and consulted the lithographs he would have found better evidence.

In the first paragraph of your letter you speak of "the present critical rating of Catlin." What I originally asked you and what, as a man who wants to give his work as much authority as possible, I ask you now, is where I can find the studies that express that rating. When I originally wrote to you I felt reasonably sure that there was little "contemporary art scholarship concerning Catlin," and your letter, those I have received from other signers of the protest, and my efforts to find articles about Catlin in the art press have strengthened my belief.

Mr. Barr writes me that he is not qualified to express judgment on my scholarship—though he did not hesitate to do so in print. You write me that you regret having questioned it, adding quite irrelevantly the obvious truth that in the field of art it is not comparable to that of the signers of the letter but omitting the equally obvious truth that those signers have as yet given no evidence of having done any scholarship at all in the one field of art which I have entered. Mr. Cahill writes very pleasantly and informatively but wholly omits to name any articles or books in the field that I may have missed. Mr. Baur relies for his scholarly background entirely on me. I have not written to Miss Miller but I find in the usual indexes no bibliographical entries which suggest that she is entitled to pass judgment on what I said. Nevertheless, all five of you are willing to tell the public that I have spoken without qualifying myself to speak and all five of you are willing to support that very serious accusation with the weight of your titles and the institutions you serve. By the standards of scholarly objectivity in my profession this adds up to something other than ethical conduct. In history one either shows cause or keeps his mouth shut.

Is it not a fact that there is practically no recent art scholarship concerning Catlin except that, good or bad, contained in my appendix? Is it not a fact also that my real offense in your eyes is not having underrated Catlin but having expressed opinions in the field of art criticism which you believe no layman should enter?

Sincerely yours,

TO HOLGER CAHILL

June 24, 1949

Dear Mr. Cahill:

I am very glad to have your letter and very grateful too. If the original letter to the *Herald Tribune* had been written in the same spirit, I should never have made any protest of any kind. I did think the original letter unwarrantedly condescending and much in the spirit with which I had been received at various museums. . . . You will understand that my feeling was not diminished by finding Mr. Goodrich's name signed to it. I deeply respect his work and should never dream of questioning his authority in any field he might have studied, but I had what I regarded as an excellent reason for assuming that he had not studied Catlin. While I was working on Catlin and on Miller I happened to be in the Old Print Shop one afternoon and complained to Miss Bartlett Cowdrey, the author of the book on Mount, that I was finding it difficult to get aid and direction about either of them. She suggested that I might phone Mr. Goodrich and when I said I did not know him, she phoned him and I talked to him. In regard to both Miller and Catlin he said I can do nothing to help you. I took this to mean I know nothing about them. Since I had seen nothing about Catlin by him when the *Herald Tribune* letter appeared, I assumed that the original condition still held, and I felt that one who knew nothing about Catlin was not precisely qualified to pass judgment on my work.

I think that some of the objections you make to what I say about Catlin are entirely correct and just and I will accept the corrections and act on them. I think that some other things you say are open to argument and if I do not get the chance to argue here, I will hope to find leisure for clear thinking and clear writing about them sometime during the summer [. . . .] Let me make some running comments on your letter now and postpone till later things that need to be looked up or formulated with care.

I think that in the end there is likely to be less disagreement between you and me on Catlin than on the Indians. I am not sure how far we disagree even there. I feel to the full the barbarous injustice of the white man's dealing with them and especially that of the American white man. At the same time I believe that, up to a very small tolerance of possibility, what happened was historically inevitable. There are historical inevitabilities and granted the American continent and the American people in the 19th century what did happen, or something only very slightly different from it, must happen. I respect and honor the Indians' fight for their country and I have tried whenever I have written about them to do justice not only to their cause but also to their ways of thinking. I do believe that we tend to make many mistakes about the Indians out of our own sense of guilt and that some of the most liberal and advanced ideas about Indians today are in fact sentimental and unsound. Thus when we praise them for their collective life in terms of a non-ownership, non-profit-making collectivity which was from each according to his ability and to each according to his need, we are making so grotesque a misapprehension that it is hard even to analyze. What I suspect you might criticize in my feeling is a refusal to identify in Indian spirituality what a good many people claim to have identified there. Where some anthropologists, rather more artists and a great many arty people tend to find a mystic consciousness unattainable by white men and possession of great spiritual truths denied us, I tend to find the dreadful terror of the primitive mind. I trust that I reverence any man's religion but whatever flowered in art and ritual from Indian religion was nevertheless rooted in awful and hideous fears that civilization has made some slight progress in dissipating. The primitive mind is to me very much like the horrible jungle of what we have come to call the unconscious mind, and if I have a religion of my own it is that freedom from the terrors and compulsions of the unconscious is more greatly to be desired than anything else in the world and that either surrender to or subjection by it is most desperately to be avoided. Again, in spite of everything that was admirable and praiseworthy in the Indians' way of life, there was also more casual cruelty, more vocational war and murder, more focus on and admiration of violence and brute force and brute cunning than I can admire. Again, there are the qualities of mind that I summed up in the name of Francis Parkman in *The Year of Decision*— the lack of intellectual coherence, the servitude not only to terror but also to irresolution and mere whim.

This in general. I will make specific comments on what you say as I go through your letter [. . . .]

Page 70. I am not saying that the rituals of the medicine lodge were nonsense. I am saying that McKenzie's phraseology and indeed the entire document and the hocus-pocus with which he phrased and surrounded it were, in the circumstances, nonsense. The Indians certainly had no conception either of what was being said or what it meant in terms of the white man's concepts. As I have already said, I respect the religious elements of the medicine lodge and though the tortures appall me, I have never remotely dreamed of calling any part of it nonsense.

Plate xxvi. To begin with, I doubt your statement that Indians "can balance rhythmical elements which we whites simply cannot follow." I myself, though no musician, have had little difficulty in following any Indian music after some study. My wife, who is a musician, needs no study at all. One against seventeen is by no means impossible to white men. Nicholas Slonimsky is, of course, something of a genius but he will produce any opposition that you may call for within a second or two. In my living room we have frequently thrown combinations at him and he has at once produced on the piano simultaneous scales with both hands in combinations of five against nine, three against fourteen, or anything else. My ten year old son attends solfège classes at Melville Smith's Longy School, where it is quite ordinary to have children of his age doing at least the rudiments of this sort of thing. Professional musicians who are on Melville's faculty can apparently all do it, if not so spectacularly as Slonimsky. I have on my shelves a number of learned treatises on Indian music, such as Frances Dinsmore on the Pawnees, and in my time have heard a good many phonograph records of chants and dance rhythms. I think they yield easily enough to study but like any music different from our own it is certainly strange and I think ugly when heard without preparation. I would be perfectly willing, for instance, to call Chinese music monotonous in these terms, and I defend "caterwauling" as unquestionably representing the attitude of the traders at Fort Union and of Maximilian [. . . .]

Page 125. "Egotism and stupidity" refer directly to the battle of the Little Big Horn and I will stick to it. Custer was up to his old trick of disobeying orders for personal aggrandizement. It had happened before in the Indian country and it happened repeatedly during the Civil War. Both Fletcher Pratt and I have made a point of examining Custer's behavior and also his army reputation during the Civil War, and there is no doubt his courage was indisputable but so were his stupidity and intransigence. He was not to be trusted outside the personal gaze of his commander. I think three different commanding generals refused suggestions that he be given independent cavalry command. As for the Little Big Horn, I will rest on Frederic Van deWater's analysis in *Glory Hunter*, though I have independently studied the court martial records myself. He was certainly disobeying Terry's order. It is impossible to believe that the massacre would have occurred if he had obeyed it [. . . .]

Your page 5. I cannot love the religion of the piney woods people. I cannot, in fact, love the excesses of any evangelism or any religion that led to cruelty or torture or self-torture or dealt in terror, whether it be Protestant, Catholic, or neolithic. I was raised a Catholic but I am a historian and do not need reminders of what Catholicism has done. I agree with you that the Jesuits were wiser not only than the Protestants but than other Catholic orders, though I might make an exception so far as the Indians are concerned of the early Récollets in Canada. If I ever do my book on early exploration, I will treat in some detail the Spanish, the English, the French, and the Americans in relation to the Indians. I believe the Spanish were the worst, the French the best, and the English and the Americans the most non-human if not inhuman. I instinctively despise all efforts to Christianize primitive peoples but especially those whose real motive was economic. The Jesuits made dreadful mistakes and the earliest ones in Canada were diseased with holiness and martyrdom. A change came about in the 18th century.

Nevertheless, what I call the neolithic mind had a logic, a perception of reality, and a pattern of knowledge and response so different from that which we will agree to call civilized, or at least post-17th century West European, that they were altogether incommensurable in the time permitted. Making all humiliating acknowledgments, I must nevertheless choose the civilized over the neolithic [. . . .]

I am at a loss how to answer what you say about Catlin, Bodmer, and the others. I think that your criticism of what I said is on the whole just and true.

At the same time I would demur, at least in part, to some of the things you say. Obviously a long evening would do better than an unsatisfactory exchange of fragmentary arguments by letter.

I am quite honest in saying that I do not find in Catlin, either in his paintings or the illustrations to his book, the sense of space and loneliness that I do in Bodmer's best work. I will not argue with you about the portraits for, as I said, I believe they are his best work, and I have no complaint to make about them [. . . .] I cannot refer you to the originals in the Smithsonian but I looked at them all several times and studied a good many of them a good deal and they seemed to me in the end and on the whole monotonous and without feeling. I claim no technical or informed knowledge but I am at least sensitive to painting and to its effects. Much of this question hinges on what Catlin intended to do. I think that in the main he intended to be realistic and that he would have objected to your finding in his work some of the things you do [. . . .]

Irita [Van Doren] cut my review [of Haberly's book on Catlin which started this whole discussion] to fit her space and not the original allotment she gave me. It ran about 250 words more than she published. Part of them modified somewhat the severity of what I said about Catlin but her cuts modified the severity of what I said about Haberly. I doubt if anyone has considered Catlin a great painter—meaning by anyone, painter, critic, or student. I doubt if you do, though I have not, of course, read your book.[1] His great historical importance is not impugned by what I say. However highly you may rate him, do you expect that anyone—in the same sense—ever will consider him a great painter? I don't think you are entitled to hold me to an absolute anyone. I am willing to amend my judgment of his painting and his draughtsmanship somewhat on the basis of what you say in your letter. Nevertheless, I still think him considerably inferior to Bodmer and to such men as John Mix Stanley and Seth Eastman. Is his draughtsmanship, in fact, or his painting either, as good as Charles Wimar's? Perry Rathbone[2] has quite vigorously asserted to me that it is not. I have not seen the paintings of George Winter but I have the Indiana Historical Society's volume with six black and white and 31 color reproductions of them. I will expose my admittedly uninstructed judgment completely and say that it seems to me that Catlin was more in Winter's class than in Stanley's or Eastman's. Good as his portraits are, are they in fact as good on the whole as Charles Bird King's? Such people as these and Rindisbacher and James O. Lewis were the ones I was comparing him with when I wrote both my book and my review. I have no training in painting and make no claim that my judgment is authoritative. If it is academic, then it is so entirely by accident. I claim merely that I have thoroughly studied representative work by all painters

1 *Art in America*, with Alfred Barr.
2 Director of the City Art Museum, St. Louis.

with whom it seemed reasonable to compare him and that I have arrived at such judgments as I make by myself with the paintings before me. As for his reputation among his contemporaries, I investigated it thoroughly and I read what at the time I thought to be everything written about him in the twentieth century, and it did not seem to me that my judgment was very far out of line with the judgment of either age. You obviously are entitled to speak with authority and it behooves me to reconsider what I have said. At the same time, I should like to know how you rate him comparatively with such men as I have named or with the group who followed very shortly after him, say Caleb Bingham. I will get your book as soon as the pressure on me relaxes a little and will study it with the utmost attention. I very greatly wanted authoritative treatises on the subject to guide me when I was working on the book and I am very sorry I missed yours.

I repeat, however, that Haberly's book is really a very bad one. That is a judgment I am not likely to modify.

I have written this letter at odd moments over a considerable time. It certainly lacks continuity and I have probably failed to make myself clear. Let me add that I thoroughly enjoyed your letter and believe that you have taught me a good deal. I hope that we may sometime discuss these matters in person.

Sincerely yours,

TO E. B. LOOMIS

*Now and then the mail stimulated by his
Easy Chair essays got under DeVoto's skin.
The one replied to below was a
contemptuous commentary on his nostalgic
tribute to Don Marquis, entitled "Almost
Toujours Gai," in the Easy Chair for March
1950.*

March 13, 1950

Dear Mr. Loomis:

I suppose you are free to write to me whenever the impulse strikes you and an unkind Providence gives me no defense. Let me say this, however: that Don Marquis passed out cold was a better man than you ever have been or ever will be, and that if you say in print what you said on your postcard to me I will take you apart in print. Of course you could not read *Archy and*

Mehitabel. You would have felt at home, however, if it had been Don's whim to get anthropomorphic about *Pediculus capitis*[1] or *Phthirius pubis.*[2] Next time you are moved to write to me be so good as to refrain from smearing dead men with your stinking ego.

Sincerely yours,

[1] The head louse.
[2] The crab louse.

FIVE
Certain Inalienable Rights

DeVoto's activities as a public champion of civil liberties and an enemy of all censorship and thought control began early and went on with absolute consistency (and increasing urgency) throughout his life. He had grown up as a part of the anti-Mormon minority in Ogden, he had been a radical instructor at Northwestern. Shortly after he came back to Cambridge to live, at the end of 1927, he had joined the rest of intellectual Cambridge in resenting the prosecution of James A. Delacey, proprietor of the Dunster IIouse Book Shop, for selling a copy of *Lady Chatterly's Lover*. It is that case to which the December 27, 1929, letter to the Boston *Herald* has reference. In September 1930 DeVoto ridiculed the Watch and Ward Society in an article, "Literary Censorship in Cambridge," in the *Harvard Graduates' Magazine*. But it was not until he acquired the forum of the Easy Chair in *Harper's*—a forum that for sixteen months was augmented by his editorship of the *Saturday Review of Literature*—that he reached his full stature as a civil libertarian.

Much of what he wrote on civil liberties appeared in the Easy Chair. Much of the correspondence on the subject that fills his Letters-In files was questions, anxieties, denunciations, or praises that came to him because of his public utterances. All his later stands—in defense of the novel *Strange Fruit*, in protest against the censorship of war news, in defiance of the snoop methods of the FBI security checks, in warning against the House Un-American Activities Committe and other congressional committees red-hot to resist the Red peril, and especially in stout defense against Senator McCarthy's cynical raid on the Bill of Rights—were taken on a single ground: that "alas, freedom of speech implies freedom of bad taste," and freedom of opinion the freedom of counter-opinion.

The curve of his civil liberties writings was from the literary to the political, but the principle remained the same. It made him wary of those who championed civil liberties for deceptive or partisan reasons (see the letter to Alice Dritz). It also led him, as in his defense of *Forever Amber* or the *New Republic*, to speak up for people and publications that he thought vulgar, cheap, foolish, or misguided. He was contemptuous of the *New Republic* all his life until it came under Senator McCarthy's threat. Then he rose up, club in hand, and would even have written for it, in its defense, in its own columns, if the chips had fallen that way.

True to his characteristic posture of independence from cliques, gangs, parties, unions, and intellectual fashions, DeVoto was politically a Mugwump. On several occasions, as during his brief alliance with Wendell Willkie and his later and deeper affiliation with Adlai Stevenson, he turned the Easy Chair into a forum for the independent voter. His loyalty was not to party but to principles of democracy. Systematic formulations in any other area moved him to vehemence or scorn, but the Bill of Rights, a systematic formulation of certain principles, had his total allegiance. His objection to systematists, whether puritan, Marxian, Freudian, or aesthetic, derived from their refusal to refer their logical constructs to the tests of facts and the will of the people, and their common tendency to impose their systems on other people for other people's good. Idealism, he said, was a cross-lots path to Berchtesgaden and St. Bartholomew's Eve. He would have agreed with Robert Frost, once his intimate friend, later his enemy, on such a man as Henry Wallace: "Henry will reform you whether you want to be reformed or not."

Democracy, by contrast, was an inductive form of political organization, and DeVoto trusted no method but the inductive. When L. J. Henderson, in a course in the history of science in 1915, directed DeVoto's mind toward the scientific method, he did a good job. The tree stayed inclined in the direction in which the twig was bent.

Except as a journalistic sniper and an avowed opponent of the idealistic and ambitious Left, DeVoto was not much involved in politics until World War II precipitated him into a campaign for morale and responsibility on the home front. By 1947, when his defense of the Public Lands began, he had been pushed into increasing political activity, had begun to know many members of the House and Senate, had begun to make frequent trips to Washington. Beginning in January 1948, he served six years on the Secretary of the Interior's Advisory Board for National Parks, Historical Sites, Buildings, and Monuments, and through all those years he was conservation's principal watchdog. In 1952, nudged along by his former students George Ball and Arthur Schlesinger, Jr., he joined Stevenson's campaign as a conservation consultant and speech writer; and during the last three years of his life, through close association with Schlesinger, John Kenneth Galbraith, and others involved in the organization of Americans for Democratic Action, he was a highly vocal part of Democratic national strategy and achieved the accolade of being publicly attacked by Senator McCarthy as "one Richard DeVoto," a Stevensonian subversive.

TO THE EDITOR OF THE BOSTON *HERALD*

December 27, 1929

To the Editor of the Herald:

Let it be observed that the season of goodwill, which began so dishearteningly for the Watch and Ward Society,[1] ended on a more hopeful note. Just at the moment of despair, when it seemed as if the society must continue its fight unaided, condemned by the unrighteous and jeered at by the damned, a new champion, desiring only honor, ranged himself on the side of purity. Few can behold unmoved the spectacle of Senator and Apostle Reed Smoot sitting down to read forty obscene books. For the corrupt, one such book at a time and at the normal intervals of literary accident must suffice. Only a person of unyielding purpose and holy zeal could sustain the boredom of forty. One thinks of the Senator from Utah keeping vigil while the heedless sleep, alone in the night, endlessly turning the pages of forty obscene books, for purity. Night after night, forty times horrified, forty times scandalized, forty times outraged, yet dauntlessly reading on. And on.

The self-sacrificing generosity of our guardians has seldom been more refreshingly exhibited. Surely the Watch and Ward will recognize in the Senator who undertakes to read forty obscene books at one high-minded effort, a resolution and a taste that are akin to their own. Surely they will give this recognition form by conferring on Mr. Smoot the privileges of membership and even office in their society. Let there be union in this cause; and they whom common desires can bring together, let them not be separated. This be their blazon: while one obscene book remains unread, the gentleman from Utah and the Watch and Ward will read it.

Politics, we are assured, make strange bedfellows; and yet, if the word be not unchaste, purity makes stranger bedfellows still. One had not expected to see Mormonism mingling with ideals so alien to it, but the recent crisis has shown that in this cause even social differences can be dissolved away. Some men, Mormons or Brahmins or mere parvenus, become aware of an inner urge, a consciousness that they are selected to watch over us and to ward away evil from us. They are our guardians, for a voice has told them so. Against the world they will defend us from what menaces us, and first they

[1] The Delacey case had brought Watch and Ward a lot of bad publicity, and many members had resigned in disgust.

will find out just what it is. They will expose themselves to what cannot harm them, who are clad in righteousness, but must surely corrupt us. It is for purity: it is for us. Be sure of that, and be sure also that they will suffer no obscene book to go unread. Yes, they will read them all. Forty at a time.

Sincerely yours,

TO ALLEN FRENCH

December 16, 1936

Dear Mr. French:

I am well aware that there are two sides to the question[1] and as I go on with it I will do my best to do justice to the other one. Nevertheless it seems to me that the side I am already committed to has overwhelmingly the better of the argument—both in theory and in actual practice. The theory is easy: no adult person is injured by reading anything, if he has a normal experience and a normal nervous system; if he is so neurotic that reading a book can influence him to socially undesirable action, he is constantly exposed to overwhelmingly more powerful stimuli than any book can contain, specifically sexual stimuli of the eye in modern fashions and modern advertising and modern movies and modern life in general, and of the ear in the music and other material that constantly assails him over the radio; the library is under no obligation to protect society from occasional neurotics, especially when such protection requires a limitation of the rights of normal people; if society must be protected from neurotics, it should shut up the neurotics and not censor the reading of normal citizens; a public library has no sanction of society to censor anything; the highest possible cultivation and the utmost possible education for all citizens is necessary for the maintenance of democracy.

The practical aspect is even simpler. You and I know that by far the greater part of the pressure brought to bear on library committees comes from questionable motives and personalities usually so distorted as to be plainly neurotic. I have had a part in resisting a good many such pressures— within four miles of your house in the Middle West and in the West. I have never yet seen a determined effort to resist such pressure fail. If library committees will act in accordance with their own enlightened judgment and then

[1] French, a troubled librarian, had written him about the pressures on librarians to censor the reading of the young, and of their possible responsibility in that regard. The stimulating cause of his letter was a DeVoto editorial in the *Saturday Review* condemning the Salt Lake City Public Library for keeping a Vardis Fisher novel under the counter.

actively resist the objections voiced to them, they will always win. When a neurotic is a member of a library committee, the only intelligent thing is for the other members to fight him (usually her) and either voice him down or get him expelled.

I have in my desk, and will publish when I can, a very realistic description of a library committee in a small Kansas town. The moral I draw from it and from my own experience in such matters is that such committees too often arrogate to themselves a moral superiority to, and protectorate over, the public they are supposed to serve, and too often regard themselves as an extension of benevolent foundations rather than as umpires of a literary and educational process. In a democracy the only tolerable censorship of books is not a moral, but an artistic one. No one objects, or can object, to a committee's refusing to buy a book on the simple ground that it is a bad book, but any taxpayer who may want to use the library has a valid objection when that committee denies him a book on the ground that it might hurt his morals. The committee has only a limited fund to spend. It should spend it according to its best literary and educational widsom—but it should leave its moral sense in the coatroom. These terms are not mutually exclusive, I know, but the more nearly the moral question can be isolated from the others and disregarded, the better for the public—or democracy is mocked.

This is my immediate response to your note. I expect to talk a good deal about various library problems during the next year and I shall certainly take this one up. I believe that the public libraries at this moment are among the most valuable institutions of democracy, and I intend to support them as much as I can.

Sincerely yours,

TO WENDELL WILLKIE

At the beginning of March 1944, while Wendell Willkie was campaigning for the Republican presidential nomination, someone called his attention to two DeVoto Easy Chairs. One, in January, had examined and repudiated the military pessimism of Colonel Charles A. Lindbergh and the defeatism expressed in Mrs. Lindbergh's The Wave of the Future. *The*

*second, in March, commented on the
apparent American fear of the coming
peace, the apprehension that war energies
could not be easily converted to peacetime
pursuits, that the censorship of wartime
might continue as a repressive force in
American life. Since these sentiments
matched his own, and moreover contributed
to a campaign issue that Willkie was
pressing, Willkie wrote DeVoto asking for
an elaboration of his ideas. In a speech on
March 24 he used a remark of DeVoto's
relating to the censorship of war information
by the Roosevelt administration and the
armed forces, and in a letter requested
documentation of DeVoto's feeling that the
American people knew less about the war
then going on than about any war in their
history. The association between the two
men, and DeVoto's rather odd position as
an adviser to the potential Republican
candidate, was brief, since Willkie withdrew
from the race after the Wisconsin primary in
April.*

March 8, 1944

Dear Mr. Willkie:

It must have been Mr. Huntington you talked to on the train. I have not been West for several years nor, though I desired it, have I had the honor of meeting you. However, I am glad that he called your attention to my Lindbergh piece and so presumably to the new one. I am very glad indeed that you are going to speak on the same subject.

Your speech is at, or very near, the heart of the problem and I agree entirely with its general burden. The fear of the peace is in large part due to our loss of confidence in ourselves, in our ability to manage our society, in our ability to master our economy. To a historian that loss of confidence is altogether astonishing. I agree wholly with you that a large part of it is due to our seeing power used irresponsibly after it had been granted in hope, to policies and procedures of the government which have tended to weaken our faith in our institutions, and to the development of ideas of government which some of us know and many more feel run directly counter to the traditions that have sustained us up to now. As you recognize, there are other elements as well in the fear of peace, but in all this and in all you say

162

about the abandonment of narrowly nationalistic economic policies, I wholly agree with you.

In fact, as a tired New Dealer, I am willing to go farther than you do in this speech. I voted for the New Deal three times and I have agreed with perhaps forty percent of its thinking and perhaps sixty percent of its ad hoc measures. Well, over the years I have come to believe that the administration —I do not mean Mr. Roosevelt but rather the whole complex of effective power—does not truly accept the democratic postulates on which it is supposed to be based. I think that it has been increasingly cynical about them, increasingly disdainful not only of democratic procedures but of basic democratic beliefs as well. I find too much willingness not only to circumvent constitutional procedures but to ignore the popular will and to be dishonest with the people. I have no idea whether or not Mr. Hopkins ever made that celebrated remark about the people being too damned dumb to understand, but I have come to believe that there is a New Deal assumption that they are too damned dumb to know what is best for them and so must be cozened, deceived, and tricked for their own good. I distrust professions of democracy which undertake to know better than the people themselves what is good for them. I find that they become actions which treat the tenets of democracy as just a lot of talk, that they turn the tenets of democracy into mere means of demagogic manipulation.

I don't know how many of us tired New Dealers there are. I think there must be a lot of us. In a couple of months I am going to write an Easy Chair explaining that any Republican candidate who is not tainted with isolationism, who will denounce isolationist support, and who will commit himself to the foreign policy to which you stand committed—any such Republican candidate can have us and no further questions asked.

Right now, however, it seems to me that the most serious offense against democracy is the timorous, crafty, or perhaps cynical failure to keep us informed about what is happening in the war—both strategically and politically. As a historian, I am sharply aware that the people of the United States have always known moment by moment far more about every other war they have been engaged in than they are permitted to find out about this one. It is our army, our navy, our foreign policy, our war, our peace to be, but we are told practically nothing about any part of it. In my opinion, that fact is the most serious threat to the kind of peace most of us hope for. I sincerely hope that you are going to make occasion to say something to the point.

Sincerely yours,

TO WENDELL WILLKIE

March 25, 1944

Dear Mr. Willkie:

This being Saturday, my secretary is not here and you will have to abide by my typing, which lacks beauty. Furthermore, since I want to get this off to you as soon as possible but must think out what I am saying as I write it, this will probably lack orderly sequence.

I should say that our experience in the Civil War and the Spanish War indicates the desirability of more government control over news than we had in either, and that our experience in this one indicates the great desirability of having much less than we are getting. With news so completely in control of the government I think it is inevitable that the administration, any administration, will use news for propaganda purposes, as in fact has been done, and the military will use the excuse of military secrecy to soften bad news for the public and to cover up military mistakes, as in fact has been done. If we are forced to choose between too much control and too little control of news, I am for choosing too little. If in order to keep the enemy in ignorance we must keep our own people in ignorance, then I am for giving the enemy information the moment it is safe to, and frequently when it is not safe.

It is most useful, I think, to set off this war against the Civil War. (There is no point of going back earlier than the Civil War since before then rapid communication was not possible and modern techniques of news gathering had not been developed.) There was very little control over reporters, correspondents, or editors, and practically none by the government itself. Stanton as Secretary of War frequently tried to stop or censor dispatches that came through Washington by telegraph but he only occasionally succeeded, never succeeded completely or for very long, and was easily out-maneuvered by the newspapers, which could send dispatches round Washington by courier or by other circuits. So completely were the means of communication in private hands, in fact, that occasionally the administration got its news of what was going on at the front by the courtesy or the sufferance of newspapers.

Apart from the Secretary of War, the only officials who could exert any influence on the handling of news were the generals in the field and those in command of departments. There is no blinking the fact that they had a lot of trouble with correspondents—that the average newspaper and the average newspaperman of that day recognized little responsibility, were quite willing to publish anything and especially if it were important or exclusive news, and frequently acted rashly, brashly, even recklessly and to the considerable prejudice of military actions. They reported what was going on in Washington and in the field so thoroughly and in such detail [that] through most of the war the northern newspapers, especially the New York newspapers, were the best source of military intelligence for Lee, other Confederate commanders, and the Confederate government. Furthermore, they made a lot of trouble. Few generals were able to control them. Only Sherman ever succeeded completely and Uncle Billy, who hated a reporter as he hated nothing else although he hated many things, only succeeded in the end by kicking them the hell out of his army—denying them access to any part of his command. They made a lot of trouble for Grant in the West and when he came East he tried to clamp down on them but he did not succeed. Some generals toadied and kowtowed to them to get publicity—and got it. A good many generals used them for their private political purposes. In the unlovely intrigues surrounding Fremont, McClellan, and Hooker, there were newspapers and newspapermen on both sides, working furiously. A good many generals furthered their own causes or attacked their superiors by way of newspapers. And so on—you know the story.

Well, it was not pretty and sometimes it was downright dangerous and did much damage. And yet—there was never a time when the people of the North did not have facts at their disposal. They knew what was happening, they could make up their minds about it, and that fact was, I think, fundamental in the preservation of Northern morale and in the eventual victory of the North. I applaud what you had to say yesterday about the Presidential campaign of 1864—I think you are absolutely right. But suppose Grant or the administration had tried to keep secret, or even to postpone, the news of, say, the Wilderness. The terrible bloodletting of those battles and their monotonous renewal to, seemingly, no decision was the hardest single strain of the war. But it was less terrible, less hard to bear, because the North knew, was completely told from day to day, just how terrible it was. There was no effort to censor that news, to delay it, or to moderate either its horror or the impact it had on the public. If there had been, I conceive that the people might have turned against the administration on Election Day. And so throughout the war. The reckless publication of news frequently embarrassed the administration and sometimes seriously interfered with military campaigns—but it also treated the American people as adults and it proved that they could take it. We are not being treated as adults now and I think there is a belief that we can't take it.

Two other influences should be mentioned. One is the fact that soldiers' letters were not censored. (There was, in fact, no censorship of mail until the first world war.) The families of soldiers thus found out what was

165

happening to the full, so far as the soldiers were able to see and understand it themselves. The other is the Congressional Committee on the Conduct of the War, whose sessions were public and whose activities were completely reported in the press. Now, the record of that committee is in many ways a black one. It attempted to usurp for Congress direct control over the military and their operations, as well as to interfere with Lincoln's functions both as commander in chief and as executive head of the government. It worked ferocious injustice on some commanders and acted with indefensible favoritism toward others. It was under the control of the "radical" wing of the Republican party and it played partisan politics throughout its course. Nevertheless, it did sift out and publicize all campaigns, innumerable actions, mistakes, failures, jealousies, and intrigues. Much of this was unquestionably in the public interest and I am not sure that the interest thus served did not considerably outweigh the obstacles which the Committee put in Lincoln's path. At any rate, this also helped to inform the people about the war and what was happening in it and helped keep them fully informed.

There can be no question that the American people were better informed about the Civil War than about any other they have ever engaged in. The excesses and abuses are easy to point out—and could be just as easily avoided by any administration which believed that the people have a right to be informed about the war they are fighting.

The other aspect is political. There is no point in rehearsing the stuff about freedom of the press; everyone knows that the administration was attacked violently and even treasonously all through the war by Democratic papers and radical Republican papers. Nor is there any point in summarizing the few suspensions and suppressions. Two New York papers were briefly suspended in '64 when they published a bogus Presidential proclamation, having themselves been three-quarters victimized by it. That was certainly close to treason. When Burnside, as departmental commander, suspended the Chicago *Times,* the *Tribune* of the period, Lincoln at once revoked his order. Two Baltimore papers, two New Orleans papers (these, of course, in or near Confederate territory), and a few others were suspended, a few were suppressed. But the point I would make is not this sort of thing but the fact that Lincoln's war policies were open and on the record throughout, as our foreign policies decidedly are not in this war. Nobody had any doubt what Lincoln's war aims were or on what principles he would make peace. He expressed them innumerable times, to inquiring editors, to Congress, in messages, in speeches, etc. It is possible to say, of course, that the aims of both war and peace were infinitely simpler than the present ones, but it must also be said that the domestic political situation and the emotional tugs on the public were infinitely more complex— and precarious. And it must also be pointed out that Lincoln both fought the war and maneuvered toward his peace aims, in all this open and public confidence, "with the enemy at our gates and powerful secret societies in our midst (and) without an Espionage Act." (The quotation is from Zachariah Chafee.) Here again, the essence of our tradition, of our democratic institutions, is full information and complete frankness. Lincoln was capable of the most delicate, secret, and exquisite intrigues in support of a policy—thank God—but he never hushed up a policy. He treated the Americans as adults.

I would also make the point that since the Civil War the press has developed a sense of public responsibility infinitely more serious and mature than it had during the Civil War. It would not endanger our success now, it scrupulously obeys the principles set for it. Any notion that it would do otherwise is cockeyed. My belief is that we are entitled to all the news that is not immediately dangerous to the success of operations actually under way or about to begin. We are not being given that, nor have we any voice in the principles that determine what we are given. I do not trust military men—they cover up for one another and their professional sense of caution is gargantuan. I think that we ought to be given all information about our war and peace policies up to the point where giving us more would actually and immediately endanger their success. I think that we ought to be given this information when our policies change, and I think we ought to be given the reasons for the changes. I think that we should be given all military and political information up to the point of immediate danger. And I think that democratic principles and procedure may frequently require us to be given information well past that point.

The Spanish-American War was a wild business, any way you approach it. The newspapers had a large part in bringing it on. They conducted themselves throughout it with little responsibility and no dignity whatever. In this they had the active cooperation of military men, including the senior Roosevelt, and sometimes of the administration. They published rumors and actual lies quite as freely as news and rather more often, since it was a foreign war and the radio had not been invented. There was very little attempt at censorship or any other kind of control. The public got an adequate idea of what had gone on eventually, but there was no way of giving it an adequate idea of what was going on. Nor were there any political issues at stake till the war was over. It has little teaching for us now.

In this war we get our news exclusively from handouts. War Department handouts, Navy handouts, State Department handouts, handouts from the press sections of the armies in the field. That system began in the first World War, but it was far from perfected then. The press was still felt to be a powerful institution and it was still acknowledged that the public had a vested right in the news. The techniques of news gathering and news transmission had not reached their present effectiveness and so coverage was both slower and more incomplete than is now easily possible. Moreover, the press had a far greater tendency than now to color facts for purposes of national propaganda—was, I mean, considerably less objective by first intention—and the roving correspondent of the time tended to be much less a newspaperman and much more a Richard Harding Davis prima donna than now. But for all this, we got more news from day to day, and that news was franker and more direct. The censorship was frequently silly but it was not as silly as it is now. No one doubts that, for instance, the mutinies in the French army or the pressures brought to bear on Pershing to brigade his troops with the Allies'—no one doubts that it was wise to censor those stories. On the other hand, the loss of an airfield or the loss of a ship would not have been held up till there was some good news to take the sting out of it. I am sure that the administration would not have stood for such finagling, and, though I may be a wide-eyed innocent, I tend to believe even that the high command would have scorned it.

It is also important that no one was ever in any doubt about Wilson's foreign policies and peace policies. He made his mistakes but also he, by God, made them in the light of open day. He told Congress and he told us—including you and me in the army.

Well, that sketches what I had in mind when I wrote to you before. I don't know if any of it will be useful to you. The supporting details are fascinating and any time you may have a moment for them, I will be glad to supply them. Or anything else I can supply you with that may serve you.

Sincerely yours,

TO ELMER DAVIS

DeVoto's campaign for less censorship of war news was accompanied during 1943–44 by numerous letters to and from his friend Elmer Davis, then head of the Office of War Information, who would have liked a far freer hand than the various executive and military limitations permitted him, and who welcomed—and just possibly incited—DeVoto's protests in the Easy Chair. The Willkie affiliation brought to a head, in the following letter, two years of mutual frustration and bellyaching.

March 28, 1944

Dear Elmer:

Certainly I've got a Program. In large part it's based on what has happened to OWI.

But first, Willkie left out of my brief original note to him only my clear notification that the stuff he did use was only part of the problem, the problem then being what I had diagnosed in the Easy Chair as a fear of peace. Since then I've supplied him with some more stuff, mostly about the Civil War. He's used some of it and I suppose he'll use some more. . . . But I don't expect to vote for him, I don't expect I'll have a chance to vote for him, and I certainly won't vote for any other Republican. I'd vote for Willkie, and not in any great belief in him either. I'd vote for him on a number of grounds. Right now, the best ground is that he is going out on the hustings and saying what's what, and he is showing a kind of guts that we are not seeing anywhere else in public life. When he told off Harrison Spangler[1] about the Irish vote the other day, I got out my remaining bottle of Glenlivet and drank to him. As late as 1944, then, the republic was able to produce a politician with guts enough to do that. I do not expect to see the like again. I do not in particular expect to see the like in our party. I do not expect to see Frank get up and tell the Irish to go to hell. I expect to vote for the Great White Father again, and in my opinion it is damn bad stuff to have to vote for a man whom one does not trust and to whom one is forced to ascribe the loss of the liberal cause. I think it's lost, I suspect you think so too, but I think Frank has to take the blame, whereas you don't. . . . Willkie, I think, as of today anyway, is likely to do us all one vast service. I think he's going to kill off Dewey, which will be a great service to the rest of us. I told you when I was in Washington that I thought Taft was the old guard candidate; I think so even more now. And that works out to the advantage of all concerned. It's possible to beat Taft, I think, and even if we don't beat him, at least he's in the open, we know what he stands for and on, and at least he does stand for and on something. Whereas what we know about Dewey is that he can be had by anyone for any purpose. He's on the town. He doesn't stand for or on anything whatsoever, and won't. Every time I think of him these days I remember Mark Hanna on Bryan, "Hesitate? Does a dog hesitate for a marriage license?"

Well, Program. I'd begin by telling people what is happening in the war and by talking in the open about our relations with other nations, allied, conquered and neutral. You know God damned well that if we mean what we say by democracy, that's the first step. You know it hasn't happened and you know it won't happen. You mistake me if you think what I want is some resounding summons from on high to get out and love democracy. When Hull writes an undergraduate theme about it, I just feel lower. What I want

[1] Of the Republican National Committee.

from on high is some simple democratic action. These things are really quite simple. The way to have an informed public opinion about the war is to inform the public what is happening.

When I say that the administration is cynical I mean a good many things besides the central one, but the central one is both simple and overpowering. It is cynical to set up OWI with the announced purpose of (as one function) keeping the people informed about the war, and then treating OWI as it appears to me to have been treated. It is cynical, in one specific instance, to leave you home when the administration goes to Teheran and then to keep you out of the White House till January 27, the last day I know about. It is cynical to make speeches about the basic freedoms of our way of life, naming a free press among them, and then permit the Army and Navy to prevent OWI from serving the function assigned it. It is cynical to set up an official agency of public information and then permit officers and subofficers of the administration to issue information to the public in the ignorance of that agency. It is cynical to make that agency the butt of public criticism when such practices as the above are indulged in. It is cynical to walk out from under, leaving OWI holding the bag, at the whim, or still worse at the political expediency of the administration. It is cynical to say officially that OWI is attending to matters which it is not allowed to attend to, and it is even more cynical to blame it in public for not attending to such matters.

It is cynical as all hell, and you know it is. I don't know about Roosevelt though I do suspect. I suspect, and this not only on the evident facts but also on years of wisecracks about the press, that he conceives the freedom of the press to be a freedom to serve the purposes of the administration. With a good many people in high places it is more than a suspicion. I know damned well that one alcove of the New Deal feels, as I told Willkie, that you don't tell the public anything except what will help you to accomplish your objects. Those objects are generally supposed to be things which are good for the public but which the public is too damned dumb to understand are good for it.

There is a hell of a lot more to it than information about the war and the peace. I do seriously believe that the New Deal has got tired, that it does not believe what it says, that it does not accept what I described as the democratic postulates. I think that in the last two or three years the New Deal has set back the cause of American liberalism, which it began by serving, very seriously indeed. I'm sore as hell. I am not, as you know, as far left as you are, but as far as I am there I am, and by God the New Deal is not. However, I would have to use up a ream of paper to discuss those things, and right now the important thing is news about the war and about our relations with other people.

Furthermore, you know damned well that I don't hold you responsible, that I think you have done far better than anyone else could have done, and that I honor you for what you have done as much as I do for what you have tried to do and been stopped. I've said so in the Easy Chair a good many times, and I've done what I could to make the Easy Chair express your point of view as I've understood it. I've even taken it in the pocketbook, since part of my trouble with *Collier's* is my prolonged explanation to Bill Chenery[2] of how much better you'd done than George Creel did. And for all that, I still say that you are not permitted by the Army and Navy or by the administration to treat the American people as adults or as functioning members of a democratic society. I still say that we know far less, dangerously less, than the tolerable minimum of what is going on in the war and what the government is doing about our relations with other countries. If Willkie says that we know less about this war than we did about any previous war we've fought, that's me speaking. By the book.

The first step in a Program, then, would be to tell us what is going on. I would inform the Army and Navy that they belong to the public and that the public is entitled to know what they are doing. (Don't forget that I spent something over two months reading secret documents and know clearly some of the things they don't tell.[3]) I would then see to it that they told. I would also forbid the administration to conduct its side of the war in the dark. In a word, I would permit OWI to serve the function for which it was publicly set up.

I don't love this Congress any better than you do. But the pat answer from my position is, first, that the administration, and in great part its cynicism, is responsible for the present state of Congress, and second that, by God, Congress is part of the government, the form of government we are committed to, and until that form is changed we have damned well got to work with it. If it comes down to fighting on the barricades, a number of us will have to fight on the Congressional side, for some of us suspect that it is no more democratic for the President to tell us we must circumvent Congress by means of executive agencies than it is for Mr. Pegler to tell the soldiers that they must circumvent it by, apparently, military soviets.

I'm afraid we're going to get Manifest Destiny but with content. I'm afraid the vets are going to be imperialistic as hell. Back about 1934 or thereabouts I sketched a deep suspicion that persuasive reasons were going to be found eventually for an American Century which would consist of an altogether benevolent but toothed expansion southward. I think that goes as originally said, and I think it will be only part of the vets' program over the next twenty years. Or rather, I'm afraid. I still think it can be stopped.

[2] Fiction editor of *Collier's*, which in January had run DeVoto's serial *The Woman in the Picture*.
[3] During late 1943 DeVoto was in Washington as the potential historian of certain World War II campaigns. Nothing came of the negotiations.

But don't call on me to give Manifest Destiny an unimperialistic content. I can't give it one while I'm kept in ignorance of what's going on. No one can, in such ignorance, except the form which Mr. Wallace gives it and I am not unique in thinking that silly.

And by God I'm not alone. The Easy Chair which brought me a letter from Willkie has also brought me an astonishing mail, and a lot of it from people who are just as anti-Republican as I still insist I am but who nevertheless feel exactly as I do. Some of them people who are on public record and can't be impugned. That mail has both astonished me and made me feel even more disturbed. One letter quoted a remark alleged to have been Bill Cowles'[4] on his return from Russia. He is supposed to have said that in Texas and in the Northwest you could find a self-confidence like the one he'd found universal in Russia, but you couldn't find it anywhere else in the United States or anywhere else in the world. I don't know whether he ever said it. But considering who he is, it makes you pause.

Well, there I am. I do not expect the house to fall—though I am not so optimistic as to expect that the Army or the Navy will permit objective histories to be written a hundred years from now. I don't expect it to fall, but I do see trouble every way I look. And I think that the administration could have prevented a lot of it by acting on its own words—and still could prevent a lot of it.

Yours,

TO A MRS. HORKAN

October 25, 1944

Dear Mrs. Horkan:

I have thought hard about your letter, which is obviously serious in calling on me for a further expression of opinion and yet, just as obviously, is written out of conceptions of literature, decency, and morality so altogether at variance with mine that I cannot hope to establish any common ground for discussion with you.

Your first question. *Strange Fruit* is a novel conceived in the spirit of truth, charged with pity and the hope of a better social justice in America, and written with high artistic integrity and great literary power. It is not obscene. No such book ever is obscene. No serious attempt to determine, express, or portray the realities or the truths of human experience can be

[4] A Spokane newspaper publisher.

obscene. You ask: then what is obscene? On the literary level, such a book as Cleland's *Fanny Hill*. On the level of popular amusement, the average dialogue or monologue of a revue or a nightclub act. On a lower level, the books sold to the boys and girls of Gainesville High School at little corner holes in the wall which also sell soft drinks. Obscenity in literature consists of a deliberate exploitation of pornographic values, something written as pornography.

Please be so good as to bear in mind that deliberate obscenity is a right of free and adult minds, so long as they do not become publicly offensive. Thus, we persecute the vendors of pornography to minors, because we believe that minors need protection. We do not prosecute the proprietors of revues and night clubs, because anyone who patronizes them does so of his own will and choice.

Your second question. *Strange Fruit* is not vulgar, cheap, or beyond the pale of good taste. You are now in a subjective field; there is no way of determining objectively what vulgarity and good taste are. Some of the books you name seem to me vulgar and in bad taste almost beyond toleration. Books are vulgar which lie about life, misrepresent experience, or trivialize emotions and values which we hold to be important and profound. In my judgment, to my taste, James Hilton is one of the most vulgar writers now writing. I would be far more apprehensive if I found my adolescent son reading a Hilton book than if I found him reading *Fanny Hill*. For at least *Fanny Hill* would not lie to him about life as Hilton does nothing but lie about it, vulgarize it, sentimentalize it.

Note, however, that I should not forbid my son to read Hilton. Neither would I advocate the passage and enforcement of a law forbidding you to read him on the ground that the exposure of citizens' minds to vulgarity is bad for the citizen and for the state. I believe that it is but I should never venture to make my judgment of taste and morality coercive. In the first place, I know I may be wrong. In the second place, I do not believe in the authority of the state to regulate taste and morality—I believe that those are private matters. In the third place, a fundamental basis of a free society immutably guarantees you the freedom to choose your own reading.

In turn, I must ask you to respect my privacy and more especially my freedom. You can be secure in your own only by respecting mine. Even if I choose to read what you consider obscene books, you must leave me free to do so, lest I in retaliation, or someone else with imperatives different from yours but just as strong, deny you your feedom to read what you consider decent and inspiring books.

That is my lesson in literary criticism and civics. I cannot forbear adding that you ought prayerfully to revise your ideas of decency.

Sincerely yours,

TO ALICE DRITZ

November 1, 1944

Dear Miss Dritz:

Your letter plunges me into a dilemma—one which I am all too familiar with. I should be glad to write a defense of the political activities of the NCPAC and to defend it in any other way within my power. I sympathize with its ambitions and approve of its actions in the present campaign. Even if I did not, I should feel under obligation to defend its right to political action, education, and propaganda.

Nevertheless, the spirit in which you want me to defend it and, more particularly, one sentence in your letter, fills me with the bewildered helplessness which I have experienced all too often in dealing with liberal thought. You say, "It would be a tragedy if the Fascist attacks of our enemies destroyed this foundation," meaning the NCPAC is the foundation of a liberal movement. I have followed the current compaign with the greatest possible attention, and though I am aware of many attacks on NCPAC, I am aware of practically none, if of any, that it is remotely reasonable to call Fascist. American liberals rightly yell their heads off when opponents call them Communists, but I have seen an all but universal willingness to interpret opposition to and attacks on them as *per se* Fascist. In my opinion, this habit of mind is at once childish and socially dangerous: it commits the very sin of absolutism which it protests and which is as Fascist as anything in the world. I am certainly not willing to say that opposition to and attacks on NCPAC are generally, or even occasionally, Fascist. In my opinion, there never can be a strong liberal movement in this country until liberals grow up politically. Part of that process of maturity involves a willingness and ability to take it as well as to dish it out. Any organization which undertakes political action must expect, in the natural course of things, to be attacked with all the weapons of politics. Among those weapons are unfairness, distortion, and the raising of smoke screens. When liberals learn to deal unhysterically with such things they will be better off politically than they show any signs of being right now.

Among the opponents of NCPAC are many honest people who honestly believe that you are wrong. They have every bit as much right to think so and say so as you have to think and say what you do. Disbelief in and opposition to NCPAC are not in themselves Fascistic. I will not maintain that they are, and if unwillingness to interpret political controversy as Fascism stamps me as a Fascist, I am afraid that to that extent you must number me among the Fascists.

Sincerely yours,

TO A MR. PORTER

The letter below was written in reply to one protesting DeVoto's Easy Chair of April 1945, which justified conscription as a democratizing force. In retrospect, it is hard to defend this advocacy of the draft, but one may note that it appeared near the end of the war that DeVoto and millions of others understood as having been waged in defense of human dignity and political freedom. Moreover, DeVoto's service in World War 1 had been, for him, part of a similar crusade, and he had seen the army at the time as a definitely democratizing force—the minutemen gathering at Lexingtons all over America to repel the forces of darkness. It is very doubtful that if he had lived into the 1960s he would have attempted to justify peacetime conscription, for he was liberty's watchdog, and despite his distaste for movements, parties, causes, and idealisms, the 1960s might well have seen him in the streets.

April 11, 1945

Dear Mr. Porter:

I have not time to answer your letter adequately, but there is one thing I should like to say. Since you seem willing to take my conclusions from my own experience seriously, I will urge this on the basis of my own experience as both an enlisted man and as an officer.

I am a good deal less troubled than you seem to be by the military hierarchy. Most of us live in a hierarchy all our lives, even those of us who, like writers, have no external marks of subordination to guide by. You yourself are part of an ecclesiastical hierarchy and are subject to an ecclesiastical discipline. Most of us have to take direction more or less subtilized, more or less direct, more or less backed by naked force. Foremen or supervisors, or superintendents or office managers, or directors or bishops, wherever as many as seven men are gathered together in a human task, one of them must be a corporal if that job is to be done.

When I speak of the Army as a democratizing force, I am speaking of what seems to me the granite and steel basis of any working democracy, realistic knowledge of man's nature. What you say about Negro regiments does not in the least impress me. No one supposes that the United States is a complete democracy, socially, politically or economically. No one supposes even that democracy itself is anything but a means to an end. We are far more nearly a political democracy than any other people have ever been, and I believe we are on the slow and painful path that makes toward economic democracy; but any kind of democracy at all seems to me wildly and even insanely impossible except as men learn to give up the myths that they tell themselves about one another. I can only say that during seventeen months in the Army I was forced, on terms which I could not possibly avoid, to associate as equals in a common task with a far wider variety of men than chance, education, or my own choice would ever have led me to know. I regard those months as the foundation of my education, and, in fact, almost all my education. In my knowledge of what life is, what men are, and what society can do, and as the basis of my belief in the capacity of Americans to keep this society better than others and make it better than it now is, that period is far more important than all the rest of my life put together. I cannot do young Americans the large disservice of believing that they will respond otherwise than I did. In fact, as I have talked to hundreds of soldiers of the present Army, I perceive that precisely the same ferment is at work in them that transformed me from a schoolboy to a thinking man twenty-five years ago.

Sincerely yours,

TO JOHN T. FLYNN

April 8, 1946

Dear Mr. Flynn:

I was not aware that the Writers' Board had sent out the letter you quote[1] and do not support the policy which it recommends. I will write to the Board expressing my dissent.

[1] I have been unable to locate this letter, which evidently scolded the Chicago *Tribune*.

Having said that, I cannot forbear saying more. I believe that the Chicago *Tribune* pays lip service to freedom of the press when its own interests are involved but, like the Communists, is absolutely ruthless in attacking freedom of the press and attacking it with complete dishonesty and cynicism in support of its interests and causes. No one need enlist my help in opposing the Chicago *Tribune*. Nothing whatever could induce me to write for it.

From this radicalism of the extreme right I cannot altogether except all of your own writing and agitation during the last ten years. Moreover, the letter which you address to me contains misrepresentations which are either deliberate and so dishonest or else the result of a passion that prevents clarity of thought. When you say that the letter of the Writers' Board attacks the *Tribune* "because it does not agree with the Roosevelt foreign policy" you are being either absurd or dishonest. When you speak of "the new school of radical bigotry" you are being a deliberate obscurantist.

When you say that you write to me not in the interest of the *Tribune* but entirely on your own initiative, you move me to a moderate doubt.

You are free to publish or use this letter in any way you wish so long as you do so in its entirety. If you publish only the first paragraph without the rest, I will publish the whole letter.

Sincerely yours,

TO THE AMERICAN CIVIL LIBERTIES UNION

December 1, 1947

Gentlemen:

Nudists have always seemed to me gentle, humorless zanies to be classified with other harmless faddists of health, psychology, or religion. Their fervent beliefs seem to me a kind of nonsense. I have no doubt, however, that many of my beliefs seem nonsense to earnest nudists and since I insist on the right to advocate my beliefs and circularize people about them whenever I may desire to I must insist on the right of people who disagree with me to do the same in regard to theirs. That the May-June issue of the *Nature Herald* has been called obscene by the Post Office Department seems to me far more nonsensical than the contents of the issue—as well as a dangerous use of an arbitrary power.

I should not like to commit myself to the proposition that the nude body cannot be photographed obscenely, for I believe it can be. In this issue of the *Nature Herald,* however, no photograph is in the least obscene or even suggestive. I cannot believe that any of them would be suggestive to anybody who was not so dangerous a psychopath that he ought to be confined for the protection of society, and I cannot imagine anyone at all who would find any of them obscene. Two or three of them are ungraceful in pose and in two or three others the subjects lack some of the qualities that are regarded as beautiful by artists but this is an esthetic judgment and I do not believe either that the Post Office Solicitor is qualified to pass esthetic judgments on behalf of the public at large or that it is within the province of his office to deny the use of the mails to anyone on esthetic grounds. I assert flatly that there is neither shame nor obscenity in the issue of the magazine in question and that the Solicitor's ruling is absurd. These people and their activities seem to me tolerably silly but that is not my affair nor the Solicitor's. I deny that anyone except a psychopath would be excited by these photographs to lustful or impure thoughts and I should regard it as a fact of extreme interest if someone were to confess that they had excited him to such thoughts. In the interest of the free circulation of ideas and in the interest of the right of all citizens to advocate their ideas as they may see fit without endangering the public I demand that the magazine have its mailing privileges restored.

Sincerely yours,

TO HAROLD TAYLOR

*During Commencement Week, 1949,
Chairman John S. Wood of the House Un-
American Activities Committee sent letters
to seventy colleges and universities
requesting lists of their offerings in
sociology, geography, economics,
government, philosophy, history, political
science, and American literature. DeVoto's
blast against this effort at thought control
and intimidation of teachers appeared in
the Easy Chair for September, and inspired
a supportive letter from Harold Taylor,
president of Sarah Lawrence College, to
which the letter below is a response.*

178

September 10, 1949

Dear President Taylor:

The arc of Mr. Conant's thinking is frequently hard to follow. Just before or just after he published an article in the *Atlantic* asserting that science must be altogether free to pursue its investigations wherever they might lead, he wrote, I am told on credible authority, the basic text of the Kilgore Bill, which would have handcuffed all scientific research in the colleges and universities to the military. As a veteran Harvard man, however, I recognize the serenity of the saints, who know that these things are mysterious only on less privileged earth.

I am very glad to have your letter—the only one I have received from anyone in the colleges so far—and especially glad that you sent me a copy of your letter to Mr. Wood. It is beautifully right both in its stand and in its phrasing and I wish it could be circulated publicly. I cannot understand why college administrations in general have not seen that exactly what you say must be said and must be backed to the limit. I believe that the ferocious heresy hunt now in progress will abate. It always has abated ever since John Adams' administration or if you like, ever since Magistrate Hathorne's time. Now, however, it seems to me there is grave danger that permanent damage may be done before it does. The tremendous sums of money now being spent in the colleges by the military services scare me and I am scared blue when I think of the federal subsidies that are certainly on the way. As I see it, to protect themselves from political dictation the colleges have just exactly as much time as there may be between now and the beginning of the subsidies. I do not doubt that they can protect themselves if they will. What discourages me is the tranquility with which too many of them have submitted to too much inquiry and dictation. If you should sometime soon feel impelled to issue a manifesto to other college presidents saying what you said to Mr. Wood, I should be heartened. . . .

Sincerely yours,

TO DANIEL MEBANE

---

*In October 1949, the month following his
exposure of the Un-American Activities
Committee's efforts to scrutinize college
curricula, DeVoto published what became
perhaps the most famous of all his Easy*

179

Chairs. "Due Notice to the FBI" objected
to the investigatory methods of the FBI
in security cases, objected to the kinds of
questions asked and the way in which
rumor, the spite of neighbors, and outright
lies got scrambled together in the raw files,
and ended with a ringing declaration: "I
like a country where it's nobody's damned
business what magazines anyone reads, what
he thinks, whom he has cocktails with. I
like a country where we do not have to
stuff the chimney against listening ears
and where what we say does not go into
the FBI files. . . . I like a country where
no college-trained flatfeet collect
memoranda about us and ask judicial
protection for them. . . . We had that
kind of country only a little while ago and
I'm for getting it back."

J. Edgar Hoover did not reply
directly to DeVoto's charges. He only
wrote a letter to Harper's denying that the
FBI investigators asked some of the
questions DeVoto said they asked, and he
also made the same denial to Daniel
Mebane, of the New Republic, which was
one of the magazines DeVoto had said
were inquired about. No great friend of
the liberal weeklies, which he thought
were often soft-headed, DeVoto was as
ready to champion their civil liberties as
he was to defend the colleges against
HUAC. He and Mebane made an extended
effort to smoke Mr. Hoover out and get
him into public debate, but without
success.

October 19, 1949

Dear Mr. Mebane:

I think it would be better if the FBI addressed me directly and in print,
and I ask you to tell Mr. Hoover so.

Since his inquiry was through you and not directly to me, I will cite
only a single instance.

I have before me a copy of an "Interrogatory" which an employee of a government department was required to fill out early this year. It is headed: "Pursuant to Executive Order —— (since I am not completely sure whether the number is that of a general directive or a specific one for this case, I omit it) and the directives of the Loyalty Review Board of the U. S. Civil Service Commission, this interrogatory is addressed to you in connection with reports of full field investigation by the Federal Bureau of Investigation under the Federal Employees Loyalty Program. . . ."

One of the numbered questions of the interrogatory reads: "Have you ever subscribed to or regularly read any of the following: 'In Fact'; 'New Republic'; 'Russia Today'; 'The People's Voice'? Please answer fully."

The next question reads: "Have you ever distributed to fellow employees, or requested or suggested that fellow employees subscribe to, read, or distribute, any of the above named publications? If so, please furnish details."

The authenticity of this copy was guaranteed to me by a member of Congress as well as by the employee in question, whom I have known for some years—and who, incidentally, was cleared.

You may tell Mr. Hoover that I have others.

Sincerely yours,

TO DANIEL MEBANE

October 31, 1949

Dear Mr. Mebane:

If Mr. Hoover requires documentary evidence, he is in a position of sitting on all there is, for it is in the FBI files. Nothing would please me more than to have my assertion checked by the production of a specific dossier from those files. I will come back to that.

The "Interrogatory" makes clear that the questions it contains are based on what both it and Mr. Hoover call a field investigation by the FBI. Quite clearly the FBI had reported in its investigation that the person in question read the *New Republic* and the Interrogatory asked whether the FBI's report was true.

I do not know whether I am a reputable person in Mr. Hoover's estimation. At least, FBI investigators have questioned me about people who have not named me as a reference. I am prepared to state or if necessary make oath that they have asked me whether various persons read the *New*

Republic or similar magazines. I am prepared to produce members of the Harvard faculty, presumably reputable people, who will state or make oath that representatives of the FBI asked them the same question. If you will consult the reports of the Coplon case[1] in the New York *Times* you will find the question in the evidence presented by the prosecution and attributed by it to the FBI. Mr. Hoover's letter says that he accepts responsibility.

I am prepared to establish that the FBI has asked even sillier questions. In the mind of at least one FBI investigator it was suspicious that the person he was investigating had published a review of a book about Communism.

As I began by saying, the only documentary evidence is probably in the FBI files. The questions asked of such people as me by the FBI are oral and I know of only one person who had the wit to call in his secretary and have the questions and answers taken down. I should like to propose something to Mr. Hoover through you. I will name a specific person about whom the FBI questioned me. Let Mr. Hoover make public the FBI's dossier on that person or merely the report *in full* of the investigator's interview with me. I say "in full" because the interview went on to take up other persons besides the one originally named to me. I should like to have this interview publicly discussed in answer to Mr. Hoover's allegation that I have misrepresented the FBI. If he consents, I will name the person in question and I am perfectly willing to conduct the discussion in the *New Republic* or anywhere else.

I take the most severe exception to the second paragraph from the end of Mr. Hoover's letter. It suggests to me that Mr. Hoover believes that the FBI should not be subjected to criticism and that to criticize it is disloyal or even subversive. My record as a journalist is in the open and I do not "smear" anyone and neither does *Harper's*. I have suggested a means by which we can get one specific set of facts into the open if Mr. Hoover will consent. If he will not, let us all three look at the testimony in the Coplon case, and Mr. Hoover's letter to you says that he accepts responsibility for the evidence entered there as coming from the FBI, which I discussed in my article—and let Mr. Hoover choose his language more carefully hereafter. I amend that last sentence to read: let him look more carefully to the language of the letters he signs.

Finally, let me say this to Mr. Hoover through you: I should much prefer to have him answer me in the press where I can answer him in turn on the same basis. Failing that, I think he should write to me directly and not to you or *Harper's*, as he has also done.

For the time being I ask you to let me keep the Interrogatory from which I quoted confidential. The man who was being investigated is close

[1] Judith Coplon, a political analyst in the Foreign Agents Registration Section of the Department of Justice, was arrested early in March 1949 while turning over typed notes from confidential U.S. documents to Valentin Gubichev, a Russian U.N. employee.

to retirement age. The investigation was a severe and prolonged shock to him and he is extremely eager to let the whole episode be forgotten—as I wrote you, he was cleared. Before I can identify him or his department I must get his consent and those of a Congressman and of a lawyer whom the Congressman consulted. I can get their consent but I see no reason to expose an already sorely hurt and harassed man to more publicity unless we can get Mr. Hoover to answer directly and in print.

Sincerely yours,

TO A MRS. GUILHERT

October 31, 1949

Dear Mrs. Guilhert:

I will gladly write your article if you will show me any evidence that women as such are any more likely to amend matters than men. Actually American politics is crammed full of women's activity and I cannot see that there is any sex differentiation. I think you misconceive the nature of politics, which is the art of bringing men to agree on a workable resolution of their diverse interests. There has never been a time anywhere in the world [when] the facts of government could seem pure and beautiful to a mind filled with ethical concepts. Men as a species, which includes women, are very mixed, very deplorable, and mostly evil. Any of us could invent offhand a theoretically more admirable species and a far finer government. Politics, however, is the art of the actual and the possible. I think we are doing well in this country and there have been few times in its history when great men were at hand. If you admire Thomas Jefferson you must know that he was a devious and frequently dishonorable politician, though an exceedingly successful one, and that his integrity was questioned by many during his lifetime and has been by many others up to now. He was a very great man indeed but he made many failures and did innumerable things which I am sure must appall the point of view from which you write. I do not believe that women will ever act politically more wisely nor more unselfishly than men and I am by no means sure that unselfishness is either a wise or a safe force in politics.

Sincerely yours,

TO DANIEL MEBANE

December 21, 1949

Dear Mebane:

My information is that Mr. Ernst[1] has gone to Europe. When he comes back I will say to him as I now do to you that his proposal is grotesque. I have talked to various people who are willing to back my statement with their personal experience if Mr. Hoover will make a public issue of it. It is quite obvious, however, that he will not and they feel, I think correctly, that nothing short of a publicly drawn issue with Mr. Hoover following the procedure I suggested to you, or some other procedure which will make public evidence bearing on my statement, would justify the discomfort and publicity certain to center on them locally, especially in the colleges. They are not interested in a sheaf of *ex parte* affadavits not responded to by Mr. Hoover with conclusive documentary evidence from his files, neither am I, and neither, I think, should Mr. Ernst be.

If you can induce Mr. Hoover to answer to the point, I am willing to go as much farther as I can. Otherwise I see nothing to do except what he obviously wants, which is to let the matter drop. I call your attention to two things. One, that of what I said about the FBI methods he has disregarded everything except a parenthetical remark about the *New Republic*, and that he has not answered this remark to the point. Two, that evidence fully establishing this point has been printed at least twice without drawing a denial from him, once in press reports of the Coplon trial and again in the articles by Bert Andrews that won him a Pulitzer Prize.[2]

I have had a good many enlightening, exhilarating, amusing, and appalling experiences out of this episode. I should like to tell you some of them sometime and perhaps show you some of the letters I have received. Among these last are a number which not only back to the hilt everything I said about FBI methods, including the *New Republic* remark, but vividly illustrate the panic among government employees that resulted from the loyalty checks. I can never use such material, of course, because it is sent to me with a request for secrecy.

Sincerely yours,

[1] Morris Ernst, ACLU lawyer. It is not clear what his proposal was, but it is clear he thought it fruitless to challenge Hoover.
[2] Bert Andrews, head of the New York *Herald Tribune*'s Washington bureau, won a Pulitzer Prize in 1947 for exposing the star-chamber methods of loyalty proceedings in the State Department. Later he had a hand in the investigations that trapped and convicted Alger Hiss.

TO MRS. FREDRIC MARCH

January 9, 1950

Dear Mrs. March:

I am very glad to have your letter and the mimeographed copy of *Counterattack*'s retraction.[1] The latter of course is lame and fumbling and does not go anywhere near as far as it should but at least it represents a victory for you and Mr. March. The whole story is disgusting and very frightening. You deserve everybody's thanks for making your fight.

The helplessness of private individuals against irresponsible accusations is one of the most appalling things about the present situation. Worse still, it is not only helplessness against irresponsible behavior by the FBI and other government agencies but against the greater part of American journalism as well. One thinks first of the Luce organization of course, which has neither responsibility nor ethics nor even consistency and has pilloried many a person in public with impunity, but of newspapers in general and even some of the few that are genuinely good. Once any accusation has been made about anyone, the damage can never be repaired by any means, least of all by a five-line paragraph on page thirty-two saying that page one three months ago was mistaken. Few people [can] afford either the time [or] the money necessary to make what small protest and fight are possible. Many others are restrained by the fact that they hold confidential positions or that by all odds the best thing for the firms or causes they work for is to let the uproar die out as soon as possible.

I see no real cure for this situation and very few ways of doing anything at all about it. It is possible occasionally to remind various sections of the public that the situation does exist and is dangerous. I have chosen to do as much as I can in that admittedly ineffective way and I am glad to say that *Harper's* repeatedly does what it can. I call your attention to the article about Dr. Condon[2] in the January issue and to the one by him which will follow next month.

I will return to the subject as soon as a strategic opportunity presents itself and I will probably make use of your release when I do. Thanks for writing to me.

Sincerely yours,

---

[1] The rightist paper *Counterattack* had smeared March as a Red, and then taken back its charges when challenged.

[2] Dr. Edward Uhler Condon, director of the Federal Bureau of Standards, was attacked in 1948 by the House Un-American Activities Committee as "one of the weakest links in our atomic security." He was given no public hearing or opportunity to make a defense. In 1951 Condon left the Bureau of Standards to become chief of research for the Corning Glass Company.

TO CAREY McWILLIAMS[1]

March 27, 1950

Dear Mr. McWilliams:

I have received a copy, signed by you, which asks me to join a committee in support of the Hollywood Ten.

I never join committees or give the use of my name to organizations without knowing who my associates are. If you will send me a list either of those who have been invited to join the committee or those who have accepted it, I will decide whether or not to go along with you.

Merely to satisfy my curiosity I should like to ask you a question. Over the years in a number of printed references to me you have intimated that I am dangerously anti-liberal and in various other ways against God and the True and the Beautiful, and once you explicitly called me a Fascist. Why do you want my support now?

Sincerely yours,

TO A MR. COLLIER

April 26, 1951

My dear Mr. Collier:

I have seen a copy of the letter which you wrote to *Fortune* about my article[2] and copies of which you sent to various people, among them the business manager of *Harper's Magazine,* my employer.

I assume that you accept responsibility for what you say in that letter. You will therefore have no objection, I trust, to my publishing the full text, including your intimation that I have Communist sympathies. This is to request your permission to publish it.

I assume too that in writing it you were not merely indulging a puerile impulse to make trouble for me at *Fortune* and *Harper's* but believe that you have sufficient reason to make this serious intimation about me. Am I right in these assumptions? If I am, then I invite you to print publicly, or to say in the presence of witnesses who will testify that you have, that I am or

[1] Editor of *The Nation.*
[2] "Why Professors Are Suspicious of Business," *Fortune* 43 (April 1951).

at some time was (whichever expresses your belief) a Communist, a Communist-sympathizer, a fellow-traveler, or a member of a front organization.

Please let me hear from you about these matters.

Sincerely yours,

TO PROFESSOR PEDRICK

December 11, 1952

Dear Professor Pedrick:

I inclose a copy of my piece about the FBI. It was published in the October 1949 issue of *Harper's*. If you can return it to me when you have finished your study, I should like to have it.

As for the episode involving Mrs. Eisler[1]—or was "Mrs." a courtesy title? I was at the time a member of the executive committee of the Massachusetts Civil Liberties Union, having joined the organization in the early stages of the *Strange Fruit* case, the first step in an ultimately successful effort to weaken the system of extra-legal literary censorship that had made Boston notorious. The others on the committee were lawyers, doctors, professors, and business men. The CLU secretary believed that such people were very busy men, whereas writers were idlers and were never engaged in important work even when occasionally occupied. It wouldn't have been nice to call a teacher from a class, a lawyer from a case, or a store manager from a discussion of his golf score. So whenever anything came up, she habitually telephoned me and I went gonging off to the fire.

Some organization, and I forget what it was (if indeed I ever knew its name), though doubtless it was a front group or at least composed of moony yearners, had arranged to bring Mrs. Eisler to Boston for a lecture— probably to raise funds for Eisler's defense, though I am not sure of this. The group had hired Jordan Hall for the lecture. Jordan Hall is the concert hall of the New England Conservatory of Music, a staid and painfully respectable institution, and was then the second largest auditorium in Boston—a larger one has since been built. It was, and still is, hired for all kinds of musical performances that could not be expected to fill the larger Symphony Hall, and for various kinds of lectures and theatrical performances. Thus it was, and still is, a source of badly needed and greatly appreciated income for the Conservatory of Music.

One morning the Boston newspapers carried a story saying that, the

---

[1] Wife of Gerhardt Eisler. Once a leader of the American Communist party, Eisler later became information head of the Communist regime in East Germany. He was a prominent target of the anti-Communist forces in the late 1940s.

previous evening, the Boston City Council had passed a resolution calling on the Mayor to revoke the license of Jordan Hall because of the forthcoming lecture. Possibly the Mayor was out of town, or more likely Jim Curley was still Mayor and a prisoner in a federal penitentiary. If Curley had been on the job there would have been no problem, for he would have disregarded the resolution. The acting Mayor was Mr. John B. Kelly, then President of the Council, later Attorney General of the Commonwealth.

I had barely read the news story when the CLU secretary phoned me and said that we had to act, as was obvious. I assembled a committee of the greatest respectability [. . . .] and that afternoon led them to the Boston City Hall. Mr. Kelly was in his own office but would not meet with us till he could get down to the Mayor's office, and there was a further delay while he summoned the newspaper reporters who covered the City Hall beat. Mr. Kelly's literacy was not so overwhelming as to embarrass either him or his listeners. We went in and I explained to him that the Council's resolution, which had been passed while he was in the chair, was against the bills of rights in both the Federal and Commonwealth constitutions, that it was destructive of the right to freedom of assembly and of speech, and that so far as I could determine by phone calls to various lawyers the Mayor had no power to revoke the license of Jordan Hall anyway. I am sure that Mr. Kelly regarded us as highly dangerous people, though that his information gave him any clear notion of what a Communist is can be doubted, but he did have some rudimentary notion of freedom of speech, having heard the aldermen hurl the phrase at one another during their intramural feuds, and a very clear and vivid notion of political opportunity. He stood up, and facing the newspapermen, delivered a rousing oration to the effect that he was a patriotic American, that America was the land of freedom, that he loathed Communism, and that he would safeguard both the freedom and the patriotism of Boston. In the course of this prose poem he intimated that he would not revoke the license of Jordan Hall. The intimation did not seem to me sufficiently binding, so when he sat down and it was possible to see again following the fireworks I kept after him till he said specifically, and in the presence of the reporters, that he would disregard the Council's resolution and make no effort to revoke the license. I thanked him and we filed out in a reverent manner and dispersed.

That was the entire episode. It was routine for the CLU, though in those days most of our energy went to rescuing Jehovah's Witnesses from various painful situations which their incorrigible trouble-making proclivities had got them into. There is one interesting feature about McCarthy's use of it. I understand that the former FBI agent who does his research was in Boston for several days, trying to dig up dirt about Arthur M. Schlesinger, Jr., who, incidentally, was a student of mine when I taught at Harvard. The Boston newspapers had devoted about an inch to our appearance before

Mr. Kelly, I am morally certain that the agent could have got wind of the episode only in a newspaper morgue, and I am personally convinced that he could have been directed to it only by a newspaper, presumably the *Post* or the *Herald*. It was a trivial matter, and, I am sure, had vanished from human memory [. . . .]

The preparation of both McCarthy and his agent was extremely superficial. In spite of his emotions about the State Department, he missed the fact that Archie MacLeish had been an Assistant Secretary of State, which would have enabled him oratorically to gain forty or fifty yards if not score a touchdown.

If I can judge by a wisecrack that Judge Wyszanski tossed at me in the library, he believes that McCarthy libeled me.[2] I myself have no doubt that he did. I did not hear his first speech but I did hear the second one, and I have heard tape recordings that were made of it. In that speech he quoted me as having made in the piece about the FBI statements which in fact I did not make, ferociously inflammatory statements. I take that to be libel. Whether or not he damaged me in a pecuniary way I do not know. I do know that an editor and a lecture agent with whom at the moment I was negotiating contracts solemnly inquired of their associates and representatives whether they would lose money if they employed me.

One thing more. McCarthy's second speech as he delivered it was more vicious and scabrous than the advance text which he supplied to the newspapers. I have been told that the same thing is true of the first speech. I have examined several hundred newspaper clippings and so far as I can see no newspaper called attention to this fact. In my opinion this is important. Incidentally, my sole function in Governor Stevenson's Research Group was that of an expert on conservation and public lands policy.

I am glad that you are making your study and hope that this letter will facilitate it.

Sincerely yours,

TO REPRESENTATIVE EMANUEL CELLER

"The Case of the Censorious
Congressman," DeVoto's Easy Chair for
April 1953, attacked the findings of the
Gathings Committee with regard to
pornographic literature. In retaliation,

[2] In the speech in which McCarthy attacked DeVoto, Arthur Schlesinger, Jr., and other Stevenson supporters.

Congressman Kearns, of Pennsylvania,
entered in the Congressional Record *certain*
comments on the affiliations of one Bernard
DeVoto. The next few letters follow
DeVoto's attempts to evoke either a
retraction or a confrontation.

May 12, 1953

Dear Mr. Celler:

Since you have been good enough to write to me about my *Harper's* piece on the report of the Gathings Committee, I venture to ask your advice about this aspect of it.

I find that in the Appendix to the *Congressional Record* for April 23, page A2248, Congressman Kearns, of the Committee, entered by extension of remarks a letter from one of his constituents severely criticizing my article. That is perfectly all right with me, but what Mr. Kearns went on to do isn't. In his own person he submitted "references to the activities of Bernard DeVoto, which speak for themselves." They add up to a couple of signed protests of the Committee on Un-American Activities and a petition against outlawing the Communist Party. (He incidentally makes an entirely untrue statement about Rex Stout.)

There was nothing secret about these matters, they were well publicized at the time, and my signature was solicited by many highly respectable people who also signed the documents. The catch is, however, that Mr. Kearns cites only news stories from the *Daily Worker*, not from any other newspaper that carried them, and lets it go at that. His plain and deliberate intent is to insinuate that I am a Communist or a Communist sympathizer.

I do not like this. I do not like it as regards the injustice done me, or as an example of a dangerous practice that is becoming commoner in public life, as the example of the unspeakable McCarthy is imitated.

I hardly need to defend myself. All my writing career and throughout such public career as I have had, I have fought Communism; I was fighting it at a time when people who are now heroes of our extreme right were members of the Communist Party and devoting their energies to the Communist attempt to undermine the American government. This is spread on the record of journalism and literature in our time. Since it is, there is this dilemma: either Mr. Kearns is ignorant of the fight against Communism in the United States, in which case his insinuation about me is an act of too great irresponsibility to be permitted a Congressman, or, and since he is an unusually well educated man this seems much more likely, he ignored it in order to retaliate for my article about the Committee report. Conceivably, to intimidate me.

It adds up to this: I criticize an official act of a Congressional Committee. Instead of replying to my criticism, Mr. Kearns, a member of the Committee, insinuates that I am a Communist or a Communist sympathizer. He does so under his Congressional immunity, and in the *Congressional Record*, where the libel is printed for the little terrorists of our time to pounce on and use as they may see fit.

I intend to comment on Mr. Kearns's action in *Harper's*, but does it not call for something more? I have thought of writing a letter summarizing it and asking you to insert it in the *Record*—or, if it would not be proper for you to do so, since you are his fellow-committeeman, asking some other friend of mine in Congress to insert it. I am sure that Gene McCarthy would do so, or Mr. Dodd of Connecticut, or my own Representative. What I should like to know is whether you think that such action would be a proper way of replying to Mr. Kearns. I am entirely sure that I must reply to him, but I should like to know whether you think I should do so in this way. I hope that you will tell me.

Sincerely yours,

TO REPRESENTATIVE EMANUEL CELLER

May 1953

Dear Mr. Celler:

I want to thank you most earnestly for your letter about my predicament with Mr. Kearns. Your advice was very sagacious and I have followed it to the letter. I wrote a letter to Mr. Kearns and requested him to insert it in the *Record*. So far I have heard nothing from him. I am leaving for a summer in the West a week from tomorrow. If I have not heard from him by that time I will send copies of the letter to the *Times* and to the papers of Erie, Pennsylvania, the largest city in his district, and will also ask Mr. McCarthy of Minnesota, a friend of mine, to insert it in the *Record*.

I must tell you that, half-way through *You Never Leave Brooklyn*, I am enormously enjoying it. I was prepared to find you saying important things, for I am acquainted with your record, and I have certainly found them. It takes me back to the excitement of the early Roosevelt years, and I am well aware that there is a full account of your labors for immigrants and their descendants still to come. I confess I was not prepared for the excellence of the writing, and I congratulate you on it. It is moving, amusing, lively, full of color and nervous strength. And yet, as a professional writer I'm not sure that I can altogether approve: if the amateurs are to write so well, where is our living to come from? I hope, however, that you will be diligent to plead amateur status to the Bureau of Internal Revenue when you report your royalties, and will demand that they be treated as capital gains. After all, you would have the excellent precedent of the President when he was writing as a General.[1]

Thanks enormously for your interest, and prosperity to all your enterprises in Congress.

Sincerely yours,

TO REPRESENTATIVE CARROLL D. KEARNS

[n.d.]

My dear Mr. Kearns:

On April 23 you entered in the *Congressional Record*, by extension of remarks, what you described as "references to the activities of Bernard DeVoto which speak for themselves." Those references were as follows:

You cited an advertisement in the New York *Times* in which I joined other citizens in calling for the abolition of the Wood-Rankin Committee. You pointed out that I am a member of the advisory council of the Society for the Prevention of World War III, "headed," so you said, "by Rex Stout, former editor of the *New Masses*." You cited the *Daily Worker* as having said that I signed a statement protesting a proposal to outlaw the Communist Party. You cited the *People's Daily Worker*, a publication unknown to me, as having denounced the House Un-American Activities Committee. You said that the files of the House Un-American Activities Committee contain the information that the *Daily Worker* quoted from an article of mine about the FBI which was published in *Harper's*.

Mr. Stout was never an editor of the *New Masses* and your readers should have been told that the Society for the Prevention of World War III, which is composed mainly of former members of the Writers War Board, is an organization of unimpeachable patriotism which is concerned solely with preventing the rise of another Nazi movement in Germany. Apart from that, I assume that the rest of your statements are true, although

---

[1] General Eisenhower, when he wrote his memoirs, asserted that he was not a professional writer, and that his writing was a sort of by-product, its income not to be taxed as the writings of professionals were taxed, but as a onetime capital gain. The IRS agreed with him, to the dismay and envy of all writers.

I am not a reader of the *Daily Worker*. Certainly I have publicly opposed proposals to outlaw the Communist Party and have several times protested acts of the Un-American Activities Committee. I may very well do so again.

I note, however, that although you might have got information concerning these actions of mine from any leading newspapers in the East, and information about the FBI article from any newspaper in the United States that used Associated Press or United Press service, you mention only the *Daily Worker* and the *People's Daily Worker*, which I take to be a Communist publication. I conclude that your confining yourself to these sources is deliberate. I conclude that you intended to represent me as a Communist or a Communist sympathizer, and that to do so was your sole purpose when you entered these "references" in the *Congressional Record*.

I assume that your misrepresenting me was in retaliation for an article of mine published in *Harper's* which severely criticized the report of the Gathings Committee, of which you were a member. I point out that you have not answered my criticism but have made the insinuation I describe. I am constrained to point out too that to criticize your official actions, as a member of Congress, is not unpatriotic, subversive, or pro-Communist. You cannot be permitted to represent that it is. I assert that your defamation of me was an effort to use your position in Congress to defend yourself against the legitimate criticism of a private citizen.

I desire to make that assertion to the same audience to which you defamed me, but since I am a private citizen I lack your privilege of inserting material in the *Congressional Record*. I therefore call on you to insert this letter in that publication.

Sincerely yours,

TO GARRETT MATTINGLY

Early in 1954 Mattingly, working abroad on a Guggenheim Fellowship, humorously suggested expatriation as the cure for the manifold ills from which DeVoto and all of America that valued its liberties suffered. He caught DeVoto in a mood of depression and pessimism; the belligerent defender of things American, the man who had never been outside the continental boundaries of

*the United States except for some brief trips
into Canada, was perilously close to
accepting self-exile.*

February 21, 1954

Dear Mat:

Maybe you're going to make a sale. But I want to make clear that it's going to be a sale, not a lease. I can see only one reason for going to England but that one is strong enough to produce a permanent removal. But why England? I may as well say here that I think the answer to this problem is probably British Columbia, but I don't mind asking you for reports on various portions of the continent of Europe. The object in view would be to find a place with a climate no worse than Massachusetts, a customary diet and cuisine no worse than those of Utah, and a populace which is not scared pissless and retains as much individual liberty as rural Georgia had forty years ago. I continue to insist that the second of these specifications rules out England. The third rules out any portion of the United States and, I gather, Spain, Portugal, and the iron curtain countries. The first appears to rule out the Scandinavian countries, and please do not suggest Ireland to me on any count. We can still further narrow it by saying that from what I've seen of the Dutch and the Swiss who roam the academic and commercial circuits here, I think I lack affinity for them and would not care to end my days among them. Maybe what I want from you is information on the climate of Belgium and the present state of the Bill of Rights in Italy. I do not doubt that the Italians, my forebears' people after all, are a hell of a lot less terrified and a hell of a lot freer than the Americans, but are they confident and free enough for a man who can remember the American Republic? As I've indicated, I think British Columbia is the answer, probably the great, beautiful, civilized, and free city of Vancouver. The only really endearing attribute of the Canadians is their dislike of the English, which is more intense than their former dislike of the Americans. They no longer dislike the Americans; they feel for them a wholly justified contempt. But they eat at least as well as I do, they drink a hell of a lot better coffee, and they are by God a free people.

The only trouble with Mencken's stuff was its date; it wasn't descriptive but it was prophetic. We were a fairly decent people in the 1920s and a much better and decenter people in the 1930s. Our behavior during the second war seemed to indicate that we had grown up. We emerged from it not only the most powerful nation in the world but unquestionably the freest one as well and in my judgment the most civilized, or maybe I should say according to my taste. That was 1945. In nine years we have become the sorriest collection of clowns and cowards in the contemporary

194

world. I hope to God you can pass yourself off as an Australian or a Scot, for even the kindliest Europeans cannot constantly shield you from their thoroughly justified opinions about the craven and castrate nation whose unofficial representative you are. . . .

I suppose this is the result of the investigating committees, but it's the indirect result for the committees themselves go on being the entirely futile circus they always have been. They simply go round the circuit of each other's performing seals and get nowhere. It's in the old home town, the state legislatures, and the courts that the official damage is done, and the unofficial damage is much worse. If you think that the scareheads you occasionally read about the bookburners is the malice of Europeans, be advised it isn't. If your book on diplomacy gets adopted for use in Texas—this is a purely hypothetical assumption, for no book with some three syllable words in it will get adopted in Texas—it will have to carry your and your publisher's affidavit that you are not and never have been a Communist and are not and never have been engaged in subversive activities. If the Texas adoption should lead to an adoption in Alabama, it will have to have the same certification but you will have to make identical affidavits about the loyalty and harmlessness of every writer you cite. If you are an immoral man, the Salinas Public Library will not admit your book—immoral as regards H. G. Wells that he committed sexual intercourse outside of the bonds of matrimony and as regards Bertrand Russell that he does not believe in God. I seem to remember that some of your relatives were or are Quakers. If the lady member of the Indiana Textbook Commission gets her way, you will not be read in state-supported institutions, for Quakers do not believe in war and that is an assist to the Communists. (Robin Hood is out on the same ground—like Jesse James he took from the rich and gave to the poor, which is giving comfort to Communists. She is now pitching out *Huckleberry Finn* and an anthology which contains a story of Sherwood Anderson's about playing hooky from school, for playing hooky is the first step in a career of crime, and careers in crime also comfort the Communists. She has lately added half a dozen other objectives, and if you think she isn't going to put them across, you are more fatuously Old American than I am.) If the word "liberal" can be applied to your book, it's out in Shaftesbury, Vermont—and I think it was when Vermont produced this one that I started looking into Vancouver and Victoria. If Rockwell Kent illustrates it, you can't get into San Antonio. For the moment you can probably be circulated in Illinois, but three weeks ago it looked as if six thousand, count them six thousand (6,000), categories were going to be proscribed. It is impossible to keep up with the committees to proscribe books for they increase between reports of the Publishers Council, which are bi-weekly. There must be close to a hundred allegedly legal ones—that is by appointment of mayors or under state statutes—and I judge that the "allegedly" will not have to be used after the Supreme Court gets a whack at them, for the Supreme Court is busily chipping away at what is left of the Bill of Rights. There must be close to five hundred private ones, private local ones I mean, and close to fifty national ones. Related statutes to the number of about a hundred, bills I should say, are currently before legislatures, and I think about a third of them will pass.

Elmer Davis says in his new book[1] that if Bricker should try to detour Congress by means of a convention to propose his amendment, there would be no way of preventing the convention from going on to reduce the immunities and freedoms guaranteed by the Bill of Rights. Irving Dilliard of the *Post-Dispatch* lately said in the Lovejoy Lecture at Bowdoin that the Bill of Rights could not be adopted now for the press would not support it. A paper at the annual meeting of AAAS said that one-third of the people of the U.S. did not know what the Bill of Rights is and another third were opposed to it. I don't know what all the shouting is about. The American people would not adopt the Bill of Rights now, they don't want it, and the truth is they have not got much of it. The Supreme Court lately affirmed the decision in a case where the evidence had been obtained by invasion of the accused's house without a warrant. Mr. Brownell[2] (who in many ways has revealed himself as the most thorough-going son of a bitch to hold his office in my memory) wants Congress to legalize wire-tapping and this is an uncharacteristic solicitude on his part for wire-tapping is routine and increasingly accepted by the courts. (You remember that the CIA started using a lie-detector on its staff; practically half the departments in Washington now do so as routine.) Margaret Smith, who is easily one of the soundest people in the Senate, has a bill to outlaw the CP. When the story of the Norwalk VFW post[3] broke, it came out that its anonymous informers were reporting the books and magazines seen in the houses of, quote, suspects—and it came out that a good many VFW posts scattered over the country, and I gather all Legion departments, have been reporting suspects to the FBI for a long time. You probably have not heard about Pro-America, which is largely Californian, or the Minute Women of the U.S.A., which is national and social as all hell, or Facts Forum, which has Texas oil money behind it— you probably have not heard of a lot of obscenities and you don't want to.

Well, no more of this. It wasn't a very free country when you left it but it was freer than it is now and is freer now than it will be when you get back [. . . .]

Yrs,

1 *Two Minutes Till Midnight.*
2 Herbert Brownell, then Attorney General.
3 The April 1954 Easy Chair carried the account of the Norwalk VFW Post's systematic listing of "known" Reds and "suspected" Reds.

TO GARRETT MATTINGLY

---

*By the time of this letter DeVoto was
physically unwell and mentally discouraged.
The long course of the McCarthy witch-
hunts had damaged his faith in the
democratic system's resilience under
pressure, and the fact that he had come to
the end of his books, and was floundering
for a new book to write, compounded his
malaise. There is, so far as I know, no letter
in all his correspondence so gloomy about
America's prospects as this one. DeVoto
lived barely six months longer, and there is
no reason to believe that his gloomy view
of America, so markedly different from the
steady faith he had shown up to 1955, was
much changed when he died. Or that it
would be much changed if he should come
to life again.*

May 1, 1955

Dear Mat:

You wouldn't care to see me in Cambridge or, these last three months, anywhere else. I've been either an invalid or a hypochondriac, with occasional souped-up intervals as a politician. In my judgment, it's an identification with F. Parkman, except that so far no eye trouble. The week I decided to catch up with contemporary fiction, I would have welcomed eye trouble. . . .

The book has not yet appeared. I will read it again forthwith, whether in bed or out of it, and who knows. The *Spectator* only acknowledged your learning, sagacity, modernity, & prose—none of which was news to me. What in hell is this talk about maybe no more books? Christ's sake, you haven't got more than two or three or four fatal diseases. I've got eight and maybe even I will write another book. On the showing so far, a lousy one.

This is a good time to be bucking up, son. Was it a year ago I wrote you about moving to British Columbia? It was a sound idea & I'd act on it if I thought there was any difference in countries. I can remember occasions when I was proud of the United States. I think I could still be if God had given us Harding or Coolidge or even Hoover all over again. We didn't know when we were well off. When I was on the Ogden *Evening Standard* the editorial page loved the word pusillanimity. Now we got it, the Democrats even more so. In two years the D. party has developed as much vested interest in being out of power as the G.O.P. did in twenty. I figure we're in for at least 20 years of it, and so does the Dem. Natl. Committee.

I was thinking about prestige, recently. Do you know anybody or any institution that's got any? In our time if J. P. Morgan, say, spoke out about something, or Harvard College, or the A F of L, or the Am. Medical Assn., or for that matter the N.Y. *Times*, it carried enough prestige so that the White House had to sit up and look into things. Christ Almighty, nobody or nothing could produce that effect now [. . . .]

The moral of our time is that the U.S. can be respected when it's scared—when it's scared about tonight's supper & next week's rent. It's scared of everything else now but not about them, and I say the hell with it. We are so God damned rich that we aren't worth hell room. I doubt if we ever will be again.

There are too damn many Americans and the Americans are too gutless. I don't know how I acquired the delusion I wrote several books about.

Well, I may be in N.Y. three weeks from now, if my gut is quiescent. A TV appearance. Do you suppose we could get together temperately, & ingest a decorous quantity of alcohol?

Yrs,

SIX

The Literary Life

DeVoto inhabited the literary world in a dozen shapes—as novelist, short story writer, essayist, critic, and reviewer; as editor and editorial adviser; as judge of novel contests and as judge of the History Book Club; as columnist and public gadfly; as teacher of writing at Northwestern, Harvard, and the Breadloaf Writers' Conference. In any of these shapes, he maintained a somewhat truculent independence, remained suspicious of cliques and coteries, and asserted, perhaps overasserted, the hard-boiled and professional attitudes of a man who had made his living by writing since the age of twenty-nine. He had his admirations and his abominations, and spoke them. He had his principles, and defended them with a singular consistency through a long literary life. He had a following, also, and firm friends and supporters both in and out of the literary profession. But the literary history of his period has been written by people of the same leftist-intellectual persuasion that he warred with in his lifetime, and if his influence is assessed from the histories written by the literary—whom he consistently disparaged—it may seem more negligible than it was. Outside of the strictly literary, on the other hand—in history and in conservation—no such diminution has taken place. And as a "cultural critic," a commentator on the state of public morals and morale, a defender of the rights guaranteed by the Constitution, and a scourge of the censors and thought police, there has seldom been his equal in America. More than one American wished him back alive when Watergate began to dominate the nation's awareness.

TO JOHN FARRAR

*It was characteristic that when asked for a
quotable line or two about each of three
books, DeVoto should have responded
with a seven-page letter containing
everything from a denunciation of
fictional dullness to an essay on American
social history. John Farrar, one of the
founders of the Breadloaf Writers'
Conference and DeVoto's colleague there
for several summers, was in 1934 a partner
in the new publishing firm of Farrar and
Rinehart, which after several permutations
is now Farrar, Straus and Giroux.*

October 7, 1934

Dear John:

I think you had better stop sending me books. God knows, with my income I am glad to have them but I must be from your point of view, from any publisher's, an unsatisfactory recipient. In the ten years of my existence before the public I have been able to report only two quotable blurbs—the one I did for Josephine Johnson[1] because I thought her book altogether fine and beautiful, and one I did a year ago for Gene Rhodes[2] because I thought that my notoriety might call attention to distinguished work too long ignored by the assured and the well informed. You've sent me three books and only one of them, Canby's, seems to me worth my time or your expense in sending it to me, and God knows whether I can say anything about that one in sufficiently brief form to be quoted and so justify the 40 cents plus postage that it cost you.

Mr. Minnegerode's glitter[3] amused me for a while, as it always does, but it's brass, John, or spinach, and it surfeits. He told me nothing that I hadn't

[1] Josephine Johnson, author of the Pulitzer Prize novel *Now in November,* was a protégée of DeVoto's at Breadloaf.
[2] Eugene Manlove Rhodes, probably the best of the cowboy writers.
[3] Apparently the book in question is Meade Minnegerode's *The Son of Marie Antoinette.*

known for a long time—for a very long time. And I'm sorry, but *The Folks*[4] is one of the dullest books I've ever read, and only a sense of obligation to you—probably a residuum of my early awe of people in the publishing business—kept me at it till I finished. I know, I know, John: it has honesty and a dozen other virtues, and it is so near to the ideal Henry Mencken set up for the American novelist that the Lord God may now dismiss Henry with a full heart and send him back to the political America, where, for my part, he's worth much more than he ever was in fiction. It simply sweats virtues, but it hasn't a single damn one of the virtues I respect. It's honest, God yes, but anyone can be [honest], honesty is the only virtue that stupid people are born with. And Henry Canby, if you'll ask him, will tell you that I'm quite right when I say that even the honesty of *The Folks* is a form of self-deception. It lacks every quality in fiction that I admire. It lacks wit, it lacks subtlety, it lacks style, it lacks technique, it even lacks the common amenities of workmanship. What it has will unquestionably appeal to many people, and the opinion of many of them will be much more valuable than mine. I can't help that: for me it's a dreary and practically unreadable book. It has no more emotion in it than a bath sponge, no more understanding of the complexities of human motives and behavior than a chiropractor, no more existence as a sensitive explanation of men and women, the only justification of fiction, than an ad-writer's nightmare about a toothpaste spread. And for all this endlessly dreary parade of pseudo-realism, of minute record as by photostat, it is a wildly romantic book. Oh, Miss Suckow is a rigidly realistic artist in her terms, and Mencken and thousands of readers will praise her in those terms, but she is as far from seeing what she looks at as even Gene Stratton-Porter was in her sweetest days. She is as painstaking as she is upright—as conscientious as her book is monotonous, on a dead-level, a sheer vacuity of feeling—but for all that she's a wide-eyed raven-tressed romantic and the book is false as hell. Canby, if you get him in an uneditorial corner, will say the same . . . It is not, let us say, my kind of book. But I'm too old now to apologize for my inadequacies.

Canby's book,[5] however, is my kind, though it's too rich and grainy to be characterized in the easy generalization that makes good advertising. Well, I offered to review it for his sheet but he preferred Red Lewis, and I've just seen what Red did. It was predictable: typical Lewis and snappy writing, but sentimental and innocent of the book's intentions, meaning and place.

I would ask Canby, to begin with, to be less tender about calling the book history. For it is history and if he doesn't know that it is, someone should tell him that systematic history is a delusion. It is a history of the sentiments in a given place during a period of change. As that, it is really two books. One is a statement of the change, the process in itself. The other

4 By Ruth Suckow.
5 *The Age of Confidence*.

is an examination of the sentiments as such, the base and reservoir of energy, the mold that gives the shape, the battery that supplies the force. For my part, the second is the better book, though both are keen and clear and very valuable today and though, also, I admire the skill with which he has imposed one on the other. But it seems to me that the first book is within the power of a good many people to write, if they would, for it takes merely honesty (again the unhappy virtue) and determination and a feeling for experience. Whereas in the second, Canby has got hold of important instruments whose existence is secret to all but a very few and which still fewer can use success-fully—as he uses them. He has derived and applied ideas of absolutely first importance in the understanding of America, past, present, and certainly to come. Ideas, I mean, which go to the bottom but which are nevertheless beyond the grasp and the rise of practically everyone who interprets America. I can only say that I have worked some of them out for myself, in *Mark Twain's America* and in other stuff not yet published, and that I hold them to be true. True and so absolutely essential to the purpose of history that those who are unaware of them are as wrong in their science as the alchemists were. In fact, American history is, over its greater area, still a division of alchemy because few of its practitioners know of these instruments and fewer still have used them.

These ideas seem to me best handled in chapters XI, XII and XIII. I would say that this passage, for it is really a continuity, is something of a masterpiece—using that word quite unemotionally. In it Canby has proved a metabolism. It isn't, of course, the metabolism of America as a whole—for only God will ever be able to see the entire organism. But it is, shall I say, a fundamental part—an enormous, enormously important and enor-mously valuable part of America has lived that way. And no one who doesn't know and use what Canby demonstrates here can understand America or should be allowed to think in public about it. These chapters are as im-portant to American history as "The Motion of the Heart and Blood" is to physiology. And that, I think, by a happy chance of metaphor, exactly says what I meant just before it. This is a fundamental document in a basic science. There is more to the field of that science than this particular docu-ment covers, but it will illuminate and clarify the rest and workers in the rest will come up to it and join on.

I get the greatest private satisfaction from the chapter on nature. The conditioning effect of nature on American life—and so on American in-stitutions[6]—has been left to geographers, which is to say the blind, and to academic critics of formal literature, which is to say the very dumb. One could have an uproarious half-hour lining up this chapter against, say, P. E. More on Thoreau and Channing or McMaster on Thoreau's period. . . . Why don't you have someone do that, John? It would be damn good fun

[6] Compare DeVoto's letter to Mattingly, p. 315.

and, I think, good publicity. Certainly it would dramatically exhibit the value of Canby's methods and instruments.

Chapters VI, VII and X are just behind the three that seem to be the best part of the book. They are quite as authentic, they are less searching and complete. I was puzzled by what at first seemed to me the insufficiency of his "Sex and Marriage." It seemed to me that he failed to make all the linkages that can be made, yet certainly no prudery or shrinking stood in his way. I think I have the answer: his failure to use the Freudian scheme. I don't mean, of course, his failure to deal with pathology, for it is the heart of his idea that pathology is not the key. Let me put it this way. The Freudian "complex" would give him precisely the same instrument he uses in chapter XII—an orientation, an organized scheme, a mutually self-dependent and interdependent organization of sentiments. It is the bed-rock idea of Ch. XII that association with nature organized the sentiments in a definite way, provided them with a definite system of response and expression, gave them an organic relationship, and so made them a powerful conditioning force on the whole shape and function of his generation. What is the difference between such an orientation and freely functioning relationship of those sentiments and a "complex"? If he had used that instrument, he would have, I think, brought his "Sex and Marriage" nearer the center.

I could, of course, quarrel with some of his exploration and some of his findings, but I take it that a publisher in search of a blurb doesn't want me to linger on that. If I ever sit down with him to debate the book, I will protest his assertion that these people knew they were Americans—and that they were the last, if not the only, people who ever did. Excuse me, the illusion has always been, and remains, widespread—and Canby is only succumbing to accord of sentiments. Okay—but! I will also ask leave to explain the tobacco-chewing politicians to him. They have always done the most important job in the world, perhaps the only indispensable one, and they are always experts. Society is inconceivable without them and no matter how his town graded them, Canby should give them an A with three plusses. But politicians are my part of the physiology. I don't ask him to put an isinglass window in that stomach.

Well, some quotable phrases. I am quite willing to say that the book is an indispensable part of the education of these days, a shrewd analysis of the period that begat this period, a profound and profoundly true interpretation of American experiences which must be truly interpreted if we are to think accurately about America. It is, in the only living sense of the word, history. It is history by a sensitively analytical mind at work on a rich material. It is history which, by illuminating the past, illuminates the present. And I say I'm damned glad to have read the book and will incorporate most of it in my own analysis.

So now, I wish you would tell me, sometime, why Canby had you send the book to me. I confess he stumps me, in his attitude toward me. I have been writing for his magazine[7] through nine of its ten years, and he frequently calls on me to do jobs which he considers important. That would indicate that he regards what I have to say as important—that he thinks my particular point of view important, as such things go in the literary world. Yet, with the exception of my Mark Twain, he has invariably delegated reviews of my books—which should be much more important, I'd think, than my casual pieces—to insignificant people who treat them casually and unintelligently. My third novel remains, after six years, unmentioned in his magazine. I am never referred to in the summaries and prospectuses that his staff write. He gives my latest novel not to a person of approximately the importance and intelligence that the display he gives my own articles would seem to establish, but to some lowly mind who cannot even understand its intention, still less pass judgment on its accomplishments. Yet, in his own person, in the B M Club sheet, he says that it is ambitious and searching. I don't know who Alvah Bessie is, but his review of Josephine Johnson's book had already convinced me that his intelligence was thin, his judgment superficial, and his understanding perfunctory. When he came to my book[8] he praised it for qualities it doesn't have and condemned it for qualities quite irrelevant to its purpose. He never even came near the theme, he didn't understand the intention, and he was so bewildered by the surface that he never got below it. Now, I submit, that is a satisfactory kind of review for a book by a person whose intelligence Canby doesn't particularly respect—and if he doesn't particularly respect mine, I have no legitimate howl. But if he doesn't respect it, why does he call on me to do important jobs for his magazine, usually at the cost of interrupting my work, and why does he give a damn what I think about his book?

Well, the literary life is a damned odd one. You have the best of it, my boy. Lolling in your palatial office—which mere writers cannot enter except by appointment as to an obstetrician or a syphilologist—you have only to consume Havanas and watch your bank balance mount. Not yours the tortures of a writer in heat, or a writer trying to float an advance, or a writer disliked by Isabel Patterson. Offer me a job, John, and I will be an ex-writer tomorrow.

I'll have more Bread Loaf pictures for you soon. Come to Boston, meanwhile, and we'll down a cup of Rhenish and forget the literary life. My best to Margaret.

Yours,

---

[7] *Saturday Review of Literature*, in whose editorship DeVoto would replace Canby two years later.
[8] *We Accept with Pleasure*, just published.

TO HARRY SCHERMAN

Around the first of April 1936, Harry
Scherman, of the Book-of-the-Month Club,
wrote asking if DeVoto would serve as a
judge for some proposed Book of the
Month fellowships to young writers.
DeVoto replied, as below, indicating
skepticism of the scheme, and a belief
that young writers might better fight the
grindstone than live soft on fellowships. He
himself never had a fellowship, and never
applied for one, though he wrote
innumerable letters for friends and
acquaintances supporting their
applications. He did not join Scherman's
committee of judgment, partly because of
his doubt of the value of fellowships in
general, but more because he feared the
commercial pressures from the donor.
Among his qualities was an intense dislike
of being used.

April 6, 1936

Dear Mr. Scherman:

I find all your material waiting for me on my return. It is a complex matter that you propose, and I don't feel competent to decide about it offhand. I should like to think about it for a while and talk it over with others of your tentative list. If you must have my answer at once, I am constrained with full appreciation of the honor you are doing me, to say no. If, however, you can wait a few days, I should like to think it over and also to have you discuss the plan with me in a little more detail.

I am troubled by a *cui bono*. Your organization is, though not precisely a publishing firm, still a business organization. You are not a foundation for the encouragement of belles lettres: you are out to make a profit. Your prospectus does not suggest that you are going to profit from the books of these young writers, but certainly you are going to profit from the attendant publicity. You are going to get a lot of priceless display space, editorial comment and word-of-mouth advertising—directly as a result of the new project. Directly, that is, as the result of your use of my name—mine and the others. Quite apart from the service to young writers, aren't you really asking for the use of whatever prestige my literary activity may have achieved, in the service of your business: publicity? Doesn't the Book of the Month stand to profit both directly and indirectly from what appears to be an eleemosynary endeavor, and may well be one, but is also a clever bid for the kind of advertising that, in the book business, is more valuable than any other?

Again, if this plan is carried through and becomes an annual affair, aren't you, in essence and in fact, setting up a board of review which has dangerous powers? Isn't your committee of writers and editors a kind of extra-legal Academy, operating under none of the constraints that a duly constituted Academy would have, and entrusted with great powers of publicity and some financial power, conceivably able to use them venally and certain to influence the young writer? And if it influences the young writer, aren't you defeating the very purpose which your prospectus announces?

I should like to hear what you would say in answer to such questions before saying finally that I will or won't accept your invitation. They represent my response to a first reading of your pamphlet, and I think that they cover matters which should be clarified.

That, in general. Privately, I am not sure that any attempt to alleviate the competitive rigors of his trade is good for a young writer, or for any writer. His job is to make his way, and if you make his way for him, it may be you will irrevocably damage him. Again, I'm not sure that the two examples you give are the happiest you could have chosen. Certainly George Santayana had, many years before 150,000 people bought one of his books,[1] a literary distinction, a literary achievement, a literary reputation even, far more valuable in themselves and far more of a reward for a lifetime's devotion to the art of writing than it is in the power of the book buying public to confer on him merely by buying his books in quantity.

I hope you will write me about these matters.

Sincerely yours,

TO FRANCES CURTIS

Among the reviewers whom DeVoto
recruited when he took over the Saturday
Review of Literature *in 1936 were a good*
many of his Cambridge and Harvard and
Breadloaf friends, including those spoken

[1] The novel *The Last Puritan*.

*of here: Frances Curtis, wife of Charles
Curtis, a Boston lawyer; Kay Thompson,
wife of Lovell Thompson of Houghton
Mifflin, and later editor of the* New
England Quarterly; *Charlotte Moody,
daughter of the president of Middlebury
College; Crane Brinton, George Homans,
and Arthur Schlesinger, Harvard
professors. Duncan Aikman was a Texas
journalist, editor of the first book in which
a DeVoto essay appeared, back in 1925.
By and large the regular reviewers could
have been called a like-minded group, and
under DeVoto's guidance they gave the*
Saturday Review *a literary and political
stance hostile to the literary Left, and at
the same time resistant to the thought
control of the Right, which in these years
was primarily literary and concerned about
obscenity.*

February 5, 1937

Dear Frances:

Jesus, you are a trial. You and Kay Thompson and the whole goddam gang of wistful amateurs that in my self-deluded moments I looked up to as a bunch of professional writers have got me down. Certainly Kay ought to realize that there is practically a complete lull in publishing books from December tenth to January first, that it is a period when quite conceivably none of the half dozen books actually published seem to me up her street, and that I can mean all the respectful and admiring compliments I send her and can refrain from sending her books when there are no books to send her without committing myself to a policy of not sending her books when there are books to send. And certainly you ought to read my sheet, since I tell you in private and tell the world through a loud speaker that you are my best fiction reviewer. If you will look at the *Saturday Review*, dear, from time to time you will find that at a rough estimate 90% of the reviews we publish are unfavorable. Don't take my word for it. Just go through three or four issues and derive your own percentages. Hardly a day goes by without a publisher writing or phoning me to inquire biliously which book I expect to praise this year. Moreover, I have repeatedly assured you and every other reviewer on my list that you can say anything you like about any book. Charlotte Moody has not yet found anything good in any novel I have sent her, except that one book looked better because she was slaughtering another one in the same review. I look back over my reviews and remember that only three of them have been favorable. I carry Crane Brinton and George Homans as trigger men, and am now adding Duncan Aikman to the squad.

I can't even remember which of your reviews we haven't run. I will have them looked up and see what the answer is. I know it in advance, however, for any review that is delayed is delayed on the basis of our judgment that the book is less important than other books which are at hand. My job is to get all reviews in on time and then to select out of material for thirty-two pages the material most important to run in twenty-eight pages. No other consideration ever influences my decision or the judgment of anybody else in the office. At any given time I have in type more material than I can run. I run what has the most important bearing on the issue as a whole and frequently my tentative decision on that importance is canceled by a realization that some book is more important than I thought it was when I sent it out. I must consider news interest, timeliness, previous importance of writers, qualities of the review itself, display space on the cover, the chance of scooping the *Times* and *Tribune*, and many other things.

For instance, I do not like to feature on the cover an unfavorable review, for it seems to be jumping on a man you have knocked down. I am willing to violate that principle, as I did with Arthur Schlesinger's review of Woodward, but do not like to. Thus, our main job in the issue going to press today is an article on Pushkin. George Stevens violently objected to making that the feature on the cover, on very good ground, that our competitors are certain to do the same. So we decided not to have a cut made until your review came in. If you thought well of the book, we would have a cut made of the Whitcomb wench and use that. If not, we could go ahead with Pushkin anyway. Your review came in and proved to be unfavorable. So at this moment George is ordering a cut of Pushkin.

Note that I have not yet read your review. I spend Friday mornings at home writing the editorial. The Whitcomb book is an important publication of this week, and George sent your review off to be set up as soon as it came in. He says it is a first rate review. I knew it would be. And what I want you to get into your giddy head is that, short of committing libel on the person of an author (it is impossible to libel a book), you are not only free to say whatever you think about any book I send you, but you are definitely informed that I will be sore as hell at you if you do anything else. I may cut your reviews if you say the same thing twice in them or if, as in the Van Druten one, you tell more of the story than you need. But I have never censored any opinion in any review and, short of the laws of libel, I never will. I will accept libel also whenever it seems to me unlikely to produce a suit—note my editorial on Sumner.[1]

What I wish you would do is first powder your nose, and then repeat one hundred times while looking in the mirror that I consider you an indispensable part of the coordinated team of fiction reviewers I have built up. If you will then spend one minute in serious meditation before the crucifix in your corner whenever one of these moods of *Minderwertigkeit* comes upon you, you will realize that only the exigencies of weekly journalism and limited space ever keep me from holding up any review of yours till I can find a place for it.

Do you now get the point I am making? It is this: say what you think and to hell with all other considerations.

I spent forty minutes pleasantly fencing with Sumner and managed to pink him once or twice. My major effort to get him to tell me what "Aphrodite" was about failed. The case has many amusing sidelights, which I can't tell you after this impassioned sermon. I spent two weeks in bed with the influenza and Bunny has spent the last week laid up with the same complaint. Avis has so far escaped. Ted Morrison[2] is coming out to stay with us tonight and I saw Ralph Barton Perry[3] yesterday, so that my communications with Jerusalem remain open. I am approaching involuntary bankruptcy and have no time to write a story, but all the colleges are asking me to make speeches and that will help. It seems unlikely that we shall get to Boston before mid-April, but if I can take a few days off then, we will stop off on our way to Middlebury, where I am going to deliver the Abernethy lecture. Avis will write to you, and I continue to adore you extravagantly, although handicapped in my passion by your moments of despondent literary vapors. Alfred McIntyre[4] reports that you are an extraordinarily fine acquisition, and Kay Morrison[5] mourns that you have probably taken her job out from under her feet. Alfred also says that the whole firm was in a condition of panic for the last week, momentarily expecting the office to become a delivery room. Kitty[6] sent me a long explanatory letter, but I am not intuiting very well since the flu and I do not make out what it is about. Josephine Johnson writes a poem in which I am described as Satan. The Easy Chair is due and I have no text.

So now be penitent and impressed and call up Kay Thompson and explain to her that publishers do not publish books in December and January

[1] His editorial of January 16, 1937, attacked John Saxton Sumner and the Society for the Suppression of Vice.
[2] Harvard teacher of writing and director of the Breadloaf Writers' Conference.
[3] Harvard professor of philosophy.
[4] President of Little, Brown and Co.
[5] Wife of Theodore Morrison, and later Robert Frost's secretary, assistant, and general manager.
[6] Catherine Drinker Bowen.

and that, if she continues to lead a pure life, she will receive packages from this family journal in due time. I was going to write her a fan letter about her article in the *New England Quarterly*, but you and she have so wounded me that I probably can't.

Yours,

TO LEE HARTMAN

DeVoto had been a contributor to Harper's *since 1927. In November 1935 he wrote the first of 243 Easy Chairs and became an intimate member of the* Harper's *editorial group, though not himself an editor. The letter below to the editor of* Harper's *is a comment on various proposals to alter* Harper's *in an attempt to weather the hard times of the Depression, and on questions of policy about the relation between editorial and business offices. Characteristically, DeVoto, who had then been using the* Saturday Review *to scourge the Left for nine months, held out for editorial independence, though his own magazine was barely surviving.*

May 3, 1937

Dear Mr. Hartman:

If the history of magazines in America demonstrates anything, it demonstrates that the most valuable business asset a magazine can have is a reputation for editorial independence, specifically interpreted as independence from advertising control. My own belief that no magazine eve[r] loses money in the long run by publishing material which its business office considers prejudicial to the interest of advertisers is amply supported by the experience of other editors and by the history of magazine reputations. It is true that individual instances occur when editorial material results in the cancellation of ads—though these instances are rare, much rarer than advertising folk-lore believes—but the loss here is trifling compared with that incurred by the weakening of the readers' respect when anything that smells of publicity or even of editorial co-operation with the business office appears in the magazine.

It must be remembered that the modern reader of quality magazines is a sophisticated and even suspicious person. He has a pointed dislike of paying for indirect publicity, and he has a shrewd ability to detect it, for it is constantly being directed at him from many directions. He prides himself on a nose for the phony and he promptly rejects everything that seems phony to him. The strictest kind of editorial ethics are the best insurance against financial loss. Editorial forthrightness is good business policy. A resolute refusal to co-operate with advertisers in the production of editorial publicity is the best asset a quality magazine can have. To survive and to make money a quality magazine must avoid not only the evil itself but every kind of appearance of the evil. Plain speaking and editorial independence are cash in the bank.

The proposal to turn *Harper's*, or any part of it, into a picture magazine horrifies me. In my opinion there is no surer way to kill the magazine. You would at once forfeit the support of a great part of your known audience, transgress the clear and obvious function of the magazine, and expose yourself to a competition which you are not qualified to meet and which would soon extinguish you.

The obvious opportunity of *Harper's* is to consolidate its leadership in the field it occupies and to take advantage of the mistakes of the *Atlantic* and *Scribner's*.

Sincerely yours,

TO FRANCES CURTIS

November 9, 1937

Dear Frances:

A Mike Arlen for you. Don't run over four hundred words, if that.

Maybe God will some time give me leisure enough to write a letter to you. I don't try to please reviewers any more, darling, or draw forth leviathan with an hook. I can only mutter that when I was a reviewer I took the dross with the gold, always observed the word limits, never missed a deadline, cheerfully put aside all my private necessities in order to serve the editor, and got paid eight months later, if at all. I have learned long since that they broke the mold after I came out of it [. . . .]

Yours,

TO GARRETT MATTINGLY

---

*By the end of 1937 it was clear that
DeVoto's editorship was not pulling the*
Saturday Review of Literature *out of the
red. Thomas Lamont, who provided the
financial backing, wanted to get out. There
was dissatisfaction among the staff, and
morale grew worse. DeVoto himself was
blamed by some of the magazine staff because he had taken the summer of 1937 off,
and gone to Vermont and Martha's Vineyard
to work on his own projects—a privilege that
he thought he had been guaranteed but that
some of the staff looked upon as a betrayal.
Never enthusiastic about his editorial job,
and loathing New York, DeVoto had
already begun to look back nostalgically to
Harvard, and would shortly be in
communication with Kenneth Murdock and
other Harvard friends in an attempt to
make his way back to teaching. He was also,
as he indicates to Mattingly, beginning the
negotiations that would lead to his
curatorship of the Mark Twain Papers,
succeeding Albert Bigelow Paine.*

December 31, 1937

Dear Mat:

   I hope that I may presently have leisure to write a decent & orderly
letter but this must be brief and is likely to be disorganized.—I am just back
from Chicago, where I griped the MLA handsomely & blew poor Bob Spiller
out of the water. I want to catch you before you leave England or I would
delay for a couple of weeks more in the hope of both leisure & more certainty about the things I have to tell. Be sure to give me at least a forwarding address when you move on to Italy.

Your book[1] is not out but is scheduled for February. I don't know what star was sighted on or what entrails consulted in that postponement. Probably Little, Brown have had no energy to spare for any activity except holding Dr. Cronin's abominable novel[2] at the head of the best seller list. If they let the advertising lag, the sales fall off like a Roosevelt estimate. It and a book about a dog are the only works of literary art, s.c., that the Americans have been buying. I will send you copies—and distribute any on this side you may want distributed—as soon as it is out.

When it appears it will be in part obsolete, and except for the horrible oaths of secrecy we are all under I would have altered the last page. I could not without letting Little, Brown know, of course, and our news has had to be protected from the publishers at all costs—even at the cost of falsifying my biography . . . The point is: it's about a 5 to 1 chance that when your book appears, when this reaches you mayhap, there will be no *Saturday Review of Literature,* and a 1 to 3 chance that, if it still exists, I shall not be editing it.

Our demise is part of what the President (by the way, I became a Republican at 7:48 this morning on reading an Ickes speech that was a follow-up of several Jackson speeches) describes as a deliberate conspiracy of rich men to bankrupt themselves. Tom Lamont can't carry it any more, and he's either selling it (with part of a one-year subsidy) or closing it out. If he sells it, the only possible buyer is Harry Scherman, of the Book of the Month Club. If he closes it out, he'll do so before January is up. Harry believes that he could make it self-supporting—and I think he could—but does not know whether he wants to take on a new major job at his age. He'll decide next week. My guess is he'll decide he can't. If he decides otherwise, it is unlikely that he'll want me for more than a few months, and still less likely that I'll want to stay on very long, even if he does.

So ends my career as a leader of thought [. . . .] Whether, in the circumstances, I can get back to Harvard or support myself in other ways is a genuine, and genuinely disturbing, mystery. If I can, why then, by God, I'll be glad to get the hell out of editing and, in the course of six months, out of New York, too. I hate this damn town with a fury that has increased week by week ever since I came to it, and the attrition it has practiced on the health & morale of my family has been all but intolerable. I'm damn tired, too, of writing about other people's books & not writing my own. I'm fed up with the literary and sick damn near to death of their ways & works. If I can get back to some kind of economic security, to a Christian country, and to my own work—well, I'll go back to the Church too, in sheer gratitude [. . . .]

I shall begin my under cover campaign at Harvard (which, by the way, don't mention to anyone) as soon as we hear from Scherman. The Hooded

[1] Mattingly's little critical book called *Bernard DeVoto: A Preliminary Appraisal.*
[2] *The Citadel.*

Ones report a certain turn of the tide. Whether or not it has gone far enough I can't begin to guess. I will also try to write a serial—whether I can again write fiction is also a question. I shall have to stay here till June anyway, whatever happens. Then—Massachusetts, Vermont, or W.P.A. There is a strong likelihood that I will be asked to examine the unpublished Mark Twain material, a considerable break, which would pleasantly fill the interstices of my time. I'll keep busy, I hope I'll keep solvent. If I do, there will be a bombproof for you in Vermont, when you get back [. . . .]

Yours,

TO CHARLES TOWNSEND COPELAND

January 21, 1938

Dear Copey:

It is poignantly true. I am fed up with editing, with New York, and especially with writing about books instead of writing books. You may expect to hear detonations very soon. Then if you know any college presidents, you may send out the burning cross.

I talk about you more often than I write about you. An antique shame sometimes keeps me from praising my friends in print, but there is no such inhibition on lectures and conversations. Either the world is full of your reverent admirers, or my happiest faculty is an ability to get into their company. I hope I may see you when I come to Cambridge briefly in April.

Yours,

TO A HARVARD COMMITTEE

As the Saturday Review of Literature
headed toward apparent collapse in
December and January 1937–38, DeVoto's
morale went down with that of the staff.
He felt himself blamed for a failure that
neither he nor anyone else could have
avoided. Understandably his account of his
departure from the editorship, expressed in

letters to Edith Mirrielees, Garrett
Mattingly, and Kenneth Murdock, is
somewhat defensive. George Stevens
does not remember that DeVoto had been
guaranteed his summers off, nor does he
remember other circumstances in quite the
way DeVoto does. Nevertheless, DeVoto's
judgment that the Depression was the real
villain seems essentially correct.

During the months when the fate of
the magazine was uncertain (it eventually
limped on under George Stevens's
editorship, and after two years acquired in
Norman Cousins an editor who brought it
to success), DeVoto was in confidential
communication with Kenneth Murdock,
Hans Zinsser, L. J. Henderson, and other
Harvard friends who wanted to get him
back to Harvard. The account of his
departure from Harvard, which had failed
to promote him into permanence in 1936,
was written at Murdock's request. His
slightly later letter to Murdock expresses
both DeVoto's earnest desire to return to
the Harvard faculty and his skepticism about
his chances. Along with this letter he
enclosed a statement, deliberately
unmodest, of his qualifications. Nothing
availed. He returned to Cambridge, but
not to Harvard.

January 1938

I submit this statement in response to the Committee's request for information concerning the termination of my appointment at Harvard in the spring of 1936.

1. 1929–1934. In May 1929 I was appointed Instructor in English and Tutor in the Division of Modern Languages. I did full time tutorial work during the year 1929–1930. In the fall of 1930 I gave up part of my tutorial work in order to edit *The Harvard Graduates' Magazine* and more of it in order to give English 31, Professor Hurlbut's old course in advanced composition, which Professor Murray asked me to take over, following Mr. Hurlbut's death. When I gave up the *Graduates' Magazine* two years later

I did not resume a full quota of tutorial work. I wanted to give up tutoring entirely—since I was not profoundly interested in it and since I felt that I was not a good tutor except for occasional students who were principally interested either in creative writing or in my special departments of Americana—but Professor Murray asked me to retain a certain minimum of it. He said that it would be advantageous to the department to continue me in the rank I held. I therefore continued to tutor one, two, or three students (the number varying) until I left Harvard. Throughout this time I was on annual appointment, teaching English 31, tutoring as I have explained, and being paid the appropriate fraction of an instructor's salary.

2. At some time during the year 1933–1934, Professor Murray asked me to give, in addition to the work I was doing, a course called "The Literature of the South and West." (I have forgotten its course-number.) After computing the time it would take for me to prepare and give the course, I decided that I could not afford, on an instructor's salary, to take that much time from my highly remunerative journalistic work. I so reported to Professor Murray. This occurrence, however, led both the department and me to face the question of my future status at Harvard, which we had not faced before. After much thought, I determined to give up journalistic work as rapidly as I could, and to give it up entirely as soon as Harvard would appoint me an associate professor. I told Professor Murray of this decision and he said he would canvass the department to determine how its members felt about my future at Harvard. Sometime later he called me in and said that the department looked forward to my eventually doing full time work. When I asked him if this meant that I might expect a permanent appointment in due course if my work proved satisfactory, he said that it did. We then discussed ways of achieving our common object. In the end it was agreed that I should prepare a course to be called "American Literature since 1900" (English 92, later English 70) which I should give the following year in addition to English 31 and my tutoring—and that I should be appointed a Lecturer in English and paid on the basis of an assistant professor's salary. I received a three-year appointment as Lecturer on that basis in May 1934.

It was my understanding from Professor Murray, and I am sure it was his understanding also, that, provided my work proved satisfactory, I should be appointed an associate professor and go on full time at the end of my three-year appointment as Lecturer.

It should be said that both the department and I made a fetish of that phrase "full time." It is a little difficult to determine just what it meant to either of us. So far as I was concerned it was a psychological evasion—I could tell myself that I was not relinquishing too much highly paid journalism so long as I was not on a full time basis. Actually, the difference between the work I did and full time work was microscopic. Teaching English 31 and English 92, I was doing four-fifths full time work. The addition of even one tutee brought it up to five-sixths full time. I did full time committee work as a tutor and read a full time tutor's share of honors theses. I also, at Professor Munn's request, took over one of the students in a 90-course of his, the Radcliffe Fellow in Creative Art, to give her instruction in professional writing. Similarly, for years it was the custom of many members of the department to refer to me for advice and instruction various students of theirs who were interested in professional writing.

3. 1934–1935. In the fall of 1934 Professor Munn succeeded Professor Murray as Chairman of the department. I went round to him and explained the burdens of my talks with Mr. Murray and my understanding of the terms of my appointment and my future at Harvard. Professor Munn told me that his understanding agreed with mine. He said that he looked forward to my receiving a permanent appointment and doing full time work. Aware that my Lectureship was a kind of probationary period, I several times, during the year, asked him if my work was satisfactory. He said that it was more than satisfactory, that he and the department were very much pleased with it. I consequently decided that my future at Harvard was settled.

During this year, in several conferences with Professor Munn and occasional ones with Professor Murdock, I made plans for developing various courses. All this was tentative and subject to change as conditions might arise, but we agreed to use my research in frontier history and literature as fully as possible. I was to give the course in "The Literature of the South and West" whenever the man who now gave it might want to offer a different course. I was to prepare a course in American Humor and another one in Frontier Literature. In addition I was soon to enlarge English 92 from a half to a full course and, at some future time, to offer its field for graduate study as a 20 course. Let me make plain that all this was tentative, plans for the future, work to be developed out of my fields—all except the course in Frontier Literature, which was actually scheduled for 1936–1937 as a "group" course. Nevertheless, although tentative, it was all purposeful and clear: I was to go on in the expectation of becoming a full-time teacher, on the basis already agreed upon.

My understanding was that I should be appointed an associate professor at the expiration of my term as lecturer. I am not sure whether Professor Munn ever said without any qualification whatever that such was his understanding also, but I believed that it was. I am quite sure that he had the same idea of my future at Harvard as I did.

4. 1935–36. Late in November 1935, a representative of *The Saturday Review of Literature* came to my house at Lincoln and offered me the

editorship of that magazine. Since my plans and desires were now centered on continuing at Harvard for the rest of my life, I had no disposition to accept the offer. I thought, however, that, in view of the offer, Harvard might be willing to give me the appointment as associate professor which I confidently expected at the end of the next college year, 1936–1937. The advantage to me of its doing so would be that I could give up all journalistic work a year earlier than I had expected to. I, therefore, went to Professor Munn, told him the terms of the offer, and asked him whether the department would be willing to give me the appointment at that time. He said that, in his offhand judgment, they would be. He said that he was in favor of it himself, that he would consult other members of the department, that he would write or cable to Professor Murdock (who was most conversant with the work in American literature, and who was then in Europe), and that he would speak to President Conant.

It happened that I had to go to the University of Missouri, to deliver a centennial address on Mark Twain. When I got back, Mr. Munn had a letter from President Conant. He read to me the decision that affected me. President Conant said, in exactly these words, that he did not at that time contemplate any change in my status at Harvard. I asked Professor Munn to ask President Conant whether that meant that I could not expect permanent appointment or full time work. A few days later Professor Munn told me that he had seen the President and that Mr. Conant had told him that I might expect to continue at Harvard on the existing basis (i.e., as a Lecturer, on part time, paid at the rate of an assistant professor) but that I could not expect a permanent or even a full time appointment.

Several days later, Mr. Munn received a letter from Mr. Murdock. Mr. Murdock said in it that he would not be in favor of appointing me to an associate professorship at the present time, that he would prefer not to open the question of such an appointment until my term as Lecturer was completed.

I thereupon asked Mr. Munn to tell me, not as an officer of the University but as one who knew me and my work, what he thought I ought to do. He said that he did not understand why the President had taken such a stand, that he thought it might be altered as time went on, and that he thought—unofficially—that I had reasonable ground for hope if I stayed on at Harvard. He repeated that the department wanted me to have the appointment that I desired. He advised me—quite unofficially—to stay on, at least until the end of my term as Lecturer. Let me make plain that he gave me this advice in the full knowledge that I wanted to stay on and that working at Harvard meant enough to me to run a considerable chance that I might not get the appointment. My own belief was that the President was not completely informed about my qualifications. I consulted various people who were informed about them, explained the situation, and asked their advice. The general opinion agreed with my own: that my request for an associate professorship (which, I understood, had been promised me by the department two years before) was not egotistical or presumptuous, that I was qualified for such a position. I therefore decided that the situation might change in the future, and so I formally declined the editorship that had been offered me.

In February the editorship was again offered me, on even better terms. I went to Professor Munn again, told him about the renewed offer, and asked him for an opinion. At this time he told me explicitly that the department had, previously, voted for my promotion. I went also to Professor Murdock, who had returned to Cambridge. He said that he had not clearly understood the situation when Professor Munn wrote to him, and that he did not now clearly understand the President's stand. I asked him—again, not as an officer of the University but as one who knew me and my work—whether he thought that, if I refused the offer, I might reasonably expect the President to alter his decision at some future time. He said that I was, in his opinion, a desirable person, that my request for promotion was not unreasonable, and that I had qualifications for promotion that would increase rather than diminish as time went on. He said that it was obviously unsafe to make any prediction but nevertheless, if my courses continued to be successful and if my frontier research developed satisfactorily, I might reasonably renew my request later on with an intelligent hope of its being reconsidered. This agreed with my own judgment and that of friends whom I again consulted. I therefore went again to Mr. Munn and proposed that, at the end of my lectureship, I be appointed an assistant professor for three years with a promise of an associate professorship at the end of that term, if my work continued to be satisfactory. This represented a heavy sacrifice to me—in salary alone, a sacrifice of six thousand dollars a year—but if there was any hope at all of advancement at Harvard, I wanted to stay there. A few days later Mr. Munn reported that President Conant had repeated his earlier answer: that I was free to continue on my present basis but might not expect full time work nor a permanent appointment.

I nevertheless again declined the editorship. I determined to go ahead on the present basis, in the hope that the situation might change in the future.

In late April, however, the editorship was again offered to me, on terms so advantageous that I felt compelled to accept it unless I could get the appointment at Harvard that I desired. I again went to Professor Munn, again received his assurance that the department was in favor of promoting me, and told him that I intended to talk with President Conant.

Here I am a little confused, for I cannot remember whether I had one interview with Mr. Conant or two. The confusion is caused by the fact that he shifted his ground, and I cannot remember whether the shift came after an interval of some days, or whether it came in the course of a single interview. The shift was this: at one point he said that he was informed that my scholarship was deficient, whereas at another and later point he said that my scholarship had not been impugned.

At any rate, I went to President Conant, told him the terms of the offer, said that I wanted to stay at Harvard and would stay if made an associate professor, and asked him to reopen the case. Mr. Conant said that I was a desirable person to have associated with the University on precisely the present terms, that the University profited from such an association and I probably did too, but that to ask for a permanent appointment brought other values to bear. He said that, according to his information, my scholarship was weak. I said that, in my opinion, he had been insufficiently or incorrectly informed, and that my scholarship was both adequate and sufficiently recognized. I refrained from specifying because I did not want to seem impertinent, but I asked him to go into the matter again and to consult with people who were informed about the extent of my research and my qualifications for it. I mentioned Professor Schlesinger and Professor Merk. I named them particularly because my project in the frontier is historical quite as much as it is literary, and because I assumed that Professor Murdock must have already vouched for its literary aspects. After the incident was over, I learned from Mr. Schlesinger and Mr. Merk that he had not consulted them.

Either at this point in a single interview or at a later interview (I am sorry I cannot say which) the President took a different ground. He now said that his former decision must be understood as involving no derogation of either my ability or my scholarship, that my appointment must be considered in relation not to me alone but to the needs of the department, the budget, and many other values. To have me on my present terms was one thing, but when I asked for a permanent appointment, he must take into consideration twenty-five years of the future. He must treat my request precisely as if I were at another university and it was proposed to call me to Harvard from there. The only question he could grant any weight to was: "Is he, considering the needs of the department, the budget, and other values, the one man we would call to Harvard at the present time?" On such a basis he would reopen the inquiry without prejudice, if such was my desire, but he would offer me no hope, for he considered his former inquiry adequate.

About a week later, I received the following letter, under date of May 6, 1936:

Dear Mr. DeVoto:

As I promised you the other day, I have re-examined the question of your appointment at Harvard and am sorry to report that my decision of this winter must stand. We shall be glad to continue you here on the present basis of your lectureship at the present salary but can not look forward to giving you a permanent appointment at full salary. In view of this fact, I feel that I must urge you strongly to accept the position which you said had been offered to you.

With all good wishes,
Sincerely yours,
(Signed) James B. Conant

I therefore accepted the editorship of *The Saturday Review* and wrote to Professor Munn resigning my lectureship.

I had no other official statements from anyone. I consulted no one else except private friends. No one else consulted me.

I want to make clear that, after the President's first refusal to promote me, I did not at any time consider that Professor Munn or Professor Murdock was speaking officially. I consulted them unofficially, in order to reach my own conclusions.

TO KENNETH MURDOCK

February 13, 1938

Dear Kenneth:

It has taken me so long to write the inclosure[1] that I may have to skimp my narrative of events if I am to get it into the Sunday collection. I feel several different kinds of fool praising myself so loudly, but I don't think the inclosure contains anything that hasn't been said of me impersonally by people who were speaking objectively, and I think that the issue at stake is so important that the things must be said, for the use of anyone who may find them useful. It is a memorandum for you. I take it for granted that you won't want to show it to anyone, but if you feel any need to, go ahead.

The campaign is in your hands, and I will follow your instructions and abide by your judgments. Whatever exterior arguments you may have, such as my usefulness to the Press or what-not, it seems to me that the main case rests on whether or not I am desirable as a teacher, investigator, and man of letters. That is what I have tried to outline herein.

I am by no means clear about what has happened at the S.R. On Tuesday I understood that Scherman[2] had finally withdrawn and that Lamont[3]

[1] DeVoto sent along with this letter an extended dossier listing his accomplishments and capacities.
[2] Harry Scherman, of the Book of the Month Club, was being wooed as a backer.
[3] Thomas Lamont, financial backer of the *Saturday Review*.

was committed to closing up at once. I felt so sure of that issue that, meeting Don McLaughlin at the Harvard Club on Thursday, an hour before the momentous dinner, I told him that the Review was folding up. But it appears that on Wednesday Lamont had summoned Noble Cathcart[4] to his office and the two of them had decided that if the paper could be kept going for eight or ten months longer, by hook or crook, someone would take it over. Just who I don't know. Scherman has flatly refused to commit himself, saying only that he will give any advice he can. Anyway, Lamont has tossed twenty thousand dollars into the pot. That is, he says flatly, his last contribution. When that is gone he will give no more. Noble undertakes to run the paper on that amount—not saying for how long, but for as long as he can.

What he intends to do is too vague for me to follow. It may be clearer when I have had the interview with him he has desired for tomorrow. As I understand it now, it runs this way. The editorial budget of the *Review* is $33,000 a year, the contributors' budget is $9,000. Noble will therefore lop off the editorial budget entirely, constrict the office space to a single room and a telephone, and pay us, when we contribute anything, the usual space rates paid to contributors. Here enters the ineffable: we are now free agents (or will be in a day or two) and are to go out and get jobs for ourselves, but at the same time we are to continue on call for full time work until April first, since our salaries are to be paid till that date. That is: we have three months' notice, on February 10, as of last January 1, and are paid a salary from January 1 to April 1, which is very handsome. But also, since our salary is paid till April 1, we are to do whatever may be asked of us, including, in my case, editing the paper.

This may be clearer to me by tomorrow night than it now is. At the moment I'm sure of one thing only, Lamont's statement that we were to do what we wanted as fast as we could, and I shall shortly go to work for *Harper's*—at least on Mark Twain, possibly in charge of the literary section of the magazine.[5] I have been asked to take that over, remodel it, and make it into something. I don't want to, and in any event won't take it for longer than a few months, to get it started. But there are psychological advantages in taking it that long, both public and private. . . . I don't think Noble can possibly edit the *Review* himself. It is quite certain that he will have to have someone edit it for him. Certain things he has said suggest to me that he intends to begin with my secretary, Mary Ellen Whelpley (she used to be with me on the *Graduates' Magazine*[6]), but I think he will soon come to enlarging his budget and taking on either George Stevens or Amy Loveman.[7] He has already hinted that he wants me to go on writing editorials—at, I

---

[4] Publisher of the *Saturday Review*.
[5] He never undertook this job.
[6] *Harvard Graduates' Magazine,* which DeVoto edited from 1930 to 1932.
[7] In the event, he kept them both.

suppose, space rates after April 1, but on my three-months notice until then. I will write them until Lamont has been consulted from Cambridge.[8] Then I won't write them.

As to what Noble has said to Lamont I can only hazard the vaguest guesses. I do know that he has complained about my absence from duty last summer, saying that it was a mistake and an unwarranted desertion. There is now a flat issue of fact between us. From the very first negotiations in November 1935, I insisted that the absolute condition of any further talk was the stipulation that I was to have my summers off. That stipulation was, according to my version, explicitly accepted at every stage thereafter. I am quite sure that it was. I told you about it at the time, I have told everyone else about it ever since, Avis remembers a flat statement of it in the Parker House, and when I left last summer, everyone in the office, including Noble, had known for nine months that I was going to leave and had at no time suggested any reason why I should not go. But, of course, I have nothing in writing. So that joins the other misrepresentations made to me, that I could count on at least three years to rehabilitate the magazine and that a vigorous promotion campaign would be instituted, as a product of my vicious and now defensive imagination.

The psychology of failure is obvious, if interesting. I am quite aware that I probably exhibit it myself. Nevertheless there can be no doubt about such matters as the summers-off business, and Noble in fact contradicts himself about it. It comes down to this: the general public admits that the *Review* improved under me and our whole force was agreed, explicitly, on November 15th that the *Review* was then the best it had ever been. But the depression slew it, and there has to be a goat. Actually it would have been slain eventually anyway, unless the business office had been cleaned out. A third of the circulation has been allowed to become deadhead, there is no advertising rate-card, the sheet does not belong to the A.B.C. and cannot make the terms that A.B.C. members can, it wastes thousands of dollars a year making advertising cuts when no other literary sheet does, there has been no advertising promotion and no circulation promotion in many years, etc. In the circumstances, however, I'll be the goat. How far I have been made one in Lamont's eyes I don't know. No one will find out from [him] direct except Conant. He was as amiable and courteous as possible to me and told me, as he told you, how brilliant I am. The one favorable sign is that he did phone Canby. . . . I'll tend to Canby in person tomorrow.

The hell with this. In public I shall have nothing to say. God knows I hate alibis, and only my friends are ever going to hear mine.

I think you may have something in Reed Powell.[9] I have never been in-

[8] Lamont had promised to give DeVoto a strong recommendation for use in the Harvard negotiations.
[9] Thomas Reed Powell, of the Harvard Law School.

timate with him but I have known him for a long time and know in general that he votes my ticket. He is also one of the men who aren't afraid to say what they think. Zinsser comes in that class too. I was sending a book to Hans for review and told him that I was leaving but told him no more than that. I think he will go to bat for me—I know that he was sulphurous to Henderson for not doing so two years ago. I think Frankfurter would too, but he is also of the Nine Old Men.[10] I doubt that Charlie Curtis would feel free to do anything directly but he will beat up the bushes as may be necessary and he may have some valuable suggestions. It is possible that my publisher, Alfred McIntyre, may also.

Well, I don't think the prospects are very favorable, but let's do what we can. I think I'd be useful to the institute of culture,[11] and that nerves a naturally shy and timorous soul to this egotistical effort. At any rate, I got an authentic thrill of gratitude and pleasure from your phoning me Friday evening. Let me know developments and any steps you may want me to take. I'm on night call, with my breeches folded into my boots and the brass rail only three feet away.

Yours,

TO HENRY SEIDEL CANBY

*Though he had long been a highly paid
writer of stories and serials for the* Post
and Collier's, *DeVoto had never had a big
commercial success with a book. That came
when* The Year of Decision 1846 *was
selected by the Book-of-the-Month Club.*

July 19, 1942

Dear Henry:

I am still reeling a little from the impact of your adoption. I counted on your liking the book and on your and Amy's being favorable toward it because you usually are favorable to me, but I have never thought of it as

---

[10] The Committee of Nine which had formulated, after some clashes with President Conant, the Harvard promotion and tenure policy. One weakness of DeVoto's position was that several of his strongest backers were on this committee, and did not feel free to champion his cause.

[11] Established in 1936, this became the program in American Civilization. It was Murdock's hope that DeVoto could be given a special appointment in it, out of the departmental winds and outside the limitations of the Committee of Nine's "red bible," which strictly limited permanent appointments.

likely to interest many people and never thought you would find a general interest in it. I am certainly not going to argue against your decision, however, and if you're staking your judgment on it I intend to be henceforth as silent as possible about what may be a great folly. I add that this is by far the biggest break I have ever had and it will enable me to tackle other jobs I have never had much hope of tackling.

Alfred McIntyre has sent me a copy of your letter to him. You can't possibly know how opaque earlier versions of that first chapter were. It is now in its third state and when I read the first state over I couldn't find my way through it myself. Getting this book under way properly is, frankly, a hell of a problem. And, frankly, I don't know how much clearer it can be made. I'll rewrite it—and glad to, for in reading proof I've been horrified by things that it would have been too expensive to change. Some things can be made much clearer, and I think I can probably write a general statement which will prepare the way and which I [can] refer back to from time to time. And I can get rid of some obliquities and ellipses.

Most of the separate things that are in it, however, will probably have to stay, though some of them can be joined and others rearranged. Hard going as the chapter is, it nevertheless pays rich dividends as the book goes on and the final effect, I'm confident, depends on it. Thus, part of the effect of the Mormons depends on Brook Farm, and part of the effect of Thoreau's rebellion against the war issues from his appearance in the first chapter. But his appearance there also supports the emigration theme and the theme of the industrial revolution, and so it is enhanced by the other literary figures. And so on.

I think the main job to be done is to be as clear and specific as possible as soon as possible about the war, the bearing of western geography on the war, and the bearing on both of expansionism. I think I can be clearer about both the crisis and the geography than I am now, and I know I can be clearer about the history of both. The trouble—apart from the natural resistance of the material—is that I too much enjoyed writing that chapter as if it were the opening of a group novel. In a sense that's precisely what the book is[1] but there is no need to practice technique for its own sake.

I also welcome the chance to tone down the rhetoric at the end of the chapter a little. I deliberately heaved it in to revive the reader after beating him over the head, but when I saw it in type I perceived I had heaved in too much.

I hope, however, you won't expect too much. I'll do my damnedest to make it easier going, and I certainly can make it clearer and less confusing, but I dunno whether it can be made to weigh much less. After all, it has a psychology, a history, and a tangle of foreign relations to clamp down under one lid.

[1] See the letter to Madeline McQuown, p. 287.

Well, I must say I'm dazzled. I have been long hardened to the belief that serious books bring no return and tripe must be the support of my family. I won't do you the indignity of thanking you, but let's say I find your judgment very refreshing.

Yours,

TO DONALD PORTER GEDDES

Defending the public interest against censors and witch-hunters was standard practice for DeVoto. By affiliation and by native sympathy he usually found himself on the side of publishers. But occasionally he felt obliged to remind a publisher of his public obligations, too. The letter below is better understood when we remember that the paperback revolution in bookmaking— the mass production of books at first designed to be as cheap and as expendable as magazines—did not occur in the United States until after World War II. DeVoto was looking upon paperbacks not in terms of what they later became, but of what they might, with responsible handling, become.

August 21, 1945

Dear Mr. Geddes:

I first thought I'd do this in the Easy Chair, but I've decided to write you a letter instead and let the public discussion slide for a while. Some day the point I raise here will have to be raised publicly and talked out by a good many people. For it's an important point.

It's just this. Granted the immense importance of the job you people at Pocket Books and your competitors are doing, in opening up a mass market, distributing books, and contributing to the pleasure, edification, and education of people at large—granted all that, as I enthusiastically grant it, there remains an editorial obligation which, it seems to me, you can by no means escape. If you are going to distribute information widely, then it seems to me you are constrained to see to it that you are distributing reliable information, not misinformation. If you aren't so constrained, if you are not to be responsible, then it seems to me that there is no social immunity which you can plead as your clergy when certain interests in competition with you, say the Retail Booksellers Association, attack you on other grounds.

The specific instance that touched off this letter is *The Pocket Book of Western Stories*, edited by Harry E. Maule. I don't know Mr. Maule or anything about him, except that he is an editor at Random House and therefore obviously a good editor. But I can pick up enough from this book to say (a) that, whatever his qualifications for other things, he probably ought not to be allowed to edit an anthology of Western stories and (b) that he certainly ought not be allowed to write an introduction to one. I say "ought" purely in terms of your organization and what I hold to be its responsibility toward the public. I assume that your organization does not want to short-weight the public in quality. I assert that it must not be allowed to mislead and misinform the public. The corollary is that you ought first to choose editors for anthologies from among experts in the fields to be anthologized, and second to give their work rigorous editorial checking before publishing it.

(An aside. A chap who is vacationing here on the Point says that Mr. Maule used to edit a Western-story magazine. If so, I am the more surprised but the fact does not in the least alter what I am about to say. Also, I do not myself want to edit an anthology of Western stories and in fact have several times refused to do so. I claim no particular authority in the field, but I do happen to know it reasonably well, as a by-product of working in the history of American literature at large. The fact that I'm not a specialist makes all the more pointed the objections which I proceed to voice.)

The less weighty of those objections deal with the book as such, with the selections. Ordinarily it is idle to quarrel with an anthologist. He is entitled to pick what he wants to pick. He likes these things; if I don't happen to like them, all I'm entitled to say is, my taste differs from his. But the title of this book implies that the selection is going to be representative and the actual selections and what is said about them in the introduction go rather beyond that—they imply that it is going to be historically representative. And it just isn't. Whole areas of Western fiction get left out entirely and, historically, there are two startling and important gaps, one of about twenty years, and the other of something more than ten years. Or put it on other grounds. What kind of anthology of Western stories leaves out the Red Saunders stories? What can you say of one that puts Zane Grey and Clarence Mulford in (or almost any other two that are in) and leaves out Stephen Crane and Alfred Henry Lewis? These are not matters of taste merely but of historical and critical foundation stones. I would have said that no one could make an anthology of Western stories that left out Phillips, Crane, and Lewis. Having seen one, I have to say that it's a bad one on that ground alone—and people who know the field would, I think, say the same, no matter what their taste may be. To anyone's eye it is two thirds an anthology of pulp-magazine, formula cowboy stories and in the other third an anthology of Western stories that disregards most of the good ones.

However, let's forget about the selection, for what I'm concerned with is the introduction. If that had been left out, I should have had no complaint; this would have been just a book, which, in my opinion, could have been better. But it wasn't left out. Some part of 150,000 people, or some part of 500,000 people, are going to read it, accept it as correct, and so acquire totally wrong ideas. For it is a thoroughly bad introduction, intolerably erroneous in its statements of fact, intolerably ignorant and false in its conjectures, assertions, and implications. I am not speaking of literary judgments, I am speaking of historical and critical information, material about which there can be no difference of opinion whatever. The public buys this introduction in good faith; it assumes that it is getting reliable information. It isn't; it is being gypped. And that, if my opening assumption is sound, is the responsibility of your organization. You are, in a very real sense, a public utility—and here you are purveying errors and ignorance.

I don't want to string this out forever, so let's simply hit some high spots of factual information and some high spots of critical appraisal and let it go at that, with the footnote that the introduction is all bad—should never, in my opinion, have been published by you or anyone else.

Page vii. I could shoot holes in each of the first four sentences of the first paragraph that begins on that page, but let them go. Next sentence: *Astoria* is not at all a novel, not in the least fictional; it is a history of John Jacob Astor's attempt to organize the far western fur trade on a Columbia River base, a strictly factual and thoroughly documented account of the exploration, commerce, and incidental excitement of the venture, as thoroughly historical as anything by Mr. Beard. Next sentence: "the movement of expansion took on its real momentum" not after the Civil War but before it— Oregon migration and the Mormons belong to the early and the late 1840s respectively, the Gold Rush began in 1849, the great days of the Northwest date from the 1850s, so does Virginia City, so do many other mining rushes. California was a State in 1850, Oregon was a State and Nevada and Colorado and Washington and Utah were Territories before the Civil War, and Nevada was a State before the war ended. Next sentence: Bret Harte went to California before the Civil War and Mark Twain during its first year. Next sentence but one: Harte and Mark met in the early 1860s, Mark left California before the war ended and Harte before 1870, they were closely associated for a number of years, they were even literary collaborators, and they regarded themselves as friends till they quarreled about 1874 or 1875. Next sentence but one: nothing in *Roughing It* was written except as a part of the book and the book contains none of Mark's earlier work and no separate or separately published stories. Next sentence: "Buck Fanshaw's Funeral" was written about two years before *Tom Sawyer* and about three years before Mark began to write *Huck Finn*.

Passing over the dubious paragraph about Harte—who was an express messenger and had little experience in the mining country—there is no "tone of patronage for the rude civilization" etc., in what Mark Twain wrote about the West. None whatever—in fact, an extremity of the opposite. Nor does Harte's stuff stand up today. Apart from no more than six stories, the anthologized ones, it is not read at all. Presumably the author of an introduction should know what he is talking about.

The next paragraph is so full of misconception, as distinguished from misstatement, that I can't possibly untangle it. What are "the stultifying literary mores" of the second great age of American literature, the age of Henry James, Howells, Cable, Harris, the rise of the short story, the consummation of Whitman's poetry, etc? What diaries of what explorers were published in this period? Most of them were in fact published in the earlier period or in the one that immediately followed. What has "the multi-volume Parkman history of early America" got to do with the West? Parkman wrote only one book about the West and that is not a part of his history, which is devoted to the struggle between the British and French colonial empires in the 17th and 18th centuries.

But why go on? It's all on that level. Now, in the first place, if my original assumption is sound, no one should write so inaccurately. But even if someone does, you are responsible for its mass circulation—and two hours of work by any clerk in your office, using no more than any standard history of American literature plus any standard history of the United States would get rid of this sort of thing. Your public isn't going to do that work: it is entitled to assume that that work has been done. What's the answer?

So let's look at it from another angle, the critical one. There was a great deal of good writing about the West in the period which Maule says was devoid of it, but let that go. The statement about "The Winning of the West" made on page viii is altogether astonishing to anyone who knows the history or the literary history of the time, and altogether preposterous besides, but let that go too. Stephen Crane and Alfred Henry Lewis preceded Wister, and a dozen others came on the scene in a dead heat with Wister, but let that go. The cowboy story had been established as a form before O. Henry started writing it, but let that go. I imagine that few critics would underwrite what is said about White, but let that go . . . What I object to is the effective implication that Western literature is a literature of the cattle business only, that there are no soldiers, no Indians, no homesteaders, no railroad builders, and no miners except Harte's and Mark Twain's in Western literature—plus the implication that one of the most absorbing areas of American journalism never existed at all—plus the downright limitation of Western literature to fiction—plus the shocking limitation of even cowboy fiction in its formative period from 1890 to 1910, to Wister, O. Henry, and Gene Rhodes. (I knew and loved Rhodes, and I wonder what he'd say to that last —or rather I don't wonder and it would have been worth hearing.) It was Phillips who gave Rhodes both a model and a start. It was Lewis, not Wister, who got home to the wide public and who fastened conventions—on the whole deplorable conventions, from our hindsight—on the form. It was Stephen Crane who first raised Western fiction to a literary level—and he wrote earliest of all I've named. It was Andy Adams and Charles Siringo— but, hell, let it go once more. Have I said enough to suggest that this introduction is misinformed, erroneous, and ignorant?

Now two things. One, there is nothing here that couldn't have been avoided if you'd seen to it that your introduction was written by someone who knew what he was talking about, and nothing that couldn't have been corrected by the most perfunctory and even rudimentary editorial checking in your office. Two, it matters damn little what anyone thinks, right or wrong, about Western stories.

But you didn't get someone who knew what he was talking about and you didn't check what he said. Also, it will matter quite a bit, in the public interest, if you are equally irresponsible about history or economics or sociology or psychology or criminology or war guilt or the race problem or propaganda or a good many other subjects you are certain to get into as you and your competitors exploit the mass market. It is certainly no business of yours to settle controversies or take sides in an argument or stand for a point of view, and God forbid that I should deny you the inalienable right of private enterprise to turn a profit in any area of the publishing business where you may think one can be found. But it is your business to see to it that you do not purvey misinformation—the more so because you are dealing with the mass market. The bigger your market, the greater your responsibility, for the greater the public interest. Which is where I enter, uttering cautions. The public is partly my business, too. It is up to me, up to my trade and calling that is, to denounce you and your calling for betraying the public interest when you sell shoddy. There is no reason why you need sell shoddy.

As I see it, there is no out for you unless you try to play it both ways. You are selling a two-bit book as a first-rate book, so you can't plead that we mustn't expect a two-bit book to be first-rate. If you are to be justified on any ground except that it only costs two bits, then you've got to be as good as it's possible to be. In fact, since you can afford editorial rigorousness and scrupulousness beyond the means of the ordinary trade-publisher, you've got to supply them or I don't know my social ethics.

This has bored you inordinately. I knew it would but I suppose part of your job is being bored in such contexts. It is simply a protest I feel obliged to make. I'd like to hear what you think of it.

Sincerely yours,

TO GEORGE STEVENS

June 5, 1947

Dear George:

Raymond Everitt's death has postponed a crisis I fully intended to precipitate practically at once. Please regard this as Secret, British Most Secret.

Little, Brown never should have published me. They have an uncanny gift for taking a book with a potential sale of 100,000 and selling 500,000 copies of it. They are not interested in the kind of thing I write and actually do not know how to publish it. I do not expect big sales or even moderately big ones, and never have. But I do think that any of a dozen, or at least any of six or eight publishers could have sold more of most of my books than Little, Brown did. I think, that is, that they had a bigger potential sale than Little, Brown got out of them. The last thing I asked Raymond to do was to send me an itemized report on total sales of all my books. I will show it to you sometime and you will be able to see whether I am right or self-deluded.

It is to be said further that nobody in the firm has ever been interested in my books. I don't know quite why Alfred[1] has wanted to publish them except that he is a friend of mine and it may also be that he feels happy in having a sort of house intellectual. I don't know quite why I have let him publish ten books except that, again, I like him a lot. Certainly he has no interest in what I write, has very seldom pretended to have any, and nobody else connected with the firm has even pretended to. When I see you at half year intervals I get more honest interest in whatever I may be working on than I get from the whole firm throughout the course of writing and publication of a book. Houghton Mifflin, who are doing my fur trade book on a one-book contract and have never suggested that they would like to do anything else of mine, have shown far more interest in that one book than Little, Brown have shown in ten.

I have gradually come to the conclusion that a chap like me is reasonably entitled to ask his publisher to do one or the other of two things, either to sell his books fairly well or to take an interest in them. That is my platform henceforth: sell my stuff or like it. You are a friend of mine and so somewhat to the surprise of the trade is Alfred Knopf—so for that matter is Lovell Thompson.[2] I have done enough publishing for friendship's sake and I propose to be cold-blooded as all hell. When the time comes I am going to put

---

[1] Alfred McIntyre, president of Little, Brown.
[2] Vice-president of Houghton Mifflin.

myself up on the counter and say to twenty-five or -six of you, here I am, how much am I worth to you in cash or unmistakable evidence of genuine interest in my kind of writing.

Presumably this unseemly frankness has already deeply offended the idealism that principally animates you, as it does all other publishers. If it doesn't, I append my present program:

1. A novel about life in Cambridge I have for fifteen years threatened to write. I am 30,000 words into it.[3]
2. A book about Lewis and Clark which is supposed to end all books about Lewis and Clark and about all early western exploration as well. I have been reading off and on for it for four years and am slowly swinging into the fundamental research right now. This is supposed to be the capstone of my peculiar western history.[4]
3. An anthology of western travel and exploration.[5]
4. A collection of uncollected DeVoto since *Minority Report*.[6]
5. Possibly the book that would round out my western stuff and enable me to say that I had covered the whole field, a narrative of Oregon emigration, most likely limited to the great year which was 1843.[7]

Let me know if you are still reading.[8]

TO PAUL BROOKS[9]

November 2, 1947

Dear Paul:

I remembered my religion, which holds that sloth is a deadly sin, and so herewith the contract.[10]

I'd like, for the record, to put down what I said to you the other day, that I had never supposed I had a fur trade book in me, that the idea was yours, not mine, and that I'm pleased, as pleased as I ever get to be with my work, by the result. I take it that part of the editorial or publishing function is to understand what a writer is capable of. It's ironical to realize that I wasn't your writer when you figured it out.

[3] It remains among his papers as the unpublished novel *Assorted Canapes*.
[4] It became *The Course of Empire*.
[5] Never done.
[6] It became *The Easy Chair*.
[7] Apparently never begun.
[8] Stevens was reading, but never got a chance to act. Houghton Mifflin's performance with *Across the Wide Missouri* caused DeVoto to stick with them as his publishers.
[9] Editor in chief, Houghton Mifflin.
[10] To *The Course of Empire*.

I told Henry[1] that, all told, I'm in a quite risky mood for a writer to be in about his publishers, and that's true. Throughout you people have been interested in the job and have assisted and supported and complemented it in a way that I had never experienced before and that has given me quite a new conception of publishing. I'm going to thank Lovell separately for the job he and his boys did in making a beautiful book and writing the only advertising matter my stuff has ever had that seems related to the stuff, but I want to thank you, and the three girls who did so much for me, for the kind of direct personal help that is invaluable. And even more for your interest in what I was doing. As I say, it's a new experience for me.

The reviews are quite a shout, aren't they? My ego is not under too great a strain; few of those who have been praising it so highly are qualified to judge it one way or the other.

Unhappily, there are some who are, and they keep rating books. I suppose my scholarly debts will have to be paid. Please send me four more copies—I am now setting myself the psychic limit of one hundred dollars for debts, relatives, and vanity . . . Well, you can always count on me as the steadiest customer for DeVoto books.

Yrs,

TO DOROTHY HILLYER

*Almost by accident, and over a period of
several years, DeVoto found himself
instructing his friends and after a while the
nation in proper drinking habits. In the
Easy Chair of December 1949, entitled
"For the Wayward and Beguiled," he
revealed the holy mysteries of the martini;
and in later essays and Easy Chairs he spoke
ex cathedra about what is drinkable and
what is not. Thousands of Americans who
could tell you nothing else about Bernard
DeVoto could tell you his recipe for the
martini: the marriage of gin and vermouth
takes place in a proportion of 3.7 to 1 and at
a temperature as close to absolute zero as
may be obtained, with no olives, onions, or
other vegetable matter, only a twist of
lemon rind. The Hour, the book which was*

[1] Henry Laughlin, president of Houghton Mifflin.

made of these drinking essays in 1951,
remains one of the lightest-hearted and
most delightful of DeVoto's writings, and
the letters that DeVoto wrote to
correspondents about the alcoholic mystique
are full of an amused gusto.

Even before the publication of "For the
Wayward and Beguiled," he was a formidable
purist in matters of drink, as witness
this letter to Dorothy Hillyer, once the
wife of the poet Robert Hillyer, later Mrs.
Giorgio de Santillana. She had been book
editor of the Boston Globe *before joining*
the editorial staff of Houghton Mifflin.
The cookbook in question is Isabel Marvin's
Bon Appétit. *DeVoto's objections to its bar*
section touch my soul in a special way
because Mrs. Marvin's book was the first
that my wife and I, as Houghton Mifflin's
West Coast editors from 1945 to 1953,
recruited for the Houghton Mifflin list.

October 21, 1947

Dear Dorothy:

I realize there is a woman's world into whose mysteries one of my sex should venture only at his risk and prepared to take stoically whatever may happen to him there. Nevertheless, I have been shocked and grieved immeasurably by the degradation of standards which the Houghton Mifflin Company is facilitating by distributing the cook book which irresponsibly and indeed with gayety and a fine élan you lately gave me to pass on to Avis. I am constrained to protest and to call on you to repent before it is too late and strive hereafter to live purely in support of the decencies.

Turn to page 236 and see what with no evidence that she is aware of blasphemy Mrs. Marvin directs you to put in a Daiquiri. If you should be moved to answer Jesuitically and say that anyone who will drink a Daiquiri deserves anything he may get, then simply go on to the last recipe on page 237. We have here a libelous name offered to the greatest glory of American culture, the martini (it has been preceded by another libel following the Daiquiri), and for this alone a life sentence to teetotalism would hardly be enough. But read the recipe and see what in the last sentence you are told to put in a martini.[1] Death to Isabel B. Marvin and confusion to any publisher who will for mere greed and gain circulate her.

[1] Orange bitters and a green olive.

As I say, it is a gynecocentric world smothered in muliebrity and swathed in marabou. Avis has expressed her admiration of the book and bids me thank you for it. I can say no more against God.

Yours,

TO CLARENCE S. BINGHAM[1]

January 2, 1950

Dear Mr. Bingham:

I am happy to send you the enclosure and to greet you with the mystic signs and grips. My taste closely follows yours but it may be I can do you a considerable service. I too avoid Noilly Prat on the ground that it has too heavy a taste and the further ground it is likely to vary from case to case and even from bottle to bottle. I used Dubonnet as long as it was available and then shifted to Martini & Rossi. Robert Blake,[2] however, must be a very great scholar indeed for he had the local purveyors import an Italian dry called Gancia. I tried it and have stuck to it ever since, finding it by far the best to my taste I have ever struck. It is entirely uniform in taste but is apt to vary in color and this causes difficulty for the impresarios who think they can mix masterpieces by their visual sense. I do not know whether it is available in Hartford. Last month I tried to get some in New York to introduce to various friends of mine and walked Madison Avenue from 45th to 95th, making excursions down every side street where I could see a liquor store. I found two or three that had Gancia Sweet and one that said it regularly carried the dry but was out. Being resolute in good works I have learned that the importer is Jules Orteig, Ltd., 475 Fifth Avenue. If you want to prod your dealer to try it out, it may be that you will call my name blessed. I like it best with Gordon's gin but would accept Milshire or Fleischman with a clear, high, and rejoicing heart.

I do not know a nobler purpose than your research into the history of the cocktail. I have sometimes thought of making that pious investigation myself. Do not neglect the amazing manuals that were issued for bartenders seventy-five years ago and more. I remember enjoying a lot of alternately snooty and bedazzled remarks made by visiting Englishmen in the 1840s and 50s but I never bothered to do anything about them.

My piece has brought in a number of heartbreaking letters from the type we used to call a gentleman, a scholar, and a judge of good whiskey. They lament the practical impossibility of getting good whiskeys nowadays.

1 President of the American Antiquarian Society.
2 Harvard professor of history, and for a time director of the Harvard Library.

I know the kind that cost $1.50 or $1.75 a full quart when you and I were young, had spent twelve or fifteen years in the wood, and was kept under the bar at most saloons lest they seem snooty to the honest man who wanted to pay only ten cents for a drink and got whiskey only eight or ten years old. In a couple of weeks I am taking off for Kentucky and later in the spring will be in rural Pennsylvania, and I hope to inquire into the matter of the small, independent distillery and see what can be learned.

I probably will have no legitimate scholarly reason to visit the Library till late spring or early summer but now that I know you belong to the fellowship I will turn into Worcester the next time I am driving to or from New York and we will perform the ceremonies.

Sincerely yours,

TO A MR. ENGLISH

February 7, 1950

Dear Mr. English:

I will not attempt to establish any test for orthodoxy whatsoever, except for the hour preceding dinner. Even there I will not set up an inquisition. I realize that some people of clean souls, sweet and kindly disposition, and even of unimpeachable taste in many respects believe that rum is drinkable liquor just as others believe that a horse hair kept in a bottle of water will turn into a snake, and still others believe that James Hilton is a writer. Surely the enlightened attitude toward them is to leave them free so long as they damage no one but themselves. Only, they must be sequestered or restrained from inflicting injury or esthetic pain on others and the gospel must be kept open to them. Furthermore, if vermouth is a poison, how splendid a one.

Sincerely yours,

TO FREDERICK LEWIS ALLEN

*Only once, in the twenty years he wrote the
Easy Chair, DeVoto had the editor send
back an essay as unsuitable, and in that
single instance there may have been an
unwillingness on the editor's part to*

burlesque another magazine. The substitute
that DeVoto knocked out within
twenty-four hours was an argument against
W. H. Auden's interpretation of Freud, and
appeared in September 1948.

July 15, 1948

Dear Fred:

You're right: the piece is lousy. I can only say that I am tired from months of overwork—some of it on behalf of *Harper's*—and half sick to boot, or more than half. On the other hand, I think that the danger of anyone's taking the piece straight would have been slight, that an occasional burlesque would do *Harper's* no harm, and that it's even in the public interest to burlesque *Time*.

It would be repugnant to my professional sense for the magazine to come out without an Easy Chair, so long as I'm writing the Easy Chair, so much that I would regard it as equivalent to suit for divorce if it did. I've canceled my weekend and will knock out another one. I'll have to tee off on what is at hand, for I've got to meet another deadline on Wednesday, and I'm afraid I'll have to use one of the obiter dicta in Auden's current piece. Guaranteeing not to hurt his feelings.

Yrs,

TO A MR. BIXLER

July 27, 1948

Dear Mr. Bixler:

I am a man whom it is easy to tempt and I confess that you seriously tempt me to break a resolution that I have been able to hold for some years. I have not read *The Armed Vision*[1] but I did look through a set of galleys reading passages here and there and it is a beautiful specimen, perhaps the most perfect I have ever seen, of the type of literary thinking that makes me bellow. I would greatly enjoy doing such an article as you suggest about it but by now I have experienced that kind of enjoyment so often that I will not risk the hangover. It seems impossible for me to write about literary criticism without uniting against me all the factions in literature's most confused civil war. If I am going to be belabored, and it appears certain that I am going to be from time to time, I prefer to bring on the brawl about real

[1] By Stanley Edgar Hyman.

things and not words. I am in a brawl now about the public lands and it has the enormous superiority to brawls about literary criticism, that we all know what we are talking about. So far as I can see—I grant you that maybe I suffer from both myopia and astigmatism—the excitements of Hyman's book are excitements about words only, not things. Some time back I made solemn oath not to discuss theories of literary criticism and by main force I am demonstrating that I have enough character to stick to it. If you want a nice piece about some segment of the objective world I am qualified to write about, take it up with me but I am true to Alcoholics Anonymous and I am not going to take that first insidious sip of literary criticism.

Sincerely yours,

TO ANSEL ADAMS

December 24, 1948

Dear Ansel:

I doubt if you are ever going to get me to do a book with you. The moral of the Yosemite one[1] is all too painfully clear. In the face of your pictures, Muir is just some unnecessary rhetoric. I cannot tell you how profoundly I admire them. There has never been a photographer in your class, which may be a bad thing for photography but is comforting for the rest of us who have to get along in the artistic world. These are terrific and I mean exactly what I say: Muir is empty and a little fatuous in the same book with them. He says immeasurably less than you do. He is a mere embroidery. I wish to God that more of your stuff were available. I am going to evangelize Houghton Mifflin about it.

There appears to be little prospect of my coming west next summer. I will depend on seeing you here or in New York. The Newhalls[2] breezed through a couple of weeks ago ecstatic and even maudlin about the new Rochester setup. I had not even heard of it but it is obviously the perfect job for them and nothing less than inspiration on the part of Eastman.

Try to let me know in advance of your coming, and do come soon. I am deeply touched by and grateful for your book. I repeat it is yours and not Muir's.

Yours,

[1] *Yosemite and the Sierra Nevada.*
[2] Beaumont Newhall, the historian of photography, who was just moving from the Museum of Modern Art to the Eastman archive of photography at Rochester, and his wife, Nancy, author of numerous books about photography, including the later *Eloquent Light*, a biography of Ansel Adams.

TO HENRY SEIDEL CANBY

This letter concerns Canby's request that DeVoto write an article for the Saturday Review's *twenty-fifth anniversary number. DeVoto never forgave Norman Cousins for printing Lewis's vitriolic "Fools, Liars, and Mr. DeVoto," and for allowing personal attacks, as DeVoto thought them, to be printed on the letters page afterward.*

April 15, 1949

Dear Henry:

As you know, I take a dim view of the *Saturday Review* these days, and especially of its tendency to wander off into metaphysical subjects of great grandeur and little or no sense. I don't know what is in the minds of you people but the subject you wired me about would seem, on the surface at least, to belong in that category. Still my regard and respect for you require me to write the piece if you want me to and I feel also that I ought to be represented ex-officio or ex-ex-officio in the anniversary number. I will write it. But please delicately convey to Cousins, first, that I will write only about my own notions about the civilization of the day, which are sure to be widely at variance with the gloom and nobility so ecstatically vibrant in the think-pieces he likes to run and those certain to be secreted by most of the contributors of this issue, and, second, that if he does not like the piece he is to reject it entirely, not tamper with it [. . . .]

Yours,

TO A MR. SLUSSER

May 2, 1949

Dear Mr. Slusser:

I am always holding myself back by the collar from touching up Wilson[1] and I intend to go on doing so as long as I find it possible to. In the first place, I took some skin from him years ago—if you are interested, look up

[1] Edmund Wilson.

a piece called "Autobiography: or As Some Call It, Literary Criticism" in a book of mine called *Minority Report,* which no one has ever read. In the second place, however he may annoy and exasperate and gravel and gripe us, he is nevertheless the only specimen in American writing today that can fairly be called a man of letters. I mean that though he is humorless and pontifical and myopic and narcissistic and at one time idiotically pedantic and idiotically arty, he nevertheless does devote himself to what he considers the literary values and literary life with absolute integrity and a single-mindedness that no one else remotely approaches. I respect this in him thoroughly, though he is usually at the opposite pole from me and though he has exactly the type of mind that I have been sniping at ever since I learned how to shoot. I agree wholly with what you say about his lack of humor, of living guts, and of the ability to regard himself lightly. He has, in fact, no lightness of any kind in him, and his blind and bland solemnity in the presence of the unsolemn sometimes drives me to the verge of despair. Moreover, he is forever, as in those pieces about the Indians, discovering with all the awe of Columbus sighting land things that have been commonplace to all sensible men and all men with juices in them ever since they learned to think, read, or see. He is at work now on a study of American literature between the Civil War and 1900. You have doubtless seen a few products of it that he has published in various places and have got the feel that, for instance, Frank Norris is at last sanctioned to have existed as a novelist because Wilson has now read him. He is going to do precisely that for two or three dozen writers whom you and I have known since we were undergraduates and who played a quite inescapable and quite normal part in forming our ideas but into whose silent sea he is going to burst for the first time. As the author of various pieces mourning the ignorance of the literary view, I am going to feel my usual exasperation—it was I who had Harper's reprint *Miss Ravenal's Conversion* and who myself reprinted *The Valley of Shadows* and I cannot remember a time when I was not familiar with them, but it was Wilson who discovered them for the literary view after I had done so—when he brings, say, Clarence King or Percival Pollard or *Oldtown Folks* or *The Country of the Pointed Firs* to the belated attention of hereafter thankful lovers of good writing. He will do it with his usual aloof and [costive] condescension and that will double the annoyance—but do not forget that the literary will thereafter be sanctioned to enjoy good books which years of effort by many of us have not been able to sanction for them. I am sure that the [?] will not suffer from either his patronage or his asininity, and the rest of us can enjoy the continuing phenomenon reflecting that he did get into *Hecate County* all the conscientiously noted small talk of his friends and may be trusted hereafter to exert similar personal deficiencies on behalf of the good life and to the amusement of more ribald souls.

Sincerely yours,

TO ELMER DAVIS

May 10, 1949

Dear Elmer:

I don't know why I think that reading an old piece of mine might induce you to write the piece I very much want you to write, but the idea has popped into what we would agree to call my mind from its unconscious storehouse and the good Dr. Freud urges us to heed the signals of the unconscious. I am sending you a book which I probably sent you when it was published but which there was no reason for you to read then and which practically no one has ever read. The piece my unconscious wants you to suffer through is the one called "Autobiography: or, As Some Call It, Literary Criticism"—alas, both parts of it. Both of us have repeatedly struggled with this problem ever since logic 1, or whatever it was we took in Freshman year. This piece is, at some strain on your credulity, the shortest statement I have ever made of where I think I come out.

I do not like any better than anyone else to be forced to think but I have been going through the motions ever since I saw you. I believe that one of the bees you are fighting, in Mr. Lincoln's phrase, is the one I have been swinging at all my life, the tendency of thinkers, intellectuals, and literary men to form abstract ideas, build them like bricks or chains into a structure, come to think of the abstractions as real things, and form judgments purely by logical deduction from abstract and therefore unreal propositions, without referring ideas for correction to experience, concrete things, and common sense. I think that another of your bees is the priority of total thinking—meaning, emotion, sentiment, instinct, and, if you like, intuition—over reason. Obviously, or I think obviously, part of what you mean is that reason by itself usually leads to error and by itself is but a frail impetus to action. Tied in with this, of course, are the endocrine secretions. Still another of your bees is the sheer inaccuracy of observation and the great gift for extending a few single examples into a universal rule that are characteristic of people thinking in public. You must, I believe, allow something for the inferiority of the intellectual's perceptions and judgments to those of the man in the street who appeals to experience, his own and that of others known to him, and to the workings of common sense instead of logic. At least one large variety of the ideas you are objecting to consists of objects hidden behind the piano in advance which are found after a scrupulously logical search for them.

It is not my present job, however, to tell you what you think. It is very much my job to urge you to obey the prompting of your unconscious on

Dr. Freud's principle—to write the piece which popped into your mind[1] and from which you have since been receiving the most industrious and convincing logic. A fanatical crusader for literary contraception, I usually do what I can to prevent books and articles from being written, but I now maintain you have something extremely important to say, so important that I summon you to say it. Nobody else can say it as well as you and the adventitious and rather silly circumstances of the anniversary number make a setting which will give it added force—for you know as well as I that that issue is going to consist of some of the most supremely beautiful and idiotic thoughts ever assembled. I repudiate your notion that such a piece might give aid and comfort to bad men, for the same is to be said of the Bible. I also brush aside the certainty that the literary will heave a lot of dead cats at you, for your public career certainly toughened you to far worse abuse, far worse and far more skillful abuse than the literary are capable of, and what is a dead cat or two in such a case?

In short, I solicit you as earnestly as I can to do the piece. When you have decided one way or the other let me know the decision. If you do it, I will go ahead with my original hunch, which was to write a piece saying that it would do no harm to intellectuals like Cousins and might even do them good to realize that there are meaningless questions and insoluble problems, to realize that much activity of the intellectuals is really devoid of meaning altogether. If you decide not to do it, I think I will tell Henry Canby that my aunt has died and grief restrains me from writing anything at all. I never wanted to appear in the damn issue anyway but felt that I was under some obligation to as a former editor [. . . .]

Yours,

TO AN UNKNOWN ADMIRER

May 9, 1949

Dear Sir:

I am sorry but you have got the goddamnedest signature I have ever seen and neither I nor any of three other people I have consulted can make out either your first or your last name, although we are reasonably sure that your middle initial is J. That does not matter in the least, however, for you have written me one of the pleasantest letters that any writer ever received. I wish I could believe that the book[2] deserves the very high praise you give it. I

[1] Elmer Davis's contribution to the twenty-fifth anniversary issue of the *Saturday Review of Literature* (August 6, 1949) was "History without Ideas," a skeptical view of the role of ideas in human affairs.
[2] Probably *Across the Wide Missouri*.

can only say that the effort, at least, is to give people something of the experience and if I have succeeded to any degree at all in giving you the experience I was writing about then I rejoice and can feel that I have to that degree legitimately fulfilled my function as a writer.

Sincerely yours,

TO WILLIAM SLOANE

For a dozen years, beginning in 1932, DeVoto taught every summer at the Breadloaf Writers' Conference in the Green Mountains of Vermont. His association there with writers, editors, agents—and students—was for many years one of his greatest pleasures. He called Breadloaf "the best club I ever belonged to." Its combination of good fellowship, tennis, conviviality, and hard concentrated teaching suited both his need for friendship and his impulse to teach—an impulse that in 1936 was frustrated by Harvard University's failure to find a permanent position for him. From then on, Breadloaf offered the teacher in him his only outlet. But by 1949, when this letter to William Sloane was written, the quarrel with Frost and a general congealing of enthusiasm had made the conference a place full of ambiguities and potential trouble to his spirit. After 1949 he did not go again, ever, as a member of the staff, though in 1955, a few months before his death, he returned for a lecture and a couple of days of reunion among the ghosts.

July 5, 1949

Dear Bill:

It is good to have better news about Mark[1] but still shocking to me that the news has been so bad. As you know, I am not only a friend of his but

1 Mark Saxton.

have a curious paternal feeling for him too. I have not yet been able to bring myself to write to Jo but will do so over the weekend and will do it on the impetus of your better news. I hope you will find out and let me know whether any of the coagulants have been used on him and whether they worked on the embolism.

I know you think of my character as massive and monolithic, held to its stern goals by a more than gyroscopic inertia, resisting exterior pressures and deterrents and impediments as armor plate resists BB shot, and scoring as weak and puerile such faint shadows of whim and caprice as occasionally arise within me. It is not for me to say that you are wrong, but I may confess to you off the record that I have been a trifle blown about by this Bread Loaf matter. My fixed and unalterable purpose has revised itself some ten or seventeen times and probably will double or triple that sum before the opening day, which by the way I do not know since in a moment of acute lack of interest I gave my circular to some young aspirant, probably Lewis Mumford. It is still an absolutely dead sure thing that I will not go but other exterior pressures as powerful as yours are being applied to me and I find additional impulses in myself which might suggest to someone who knew me less well than you that my decision is crumbling along the edge. A very accomplished thumb-twister has twisted both my thumbs since you were here. Probably I will still be unalterably refusing to go when I drive into the yard of Treman and start bellyaching about Fletcher's martinis. Or shall we consign the outcome to fortune, Providence, the fall of the dice, or the flutter of a handkerchief.

Actually you could do the job a damned sight better than I. You are not yet anguished with boredom at the sound of your voice coming back from the same damn wall saying the same damn things for fifteen years to the same collective, submissive, inexpressive, and certainly damned face. The juices of youth that have long since been fried out of me, though the verb is perhaps unfortunate, still foam and bubble in your veins and make your un-lined face ruddy and your unwearied heart buoyant. I have even surprised you in moments of enthusiasm if not indeed idealism so strong as to suggest to me that the secret wish of your soul is to add an inch of diameter to your pipe bowl and half an inch of fuzz to your jacket and become a professor at Princeton if not indeed a master at Hill School. If we make a hypothesis contrary to fact and prophesy and assume that Columbia's gift to me[2] eventually noses into that front yard, I think you had better be the lead and me the understudy. I also think that somebody had better put our minds to work on back-stopping Fletcher.

The truth is I mortally hate the place, its hysterias, its psychoses, its double-bitted axes, its miasmas, blights, poisons, obsessions, shuck mattresses,

[2] The car he bought, or partly bought, with the Pulitzer Prize money awarded to *Across the Wide Missouri*.

dining room regulations, Ophelias, Lady Macbeths, Meg Merrieleeses, Pistols, Olsens, Johnsons, somnambulists, insomniacs, and most of all, by Christ, its glee clubbers. The truth is, further, that it terrifies me and infects me with manias, depressions, and blue funks. Beyond that is the further truth that there are increasingly acute reasons why I should not come, and beyond that is the concentric truth that I always have the best time of the year when I am there.

I see by the paper where it says that your firm is going to publish a book by one Edward Nicholas—my God, a Harvard-Princeton man, that is to say, a Persian terrier—which includes a piece about Margaret Fuller in this month's *Harper's*. If any other part of it is as good as this chapter, then that's a book I want.

It was very swell to have you and Julie here. In fact it was the one bright day in an otherwise dolorous summer. I wish to God you would take over Arthur Williams' job and stay for a week. You may state to Julie as much of my complete adoration as you may see fit and add that I am nevertheless someday going to lead her up to a millpond and make her throw a horseshoe in it and see what happens.

Yours,

TO A MR. WOODFORD

April 3, 1950

Dear Mr. Woodford:

Of course you have my permission to use the quotation from *The Year of Decision* you ask for.

Incidentally, I solicit you not to assist the growing conviction of publishers that permission for quotations has to be asked and if possible paid for. The law is quite clear: "reasonable" quotation, which may run to many hundred words, is everybody's right. It is only when a writer stands to profit from the work of others rather than his own that he is infringing any law or any custom of the publishing business. If a man is merely editing someone else's work, as in an anthology, he ought to pay for it. If, however, he is commenting on it or using it illustratively he is entitled to use as much as he likes and the courts will so find. Ethically and culturally a man who publishes a book puts it at the disposal of anyone who wants to use it. If there is such a thing as cultural heritage, then it belongs to everyone and only those who expect to profit from it should pay.

I look with distrust on the habit publishers have formed in recent years of trying to turn an illegitimate penny by making difficulties or by intimidation. I regard my own stuff as freely available to anyone who wants to use it and as a matter of principle I do not ask permission when I quote.

Excuse the sermon but I regard the point as important.

Sincerely yours,

TO A MR. OBERHOLTZER

April 3, 1950

Dear Mr. Oberholtzer:

Occasionally I have blown off steam in *Harper's* about primary and secondary school and college students who call on me and others like me to do their work for them. Your letter is the first time that a person at the head of a school system has ever made what seems to me a thoroughly unwarranted and illegitimate request. If your Association is drawing up a program, it certainly has people qualified to make a bibliography. There is no reason why I should interrupt my work to do the Association's. Delegate and pay one of your committee to do the research required. If you lack confidence in the results when it has been done that is the time to ask for the critical judgment of someone else. If that time comes, I suggest to you that there are plenty of experts in conservation in Denver, at Denver University, and elsewhere.

I am also moved to wonder how good your Yearbook is going to be unless some of those who write it have first hand knowledge of the subject.

Sincerely yours,

TO ANNE FORD[1]

May 22, 1950

Dear Anne:

I love Barzun's stuff but two volumes—dear, it ought to be forbidden by law. I find, however, that you have sent me both Kitty Bowen, for which I will certainly give you the heartiest plug I can write as soon as I have read it, and Lloyd Lewis, which I have been honing to get hold of.

I am just back yesterday from the Missouri and the stratosphere. I grant you that you are a great expert at your job but I assure you that so far as

[1] Publicity director for Little, Brown and Company.

publicity is concerned you and I and all the world are innocents compared to one William J. Lederer, Commander, United States Navy. He now has them selling *All the Ships at Sea* in every saloon, tobacco shop, and garage within a hundred miles of the Missouri River throughout its length. I would be willing to pay high just to watch him in action. If you read your *Globe* yesterday you saw the carefully unrehearsed photograph of Bud [Guthrie] and me throwing him into the Platte River. When he first sprang that one on us I was for doing it from an airplane.

Yours,

TO A MR. CHAMBERS

May 22, 1950

Dear Mr. Chambers:

You find me in a captious mood. Maybe I ought to address George Stevens, who wouldn't give a damn.

In the first place, I feel that a publisher who sends a book to a writer uninvited has to take his chances. There is yet no statute that compels a writer to read it unless he feels like it or say what he thinks about it unless he wants to.

In the second place, there is something screwy about a publisher's requiring a writer to comment on a book which has not been sent to him. So far as I am aware no copy of *Guests of Don Lorenzo* has appeared at this house and no copy of any other book by Mr. Robert Pick.

It is possible, of course, that you sent me galleys. If you did I certainly threw them away without looking at them, and I will add that in the third place, a publisher who asks anybody to read galleys has forfeited the ordinary immunities of citizenship and would not be entitled to kick if the grizzly bit him, I hope to God.

Sincerely yours,

TO A MR. BURT

In the Saturday Review *for April 25, 1936,
DeVoto published "Genius Is Not
Enough," a destructive review of Tom
Wolfe's* The Story of a Novel. *In the*

*Atlantic for January 1940 he included some
equally destructive comments on* The Web
and the Rock *in an omnibus review,
"American Novels: 1939." In 1950 he
denied, in a footnote in* The World of
Fiction, *that he had persecuted Wolfe, as
Wolfe and some of his friends had said.
Since the two reviews cited above are almost
all he ever wrote about Wolfe's work, his
disclaimer would seem valid. The letter
below is in response to a correspondent who
challenged* The World of Fiction *footnote.*

May 29, 1950

Dear Mr. Burt:

I do not quite make out what you are accusing me of. I do understand you to say that I have misstated facts and this is the only part of your letter that concerns me. Disagreement with my opinions and dislike of my work are the ordinary hazards of my trade and though I may regret them, there is nothing I can or would do about them. To be accused of misrepresentation and lying, however, is a different matter.

I do not know how large the Nashville Public Library is but if it is large enough to serve a city the size of Nashville you can find the kind of statement my footnote was referring to in half a dozen texts within fifty feet of your desk. If you will then go to Vanderbilt and look at the kind of critical anthology of modern American literature now being increasingly used in college courses, you will find several more such statements, including the one which I quoted in my footnote. I think it would have been courteous and even scholarly to have done the required bibliographical research before writing to me.

I have no idea how many people believe there was what you call a vendetta between Wolfe and me or that I have written a very great deal about him. I do know that I repeatedly run into them in various parts of the country. I long ago got fed up with being introduced to college audiences or to literary strangers as a notorious contemner of him, and with receiving heated letters, many of them unsigned, which had the same burden. I think that Wolfe himself had a good deal to do with creating this fictitious reputation for me. At least friends of his have told me so and there is evidence in some of his published letters and in unpublished ones in various collections which have been quoted to me by people who are studying him. There has been enough of this, as my footnote says, to deter me from discussing Wolfe's work in connection with literary studies I have had occasion to make. It was for this reason that I wrote the footnote. I could not say what I wanted to say about fiction without writing what I did write about him.

I hope you have kept a copy of your letter to me. You say that "Genius Is Not Enough" is "not a single review, as you put it." Please refer to the footnote. The second sentence calls it a 2500-word article. The third says it was a review of Wolfe's *The Story of a Novel*, and so it was.

You have a point about that photograph,[1] but I had nothing to do with its circulation. It was taken by a friend of mine as a joke and I gave it to Alfred McIntyre, president of Little, Brown, who was my friend and then my publisher, to add to a collection of informal photographs of Little, Brown writers that hung in his office. It was not intended to be circulated for publication. Mr. McIntyre did not authorize its use and I did not know it was being used. An ill-advised publicity man at Little, Brown had it copied and sent out mats to various newspapers without my knowledge. Its publication in the *Saturday Review* was the first intimation I had of what had been done. I have no doubt that George Stevens, the managing editor of the *Review*, enjoyed using it in that context, but I did not enjoy seeing it there. I at once made Mr. McIntyre recall as many of the mats as he could. He got all but two or three, or at least the cut was used only two or three times.

I note that the date of publication of "Genius Is Not Enough" was April 25, 1936. At that time I had twice been offered the editorship of the SRL and had twice refused it. Several weeks later when the offer was renewed I accepted it, but when Mr. Canby asked me to review *The Story of a Novel*, which had first been published in the *Review*, both of us were sure that I was not to be his successor. I was, however, and had been for some years, one of his first string reviewers. I did not volunteer to review the Wolfe book. Mr. Canby sent it to me, prescribed the length of the job he wanted, and asked me to treat the book in connection with Wolfe's novels.

I do not know what the job of a reviewer is unless it is to say truthfully what he thinks of the book he is reviewing. I have never supposed that my literary beliefs are sacred or my opinions final. I have never tried to impose either beliefs or opinions on anyone else, but I have undertaken to say what they were, to give the reasons for them, and to let my case speak for itself. If you will read the preface to *The World of Fiction* you will see me saying that I believe the way I look at fiction is a valid way and true so far as it goes. What I wrote about Wolfe differed in no way from what I have written about many other writers whom I have treated from my point of view. I have said of them all what I thought of them all. As it happens, I have praised far more than I have condemned, but that is incidental to the fact that I have written about them what I thought about them. As I see it, that is my critic's obligation.

I do not well understand what you mean by "a pretty easy prey" or "manifestly poor sport" or "subtle vituperation." As I see it, my job was to

[1] A photograph of DeVoto standing at raised pistol with a .45 automatic, prepared (so the implication went) to shoot the eye out of any disagreement that dared poke its head up.

say what I thought. It depends on how seriously one takes literature. I happen to take it very seriously and I was paying Wolfe the highest tribute a critic can pay a novelist by taking him with the utmost seriousness. I thought and still think that he was a bad novelist and that the example he, and especially the critical praise heaped on him, gave to young novelists was a bad influence for American letters. I have seen the cult rise and rage and decline. I am glad for the sake of American literature that the young do not admire him anywhere near so fervently or so extensively as they did ten years ago. As I see them at colleges I visit and see their manuscripts as an editor, I am relieved by the recession of an influence which, for the reasons I have given in my new book and gave in my review, I considered harmful.

This has nothing to do with sport or taste. It has to do with what I consider the bases of literature and nothing else. It is your right to disagree with me altogether, to consider me wrong, wrong-headed, stupid, blind, or what you will. I do not see by what right you are entitled to impugn my honesty because my opinions differ from yours.

You are manifestly wrong when you say that Wolfe has been "without a voice to answer for him." Look through the indexes of the books and continuations [sic] on your shelves. You are manifestly and, if you will excuse me, absurdly wrong when you say that I created "the legend of the Wolfe who couldn't write without Papa Perkins." It is no legend but a fact so widely established that I wonder you have missed it that at any rate he did not produce novels without Perkins' and later Ed Aswell's symbiotic editing. What I said in my review was based wholly on what Wolfe himself said in *The Story of a Novel*, and, again, it would have been considerate of you to refer to that book before accusing me. I did not go beyond what he himself said, though as one who knows Perkins and had the common knowledge of literary circles in New York at the time, I might easily have done so. The story of how his books were made has never been told. It is hardly even glanced at in the discreetly edited collection of Perkins' letters that appeared some months ago, though if you will glance at that you will get some hints. I think the story will be told sometime and I judge it will distress you much more than my review did. Meanwhile, if you think that Wolfe exaggerated in what he said or that I lied in what I said, the Harvard College Library has a considerable collection of Wolfe's manuscripts and some study of them would be a wholesome, or perhaps shocking, experience for you.

In the second paragraph of your second page I am again at a loss. I suppose my book is full of personal statements in that I carefully try to describe a point of view toward fiction which I have with equal care said I know to be neither complete nor final. The statement about myself in the footnote, however, is of an entirely different kind. Again, you are privileged to consider the inclusion of Wolfe, with others, on page 22 of *The Literary Fallacy* anything you may choose to. Note, however, that it was an incidental mention in support of a very important point, and note also that I have written many times about everyone else mentioned in that sentence but only twice about Wolfe.

I have been around for a long time and have touched the literary scene at a good many places and known a good many writers. I have found it both safe and useful to assume that serious writers are honest in what they say however wrong I may judge what they say to be. Dishonesty in literary criticism, I have found, is uncommon. I suggest that when you disagree with somebody who is writing with obvious seriousness, you confine your doubts to his intelligence and not assume that he cannot honestly and honorably differ from you.

I never knew Wolfe either.

Sincerely yours,

TO PHILIP GRAHAM[1]

December 22, 1952

Dear Phil:

I'm sorry but I don't think any of your points are valid. Put it at its simplest: what happens if I write to you and say I believe like hell in the value of stirring up interest in books and since the *Post* is known for its service to culture it ought to stir up interest in books by giving my new one a quarter of a page of display space without charge to me?

All right, you show a deficit on a luncheon. What of it? The whole thing is promotional institutional advertising for the *Post*. Nobody can talk about it without talking about the *Post*, you advertise it in your own columns and you're advertising the *Post*, you report it the next day and you're advertising the *Post* some more. Well, if you want the services of an advertising agency, a billboard, a copy writer, or a press agent, you expect to pay for them. You don't ask them to contribute their services for the love of either culture or the *Post*. Why ask a writer to?

All right, you don't solicit ads from the publishers, but the booksellers think these occasions are just wonderful and you do solicit ads from the booksellers. Furthermore, if you can build the *Post*'s book page up sufficiently, and these luncheons are maybe a promising way to do so, you will solicit ads from the publishers.

I can tell you a better way. Pay enough for reviews so that you can get good reviewers and devote enough space to the enterprise for them to discuss books at decent length.

1 Editor of the Washington *Post*.

I also believe that it does people some good to have some association with books. But my proper activity in regard to that belief is writing books for them to associate with. Nobody is associating with books when he, or rather she, comes to look at and listen to me. More likely, it works out the other way. Have your read DeVoto's new book? No, but I heard him at the *Post*'s luncheon the other day.

I don't run a gas station or a shoe store that goes on making money for me when I'm out of town. I'm a professional writer and any time I take off from the job is a dead loss. I lose at the very least two days if I go to Washington to do the stunt, and the habits and reflexes of writing are such that I'm lucky if it doesn't amount in the end to four days. If I happen to be writing a piece for *Woman's Day*, which represents the median of the fees paid me, two days means four hundred bucks.

Why don't you set up a book luncheon at which three teachers of English in the Washington grade schools talk about books? By and large they'll talk about them just as well as three writers will. You don't because my name has got publicity value. Sure, that's why I'm in Colston Leigh's[2] stable. Apply to Colston Leigh and he'll say, for a one-shot job, whether it's ten minutes or an hour long, I get five hundred bucks for DeVoto.

Look, I used to be a newspaperman and I'm still a reporter. I know about all these benevolent public services—fresh air funds, hundred neediest families, gold gloves tournaments, and whatnot. They're public spirited as all hell but the idea is to sell the papers. Any names that can be got to commend them, appear at them, or do some work for them will be just fine. But the staff you assign to run them get paid their regular salaries and if any union labor is involved it gets the union scale. Tell a carpenter, a stage hand, or one of your own staff that he ought to contribute his services gratis just because people ought to have some association with books, and see what he says.

What do you think about the radio programs that ask me to appear on them free of charge?

I'm willing to put it on a barter basis. Send me a schedule of your advertising rates. Then the next time you set up one of these luncheons I'll figure out the cost to me in time and expenses and I'll trade you even up and write the copy for my ad. Sure, I have no love of culture. I can't afford to have any. I know damned well that the *Post* can't afford to, either.

Yours

[2] The W. Colston Leigh lecture agency, to which DeVoto was under contract for several years during the early 1950s.

TO A MR. KLARNET

December 26, 1953

Dear Mr. Klarnet:

It was agreeable of you to send the brandy, but I can't accept and have taken it back to the Harvard Provision Company. If the Easy Chair has any merit or standing, it is because I follow only my own impulses in it. If someone gets publicity or makes a profit from what I write, it is only after the fact. I cannot be, or even appear to be, under any obligation to anyone, nor can I accept gifts or gratuities of any kind, however pleasantly intended. Every year several hundred people try to get me to write about their products, but if I followed the prompting of any of them there would be no distinction worth making between the Easy Chair and the *Harper's* advertising columns.

Sincerely yours,

TO ARTHUR HAYS SULZBERGER

The Easy Chair for December 1953,
"Always Be Drastically Independent," had
been a hymn of praise for the St. Louis
Post-Dispatch, *during the course of which*
DeVoto had compared the New York
Times's *editorials unfavorably with those of*
the Post-Dispatch. *The letter below is*
DeVoto's reply to the pained protest of the
Times's *owner.*

December 29, 1953

Dear Mr. Sulzberger:

Unless I am to write a long treatise, I will have to answer you in purely personal terms, though I believe that what I said about the *Times* editorial page is not solely my own view. As a matter of fact, it was the gist of a long conversation I had just had with several very good newspapermen.

For years I have gone through a regular cycle. There will be a stretch when I read the *Times* every morning. It is a long chore for the *Times* is a long paper—its greatest strength is its big coverage. Because it is a chore but also because of something else which is the heart of the present matter, there eventually comes a time when I rebel. I stop reading the *Times* and—there being no newspaper in Boston—I start reading the *Herald-Tribune*. As a former independent but now a convinced Democrat, I allow for the partisan-ship of the *Herald-Tribune* for two months every second year and four months every fourth year. I expect it to be partisan and I enjoy reading its partisan editorials, as I enjoy reading its columnists and special writers on Sunday. That is the whole and very simple point. They are more pleasantly and more seductively written than *Times* editorials, they are livelier, they are more forcible. Because they are, I read the *Herald-Tribune* for a longer stretch than I can justify on any other grounds. Then there comes a time when I am fed up with it and shift back to the *Times*—with rejoicing in the *Times* as a newspaper but with what I can only call resignation about its edi-torials.

I do not dissent at all from what you said in your letter to me. The *Times* is not only a great newspaper but a liberal one as well. But what you call crusades are really, I think, stands. The stands are massive, magisterial, stub-born, and most of all tireless in searching out the news. It is a fine feeling to have the *Times* on one's side but the editorial stands seem to me in-stitutional—without fire, without the élan that I find in the *Post-Dispatch* editorial page. *Times* editorials lack the charm and the sagacity of good writing, and in my judgment they lack vigor. As I said in my piece, I suspect that they are kept under wraps through an honorable motive, not to over-balance or overshadow the news columns, but still they are under wraps. I'm aware that during the last two or three years the editorial page has given up some of its institutional gravity; it is a livelier page than it used to be but still it is not, I think, a vigorous or a particularly well-written one. And it simply does not throw its shoe over the barn, throw away its scabbard, or whatever the figure is for intensity of belief and all-out resolution to attack.

And that is just what I do find in the *Post-Dispatch*. Its editorials are luminous, just, informed—but most of all they have a passion of belief that I simply do not find in the *Times*. And it is written with most admirable art. In these anxious days it is a great comfort and several times a week it says something that makes me want to cheer—which is not the mood in which many people put down a *Times* editorial. I have had frequent occasions to compare *Times* and *Post-Dispatch* editorials, and the *Times* very seldom comes out ahead. When I am out crusading for something, I am glad if the *Times* comes out on my side, but I know I can use what the *Post-Dispatch* says.

This may be merely to expose my own limitations or bias, but it is what I truly feel.

Sincerely yours,

TO JOHN FISCHER

For the last ten years of his life, DeVoto was deeply involved in the struggle to save the Public Lands of the West from the designs of stockmen, lumbermen, and the dam-building bureaus of the federal government. Both in the Easy Chair and in full-length articles, he battered away at the opposition steadily—so steadily that first Frederick Lewis Allen and later John Fischer suggested that he was in danger of flooding the magazine with conservation stuff. DeVoto, as witness the letter below, did not agree. He had always had full independence in his choice of subject for the Easy Chair, and he continued to insist on it, particularly since the controversy at issue here—the fight over the proposed dams in Dinosaur National Monument, with their threat to the entire national park system—was at the time acute and in a dangerous stage.

July 16, 1954

Dear Jack:

It depends on what you mean by "a definite moratorium."

The point about the latest piece is that the printed hearings are just out. The *National Parks Magazine*, with a circulation of a couple of thousand, will pick up the juggling of figures by the Bureau of Reclamation, with hundreds of millions of dollars and the national parks system involved. Nobody else will, not even the *Times*. The offense is flagrant and the danger great; publicizing them is important and, I think, it is good journalism too. I would say that if I had run twelve pieces straight on the same subject, as I haven't.

If I let my mail influence my choice of subjects, I'd end up writing about nothing, for it cancels out. My indications are that the Nero Wolfe piece was a bust: lots of people bawl me out for wasting space on a triviality. That does not bother me, though I'm willing to grant that the piece could have been a lot better than it was, and I don't think it should bother you. I don't think an armful of bellyaches that I've been writing too much about the West should bother you, either. Balance this one with the applauded statement in Washington last night that "*Harper's* is the only magazine in the country that pays any attention to these things and we'd have been sunk long ago without it," and prepare yourself for an armful of bellyaches about me on other grounds presently.

In twenty years I haven't, I think, failed to write about anything the office wanted me to tackle. On the other hand, the theory has always been that no limitation would be put on me, that I'd decide what the Easy Chair was to be about. With the inherent proviso that if I got senile, tiresome, the office would give me my time and get somebody else to write it. I'd much rather accept the proviso than abandon the theory, for any worth the Easy Chair may have had in my time originates in the fact that there haven't been any moratoriums.

Yours,

SEVEN
The Writing of History

To Garrett Mattingly, May 10, 1933(?)
To Garrett Mattingly, Summer 1933
To Elmer Davis, November 26, 1943
To Henry Steele Commager, April 30, 1944
To Garrett Mattingly, November 1, 1945
To Dale L. Morgan, December 28, 1945
To Garrett Mattingly, December 28, 1945
To Henry Steele Commager, April 29, 1946
To Samuel Eliot Morison, December 1946
To Catherine Drinker Bowen, n.d.
To Madeline McQuown, January 3, 1947
To Garrett Mattingly, July 11, 1947
To Garrett Mattingly, December 1, 1947
To Garrett Mattingly, March 14, 1948
To Mae Reed Porter, May 24, 1948
To Garrett Mattingly, November 16, 1948
To Garrett Mattingly, December 2, 1948
To William Sloane, December 3, 1948
To Garrett Mattingly, n.d.
To Garrett Mattingly, September 11, 1949
To Dixon Wecter, June 12, 1950
To Garrett Mattingly, October 28, 1950
To Garrett Mattingly, December 4, 1950
To Frederick Merk, July 30, 1951
To Wallace Stegner, January 13, 1952
To Wallace Stegner, July 7, 1952
To Wallace Stegner, March 14, 1953

Like many of his opinions, DeVoto's opinions about history, historians, and historical method were vehement and not absolutely consistent. On the one hand, he felt his lack of formal training in historiography, and sometimes assumed a deceitful humility, calling himself an amateur and a journalist. On the other, he had a relatively scornful view of the rank and file of the profession, especially the monographers and academic historians, whom he thought narrow of view, timid of judgment, and awkward of prose.

Yet individual historians—Frederick Merk, Paul Buck, Samuel Eliot Morison, Henry Steele Commager, Walter Webb, and especially Garrett Mattingly—he respected and liked, and he preferred their company and conversation to all other except the company and conversation of scientists. When he was engaged in an enterprise where he felt his lack of knowledge, he consistently sought their advice and help, and on Mattingly in particular he relied as a bright and imaginative student might rely on a favorite professor. Mattingly had been his colleague at Northwestern and remained one of his closest friends. The correspondence between them over a period of many years contained a running discussion of history, historians, historical problems, and historical methods. What undoubtedly also went on in conversation with Morison, Merk, Buck, Arthur Schlesinger, Sr., and the literary and cultural and intellectual historians Perry Miller, Kenneth Murdock, and Howard Mumford Jones, who were all his neighbors in Cambridge, got preserved in letters to Mattingly. Mattingly gave DeVoto criticism, calmed his exasperations, provided bibliography and trained advice and steady friendship, but actually the Cambridge historians, who were Americanists and who impinged on DeVoto's chosen field of the frontier and the westward expansion, probably had more to do with the shaping of his mind and the formulation of his books than Mattingly did.

And all of them, together and individually, had his respect. He might disparage monographers and clutch his head at historical prose and rage at those who tried to make history into a science, and fume at those who approached it like literary men, whom he accused of having an inadequate respect for and capacity for facts—he might thunder against all the debasers of history, but true historians he respected, and a true historian was one of the things he most earnestly aspired to be. That his own histories should have been described by the profession at large as "literary" should not have surprised him. They were—intentionally, as he makes clear when he defends the method of metaphor to Dale L. Morgan or describes his historical practices to Madeline McQuown. He was a literary man writing history, but a literary man trying to be more respectful of facts than he thought the literary customarily were.

TO GARRETT MATTINGLY

---

*DeVoto's trilogy of histories about the
westward expansion—*The Year of Decision
1846 *(1943),* Across the Wide Missouri
(1947), and The Course of Empire
*(1952)—occupied even more of his time
than the two-decade span of their
publication dates would indicate. They were
in his mind as a trilogy as early as May 1933.
By the summer of that year he had
discovered James Clyman, who as "culture
hero" committed him to his characteristic
historical method.*

May 10, 1933[?]

Dear Matt:

[. . . .] I'm damn glad you like the book.[1] I can say it was an honest job—and also that I don't think I'll ever again tackle a literary subject. I think that half of my odd dichotomy is a historian, not a critic. What enables the Mumfords of this world to flourish is that it's impossible for critics to mean anything. In history you know what you're talking about—or, he qualified with due thought, at least you partly know. About all that criticism is is a way of giving one's prejudices, or one's ignorance, the dignity of a pseudo-logic. At least, in history, words can be given an occasional correspondence with things. . . . That particular half of my dichotomy decided to do a book about the Civil War, gathering material for it while my new novel should spin itself out in the intervals of earning a living. I even got a promise of $350 Milton Fund from Harvard to "investigate the origin and alteration of social mechanisms, North and South," which seemed to me an expertly devised title for one asking money, and capable of covering any whim I might develop.

Well, in those brief intervals, my novel is now spinning but it seems I'm not going to do a book about the Civil War. Two things happened. Lloyd

---

[1] It is not clear what book, but from the internal evidence, which dates this letter in 1933, it would have to be *Mark Twain's America*, published in the fall of 1932.

Lewis's *Sherman* came out and proved to have done about half of what I wanted to do—the daily-life-in-the-army thing and the danger's-bright-face. And Fred Merk and Arthur Schlesinger reasoned with me. Their story was (a) about everything worth doing had been done with the war, unless I wanted to try one of the remaining biographies, which I emphatically didn't want to do, and (b) that it was silly to waste some packed years of study about the frontier. In the end I bowed to that last consideration. So, megalomania growing on me, I now contemplate no less than three volumes about the frontier. DeVoto's Digest in annual installments or something of the sort. They're too complicated and too nebulous to describe here, but the one that most clearly emerges so far ought to amuse you: The Technology of Frontier Life, or how the woodsman felled the tree and made pemmican, that sort of thing [. . . .]

TO GARRETT MATTINGLY

Summer 1933

Dear Mat:

[. . . .] The first volume of this frontier trilogy—tetralogy?—polyology? —or perhaps teratology?—would appear to be the book you draft me for. The Indispensable Information Item is the second. The first is an effort to isolate the frontier bacillus by selecting a year when it was most in evidence and describing that year as completely as possible, following all lines of fuse[?] back to their origin. Fill the book with as much marching & countermarching as possible, hullabaloo, off-stage noises, red fire, wind machines, and sidereal auroras. If anybody should ever ask you what year would best serve that purpose, you ought in friendship to say there isn't any. But meanwhile whenever you think or hear of anything at all that happened in 1846, send me a memorandum of it. I've found a culture hero. Look at his career—and it's history, not my invention. Born on G. Washington's land in Fauquier County. Met the Gen'l in person. Down the Ohio in time to be present at Tippecanoe. Militiaman in 1812–14. Helped Alex. Hamilton's son survey national lands in Indiana & Illinois. Got to S. Louis in time to join the 2nd Ashley expedition which opened up the Interior basin. On the party that found South Pass. One of the four who explored Great Salt Lake in a skin boat. Five years as a fur trapper. Present at practically everything that happened in those years. Then back to Illinois, where he bought land. In Abe Lincoln's company in the Black Hawk war. Pioneered in lumber & then in farming in Wisconsin. The milksop Winnebagoes shot him twice—& he'd

fought Blackfeet. Got asthma & went west to cure it. To Oregon in the first
1844 emigration. In Oregon, was with the Applegate party that blazed the
trail to California. Bear Flag revolt as an associate of Fremont. Helped
Hastings make his cut-off, quarreled with Hastings about its safety & denounced H's book. Met Lillburn Boggs & turned him from Cal to Oregon.
Met the Donner party & advised them not to take the road they did. Met the
Mormons. Came back to Wisconsin & was employed by the Mecomb party to
guide them to Calif. Got to Sutter's in time to see the first gold. Married one
of the Mecomb girls, bought a ranch at Napa, and lived halfway through the
administration of Rutherford Hayes. . . . Think that career over. And I didn't
invent a comma of it. . . . But, to answer your question, I can't ever be a
historian for I hate detail & can't spare the time for original research. I'm a
journalist, my boy. Besides, the historians being the only group in America
who approve of me, it would be a pity to alienate them as I certainly would if
I announced I'd forfeited my present immunity—as a mere literary gent who
can be a nice press agent for history [. . . .]

TO ELMER DAVIS

---

*During the fall of 1943 DeVoto spent many
weeks in Washington, hoping to receive an
assignment to write some element of the
war's history. His friend Elmer Davis, as
head of the Office of War Information,
aided his effort in every way possible and
kept him advised of the latest state of mind
among the officials of the War and Navy
departments, but their joint exertions and
DeVoto's manifest eagerness to be of some
use in the war effort came to nothing: first
the North African campaigns, then
Guadalcanal, then even Attu, were
suggested, nearly confirmed, and then
taken away. Samuel Eliot Morison advised
DeVoto not to take on anything unless
he was promised full access to all documents,
including battle reports. When it was clear
that he would never get that sort of access
to anything, DeVoto gave up and went*

home. The present letter, one sample only,
details the sorts of indecision and
bureaucratic cross-purposes he ran into in
his attempt to resign his civilian status.

November 26, 1943

Dear Elmer:

I would have written before this except for one of those fantastic serial catastrophes that in the last few years have become the routine expectation of the DeVotos. Avis met me in New York and we rioted mildly for a couple of days. Whereupon we got home to a house where one kid was sick and the maid was leaving. Avis developed a sudden arthritis in her knee and it grew to the size of a water bucket before it could be reduced. I expressed my Washington frustrations in a two-day migraine, developed a cold on the third day, and then took my third typhoid shot, as apparently one should not do with a cold. I was loopy for two days. At one period I thought I was inside the radio, which may be an identification with you. I hope I get to read the Easy Chair which I wrote in that condition. It was on the Lindberghs.

Naturally, I haven't written to Surles and McCloy.[1] I will do so tomorrow. As soon as may be convenient and useful thereafter, I'll come down to Washington and try again. If the Guadalcanal project goes through, so much the better. If not, I'll simply put myself in Surles' hands and volunteer for any odd jobs he may want done, unless you can suggest some specific ones I might volunteer for.

I take it that you believe the Guadalcanal job is a worthy undertaking. Well, the Navy stuff is ready and the Army has got a hell of a lot more stuff on it than anything else except Buna. Furthermore, it's a lot tidier than North Africa. It stays put, you don't have to go charging from place to place. Finally, a hell of a lot of veterans are in easy reach. At a guess, I could get right to work on it. Provided.

You know what the provision is. There isn't any point in getting started on it unless I can get a 16-inch authorization, or at least a 14-inch, and I hope you can suggest as much to McCloy without quoting me. In eleven days in the Pentagon I saw at least twenty-two different runarounds. That's inside the War Department, whereas Guadalcanal involves three different services and the runarounds are certain to increase with the cube. If somebody sufficiently high up can be interested in getting the job done, it certainly can be done. But I'd say that without a clear directive of considerable weight difficulties, hiatuses, and lacunae will pile up till the whole thing will bog in them. I can't say this to McCloy or Surles but you can. I don't know where

---

[1] General Alexander D. Surles, then director of the Bureau of Public Relations, War Department; John J. McCloy, then Assistant Secretary of War.

the pressure has got to come from—I guess McCloy himself—but I know damn well it's got to come from somewhere.

McCloy and Surles were the only people I met in the Pentagon (with the exception of a humble captain on whose PhD board I sat, years ago) who seemed to me to want the stuff to come out. They obviously do want it to; more or less obviously, nearly everyone else either doesn't want it to come out or wants it to come out in a particular way, under particular offices, to the good of some particular organization. Again don't quote me to McCloy, because if I'm going to work with historical stuff these are the boys I'll have to work with, come hell or a hayrack—but the Historical Section is convinced that, shall I say, we must not be hasty or premature in these matters, there's a long, long way to get yet before even the groundwork for eventual writing can be laid down, and when the far off day comes and we're ready to write at last, the proprieties suggest that it had better be the Historical Section itself which does the writing, not some outsider. An old friend of mine who is in it said to me quite flatly, "Well, if that's the kind of book you want to write, you'd better come down here and join us." And hell, the Historical Section is just one part of the hierarchy.

It's the old army game and, on a humble plane, I was quite adept at it when I was in the army. You beat the army game by rank. A big shot says I *want* this book written and then the obstacles yield. Whoever writes the book on Guadalcanal, or on anything else at this stage, has got to be able to say, when expedients and avenues and oil and crossfire have been exhausted, but a big shot *wants* it written. He's got to have a directive or a phone number or whatever, when it develops that such and such documents are missing, or a smokescreen is going up here, or somebody thinks that it would be better if another department had jurisdiction.

For my own sake, I don't give a damn. I'd like to have some minute share in the war somewhere, I've got enough money to afford a period of patriotic endeavor, and obviously I'm a writer if I'm anything. If Surles or McCloy want me to write about truck repair courses at Camp Audubon Gregory, well, okay. If they think I'm useful as a historian, fine. If they want me to undertake Guadalcanal, I'll be damn glad to. But somebody of McCloy's size and weight has got to convince the boys that he really wants the job done or it's perfectly clear to me it won't, in the end, get done by me or by anyone else. I happen to think that books of that sort are in the public interest and well within the public's right. I know you do and I know McCloy and Surles do. But damn me if I met anyone else in Washington who thinks so. Except Joe Greene.[2]

This is merely to say that I can't say such things to McCloy and you can't say them in my name, but if anybody is going to write that kind of book somebody upstairs has got to understand that they're so. Reasonably

[2] Colonel Joseph Greene, editor of the *Infantry Journal* and an old Breadloaf companion.

269

informative books won't be written till 4 P.M. the day before Doomsday if the boys I dwelt among have their desire, unless somebody upstairs directs them to be written.

Well, I'll get off the promised reports to McCloy and Surles, considerably less direct than this one, and in due time I'll be down and try again. I do think that you can help matters by suggesting to McCloy that he's got to manifest his interest in such projects, and manifest it quite clearly, and be ready to manifest it again on call.

What did I tell you about Pearson? I heard that Patton story from the newspaper boys in New York on my way down and it was a hell of a lot less picturesque than it was on his broadcast. Further thoughts on the matter I will confide to your ear, not to paper. My love to Fliss.

Yours,

TO HENRY STEELE COMMAGER

At the time when DeVoto wrote Commager, following his own formula for how to become a historian ("Go to the experts and be helpless"), he was planning to go directly ahead with a book on the Lewis and Clark expedition. He had half agreed to do some captions for a book of Alfred Jacob Miller watercolors of the fur trade proposed by Emery Reves and Mrs. Mae Porter, but conceived that as the job of no more than six weeks, part-time. As it happened, the fur trade took precedence over Lewis and Clark, and the Miller paintings themselves, and the travels of Sir William Drummond Stewart on which they had been made, became "just a line to hang the whole fur trade on." What had begun as perhaps 20,000 words of captions became a rich and complex and colorful book, perhaps the best book DeVoto ever wrote.

It is worth observing, as an indication of the energy and multiplicity of DeVoto's

*literary life, that when he wrote this letter
he was conducting his feud with Sinclair
Lewis, Norman Cousins, and the rest of the
literary world about* The Literary Fallacy,
*being the flag-bearer against the censorship
of Lillian Smith's* Strange Fruit, *writing a
monthly Easy Chair, working on the novel*
Mountain Time, *advising Wendell Willkie
on how news had been handled in
America's several wars, and carrying his
usual load of reviews, casual essays, and
diverticulated research.*

April 30, 1944

Dear Henry:

As the man who discovered I'm a bum novelist before Red Lewis did, you've got certain obligations. The one you're held to at the moment is to give me advice. I'm playing with the notion of getting to work—in a minor way, since I won't be able to go all out on it for some months—on a historical job. Paul Buck is willing to license me to practice history, under the simple rule of *caveat emptor*, but this job is out of his field. All the other historians in Cambridge regard me as a phony, a charlatan, and a menace to the public peace and dignity of considerably more horrifying aspect than the one the literary critics have drawn. Naturally I turn to you, as one who has handed his gun to the bartender before striking up conversation with me. I'm going to ask Julian Boyd some questions too but they will be mostly specific, whereas what I want from you is mostly general.

The job I'm eyeing is Lewis and Clark. You probably agree with me that Mr. Peattie's recent villanelle[1] doesn't impair the flat statement that there is no narrative account of their expedition. I propose to draw on the narrative talent that is denied me in the current reviews[2] and write a narrative history of the expedition. That's that, but naturally I want the book to be as complete, as understanding, and as widely useful and applicable as it can be made without breaking up the narrative. I want to learn as much as I can. I also want to shorten the learning process as much as possible. I want you to save me as much time and as much wasted effort as you can. I want general advice from you. Also advice on what to look for, what to high light, and above all where to look. Also advice on what not to do.

What I know of general American history begins with about Martin Van Buren. I have, however, got a pretty good specialist's knowledge of

[1] Donald Culross Peattie, *Forward the Nation* (New York, 1942).
[2] Either of *The Literary Fallacy* or of the John August novel *The Woman in the Picture.*

the mountain fur trade, beginning with Ashley, and a not bad knowledge, one that could easily be made tolerably good, of the western fur trade generally from Astoria on. That may be of some use to me with Lewis and Clark but not a whole hell of a lot. You see, I'm taking a backward leap into a field where I'm virginal, bucolic, naive, wideeyed, trustful, and practically as ignorant as Red Lewis. So, the idea is, you take me by my little hand and lead me in.

I want to know about Louisiana. I want to know how the sense of that vast, unknown area began to penetrate the American consciousness, in what form, with what speed. I want to know how people thought about it—and how to find out what they believed about it and what they knew about it. So you tell me how to go about learning that, and where to look, and whom and what to look for. The idea of Louisiana before we got it. And, as a lead out of that, how much can I get in Jefferson and how do I go about looking for it?

That's the heaviest job. But I also want to master the purchase itself and to do so with as little waste motion as possible. I want to master the essentials on the spot and at the sources, French and American—and Spanish too, if they're essential, and I'm too damn dumb to know—and also in the judgment of modern historians. Let's make this last as brief as possible—you tell what's vital in the current production and forget the rest.

Again, I want to know where and how to work with maps. Hell, I don't know anything about maps of that period. Here you r'ar back and say anything at all and it will be pure gold.[3]

I think I can get the Indians for myself. Some time ago I got an urge to read more about them and so I've been laying down something that turns out to be useful. But if you have any notions, just run them in.

And General Remarks. You're Old Killbuck in person, and here I am, a greenhorn, a *mangeur de lard*, just starting off into the hills for the first time. With a horn or two of Monongahely under your belt you're feeling genial and you decide to prepare me as well as you can for the first sight of the buffalo and the Blackfeet. You think it's a shame that as nice a guy as me should enter the wilderness so poorly equipped. You're going to give me all the general advice that occurs to you, in the pious hope that I'll be able to save my scalp.

Sure, I know this is unconscionable and you have more to do than you'll ever get done and who the hell am I to bust in on a busy man, and all that. On the other hand, you've got a stern obligation to your profession, and if amateurs will insist on trying to practice it, you've got to do what you can to keep the resulting damage at a minimum. Right?

Yours,

[3] Compare his advice to me on the same subject, pp. 320–321.

TO GARRETT MATTINGLY

November 1, 1945

Dear Mat:

[. . . .] I find, after prolonged scrutiny, that there is, as I have hitherto not believed, a literary ethics. On one or another occasion when we were batting it about, you parenthetically, and I doubt not with a negligence of a saying for that date and train only, emitted a gem, one of your usual gems, that has gone on working in my mind. "American history," says you, with the confidence of a man who boasts that he knows nothing about it, "American history is history in transition from an Atlantic to a Pacific phase." If you didn't say it that way, don't revise it now, for that's the way I want it. As I say, there is a literary ethics: I will steal what I need as I need it, but not from my friends. And I think I'll begin my book,[1] or end it, or both, with those great words, like the couriers that are stayed not on the frieze. Do you want to be accredited in the text or in a footnote?

For my private information, how the hell good is your mind? I mean, I think, how accurate? This morning I four times got up from my desk, at one end of my study, and went to the map at the other end and looked up the direction of flow of the two forks of Snake River, then went back to my desk, wrote down the information, was not pleased with it, went back to the map, found I'd written it down exactly wrong after walking a measured eighteen feet, and corrected it, and not liking the correction, went back to the map, etc. Four times, and after the fourth time I still had it exactly wrong.

Or is that par for a historian? Another superstitious awe of mine is beginning to fade out, at least along the edges. The ethnologists, I find, don't know any more than the rest of us, or any better. Yesterday I won five dollars from my chief guide and counselor at the Peabody, an authority on the Plains Indians, who didn't know and backed his ignorance that these Indians used perfume, but I did [. . . .]

Yours,

[1] *Across the Wide Missouri.*

273

TO DALE L. MORGAN

DeVoto's review of Fawn M. Brodie's
biography of Joseph Smith, No Man Knows
My History (New York *Herald Tribune*
Books, *December 16, 1945), drew a long*
letter of disagreement and disapproval from
Morgan, who as a Mormon historian and a
friend of Mrs. Brodie's objected to
DeVoto's view of Joseph Smith as a
paranoid. The irritation evident in
DeVoto's reply, though some of it had been
simmering for a good while, reflected partly
the heat of argument and partly the
profound differences in personality and
historical method between the two. But
squabbling was not their characteristic
relationship. Both before and after this
altercation, DeVoto drew on Morgan's
encyclopedic knowledge of the West and
the fur trade, and valued him both for his
learning and for his generosity with it. We
all did. On his part, Morgan reviewed
Across the Wide Missouri, *when it appeared,*
with admiration and enthusiasm. And he
was never quite as obtuse about metaphor
as DeVoto suggests here. He may have
been—many were—somewhat baffled by
DeVoto's difficult and allusive style.

December 28, 1945

Dear Morgan:

    After my '46 book came out you wrote me a long letter. I didn't answer it. I didn't answer it for a reason that discourages me from making any sensible answer to your new letter. You listed a lot of mistakes in my book. About half of them were mistakes: plain, flat, blatant errors. That was okay. Nobody knows any better than I do, or in fact half so well, the defects in my intelligence and in my work, the hiatusses, the superficialities, the plain stupidities. If I were reviewing my stuff I could give it a far more thorough kicking around than anyone has ever given it. Moreover, I have written a lot of books, seen others write a lot of books, read a lot of books—and know (a) how impossible it is to write so much as a page without making mistakes, and (b) how necessary it is to have mistakes corrected. For the corrections you made in your letter I was and remain thankful—though, let me say, I chased some down, after your corrections, and found that I was right and you were wrong. I corrected the corrector. Those corrections, yours I mean, are entered in my shelf copy of the book and if it ever comes to getting out a new edition I will review it in line with them and duly confess error and duly thank you and others who have pointed out where I was wrong.

But what made me refrain from answering your letter, what in fact made me feel altogether incapable of answering it, was the other half (look, I'm writing from memory, maybe "half" is not mathematically correct) of what you listed as mistakes. They weren't mistakes. I could not imagine anyone's understanding them as mistakes. I had never experienced the kind of mind that could think of them as mistakes. There was no way my mind and yours could meet over them. Part of the time you were solemnly holding metaphors up to your calibrating machine—that's a metaphor—and taking me to task for saying that the sun set in the west whereas I ought to know better or objecting that I ought not to say someone had added a cubit to his stature when both the Bible and natural science informed me that no one could and so this one hadn't. That sort of objection always leaves me helpless. I experience no difficulty with metaphors when I read them in someone else's work, I write them naturally and also because I want to make the reader's lot as easy as possible, and I take it for granted that a metaphor I write will be recognized as a metaphor and not as a mendacious or ignorant misstatement. But more often you were quarreling with something I'd said for no reason I could find on the surface. The statement I'd made seemed, on re-examination, to be quite okay, and what you said about it seemed to be quite irrelevant—there didn't seem to be any clash between what I'd said and what you said I ought to have said. After applying my own calibrations I finally made out that you were engaged in some kind of verbal analysis. I'd say, maybe, "preface" and you'd say I ought to have said "foreword"; or I'd say "league" and you'd say I ought to have said "three miles"; or I'd say "assumption" and you'd get worked up because I hadn't said "hypothetical thesis." There was simply nothing I could say in answer or comment that would make sense or, I thought, bring our minds any nearer. So I didn't say anything. I have low impulses and when your—damned good—Humboldt book[1] came out, I was under strong temptation to send you a list of factual errors, misconceptions, metaphors, and debatable verbalisms I could find in it.

So now your blast about my review of Mrs. Brodie's book. I can't say

[1] *The Humboldt*, Rivers of America (Farrar and Rinehart, 1943).

anything, I'm sure, that will bring us any nearer. The point you debate so exhaustively is pure verbalism and there is no possible appeal from it to anything except experience. Your minor point is a question of value judgment exclusively and there is no such thing as an appeal to the facts, though you might wholesomely realize that when it comes to value judgments my rights are quite as inalienable as yours—or maybe that you'd better recognize a value judgment when you make it. I can't, I repeat, hope to meet your mind. The best I can do is to explain how mine got that way. Perhaps if I do that it will keep you from debating an unreal issue when you come to write your book.[2]

But I can, as a preliminary, protest your all-too-easy assumptions and accusations. I'm fed to the teeth with the cheap sneer that the reviewer didn't read the book attentively and the equally cheap one that he imposed his own notions on it. So far as the first is concerned, you are wholly and flatly wrong, and you had damned well better revise your own thinking to take account of the error. So far as the second is concerned, I can only say that I take ideas seriously and, within the limits of mortality, I try to state as clearly and justly as possible what the ideas I'm reviewing or commenting on are. I tried to when I was reviewing Mrs. Brodie's book.

I did not want to review it. The reason Irita[3] was two weeks late with the review was that I several times refused to review it. I agreed to review it only when Irita solemnly asked me to on the basis of a long association and, she said, her belief that I could do a better job than anyone else she could get. I took a week I could not afford from a book I'm writing and from the urgent job of making a living. I read the book as carefully as I could, as carefully as I ever read any book. I looked up a good many things in connection with it. I rewrote my review twice. If I had had a month to work in and space for five thousand words of comment I could have been much more just to Mrs. Brodie and—don't forget this—to my own ideas. I didn't. And in fact Irita, to make space, as one has to in weekly journalism, cut out a full typed page of my review, about 400 words. She cut the passage in which I enlarged on the idea that the Book of Mormon is like a novel. It would behoove you to take account of such limitations on what I or any other reviewer, yourself included, can say.

Furthermore, it is not always safe to assume that your erudition is greater than mine. Thus, as a minor point, I conclude from your letter (and why not, since you are always concluding from my stuff) that you have not actually seen the Palmyra *Reflector* with the pre-publication excerpts from the Book of Mormon, and you certainly assume that I haven't. But I have, seen and hefted and handled with my hands. (Jocosity) But more to the

[2] For many years Morgan gathered material for a history of Mormonism. He died in 1971 without having completed either it or his comprehensive history of the fur trade.
[3] Irita Van Doren, editor of the *Herald Tribune Books*.

point is something else. I can fairly claim to be a student of Mormon history, but I cannot claim to be a specialist in it or an authority about it—I have nowhere made such a claim, in fact I have repeatedly denied it in public and at the top of my voice. In matters of Mormon history as such I cheerfully yield to your infinitely greater knowledge—and publicly yielded to it in my review. But American life of that period is something else, and American life of that period and in those places is also something else. I am not sure that I can yield to your judgment in such matters on the mere assertion. What do you suppose I have been doing all my life? What do you suppose I do with my time? I beseech you by the bowels of Christ to consider that you may be wrong (quotation from Cromwell)—that when it comes to talking about what was general or even specific about the society, the people, the individuals, the ideas, the states of mind of that period and place I may know what I'm talking about. And on the same oath I beseech you to consider that I do not lightly or *a priori* toss about psychiatric ideas.

Here I had better stop—and I am still short of making the only point I want to make—to explain why I flow naturally into psychiatric judgments, why, if you will, I am warped and writhen and tied in a double lover's knot in that direction. Permit me to hazard a guess that you are a spoiled sociologist—at least it appears to me that when you have found an environmental explanation of something you are content, you feel that you have settled matters, and depart about some new and proper business whistling in the carefree consciousness of a job well done. Well, I am a spoiled psychiatrist. The only reason why I ended up as a writer was that, at the end of the last war, I was too old and too broke to go to medical school on the way to the career in psychiatry I had always looked forward to. I read psychiatry. I associate with psychiatrists: in twenty years there has never been a time when I was not hashing out the actual behavior of actual neurotics and psychotics with several psychiatrists who were intimate friends of mine. And that is, in this central issue, important. For when I believe that Joseph Smith is a paranoid, I am not talking about Henderson and Gillespie, though I referred to it in my article (for the reader's sake). I am not talking about any textbook or any formalized or theoretical statement. I am talking about patterns of thought, emotion, and behavior which I have actually seen over a course of a good many years, more than a quarter of a century in fact, and have exhaustively talked out with experts, and have seen experts work out on.

And right there is the issue between you and me. And, I think, you meet it with a verbalism. Now no one knows any better than I that there is no such thing as proof in such an issue, that the retrospective psychoanalysis of a dead man is at best uncontrolled and speculative—I warrant you I have said that more loudly and more repeatedly than anyone else in this writing generation. Nevertheless, when no better instruments of appraisal are at hand we must use that one—and you have not, by God, supplied a better instrument. We cannot reproduce the environment, as proof of your thesis would require. But we can observe the pattern of behavior in an almost illimitable number of cases, on record, before our eyes. When I say that Joseph was a paranoid and became a paranoiac I mean that, in reference to what we observe about such people around us every day, he presents that pattern—and presents far more of it than is required for diagnosis when a case comes into the consulting room. Nor do I see anything in Mrs. Brodie's book that vitiates that statement; on the contrary, I think she vastly increases the evidence. I am going, in the natural course of things, as mere routine, to have one of my professional friends read her book, without any argument from me, and see what he makes of it. At the time I revised my article on the centennial[4]—the time, you will remember, when I went through as many of the sources as are available in the not inconsiderable Mormon collection at Harvard and publicly announced that my earlier championship of the Spalding theory had been ignorant—I made as complete a statement of the psychological evidence as I could and laid it before a friend of mine who was a distinguished psychiatrist. He turned in a finding that agreed with mine—which I had not communicated to him.

Now I repeat, all this is speculative, uncontrolled. But so is your thesis, and in particular so is the comment in your letter to me. You depreciate the significance of a man's saying that he had seen and conversed with God the Father, Jesus, some angels, and some Old Testament characters, etc. You would want, you say, to know something about his social background—and I know something about it, quite a bit in fact—and you would find it less strange if you found therein some preachers who were announcing the millennium, some others who were saying they were God, and some neighbors who had seen mysterious things in the sky. I'm sorry, social background or social backhouse, there is no difference between such a statement in New York in 1830 and such a statement in Alexandria, Virginia, today. There is, and was then, a fixed, immutable difference between the kind of subclinical monomania which would induce a man like William Miller, say, who was a screwball but not screwy, to say that mathematically the millennium could be predicted as on its way and due to arrive at half past four on some future date—between such a man and a man who said that the millennium had arrived. The former was subclinically an enthusiast or clinically an obsessive—that is to say a little over-balanced but as rational as you or I, which I grant you as a clinician is not very rational. But the latter, if honest, was hallucinated. The millennium had not arrived. The preacher who claimed to be God was not in fact God, and if honest, then in the lay word crazy. In Joseph Smith's time as in ours there was reality, there was the ability to distinguish

[4] "The Centennial of Mormonism," first published in *American Mercury* for January 1930, was reprinted in considerably expanded form in *Forays and Rebuttals*, 1936.

between reality and phantasy or delusion or hallucination, and that ability was the test of sanity.

Sanity is a wide, vague, elastic, adjustable conception. Nobody knows that better than a psychiatrist, who will cheerfully reverse his definition for you verbalists and call the maniac sane and himself a maniac—*provided always you adhere to the terms of the definition*. Futhermore, even after you have drawn the line which for purposes of getting on with the job you must draw somewhere, sanity expands and contracts, and the X that marks the very center of sanity today may be near or at the edge of sanity tomorrow.

It nevertheless remains absolutely necessary to draw the line somewhere. I cheerfully admit that I may be drawing it in the wrong place. I may be 89° wrong and no one can be more than 90. But you do not draw it anywhere. The question is not how vivid and lively an imagination a man has got: the question is whether he can distinguish between reality and imagination. You ask where is the man who doesn't suffer from delusions about himself. But that is a pun. If he has delusions then he belongs in the booby hatch. The man who thinks he is a great hand with the gals is subject to the correction of fact. If he makes a pass at a gal and fails, he is sane if he knows that he hasn't slept with her, but if believes that he has slept with her then he is hallucinated. We can speak loosely of men with a strong drive for power as thinking that they are Napoleon, but if they actually think they are Napoleon —if they start writing letters to Josephine or dictating orders to be forwarded to Lannes and Ney, then they are crazy. Nor does it make the slightest difference how many people believe them when they say they are Napoleon, how many take orders from them as Napoleon, or how many other Napoleons there are in the vicinity. From your point of view, it would be perfectly okay if there were a lot of French Revolution study clubs in Westchester County, if Scarsdale put on an annual festival of the Consulship, if there were a pageant in White Plains depicting the whiff of grape, if a lot of school children started playing Jena, if here and there some gents put on cocked hats, thrust a hand into their cloaks, and said they were Napoleon, and presently a lot of people decided that one of them was. You would admit that the people who accepted him as Napoleon were deceived but you claim that the Napoleon himself was only self-deceived, whatever the hell that means. I don't know what it means. Did he believe he was Napoleon or didn't he? He wasn't Napoleon, and if he couldn't tell the difference, then he was hallucinated.

Is there any doubt in your mind that Joseph Dylks[5] was crazy? Would it have made the slightest difference in his insanity if a lot of people had accepted him and a church in his name had come down to today? At a more speculative level, can you have any doubt that Mary Baker Eddy was

---

[5] The Ohio enthusiast who was the source for W. D. Howells's *The Leatherwood God*.

an obsessive to begin with and that in the last years of her life, particularly in the last two or three, and with special reference to the praying circle defending Mother from Malicious Animal Magnetism, she had hallucinations? Is the fact of her hallucination in any way altered by the fact that a church remains—or does her hallucination in any way affect the validity of her teachings, whatever that validity may be?

Now Joseph Smith is on the same basis. It is quite, quite true that I can't prove him a paranoid. I can only point out the remarkable correspondence between his behavior and the established, verifiable pattern of many thousands of paranoids. I solicit you, however, to realize that there is no such thing as a psychology that can be explained in purely environmental terms. You talk about dynamics in psychology—be advised not to dismiss dynamic psychology so cavalierly as you do. In fact, as seriously as I am capable of speaking, I recommend to you, before you finish your book, to spend a considerable time actually in the clinic. Observe the actual dynamics of hallucination and the behavior of hallucinated people—especially of those who retain some capacity sometimes to distinguish between their vision and the objective reality but who at other times lose that capacity. It is too damned easy for you to sit back and talk about my "assumed" correspondences. They are only what Smith himself said, what I take to be true in what others said about him—and both much stepped up by Mrs. Brodie's book and especially her Appendix A. I am pointing out what I take to be correspondence. I may be wrong, but there is no assumption whatever, I am talking about objective things already on the record before she wrote and now quadruply on it as a result of her work. In fact, "assumed" and "assumption" are words you would do well to turn upon your own thesis, for it, and your letter, are full of things taken for granted which need the most critical scrutiny. There are a very great many things in Smith and in Mormonism which I cannot accept your explanation as explaining. I cannot take time to list them here, but I can again beseech you to consider that you may be wrong, that your thesis may not suffice.

But I feel profoundly that all this is idle, that as I began by saying it will not mean anything to you, as much that you say means nothing to me. I am, in fact, much farther from accepting what you say than I am from accepting what Mrs. Brodie says. It seems to me that your vast factual knowledge of Mormonism, your enormous store of data, rests on and is implemented by conceptions that have only a verbal meaning—or at least that as you express it to me, and furiously find fault with my conceptions, you deal with pure verbalisms as if they were realities as solid as bricks. What seems to me to weigh a pound seems to you to strike C-sharp and there is no way of bringing us to discuss things in the same terms. I can come to issue with Mrs. Brodie over objective events which she interprets as a growth in wisdom and

I as a falling off of the sense of reality. But the concepts you hold, or at least those which you express, are so different in kind from mine that I seem wholly unable to see the thing which I take you to be looking at. I feel the same helplessness I felt when, in your earlier letter, you took me to task for something which I could not find on the page or attribute to the page by suggestion. When she says, of the revelations I grant you, not the B of M, that "he appropriated the lyrical style of the Bible so expertly that the instrument sounded under his touch with astonishing brilliancy and purity of tone," I can always ask her what passages she means and we can come to grips. But when you say "the history of the book itself is a denial that it altogether lacked in some kind of form and structure" I simply do not know what you are talking about, and since I don't know I am forced to conclude that you are not talking about anything I can deal with. What happened as a result of the book has nothing whatever to do with the question of its form and structure, in terms of the issue I was talking about, and to say it proved something about them compacts a dozen fallacies, some of them formally named in Logic, as *post hoc ergo propter hoc*, and more especially *non causa pro causa*. Mrs. Brodie says "novel." I point out that she is thinking in terms of twentieth century literary concepts which do not apply. In that sense there is no form and structure in the Book of Mormon, a simple question of fact. In that sense, there was no novelist in America in 1830. In that sense I can, I think, demonstrate by the ordinary means of textual analysis that Joseph was not writing as novelists write, even as novelists of 1830 wrote, even as up-state New York novelists of 1830 wrote. But when you say that the reception of the book proved it has form and structure *in that sense* we are not even in the same world.

Will you now read pages 48, 49, 62, 63, 69, 73 of the book and see whether I distort what she says about the imagination, style, and structure of the book any more than you do.

I cannot, however, keep this up, especially since I am convinced that it will not get either of us any farther along. I can merely say, look to your own preconceptions and be a little more careful of your own statements of fact. But most particularly this: when you think of Smith as "a product and exemplar of his times," take care that you sufficiently realize that those times did not, anywhere outside his church, center on him. In short, if you are going to deal with him on the basis of what seems to you a historical theory but is, if I diagnose it aright, a sociological theory which accepts only a static psychology—then make sure, make a damned sight surer than it appears to me you now do, that you avoid the cardinal fallacy of practically everyone who writes about Mormonism. Mrs. Brodie is a lot more successful in avoiding it than anyone before her, a lot more successful than I believe you are, but not completely successful. That fallacy consists in overstating the importance and the typicalness of Mormonism in the United States of its time. It was not typical of American life at that time and it was, even in sum total, of exceedingly minute importance in or to American life. It is at best a minor thing in America as a whole, and at best an aberration of the principal American energies involved in it. Something of the state of mind of the true believer seems to linger on in everyone who writes about Mormonism, some sense that this was the central meaning of American history, that this was the most important experiment that nineteenth century America ever made. It was not. Mormonism is peripheral to American life, not central. It is a minor and unimportant footnote in American history, not the principal theme. With the greatest solemnity I am capable of, I urge you to bear that in mind when you come to explain either Joseph Smith or his church in terms of what you call the social background and the life of the times.

And, though I will suffer correction from you gladly in Mormon history, I am afraid I will not acknowledge that your ideas about American life at large in the first half of the century are any more authoritative than mine or rest on any more intimate or more detailed knowledge.

Beyond that it seems no more than fair to ask you hereafter to think twice before accusing me of misrepresentation or misstatement or inattention or superficiality, at any rate to wait long enough to see if what you really mean may not be merely that I come out at variance with your ideas.

TO GARRETT MATTINGLY

December 28, 1945

Dear Mat:

You are a damned softie and the inability of your critical intelligence to function in relation to your friends confirms and accelerates my progressive disenchantment with history. However, the principal dilemma solved, the lesser one yields to folk wisdom and the philosophers. *Across the Wide Missouri*, whether or not under that jeweled name, is in the hand, whereas we know not of Lewis and Clark and time and chance happeneth to them all. I may not live to write it, I may live to learn better than to write it, it may turn out to be about Lewis and Conger. I say, if you have no proper sense of professional dignity, you get the present one and you will, by God, signify by raising the right hand that you were clearly warned and had opportunity to avoid it.

And I am not going to join you any longer in the pretense that I have the kind of mind that can write history. The sole difference between me and

THE WRITING OF HISTORY

Lewis Mumford is that I'm brighter than he is.[1] I am quite incapable of
determining facts, recognizing facts, appraising facts, putting facts in relation
to one another, confining myself to facts, guiding myself by facts, or even
recording facts. My mind is an instrument superbly designed for inaccuracy.
On the way through it the clearest statement of the simplest fact gets
transformed into nonsense, and nonsense which is supported by what can
hardly even be called intuition and is probably some molecular concatenation
of accident. There is a kind of awe and wonder about my mental processes.
I sit back and read what I have set down in ink and I am consumed with
admiration of the ingenuity of God or Nature, who has given me a
faculty of dynamic otherwiseness that can transform sense and knowledge
into absurdity with the speed of radio waves. No man unless it be Mumford
himself ever made more of less, or for that matter less of less, than I do offhand and repeatedly and by habit and invariably. By God, put into me one
million bacilli influenzae, four ounces of cthyl alcohol, and three grains
of phenobarbital and my mind is indistinguishable from his at thirty-six
inches [. . . .]

                                                                    Yours,

TO HENRY STEELE COMMAGER

---

*In the spring of 1946, Commager asked
DeVoto to write* The Far West, 1830–1860
in the thirty-seven-volume series The Rise
of the American Nation, *of which
Commager was one of the general editors.
Undoubtedly the offer was a temptation,
for the series was sure to be a distinguished
one and Commager was one of the
historians DeVoto liked and respected. In
the end, he was dissuaded, not only
because he felt himself lacking in the
qualities of the academic historian, but,
one suspects, because he would not have
felt at home in a series.*

[1] Mumford, always one whose name raised DeVoto's blood pressure, was on his mind at this
time because he had heard rumors that Mumford, Brooks, and Allen Tate were all being
considered as replacements for Robert Hillyer in Harvard's Boylston Professorship of
Rhetoric, a position for which (rumor also said) DeVoto had himself been considered and
rejected.

April 29, 1946

Dear Henry:

I think you and I had better sit down and talk this matter over. It is an extremely flattering request—though if it means that your guild is beginning to look at me favorably maybe I had better start searching my conscience—but I am by no means sure that I am competent to write such a book or that I could qualify myself to this side of Judgment Day. That is what we will have to determine.

I see history as primarily processes of individuals. I probably know enough about individuals in the period and place you offer me to write a book and probably I know more about the explorers than anyone else you could get and as much about the fur trade. The emigrations and the mining rushes are also perfectly familiar to me and I know enough about the relationship of all this to the coming of the Civil War to do an intelligent job on it. What I lack is the vast statistical acquaintance with people, places, racial stocks, frontiers and counties and settlements, crops and finances and elections, congressional debates, and all the paraphernalia which such a series as yours must find essential to such a volume.

The ominous thing is that I am working in the other direction, toward 1800, not toward 1860. Whether or not I could acquire the necessary learning would depend on a great many variables. Perhaps the most important question to ask is when would you expect the book?

I have probably paid my last visit to New York before fall and am preparing to start west about June 10. Why not requisition an expense account from Harper's and come up and spend an evening drinking with me?

Yours,

TO SAMUEL ELIOT MORISON

December 1946

Dear Sam:

The humiliating truth is that I emptied my history tank with the fur trade book and am only now beginning to refill it with Lewis and Clark. As a historian I have to operate on a small capital with a rapid turnover. Every book I write represents the sum total of my knowledge to the date signed to the preface.

This is to say that I cannot by April of this year produce a paper that would be worth the Society's[1] attention but that as the year develops, my

[1] The American Antiquarian Society.

tank will be refilled to the point where I probably can produce one for April of 1948. I am asking you to pass over me this year and do me the honor of inviting me to write one next year.

Please get in touch with me when you come back to Boston as I should like to open a bottle of wine for you and sit around for a while quarreling with you about how to settle the universe. I am afraid that the wicked are increasing. My recent trip to you signalized the arrival of a rear quarter of venison from Wyoming. Maybe there will be another one later.

Yours,

TO CATHERINE DRINKER BOWEN

Mrs. Bowen, who met DeVoto at Breadloaf in the summer of 1933, adopted him, instantly and with enthusiasm, as her guru in all matters relating to writing and especially in those relating to American history. When she wrote him that a professor had put her down, saying that her addiction to American history was romantic, DeVoto dashed off a reply— dashed it off, but liked it so well when it was done that he kept three carbons for his files. Mrs. Bowen published the letter in her Biography: The Craft and the Calling, *1969.*

[n.d.]

Dear Kitty:

Sure you're romantic about American history. What your professor left out of account was the fact that it is the most romantic of all histories. It began in myth and has developed through three centuries of fairy stories. Whatever the time is in America it is always, at every moment, the mad and wayward hour when the prince is finding the little foot that alone fits into the slipper of glass. It is a little hard to know what romantic means to those who use the word umbrageously. But if the mad, impossible voyage of Columbus or Cartier or La Salle or Coronado or John Ledyard is not romantic, if the stars did not dance in the sky when the Constitutional Convention met, if Atlantis has any landscape stranger or the other side of the moon any lights or colors or shapes more unearthly than the customary homespun of Lincoln and the morning coat of Jackson, well, I don't know what romance is. Ours is a story mad with the impossible, it is by chaos out of dream, it began as dream and it has continued as dream down to the last headline you read in a newspaper, and of our dreams there are two things above all others to be said, that only madmen could have dreamed them or would have dared to—and that we have shown a considerable faculty for making them come true. The simplest truth you can ever write about our history will be charged and surcharged with romanticism, and if you are afraid of the word you had better start practicing seriously on your fiddle.

Yours,

TO MADELINE MCQUOWN

DeVoto made his last effort to be a novelist in Mountain Time, *whose manuscript he completed almost at the same time as that of* Across the Wide Missouri. *He handed* Mountain Time *to Little, Brown and* Across the Wide Missouri *to Houghton Mifflin just before leaving to spend the summer of 1946 in an extensive tour of the West. Both in the prepublication months when the manuscripts floated around among his friends, and after they appeared in print, the two together led some of his friends to comment on his qualities as novelist and historian (generally to the disadvantage of the novelist) and led DeVoto himself to ponder his own intentions and methods. Thus in his letter to Madeline McQuown, a librarian friend in Ogden, he defended his practice somewhat belligerently, both fiction and history. But the history he described in the McQuown letter was the narrative kind, tightly circumscribed in time, multiple in story, utilizing the devices of the test-boring and simultaneity that he had developed first in* The Year of

*Decision 1846. The history he embarked
on after the completion of* Across the
Wide Missouri *turned out to be quite
another kind—expansive in time, limited
in its opportunities for the sharply
fictionalized scene and the sharply
delineated character, too broad in its
coverage for symbolic culture heroes. His
letters to Mattingly through the next
three years are one long howl of
exasperation at the morass into which he
had all unwittingly floundered. When he
wrote to Mrs. McQuown at the beginning
of 1947 he thought he knew exactly what
history was and how he wrote it. By the
end of that year he was already deep in
what Mattingly diagnosed as* regressus
historicus, *chasing "the background of the
background of the background" back
through the centuries and hating it all the
way.*

January 3, 1947

Dear Madeline:

I answered your letter about three weeks ago but was under pressure of
haste—when am I not—and decided that I hadn't said anything worth
reading and tore it up. The idea was I'd sit down tomorrow, as I'm at last
doing, and give you the rest of a kind of analysis your letter suggested. I
don't know precisely what, except that I am a professional corrector of errors,
and you make some screwy ones about me, and when I do embark on self-
analysis I seem to want to do a three-volume job.

I'm glad you like the new book.[1] I don't underrate it, though I am not
much concerned about my critical status and not much given to wondering
how good my books are. I think that it and its predecessors (and prospec-
tively its successor, I hope) say some things previously unsaid about the
West in relation to the country as a whole but important to have said.
Especially, I think, they uncover interrelationships of some importance heretofore not widely recognized, perhaps not recognized at all. I think that in
some small degree they will affect thinking and writing about this part of
American history for a while. In fact, they already have. Whether or not they

[1] *Across the Wide Missouri*, which Mrs. McQuown had seen in manuscript. Her comments
had been favorable on the history, unfavorable on *Mountain Time*, which she had read,
if at all, in the *Collier's* version.

are history I don't know or care. The academics say they aren't, so does Morgan. Words don't matter—they're history as I use the word, let anybody else use it any way he chooses to. I think the job I've done is of some value. It's a representative achievement of the caliber of writer I am, neither little nor big but of some capacity, some thoroughness and honesty, considerable intelligence, and all-out—that is, doing things without reservation [or] to the limit of one's ability. Is that a fair statement? I think it is.

What is valid in your remarks about the books is your perception that they are *written*. Very few historians of our time, practically no academic historians, realize that history is not only knowledge, not only knowledge and wisdom even, but is also art. I do. My books employ the methods and techniques of literature and especially they have structure as literature. They have form. What's more to the point, and what distinguishes them sharply from a book by Allan Nevins or J. G. Randall, say, is that form is used to reveal meaning. The meaning is the end in view. But a much more sophisticated and expert technique is used to make it clear, to communicate it, than anyone ever realizes unless he studies my stuff very closely indeed. You are quite right in perceiving that the books are like novels—they are constructed and written like novels to exactly the same end as novels. I expect this to have some effect on the writing of history, and again it has in fact already had some effect beginning with *M T's A*. Finally, the materials of history have grown so multifarious that, I think, from now on some kinds of history can be written satisfactorily only by methods which I have used in all three of my books, and may possibly be the first to have used them, methods which I can designate roughly as the test-boring and the focus on simultaneousness.[2] Some fairly exalted names have used just those words. I'm content to speak of dynamic narrative.

What is not valid in your remarks about them, what makes you both overvalue them and at the same time partly distort them, results from subjective matters in your approach to them. You reveal part of it when you speak of yourself as "incurably a Westerner." In your response to my books various phantasies enter quite clearly. Most of all there is your complex phantasy about the West itself but there are such additional ones as your phantasy of yourself as a writer about the West, of me as a person, of me as a writer, of me as the Westerner writing about the West and so fulfilling part of your own phantasy. And so on. The valuation you set both on the kind of thing my books do and on their achievement is oriented from these phantasies. They shape the books in your thinking—give them, I mean, a different

[2] By "test-boring," DeVoto meant sampling, the use of the part for the whole, synecdoche. By "focus on simultaneousness," he meant the handling of multiple strands of narrative, as in the stories of the Mormons, the Donner party, the Missouri Volunteers, and other elements of the 1846 emigration, and trying to give the impression that all were happening at once, as of course they were.

shape from what they have to me and have, I believe, objectively. What seems to me the important thing about them is their progressive description of the part the West played as *one* of the forces that made the nation what it is—their analysis and exploitation of the Jefferson-Lincoln political geography plus mystique. Autobiographically they are my evasion of a once self-imposed obligation to write about the Civil War. The Civil War is the best single lens through which to look at American history and a book about it would say at the center of the circle precisely the things I'm saying not at the center but farther toward the periphery. Continental expansion, I'm saying, is the next best lens, and I chose it because I wanted to do other things as well as write my understanding of American experience—and a Civil War book of the kind I'd write would require a whole lifetime [. . . .]

Yours,

TO GARRETT MATTINGLY

July 11, 1947

Dear Mat:

Jesus Christ, look who's telling me how to get about Connecticut in an automobile. Before we go any farther with this, I want you to answer a placement and aptitude questionnaire, just for my guidance in dealing with the situation. Time, four hours.

    a) What makes the car go?

    b) How does one stop it?

    c) Which of those guys in the front seat is the driver?

Candidates are required to answer one of these questions correctly before the discussion can proceed.

I hate to say this, but maybe you'd better tell me where you're going to be in Vermont and also the dates of a) leaving Connecticut and b) arriving in Vermont. Besides cursing the medical profession, being both parents to two abandoned children, and signing checks for the trousseau that is going to wow the fashionables of Houghton,[1] I'm being Helen's[2] stand-in at Radcliffe in Publishing Procedures—her summer health is proving even lousier than mine—and I don't seem to get much time to myself. Let's be clear about this. I been to Vermont. Just tell me where you're going to be

---

[1] Avis DeVoto was visiting her home town of Houghton, Michigan, during this summer.
[2] Helen Everitt, then a Houghton Mifflin editor, conducted a summer course in publishing procedures at Radcliffe.

and how far off I have to go to get a bed. As a matter of fact, why the hell don't I load both kids and a barrel of Paris green in the car and go anyway? Hell, I wouldn't need the Paris green. If I put both of them in one automobile I'll probably get out of it and maybe one of them will, but you can be damn sure that they both won't.

I will say that this gives me the greatest pleasure I've had since the Rev. Father Cushnahan's pants caught round his ankles underneath the cassock—Jesus, do I mean chasuble?—when I was head altar boy at St. Joseph's Church . . . Pytheas, son? Why he was part of the $8000 worth of work I've done on your God damn Welsh Indians so far, and I must say at the moment he's worth $48,000 cash to me. (You can get a preview of my appearance on Oct. 15—When Brigham told me that I couldn't any longer avoid the obligations of an honorable member of the American Antiquarian Society, I told him I'd inform the brotherhood in regard to the Welsh Indians. I added, out of my wisdom, that I was preceded on that subject and before that audience in 1854.) Well, seems he [Pytheas] was a Greek who lived at Massalia and determined the latitude thereof something like a hundred years before anybody else determined any latitude whatever. This was maybe 330 B.C. That was just cram stuff, though. He was prepping himself to sail through the Gates of Hercules, sneak through the Phoenician patrol by night, and be off to see what he could see. Damn if he didn't do just that. Cadiz, Cape St. Vincent, the Bay of Biscay, northwest Gaul, Ushant. Okay, so he liked it, spit on his hands, and headed out to sea, and damn if he didn't discover Britain. He visited the tin mines and seems to have wowed them. Then by water past the tip of Scotland and the going still looked good so he headed out to sea again and this time what he fetched was Iceland. He seems still not to have [had] enough, so he sailed a hundred miles north of Iceland. He'd still be going but the ice stopped him.

So far the texts. I must say it all clears up a number of things that have been bothering me. That's where the Mandans got those blue eyes, all right, and I can't doubt that it was old Pete Pytheas who buried those crosses that Hamlin Garland kept finding in the hills above San Francisco Bay. I don't think I believe in getting educated. It makes people too damn credulous and I don't like to be credulous. God almighty, at my age I should learn about the guy who invented the Western Hemisphere. Before I studied history I used to think of historians as the hardheaded people who couldn't believe anything, more or less what I was shaping my image by in those innocent and sunny days, but when I started to get educated I found out that a historian is somebody who keeps having to believe something else, and by God I admit it now. I'm a historian. If you want to tell me that among the first five or six thousand discoverers of the American continent from the east was St. Patrick, that's all right with me. I've come to accept St. Brendan,

I'm on the verge of accepting Judas as [on] his passenger list, I'll have the stone boat explained by the end of the week, and why not St. Patrick? It was some of St. Patrick's nephews on that dock on Boston Neck when Capt. J. Smith sailed by and they made lewd signs at him . . . Look, Mat, it was a good many years ago when I stopped being surprised by the traffic in Cumberland Gap fifty years before Dr. Walker discovered it, and long before I ever did any work on Lewis and Clark I knew that the trail they blazed carried more cars than the Lincoln Highway before they were born, but this transatlantic stuff is too damn much for me. I wish you boys would get together and establish a few conventions and adhere to them. I don't mind the Norsemen in North Dakota, I don't mind the Irish they found in Iceland three centuries before they had seen Iceland when I went to college, but if Thule was European in B.C. I'm ready to go back to the practice of literary criticism. There's a field where you really know something when you know it, and if you know it you don't have to know anything else for it stays put. You started something when you assigned me to the literary [historical?] beat. I'll come out of it knowing for sure that Madoc settled the U.S. And what's history got that the Book of Mormon hasn't? If Brendan, why not Mormon? If the Irish are in Iceland in 700 A.D., and beginning to be decadent, why not the Nephites in Zarahemla seven centuries before? Do you people happen to know where North America is? . . . .

Yrs,

TO GARRETT MATTINGLY

December 1, 1947

Dear Mat:

[   ] Hell is not hot enough for you. I wish you would, in a decent humility of spirit, repair to the nearest psychoanalyst and find out why in the name of Christ Jesus you ever put this spell on me. I am so damn fed up with Welsh, Irish, Scandinavian, Mormon, and Australoid Indians that I could throw up.[1] In fact I have thrown up—I've thrown up history, the art of prose, and the life literary, for all time. Comes today the news that Appomattox is a Welsh word and a long bibliography from Sam (Young

[1] Examining the early explorations of North America, DeVoto had got led back into the mists of legendry, trying to unravel the stories about Prince Madoc and other pre-Columbian immigrants. Too fascinated to let them go until he had got to the bottom of them, and too exasperated by the time they cost, he did not pursue his researches with a calm mind. As usual, Mattingly was called upon to provide therapy.

Columbus) Morison about the weaknesses in the notion that the Norse had anything to do with the continent of North America. Comes also a book by one who describes himself as a heretic in archeology and anthropology with what he describes as plain proof that between the fifth and third centuries B.C., which was some time before Madoc, the said continent was invaded by a race of black-bearded men from the East Indies, and they were the babies who really put the Indians on the right track. During the week (a) William Cullen Bryant entered the picture with a bibliography from here to there four times about the Chinese discoverers—hell, I had supposed I had that one not only covered but coppered—of North America, and (b) the Egyptians entered with more damn blowing of trumpets, dancing of slave girls, and orchestral climaxes in ascending octaves than there are when the breech-clout boys carry in Rhadames. And look, I'm under no contract to settle Egyptian history for you or anybody else.

You think I'm making jokes, you think this is a literary expression of something or other. You're damn wrong. I make solemn oath that I've had enough—enough history, enough literature, enough literary endeavor. The sacred honor of Ogden will keep me on this job till I've wiped it up. Then I'm through. . . . I took home a patient last night, after he'd made my evening joyful. I walked him part way, I taxied him part way, and the last two hundred yards I carried him over my shoulder. And every fifty feet, in whatever vehicle or posture, he announced "I don't give a f—k for Harvard." Well, that's what, from this moment forth, I don't give for literature, see? I'm too old. It shouldn't happen to Jim Conant, let alone me. There's a guy who thinks I'd make a good partner for a provincial bookstore endeavor. I think he's right as hell.

Who is Ckio, what is she, that I should get duodenal ulcers of the soul over her? You know the answer to that one, Mattingly?

That isn't supposed to be Ckio. It's supposed to be Clio. It's as accurate as you boys usually get, at that.

Go back to the sacred honor of Ogden. For the duration of this run only—then I'm going into the bookstore business. Till then:

1) In the name of god what is a purgatore? Don't start looking it up in dictionaries, it isn't in them, just pull it out of your erudition. St. Brendan started out on his voyages as a penance laid upon him by his confessor. Penance for what? For the sin of disbelief or skepticism. There were a lot of things the Saint was skeptical about that I follow him in and back him up, as for instance the sea serpent. But historical criticism marks time till I find out what a purgatore is—and it is neither a physic nor a limbo—because among the things Brendan was skeptical about were nine purgatores.

2) We're back to the Spanish Empire in North America now, and I find out that among my complete ignorances the Spanish Empire in North

America occupies a conspicuous place, though I will not go so far to say, among superlatives, first place. All right, I'm willing to read one (1) book about it. I won't read a book by Haring but I will read any other one (1). Which *one* book will most usefully reduce my ignorance how far?

3) You said you'd settled the Brazil (bakkam, braisier, baxa, braseiro, braser, braciere, brasilli) wood business. Well, settle it for little Peterkin damn fast. I would even read *one* book about that, but I'd prefer a nice summary on a 4×6 card.

4) Have you any suspicion that Cabeza de Vaca was contaminated with Celtic blood? Or who built Harahey and Quivira?

Peg may not be the right noun and square may not be the right adjective, but I damn well don't fit in the hole you've been trying to drive me into these last forty years [. . . .]

Yours,

TO GARRETT MATTINGLY

March 14, 1948

Dear Mat:

The other night, in the presence of a learned gent, I said something like this: I doubt if the myths of the Plains Indians we have to deal with are more than three hundred years old at the outside, and I don't trust an Indian tradition farther than grandpa, if that far. The learned gent remarked, "That's exactly what Lord Acton said." Maybe he did but he might as well have been Hammurabi for all the clues I've got about how to find it. Where do I start looking?

By infinitely slow stages I got L&C from the Sioux to the Mandans, where they are stuck not only for the winter of 1804–1805 but for whatever additional time it takes me to chock up American history on blocks, turn it around, and give it an entirely new orientation. It is now clear to me that the Mandans[1] are American history and we have all been wrong, you as well as I. They explain the Essex Junto, the industrial revolution, U. S. Grant, and Douglas MacArthur and everything that fills the interstices. I want to run one for President.

[1] For a time, because of a tendency toward light skin and freckles, the Mandans were rumored to be descended from the Welsh of Prince Madoc.

TO MAE REED PORTER

---

*Mrs. Porter was the instigator and in a
minor way a collaborator in* Across the Wide
Missouri. *She discovered and bought about
a hundred Alfred Jacob Miller watercolors
in the Peale Museum in Baltimore in 1935.
Becoming acquainted with Emery Reves, a
Hungarian émigré who was trying to
establish himself in the American literary
world, she fell in with his scheme of making
a book on the "Stewart-Miller
Expedition" of 1837, during which Miller
had painted the mountain fur trade at very
near its climax. Reves sold a spread of the
pictures to* Fortune *(January 1944), and at
about the time of their appearance, came to
Houghton Mifflin with the book proposal.
He wanted some competent historian to
write 20,000 words of captions.*

*From that beginning, by tortuous and
not always good-tempered negotiations,
developed* Across the Wide Missouri. *Very
early it was clear that Mrs. Porter was not
competent as a historian. Just as early it was
clear that Reves's involvement was
somewhat irregular. As owner of the Hyperion
Press, a defunct publishing house, as agent
for Mrs. Porter, and as entrepreneur on his
own hook, he appeared to want a cut as
publisher, author, and agent all at once.
Houghton Mifflin, who had dealt with him
before and would deal with him later (he
was instrumental in obtaining Winston
Churchill's memoirs for them) thought
Reves simply unacquainted with American
publishing procedures; DeVoto questioned
his good faith. In the end Reves settled for*

*something less than he wanted, and was
out of the negotiations. Mrs. Porter got her
share as owner of the Miller pictures and
author of the foreword describing their
acquisition. DeVoto wrote not 20,000 words
of captions but the most brilliant evocation
of the mountain fur trade in historical
literature, which won the Bancroft and
Pulitzer prizes in 1947.*

*The letter reproduced here is the last
item in more than two years of
correspondence between DeVoto and Mrs.
Porter, and recapitulates DeVoto's side of
the matter. As he said in his self-portrait
written for Miss Burke, he hated amateurs.*

May 24, 1948

Dear Mrs. Porter:

In your undated letter to us of about two weeks ago, you ask "Am I entitled to a small slice?", meaning a part of the Pulitzer Prize awarded to *Across the Wide Missouri.* I think you are not entitled to a part of it and that would seem to be the opinion of Columbia University, which addressed the announcement of the award to me only, and of the committee of historians who made the recommendation to Columbia without mentioning you. Since I did not care to decide the question myself, however, I submitted it to Houghton Mifflin without comment. Their judgment is that the award was properly made to me only.

The rest of your letter and certain remarks and claims attributed to you in various newspaper stories, however, suggest that the time has come for me to remind you of the realities. As you know, I submitted to Reves's getting a portion of the royalties to which he had no moral or legal right, in order to prevent his making a public unpleasantness about the book. I have wanted no public unpleasantness of any kind and so I have also made no protest about various claims of yours to credit that does not belong to you and to a share in the making of the book which you did not have. I have no objections to your getting any kind of satisfaction that you can from the book but you are now making quite false claims and they are getting printed. I therefore feel that I must remind you of the facts.

I have again gone over the notes I made during my various visits to Baltimore, my research notes on Miller, your letters about Macgill James,[1] and other documents bearing on Mr. James's connection with Miller, in-

[1] Of the Peale Museum, who discovered Miller well before Mrs. Porter did, and provided her with much of her information about him.

cluding letters from him that summarize the history of his work. After reviewing all this, I find no reason to alter any of the statements I make in the book about Mr. James. Actually, what I say does less than full credit to him and more credit to you than the facts justify. If you care to make a public issue of this, the material I have will make that fact fully evident. I'm sorry if it grieves or offends you, but the statements made in the book are going to stand as they are printed.

There is another set of documented and fully demonstrable facts that bear on your claims, now grown to preposterous size, that biographical and historical research of yours went into the book. Your conception of your role in the book has, as I have already said, got entirely out of touch with reality. This does not surprise me, since you have persuaded yourself that you discovered Miller, whereas your discovery consists of having had your attention called to him—to a man of whom, by your own printed statement, you had not previously heard—by the secretary of a museum where some of his pictures were, some years after a public exhibition of them had been held and biographical material about him gathered and in part printed. I cannot see that this constitutes discovery in any accepted sense of the word, and I find it altogether impossible to understand why you suppose that your "research" on Miller, Stewart, the fur trade, or Western history in general played any part in the book as it was written and published. Actually the part your research played was to delay me for a couple of months at the beginning. When I got to work I assumed that you knew what you were talking about and so I accepted your material in certain places which my own knowledge did not then cover. I soon found, however, that your material was not acceptable and was forced to go back and dig the stuff out for myself.

You have worked yourself into what seems to me a curious state of mind about this. When you insisted on inserting the phrase "with its attendant research material" in the last sentence of your Foreword I let it go because it seemed harmless enough. It now proves that I should not have let you insert that phrase. Your unfounded claims, made in conversation and public lectures, to having had a part in the scholarship and writing of the book did not disturb me, but I cannot let them go unchallenged when newspapers print them, presumably after talking to you. The Kansas City *Times*, May 4, 1948, says "The first drafts of Mrs. Porter's work were begun in 1941 and later were turned over to Mr. DeVoto who wrote the material as it was published, adding some of his own material." The Marshall *Democrat-News*, May 6, 1948, says, again obviously on your authority, that the book "owes much of its source material" to you. My clipping bureau has sent me clippings from other newspapers in which the same or equivalent claims are made.

I am not going to ask you to correct misrepresentations such as these that are already in print, though in honesty such a correction should be made. I do ask you to make sure that they do not appear in print again—they or their substance or any claim to a share in the scholarship of the book except in strict accordance [with] the facts as I now proceed to state them.

The material that Reves turned over to me which included your "research" material, was in general of two kinds, biographical material about Miller and Stewart and a couple of curious manuscripts of yours that dealt with Stewart's 1837 trip west and contained some miscellaneous background material about the fur trade. One of these manuscripts was the basic document out of which your Foreword evolved—after I had corrected errors in it. The other was called "Research Material on the Stewart-Miller Expedition (1837–1838)"—and you will observe that even the title contains a basic error. Even this second manuscript, shot full of errors and misconceptions as it is, appears not to have been solely your work. It shows evidence of having been in part amplified and in part corrected by Aimee Crane or someone at the Hyperion Press who was working under her direction and by some staff researcher at *Fortune*. (The text accompanying Miller's pictures in *Fortune* is on the whole more accurate than this document but nevertheless contains many statements which anyone who knows the history of the period must recognize at sight as misconceptions or errors of fact, but which you did not identify as such.) I assume that your claim to a part in the scholarship of the book is based primarily on this second document.

That document is based on Miller's notes, from which it repeatedly quotes, either directly or indirectly. You were not competent even to recognize Miller's errors of fact, still less his misconceptions or his later amendments of his text. For the rest, the narratives and analytical account of the 1837 expedition and such background material as it parenthetically contained, the document was absurd at sight. It was absurd to me and will be, if you submit it to one, to any historian who knows anything about the fur trade or Western history in general. It contains scores of errors, scores of misconceptions, and scores of naively proposterous statements. It also contains allusions to a text that does not exist, one which when I asked you where you had found it, you said you had invented for artistic effect in a lecture—in plain words, a historical forgery.

A single reading of this document showed me, and would show any historian, that it was the work of a novice without background in Western history, unused to historical inquiry and investigation, ignorant of the historical matrix in which the narrative it purported to tell would have to be set, so ignorant also of the immediate subject that she could not tell specific errors from fact, incapable of analyzing historical evidence and appraising its worth, and, on the showing of the document itself, incapable of determining even the most superficial facts about the one summer (though you thought it was two summers) with which it dealt. The document was worthless. I am sorry to speak so bluntly but that accurately describes your "Research Material." Any competent historian to whom you may submit it will be forced to describe it in exactly the terms I have used. I trust you will not want me to waste time pointing out page by page and line by line how what I have said about it applies, but if you want me to, or if you care to challenge what I say, I will do so.

I therefore discarded the "Research Material" altogether. Nothing in the text or footnotes or appendixes of my book rests on it. That fact, also, will be established at once by any historian who may compare your document with my book.

When I got to work, I knew little about Stewart, though considerably more than you did at that, and nothing about Miller. As I have said above, I began by assuming that you had worked on both of them carefully enough for me to trust your notes. I began with Miller. I soon found glaring inaccuracies in your notes (some of them are stubbornly adhered to in your letters to me) and I saw that I must do the job myself. Hence—besides my research in libraries and museums—my repeated trips to Baltimore and Washington and my detailed correspondence with historians and critics of art. As my investigation progressed, I came to see that the only parts of your material which it was safe to accept were those that had been furnished you by Mr. James. I know that this fact is repugnant to you, but you seem to have forgotten that much of the material which you—or Reves—turned over to me was in Mr. James's handwriting. I did not find out whose handwriting it was until I had done enough work of my own to verify much of his work and invalidate much of yours (though your own work on Miller was small in bulk as compared with his). I found out whose handwriting it was by chance. On one of my visits to Washington I took a briefcase of material to Mr. James in order to ask him for further leads and for ways of checking up on my own investigation. He, of course, recognized his own handwriting, and he also identified as having originally been made by him a large album of material which by then I had independently proved to be reliable. Again, your own statements show that Mr. James's work had long preceded your own. The material itself shows that your work on Miller had not progressed far beyond Mr. James's by the time the material was turned over to me, and that in what you had added to his you had repeatedly erred. There it is, on the record, plain, capable of being checked by anyone who inquires into it.

I understand several of your letters to assert that this was not Mr. James's work but Miss Whyte's. In letters to me Mr. James freely acknowledged, as he did in person when I talked to him, his debt to Miss Whyte, who, however, worked under his direction. But the first point is that the fundamental biographical material about Miller is in his handwriting, which obviously is not Miss Whyte's. The second point is that all this work, whether his or hers, is not your work. The third point is that, whosoever work it is, it long preceded yours. The fourth point I have already made:

your own work was not dependable. It was loose, inaccurate, contradictory, full of hiatuses, eked out by sheer guess, out of accord with the facts which it had become necessary for me to turn up. I had to make my own investigation in order to determine which parts of the material turned over to me were dependable, and by the time I was able to determine that those parts were Mr. James's work I had qualified myself to write about Miller. None of what I say about Miller anywhere in my book rests on your material.

Again I trust you will not want me to waste time pointing out line by line the unacceptability of your work on Miller. But if you want me to, or if you insist on making a public issue of it, I will do so.

Here I must point out two facts. My book contains an appendix on the first illustrators of the West, so far as I know (except as Dr. Taft's[2] work intersects it) the only detailed, comparative, historical treatment of the subject so far written. Any historian would recognize such a discussion as the foremost obligation of anyone who was dealing with Miller—anyone who did not recognize that obligation and do his best to fulfill it could not be called a historian. But in all your material there is no recognition of that obligation, no effort to fulfill it by so much as a single sentence, no mention of any of the painters it deals with except Miller, and no attempt to see Miller or his painting in their historical context. The second fact is this: you had nothing to do with the choice of illustrations in the book. Lovell Thompson[3] and I made the choice. I went to Baltimore twice and to Long Island once and to a great many museums and libraries for the sole purpose of comparing pictures and deciding which ones would make the best illustrations. On one of my trips to Baltimore and some of my other trips Mr. Thompson accompanied me, and he made similar trips for the same purpose without me. The first approximation was made on those trips; the final choice was made in the Houghton Mifflin offices. It was made exclusively by Mr. Thompson and me; no one else had a voice in it, you had no voice in it, and though we called on other members of the firm for expressions of taste and opinion we did not call on you. In so far as determining what pictures to use may have played a part in such excellence as the book has, this is a fair statement: some of the illustrations are by Catlin, some are by Bodmer, and the rest are by Miller; of the Millers, the larger part but by no means all belong to you. In the illustrations you appear solely as a collector of pictures.

I do not propose here to go in detail through your "research material" relating to Stewart. Most of it is covered in what I have said about your document on the 1837 trip. What I have said above applies to it and to your

[2] Dr. Robert Taft, a chemist at the University of Kansas, whose interest in western pictures resulted in *Photography and the American Scene* and *Artists and Illustrators of the Old West: 1850–1900*.
[3] Then vice-president and production manager of Houghton Mifflin.

letters to me in answer to questions of mine. Your material about Stewart was untrustworthy, inaccurate, undependable, misconceived, shot full of errors and misconceptions, innocent of historical background. You did not even know how long Stewart was in the West, until I pointed it out to you. You confused the trips you did know about. You did not have the dates of his baronetcy right. You made wholly unsupported guesses about him and presented the guesses, which were wrong, as facts. You misconstrued what the Army Lists said about him. You had not even heard of The Red Book of Grandtully, the basic document concerning his lineage and service, till I mentioned it to you. You accepted fiction as fact. You presented rumor and hearsay as fact, and you made wholly unjustifiable deductions from them. Much of what you had rested on inquiries in Scotland, made by others, unchecked. But the greater part of the available information about him you had never even heard of. In short, your work on Stewart was meager, amateurish and wholly untrustworthy. I rejected it altogether and, with the exceptions which I will list in a moment, it made no contribution whatever to my book.

This too can be verified by anyone who checks your material against my text. I trust you do not want me to analyze it in detail but, again, if you want me to or force me to, I will.

I will now state what parts of my book rest on your material. There is a single statement, less than a paragraph long, that rests on a document with which you supplied me and that I have not attached your name to in a footnote. I will not identify the statement here because I have come to suspect that the statement is wrong, and I propose to seek out the document for myself and determine whether or not you copied it correctly, as I now think you did not. Every other statement made in the book to which your work contributed anything at all is specifically accredited to you in a footnote, mentioning you by name. You can thus figure out for yourself the full extent of your contribution to the book. All these statements refer to Stewart's 1843 trip or to his later life in Scotland, both of them outside the province of my book. I attached your name to them for two reasons; I wanted to make absolutely clear what you had contributed, and I also wanted to disclaim responsibility for statements that rested on your work, for in my opinion these are no more trustworthy than the rest of your findings.

I repeat, this letter completely covers your connection with the book and gives in full the part your "research" played in the ultimate text. I can prove everything I say here by the documents.

I trust that you will not force me to prove it in public. From the beginning I have tried to avoid unpleasantness, though your insistence on being credited with work you did not do and your claims to having had a larger share in the book than you actually had in it have irked me. Any public airing of your claims would be repugnant to me, but [it] would also be disastrous to you, and I trust that you have therefore an even stronger desire than I have to avoid a public dispute. I propose to do nothing in public—or in private, either—if the matter end as it now stands. But the statements which are now being printed and for which you are certainly responsible are a very serious distortion of the truth, and they reflect on both my honesty and my professional competence. I will not permit them to go any farther without public protest, without making the whole case public.

I earnestly hope that you will not force me to, that you will be content with the full credit given you in my preface for initiative, energy, and the most admirable courage and doggedness in trying to make Miller known and getting him his public due. If you are not content, then I must remind you that there are very clear and very firm standards of historical propriety and that as a historian I cannot permit you to impugn my work by departing from them.

My secretary has now finished checking the copy she made of Miller's notes on his sketches. I will presently send it to you, along with your "Research Material," which I have had microfilmed, and the prints you spoke to me about. I will return to Mr. James the album he made and the various notes and documents in his handwriting. He told me that he only lent them to you and asked me to send them back to him when I had finished with them.

Sincerely yours,

TO GARRETT MATTINGLY

November 16, 1948

Dear Mat:

Questions. Not that any of them is worth 64¢

I've tied up Vérendrye. . . . I don't know why. I don't know a damned thing now that I couldn't have got, that I didn't get, by adding Crouse to Burpee to Brebner.[1] Except that if anybody tried to figure out what ideas he was working on, nobody bothered to set them down. But I was uneasy, I wouldn't have felt right, so I did the God damn job. I can't go on that way. I've taken an oath to jump all the way to Carver and take the scholars' word

[1] Probably N. Maynard Crouse, *The Contribution of the Canadian Jesuits to the Geographical Knowledge of New France, 1632–1675;* L. J. Burpee, *The Discovery of Canada;* and John B. Brebner, *The Explorers of North America.*

301

for what's in between. And, taking it, get to work on one St. Pierre, who criticized V's suggestions ten years later—in misspelled, uncapitalized, 18th century, frontier Canadian French and never heard of periods. Did I say 50 years? Make it 150. . . . Well, what I want to know is, why do I like the Frenchmen and don't like the Spaniards or the English? Explain me or explain history, take your choice.

This Vérendrye is a hell of a lot like Champlain, maybe he was better than Champlain, some ways—at least he understood the businessman bastards. He had iron and guts in him and he did what he started out to—as close as a man is allowed to—in spite of the God-damnedest set of snooty bureaucrats in Paris asking him why the hell he didn't travel 1500 miles of rapids and portages in three weeks and why the hell should he expect the king to pay him anything for doing the king's business. Nine wounds, a couple of them at Malplaquet and the poor boob thought it was important to get out to the Western Sea and damn near did. With a kind of flourish, and he liked the medal of St. Louis Maurepas sent him instead of a draft, and he liked Indians, the French all liked Indians and didn't like killing them. Well, why does he, why does Champlain, why does La Salle, seem not only heroic but admirable to me? Why do I like them? The damn 18th century English make me as mad as they made each other, and that goes for practically everybody you can name, and especially it goes for Alexander Henry and, redoubled, for the great Mackenzie. There was only one Hearne in a carload of them and I think he must have been a Wop. Why? What gives me the pip about the English? And why is Champlain rotting his gums out with scurvy a great and intelligent and devoted man to my mind, whereas Coronado seems a kind of fathead? Why do I object so to all the Indians the Spanish kill? Is it because I can't read Spanish?

Yes, and I haven't read Madariaga's first volume and now he's got another one, and do I have to read them? Also, if the Spanish didn't kill any Indians but cherished them lovingly, as I understand him to say, as God is his witness, what happened to all the Caribbean Indians and what were all those primates they were killing from Mexico City north and from Key West inland?

Do I maybe think I'm Francis Parkman?

What do you do about geography? I mean, what do I do about it? Have I got to go up the Saskatchewan too? Or Lake Winnipeg? This guy Burpee appeared to know which peak was up but I got stalled when he had the Red River flowing both north and south in the same stretch. That turned out to be his faith that Vérendrye would have put in a period and a capital if he'd stopped to think, but what do you do? I wrote you a belch about this guy Brown that my secretary says used to be so charming to his students. I damn well need to know about the stuff that's in one half of his book, but the trouble is I damn well do know about the stuff that's in the other half and it gives me no great confidence about the first half. Christ, Mat, I can't dig out the background of the background of the background. How the hell do I learn historical geography?

For that matter, why should I? What the hell am I doing farting round with Charlevoix and who was where in 1690 and was there anything in that yarn of Marquette's and if so what did it get bent into why? This was supposed to be about Sacajawea, wasn't it? I figure I can clean up the predecessors of L&C in 30 years more, oh, easy. I figure I can do the empires and the wars in less than 10 years more and the trans-Allegheny U.S., the state of scientific thought, symmetrical geography, the diplomatics and American politics in another 10, and maybe in 5 years I can get Napoleon and La. straightened out, though not as easily as F. Pratt could in five minutes. . . . Well, God damn it, twice now you've been able to tell me what book I was writing on the basis of a first draft. We haven't got time for that sort of thing any more. You damn well tell me pretty soon what book I'm working toward now or I'll get buried under it. What's in my mind? No, that's a crass question. What book am I aiming at?

Buried? Sunk without a trace. You had to go and quash the only intelligent idea I've ever had about the job, which was to cut the loss and get out. That idea quivers toward intelligence again every time Kenneth Murdock tells me all I'd have to do to write a humdinger about Salem witchcraft would be to read eight or ten books, printed and in English at that, and sit round on my can and think about Freud. Bring that one out and set it up against, well, forget about Louisiana, just set it up against finding out what Jefferson was thinking about. I say we damn well need a good book about witchcraft and we'll damn well have one unless you pretty soon tell me what I think I'm up to.

Don't tell me nobody wants to read about witchcraft, either, for nobody wants to read about Vérendrye.

Dirge. I got badly stuck and had to cook an Easy Chair in one day. There was simply nothing to do. I did the damn Welsh Indians. Good subject wasted on four pages. Also botched.

I wish I could tell you how good that piece on Frisky[2] is. I wouldn't be so scared of history if I had a mind, maybe—that's the moral I draw from it. I guess there may be something in education too. Harvard did more by you that it did by me, I mean proportionately.

Please explain history to me.

Yrs,

[2] Roger Bigelow Merriman, the Harvard diplomatic historian under whom Mattingly had trained, was universally known, in affection or derision, as Frisky.

TO GARRETT MATTINGLY

December 2, 1948

Dear Mat:

This is a dirty trick but it won't take you more than ten minutes and a postcard.

It is clear to me that my French boys, and later even some of the English, were getting information about the Western Sea that consisted of three separate elements (besides pure fantasy and lying) which they took to be only one, single thing. Most of them had to work through at least two interpreters, some of them needed three sometimes, and so far as I can see none of them spoke the language of any tribe that actually claimed to know somebody who'd been there or claimed to have been there themselves. Sometimes, as with the senior Vérendrye, they had to do it by signs. . . . Well, they thought they were getting dope about the Western Sea. Actually they were getting straight dope about the Pacific, about New Mexico, and about Kaskaskia and Cahokia, plus some Indian confusion and misunderstanding, plus some happy Indian lies. To which they added their own misunderstandings and prepossessions.

Well, the next time you're in the library with ten minutes to spare, get out Lawrence J. Burpee's Champlain Society edition of *Journals and Letters of La Vérendrye and His Sons*. Read pp. 366–372 (this is La V père) and pp. 414–417, which is the Chevalier, his son. Better read the French, for B's translation gets high, wide, and handsome sometimes and misled me at some critical points till I learned better, and misled him. . . . Well, I'm sure you will see the same three elements that I do, but I want your verification that there is some solid dope about New Mexico here and I particularly want a comment on the last paragraph on p. 371. The bridle and bit are Spanish as all hell—I've seen them in the museums—what about the marching in column, and most of all what about the *cuirasses de fer maillé?* After all, Mat, this is 1738. I *know* that forty years later nobody was wearing any kind of mail out of New Mexico—unless drunk—but these damn men in armor or some kind of fragmentary armor keep turning up in all the Indian yarns about the wonderful Frenchmen on the seacoast. What about it?

Put the two passages together—the second is 1742. I consider that we here get the first solid information about New Mexico that came to Canada, no matter how incrusted and mixed up it may be. It happens to be blended with some straight dope about the Rockies and the Pacific, and to be embroidered with some stuff out of the Illinois, and the French were beautifully unaware that there was a mixture, but it's solid New Mexico nevertheless—or I'll quit and write science fiction. So far as I can see it's the first. I've read so damn much stuff earlier than this that when I sweat Pierre Margry wipes his forehead, but this is the first I'll take a stand on. Okay?

After reading your letter and meditating on our talk I have come to two conclusions: (a) that I will abandon all the seventeenth century I haven't so far covered and all the eighteenth century between Vérendrye and Robert Rogers, and pick this stuff up whole from Brebner and his colleagues, and (b) I haven't succeeded in making clear to you what really oppresses me with a sense of my unfitness to do the job. The first is with reluctance, for the movement of these boys across a map that is not the map they have in their minds fascinates me, but it's realistic, and the fact is that the L&C story proper begins with Rogers. The second is simply this: in the odd moments during which my, shall we say, mind has been working on the material for this ectoplasmic book, I have somehow crossed the frontier into, shall we also say, Historical Ideas. I say the hell with them but there I am. What some of them are, or seem to be shaping up as, I told you at the Century. Being of the uncircumcised, I don't know how important they are—which is part of the impasse—but I do know that they're fairly sizable. I told you there has to be a third leg to Parkman's stool, which has just two. I seem to be swarming like bees round that third leg, and, as a case history in the vagaries of the psychopathic personality, I seem to have started swarming as far back as MT'sA and to have been more or less working toward an eventual destination ever since, more or less the way you might go to Worcester from Boston by way of Key West, Rio, Nova Scotia, and Pittsfield. At any rate, the symptomatology is that I'm running some ideas. And I just don't know enough and I just don't see how it's possible to learn enough in the remaining time that this machine is to me. It isn't a question of not knowing how Jefferson knew he was going to buy La. six months before he did know it—I'm perfectly willing to follow your theorem and tell the reader, look, I don't know. It's a question of an all-encompassing ignorance of the field in which alone the ideas I've spawned have any meaning at all and in which alone their validity can be tested. The L&C expedition was not primarily what Brebner, the best of the lot, wrote it off as, the beginning of a new era of exploration of the North American continent, the methodical, so to speak industrial age era and no damn nonsense. It was, unless it was just some soldiers that Mr. Jefferson sent to find out how he could protect the sea otter trade from British sea power in case of war, it was a turning point in world history. And what the hell do I know about world history? That's easy: nothing. And how do I learn enough about world history to either complete my, as we say, ideas or to find out whether they're worth a damn? That's even easier: I can't.

There's no reason to write a book about how a well-conducted party got to the mouth of the Columbia and back. John Bakeless, in the Bakelessian prose, has written it.[1] Better men have written it in better prose. There's no reason to produce a one-volume summary of Parkman or a modernization of Justin Winsor—who was a great historian, and why in hell don't people say so? The only thing worth my writing or anyone's reading is a book that says, hey, this seems to have been left out of the picture. And before I write it, I'd like to know whether it's nonsense.

Diagnosis: intellectual palsy or elephantiasis of the ego. Prognosis: doubtful. Consultation requested [. . . .]

Yrs,

TO WILLIAM SLOANE

Among the things that brought DeVoto
near to intellectual apoplexy was the
"revisionist" view of the Civil War
increasingly propounded by Southern
historians—the view that the war was
brought on by Northern radicals, that it
need not have happened, that those who
thought slavery a moral issue were guilty of
precipitating the fratricidal conflict. In the
Easy Chairs for February and March 1946
he had denounced the attempt to butter
over the real issues of the war, had attacked
such revisionist historians as Avery Craven,
of the University of Chicago, and had said,
in thunder, that it was not the War between
the States, it was the Civil War, that it was
fought over slavery and secessionism, and
that the right side won. One wonders what
he would have said if he had lived to hear
the public relations reconciliations of the
Centennial years, with their visions of the

[1] John Bakeless, an old acquaintance from student days at Harvard, beat DeVoto to the Lewis and Clark story in *Lewis and Clark*, which DeVoto reviewed in the New York *Herald Tribune Books* on December 21, 1947. For a very brief hour, until he thought how much else he was bringing into the story, DeVoto was afraid his subject had been cut from under him.

boys in blue and gray linking arms and
singing, in harmony, "Tenting on the Old
Camp Ground."
     The letter below seems to have been
stimulated by word from Bill Sloane that he
was considering, for his publishing firm,
William Sloane Associates, a revisionist
history.

December 3, 1948

Dear Bill:
     A calm, temperate, judicial man myself, I am a little puzzled by your
note which seems to have been written in a moment of what I could almost
call emotion. Many years ago I was operated on for an ailment that had no
relevance to this discussion and was not even in the area of it. For several
days after I came to little pockets of ether would periodically open up somewhere in me and discharge that nauseous smell into my nostrils. One of
many fascinating things about our relationship, my boy, is the way little
pockets of idealism and innocence keep opening up in you as I pursue my
inquiries, which may be described as psychological, taxonomic, and religious. I will continue to do my best to heal you of these diseases but I know
how inexhaustible is the capacity of the human race, and especially that
subgroup of it known as publishers, for credulity.
     To begin with, be warned by my example ere it is too late. This thing
could get a grip on you as it did on me and I want you to spend your life
more fruitfully and with better success than I have spent mine. I have devoted at least two generations to pointing out to my contemporaries and
yours that by congressional and executive fiat and the usages of nations it
is *the* War of the Rebellion and that by the infrangible idioms of this
sweet American tongue it is *The Civil War*. I have shed so much blood that
the MGH[1] maintains a special serum bank with my name on it from the
wounds that you so gallantly and idiotically propose to submit yourself to,
including innumerable proud declarations by Gallant Southrons that they
were Rebels and coterminously Johnny Rebs. I have labored with my betters
and inferiors, if any, in the profession which your Mr. Pratt[2] and I adorn
to persuade them that the Civil War had something to do with secession
and something to do with slavery. I have further lost weight, sleep, skin, and
temper pointing out that there were various armies on the side of the
North—the Black Republican Nigger Lovers to you—and that though they
were one hundred times as large as any pitiful but dauntless group of
Southrons that ever opposed them and though they invariably fled headlong

[1] Massachusetts General Hospital.
[2] Fletcher Pratt, historian and Breadloaf colleague.

307

at the sight of Jeb Stuart's rose—a noun you will please not misinterpret—or any other Southron, somehow they won *the* war. I could go on listing my idiotic efforts but I merely point out to you where they got. With each succeeding volume of Mr. Freeman's works[3] I called his attention in front page reviews to the fact—which I can establish—that there were Union armies and that they had something to do with Lee's lieutenants. You will search Mr. Freeman's work in vain for any awareness of that fact. That, however, is far from the worst. It is now an established principle of American history that the War of the Rebellion was not as you with such prejudice put it, an unpleasantness—it was instead a hideous by-product of a conspiracy of hireling, maniacal abolitionists and owners of heavy industry.

Against this, my boy, the watchman waketh in vain. If you want to accomplish something within your lifetime, join the Union Club and start preaching the essential economic soundness of the New Deal. Nothing whatever can be done about it and I am sure that you are far too precious to many people, me among them, to waste your substance toward a bitter end. It was probably my successor Dumas Malone of the University of Virginia, suh, who rejected the filthy if belated piece of propaganda you are trying to put over on people in the even more idiotic belief that perhaps some Southrons would read it. This thesis, however, is open to one critical objection, that if he did it is the first known positive act of said Malone.

I have had no word from or about the History Book Club since I left it. It ran on my suggestions for some four or five months and among them was an italicized determination to get a book on the Civil War as soon as one should appear. They have obviously departed from gospel. I have two suggestions: one, provide yourself with the collected works of Avery Craven; two, go down to Richmond and seek out Virginius Dabney and tell him you are discontented with the Southern intellectual. You must know that Abraham Lincoln was a by-blow of Jeff Davis' grandfather, that Thad Stevens had a yaller gal to sleep with and wanted to hang—hang, suh, all Confederate gentlemen above the rank of first lieutenant, and that truth crushed to earth shall rise again but error wounded writhes in pain and dies among her worshippers. If you don't, then I will be willing to instruct you in some of the eternal truths week by week for a modest fee. Also, your alleged associate, Mr. Saxton,[4] was going to send me a copy of the book but so far has not done so.

Yours in the sacred memory of Varina.

[3] James Southall Freeman, *Lee's Lieutenants.*
[4] Mark Saxton, once DeVoto's student at Harvard, and son of his old friend Eugene Saxton, of *Harper's Magazine.*

TO GARRETT MATTINGLY

[Postcard, n.d.]

Please drop in on Brebner and shoot him. *Le Métis Canadien* has 1293 royal octavo pages. You know my other historical weakness: I have to read all of a book.

B

TO GARRETT MATTINGLY

September 11, 1949

Dear Mat:

[. . . .] Something has begun to divide the waters from the waters. As soon as may be practicable, you are to tell me what the book is about,[1] but I've decided to start writing it. No, it says in my abandoned novel[2] that we don't make decisions, we merely find that they have been made. Early August informed me that this one had been made [. . . .] So pretty soon I'll be off for the Western Sea, a hell of a long way, and a hell of a lot of stuff to get into five or six hundred pages. Why is it so much easier to write five thousand? Maybe crystallization began when I finally got a rope around the displacements and economic wars of the tribes. When I confidently told you that that was one of the major forces in American history, I had no idea how important it was. There was a lot to do this summer, and thank God, but I turned up some key pieces in the jigsaw, and if anyone has ever known as much about the subject as I do, he's guessed a hell of a lot harder than even I have. And yet, it's a long way till we get to them. You are to explain the Spanish Empire to me: I'm checking that to you. I appalled Helen[3] by saying that I ought not to start till I'd learned something about the Crusades, and except for the winged chariot I wouldn't, for, properly speaking, Ch. I of this book would be about the last withdrawal of the ice cap and Ch. II would pick up with the Crusades.

1 *The Course of Empire.*
2 Called *Assorted Canapes.* Several versions exist among the unpublished papers.
3 Helen Everitt, then a Houghton Mifflin editor.

I still know as little as ever and I'm oppressed by it. But also I'm suddenly oppressed by how much I know, at least how much information I have, and how hard it's going to be to impose form on it and make it readable. I suppose there is a structure; I know it's going to be hell to find it. This pre-delivery stage is always a holy horror and I wonder anyone writes books. I've got some odds and ends to do and I hope also to pick up a little cash from the journals of fashion and thought before I begin. Then dip the pen and write "Verrazano." Or maybe "Folsom Man." The odd bits are maps in the Am. Geog. and the Library of Congress, and a search for someone in the National Archives who will be happy to do my work. I'll write as far as I know, then stop and find out, then write some more [. . . .]

Yrs,

TO DIXON WECTER

For a man who professed to be untrained in history, ignorant of the professional mysteries, one of the uncircumcised, DeVoto gave an astonishing amount of detailed and cogent advice to other historians and biographers, and was willing at all times to argue for his historical judgments and defend his historical facts. Thus even while he was taking out on Mattingly the frustrations of history, he was advising Kitty Bowen, Dixon Wecter, and others on the conduct of their own historical work, and was robustly defending against Frederick Merk his theory that Jefferson understood from before the purchase of Louisiana precisely what imperial or continental results must be sought on the Pacific Coast.

Wecter, author of The Hero in America, When Johnny Comes Marching Home, *and other books, succeeded DeVoto as curator of the Mark Twain Papers at the end of 1948. The full biography*

referred to here was never completed,
being cut short by Wecter's death. The
first section was published posthumously
as Sam Clemens of Hannibal.

June 12, 1950

Dear Dixon:

By the time I got back from the Missouri it was too late to intercept you with the word, which I had already conveyed to Paul[1] when he phoned me before I left, that I would be in New York to talk to the booksellers. I hoped to see you in New York and was grieved when I got your wire on the morning of the 6th. I tried to get in touch with you by phone but could not locate you.

Of course the ultimate advice I can give you and the stand in which I will support you is to write the book as you think best regardless of what anyone else may say. It is your book and you must be the final judge. That being said, however, I want to urge you as strongly as I can to confine it to one volume if that is possible. My grounds are not commercial, though certainly you will make more money from a one volume book than you would from a two volume one, they are purely literary. You can get up to 300,000 words in a single volume of reasonably convenient size, and that is enough words for the life of Christ and all the Apostles. I cannot tell you how strongly I feel about writing a biography at decent length and with proper subordination of part to part and parts to the whole. Unquestionably this puts the most severe requirements possible on the biographer as a literary man, but unquestionably also the results in clarity, and especially in form, are worth all the labor it takes. Certainly you are full to the bung with fascinating detail about Mark and about his boyhood, much of it unquestionably your own discovery. It gripes you and breaks your heart to give up any precious morsel of it. I say, nevertheless, that a decent regard for letters and for literary form impose on you the duty of giving up everything that is not entirely necessary for the ultimate effect. Nothing is worse than a long biography—I mean nothing is soggier literature or more flaccid writing. Your job is to write a man's life in full with due proportion and full illumination—and to do this in one volume.

I am very sure that 90,000 words for Hannibal is less effective than 50 —or better 40,000, would be. I say this regardless of what the words you have written are. I am also sure that the 90,000 contain a lot of stuff which you can squeeze out of them and that if you do squeeze them out, the book will be much better. I will even bet that the material you can squeeze out is of such a nature that you can transfer it practically as it stands to scholarly publications. If you can do that, it certainly has no place in your book.

[1] Paul Brooks, of Houghton Mifflin.

Biography is a demanding and an exhausting art. This Mark Twain job calls on you for more sheer craftsmanship than any other book you have undertaken. That is too bad and I sincerely sympathize with you, as I do with any honest man who has to grapple with the fearful problems of artistic form. Nevertheless, in my judgment, there is no way in which you can escape grappling with them and no solution of them that would sanction you to go on into a second volume, considering what dire and inescapable results would automatically follow. Grant me some awareness of what a biography of Mark Twain involves. If I were writing it, I would hold myself to a maximum of 200,000 words, guarantee to do the job at no greater length, and diligently labor to do it in less. Add 50,000 words, 25 per cent, to allow for developments and possibilities I am ignorant of. I regard that as the topmost limit you should consider. I think you will fall short of your possibilities and your books if you go beyond it. I think you are running a very desperate risk of changing the character of your book and curtailing its artistic effect and literary influence. I would rather see you take up spiritualism or polygamy.

I repeat all the foregoing at the top of my voice, an octave higher, and with the blower on.

It is easier to write long books than short ones. It is also easier to write verse than prose. Nevertheless, we have got to immerse ourselves in the destructive element and make it bear us up. If one volume takes you a year longer than two would, that may be hell on you but it is all right with me and the art of biography.

That's where I stand and I can do no less than tell you so. All books are written as needs must and nobody but you can determine how this one must be written. But if it is humanely possible to write it in one volume, then, by all I have learned about writing, you have no choice.

And just to be dirty, have you considered the possibility that you may get confused with Mr. Paine? [. . . .]

Good luck to you and retire to your favorite house of worship and search your soul about the problem of literary proportions.

Yours,

TO GARRETT MATTINGLY

October 28, 1950

Dear Mat:

[. . . .] If I am forced to express a judgment on your spirituality, I am afraid the march of events has brought me to a position where I can no longer escape the I assure you unpleasant dilemma of finding either your morality or your intelligence defective, in fact unspeakably awful. It is entirely your fault, and neither God nor man will forget it, that I am embarked on the God-damnedest fool literary, or if it pleases you to say so, historical, enterprise this side of John Bakeless or the far side of Bedlam. An advocate would plead in your defense, though not successfully before a jury of imbeciles, let alone half-wits, that years before senility and elephantiasis overtook me, I did show superficial evidence, or what might look like it to a hasty and shallow mind, of being able to say something, or if you prefer nothing, in less than seven hundred thousand words per parenthetical subtopic. But if you are fitted to instruct the young and pass as an equal among the intelligences of a college faculty, then we must assume that you are also too bright to be taken in by such evidence as was offered you. I say you will fry your ass in hell forever, as I stew mine daily in the dullest broth of watery, uremic, and flatulent prose ever compounded, of which there is not only no end but not even a middle. Middle? hell, there is not even an approach, there is not even a beginning. It takes me thirty thousand words to draw even with where I was when I began them. To begin a chapter is enough to make sure that I will be farther from the end of the book when I finish it—farther by twice as many words and God knows how many years. I run furiously, at the extremity of my (waning) strength, and the sweat that pours off me is all words, words, words, words, words by the galley, words by the thousand, words by the dictionary, and I sink forever deeper into them, I don't get any farther forward, I only drift back and disappear under them. And Jesus Christ, what words, shapeless, colorless, without sound or substance or taste or perfume or indeed existence, words of immense viscosity and no energy or luminescence whatsoever, words out of a lawyer's brief or a New Critic's essay on Truman Capote or the ghost who writes MacArthur's communiques, words of unbaked dough, of glucose thinned with bilge, words less than a serum and somewhat more than an exudation, and in all the mess and mass of them not a God damned thought that would trouble the intelligence of Norman Cousins. It is your God damned fault. You are responsible and you will damn well answer to Almighty God.

I have, *in nomine Patris et Filii,* this day got the French out of North America. One year to the day, and three million words, after I began a book that had no intention of getting the French into North America. If you are bright, or intellectually honest, enough to associate with Allan Nevins—and who said you are?—you would have clapped me into the booby hatch before I started. You didn't and that too shall not be forgiven you. You [should] have locked me up in the public interest and in my own too, being perfectly familiar with the two tenets of Holy Church which say that every soul, including mine, is worthy in the sight of God and that self-destruction of the corporeal envelope that incloses even my soul is mortal sin. The good book says something too about shielding the innocent and suffering fools.

It is not Purgatory you will pay for it in, it is hell, where you will be chained to the side of Pitirim Sorokin,[1] who can also blow five words up into five million and fall short of saying one. And I now perceive an error in what I have set down here, an error which flows inevitably from my total incapacity to handle facts. It is not three million words I have written getting the French out of North America, it is thirteen million. Well, to be sure they compose, so far, what would only be a good fat third of a book for Jim Farrell or thirty-five books for Fletcher Pratt, and we may observe with interest that it took Francis Parkman, that elegant Brahmin who was plagiarizing me anticipatorily eighty years ago, nine books or eleven volumes to get as far as I have. So where are we? With thirteen million words written, or by our lady some two score million, we have now accounted for 229 years that do not enter at all into my book and have only forty more years to go, or say an even million words, if in the meantime I can learn something about concentration or alternatively get a tight cinch on my bowels, before we reach the beginning of my book and, with a sigh of infinite satisfaction and a suffusing glow of happy realization that only ten million words lie ahead, take up a blank, virgin sheet of paper and write at the top of it Page One. And all your fault. It may be of God's intent or my own sin a case of ambulatory and dropsical logorrhea—for my infection I impute no fault to you—but by God it is your fault I turned the discharge in the direction which your antic mood or mere witlessness chooses to call history. I suppose we must accept the premise alike of philosophy, religion, and the theory of probability that in order for anything to be possible all things must be possible, and so it is possible that eventually, millions and millions of words and reams and reams of Goldenrod Bond from now, the drip will cease, the wind will drop, the bowels will stop echoing, and the God-damned thing will end. It is even, if we must hold to our premise in the hope of light, it is even possible that I may begin another book. But not, this time [history], if you are as bright as various hands, including me, have somehow been led to suppose.

You will not pay for it exclusively in hell. With Chapter VI, untitled because the only title appropriate would be obscene, we reach a problem which I truly relish. I have got, I say, the French out of North America. And now, by God, you have got to correct Ch. VI, untitled, for history. And that, so help me Mary the Mother of the Infant Jesus, that will hold you.

Yrs,

[1] Pitirim Sorokin, once a minister of the Kerensky government in Russia, condemned to death and then banished by the Bolsheviks, wound up at Harvard as professor of sociology. During DeVoto's later years in Cambridge he was as famous as Casey Stengel for his jawbreaking jargon.

TO GARRETT MATTINGLY

December 4, 1950

Dear Mat:

These things happen. I was gabbing about this with my editor, to whom please forward it with usual carbon and memo, when either she or I, I'd like to believe I, perceived that the damn thing ends where I have now ended it. That means that the remaining two sections, so far unwritten, get prefixed to the next one. That means, probably, that part of the next one gets detached. And that means that T. Jefferson probably gets a chapter to himself. And that suggests:

I put it up to you. It only hit me last week as an idea. If this stuff is five per cent as good as you hold when drunk or five thousand per cent better than my more realistic intelligence judges it to be, then by the end of page 2626 herewith something to an implicit point should have made itself apparent to the reader's, if any, mind: that the land has by now affected the shape of the consciousness (North American). I succeeded in writing the '46[1] thing without feeling I had to make the implicit explicit and I think that the reader, again if any, got there without my help. But I am not the gay young swaggerer I was in those days and I no longer feel if the dumb son of a bitch won't work at this, so much the worse for him. I'm not only grateful to him, I sympathize with him very deeply, and maybe I ought to send out the rescue squad. It occurred to me that five to eight pages might undertake to set down in words, the simplest ones possible, that you learn to plant corn in hills, you then find you are making corn shocks that are architecturally and functionally different from the way they pile wheat in England, presently your house has the logs lengthwise instead of on end, by damn the helve of the axe you felled them with has a curve in it as no axe did before, you think entail ought to be abolished, and by God of eternal and manifest right there must be no limeys on San Francisco Bay where rolls the Oregon. Even to try to phrase this would be as idiotic as a Harvard quarterback's calling a power play through the middle of the Princeton line, it's a literary problem so fantastically hard that discretion is obviously the best mentor and don't even try. Still, there it is as a problem, and if anywhere, then at the end of the T. Jefferson chapter, which is not T.J., really but The Young Republic. And nice too, for Tom believed of 18th Century right reason, and said so repeatedly in pellucid prose, that

[1] *The Year of Decision 1846.*

315

of course this continent is so damn big and the Pacific is so damn far away that the Young Republic won't get there and what we got to work for is a free and independent Republic of The Pacific, dowered with our own inspired political institutions, populated by manly freemen of American blood, and bound to us by the ties of friendship, philosophy, and the dollar balance. So he said of good right reason. And nevertheless, beginning with the time when the Rev. Maury was beating Greek verbs and the unity of continental geography into his head right on to L&C, he put on a perfectly straightforward, coherent, cumulative series of measures and deeds which would prove to anybody who hadn't happen to hear him talk that by God what had to get to the mouth of the Oregon was the United States.

Well, there it is. I add that it might have the additional merit of making any treatment of L&C superfluous. Should I do it?

I can now say clearly that the principal reason why I am disgusted with this book is that it is a different kind of stuff from its predecessors and I don't relish the dilemma, for if one is history the other isn't, and who am I? [. . . .]

The hell with it. Read any good Nevins books recently?

Yrs,

TO FREDERICK MERK

July 30, 1951

Dear Fred:

I am getting all the last-minute things done before taking a plane to Montana tomorrow morning and can't possibly answer your letter. I wish I could. I will pry you loose from an afternoon or evening when I get back, and prophesy unto you.

I don't care in the least how the ideas in that quotation from Lincoln[1] have been used, whether for propaganda or whatever; I'm concerned with how *true* they are. And I believe that there is more in them than you perceive, or at least than you remember.

[1] Used as one of the epigraphs in *The Course of Empire*. The key sentence: "That portion of the earth's surface which is owned and inhabited by the people of the United States is well adapted to be the home of one national family, and it is not well adapted for two or more." The notion of a geographical basis for the continental unity of the United States DeVoto had got both from Lincoln and from Lincoln's appointee to the Governorship of the Territory of Colorado, William Gilpin, author of *The Central Gold Regions* and ardent proponent of a geopolitical form of Manifest Destiny. See DeVoto's "Geopolitics with the Dew on It," in *Harper's*, March 1944. It was his contention that Jefferson had very early seen the same vision.

That the United States occupies the continental territory it does occupy is not a matter of chance, accident, or statistical averages. It is the result of the complex operation of a great many forces. I think that there can be no question that *one* of these forces is the nature of that continental unit itself—its geography. If you want to call this the geopolitical factor, that's all right with me. At any rate, the geography was one impelling force in the occupation of the continent by a single political unit. I do not say (though I happen to believe) that it was the most important or most powerful single force. I do say, and I believe I can establish, that it was one of the basic and fundamental forces and that it affected most of the others.

Since this geographical determinism, if you like that phrase, gets at least two hundred pages in my book, I can't undertake to summarize it here. But take a single example, such as Why did the bulk of the Oregon emigration go through South Pass? or Why did the Oregon Trail follow the route it did from the forks of the Platte to the Snake River? The answer to the first one is, approximately: because there was only one other route across the Continental Divide that wagons could use, Marias Pass, and that was blocked by snow during most of the travel season, and was exposed to the Blackfeet besides. The answer to the other, besides South Pass, is roughly: because horses and oxen needed grass and they and men needed water, and the route, besides being traversable by wagons, had to go where the water and the grass were. These are all geographical factors and they were, historically, determining factors.

Or, even simpler, Why did the Union Pacific go through Bridger's Pass? Because the best gradients were there. That is an absolute factor and it's entirely geographical.

Or, much more complex, take your own studies of Indiana and Illinois south of the moraine.

I believe, and I think I can establish, that geographical factors adding up to a very powerful force indeed had their part in determining the size, shape, and government of the United States. I believe that Lincoln was speaking the exact, literal truth, literal as all hell, when he said, on the basis of the geographical data he summarized, that the land itself demanded Union. I believe that that is one of the basic truths of our national experience. It doesn't matter in the least, so far as I'm concerned, that he was using this physical fact, this true statement, for political or propaganda purposes, or that others so used it. It is, I insist, literally true. Not only manpower, economic power, industrial and agricultural power had a part in winning the Civil War for the North: geography fought for the North too. Indeed, geography was a strong element in its manpower, economic, industrial, and agricultural power, and in its diplomatic power too.

Why do you object to syntheses of relationships which you accept at a lower level? A river route of travel, communication, and transportation is in part pre-determined geographically. That's all right with you: there was going to be a city at the mouth of the Hudson and another one where St. Louis is. Geography said so—and you say so yourself. Okay, then along comes a railroad. Where it is going to be is in part pre-determined by where St. Louis is—they damn well aren't going to miss the St. Louis freight. So, even if keelboats and steamboats are now obsolete, the route of this railroad is in part geographically conditioned by the original conditioning, by the rivers as water routes. (In detail, of course, its mile by mile line of track is geographically pre-determined.) Now add in the other big towns on its route, all of them at sites originally dictated by geographical factors. Add in the kinds of freight that railroad will be carrying—this kind of crop from this kind of soil, that kind of ore from that kind of vein, machinery to work such and such outcrops, food for so many families, etc. Pretty soon it begins to look a hell of a lot like a pre-determined railroad.

You haven't any objection to recognizing reciprocal relationships at that level. Well, what I'm trying to do is to recognize them in more intricate patterns. The more intricate the relationship, the more generalized the statement that can be made, and the more tentatively it must be made. But I nevertheless believe, and I think I can establish, that a geographical factor can be made out, stated, illustrated in its working, and asserted as one of the formative and shaping influences in the history of the United States.

That's what I'm trying to do. I'm sorry you won't string along with me. I'd rather have your approval than that of anyone else writing American history—in fact I only want the approval of half a dozen others besides you, only one of them a historian and he not an American historian. I will duly modify my statements whenever you can show me that I've got my facts wrong, and when the Louisiana Purchase chapter appears it will be considerably modified from what you read. But I will have to follow my own light wherever it leads, and in this matter, the geographical conditioning, I have no longer any doubts.

I am perfectly willing to forgo the word "history" and say that I'm not writing history, if that will help. But it seems only a quibble, for I make no judgments outside the area of historical facts and, I believe, I say nothing that I cannot factually establish. I am as scrupulous as I know how to be, and I gladly amend any statements or ideas when I find, or have pointed out to me, that the facts won't justify them. But I am entirely sure that the geographical factor exists and is important, and I believe that I can in part define it.

Well, that's the effort, anyway. I'm sorry this is hasty and jumbled. Let me talk to you when I get back from Montana. In the meantime, as always, thanks for your interest and time and generosity.

Yours,

318

TO WALLACE STEGNER

In the winter of 1951–52 I was working on
Beyond the Hundredth Meridian, *a*
biography of John Wesley Powell, and
because I was at least as untrained in
historical research as DeVoto himself, I
was feeling my limitations. As he leaned
on Commager, Mattingly, Merk, and
others, I leaned on him. I include the
following three letters to illustrate the
detailed concreteness—and the wide-open
generosity—of his assistance, his total
willingness to put aside his own work,
however pressing, to help steer a friend past
a hard place.

January 13, 1952

Dear Wally:

I carried off to New York an uneasy feeling that I'd counted the Pacific Railroad Reports volumes wrong for you. If you can count above ten, as I apparently can't, that will be all right, however.

Taft will take care of your illustrators problem and very handily. He oozes bibliography at the pores and you can go as far beyond his text as you may want to, which I suspect won't be very far. He has the comforting quality that you can depend on him completely. When he says something it stays said. Me, I think Stanley was the best damn artist of the lot. Most of his surviving stuff is at the University of Michigan, whose library has published a handsome little book. There's a list of his paintings in the Smithsonian before the fire that destroyed them in some damn annual report I'm too lazy to look up for you. You'll run into it soon enough, and it's probably in *Across the W M* anyway. Yes, by God, it is, I'm not too lazy to go to the bookcase. P. 451, Smithsonian *Publications*, No. 53. Probably also in Smithsonian *Annual Report* for 1885, the Catlin catalogue.

Mrs. Dean Acheson is Stanley's granddaughter. She's something of a painter and back during the war sometime she had an exhibition in Washington, her pictures, some of grandpa's, and some by somebody in the intervening generation, either ma or pa, I forget which. I thought I had a catalogue of it but find I haven't. Your library probably has.

Stanley illustrated Emory's report, among other things.

Most of your map problem will be easy too. The rest will be so God damned hard you'll wish you'd stuck to fiction, or to Mabel Souvaine,[1] who recently asked me why the hell you aren't writing pieces for her. (I said, come west with me and ask him in person.) What makes it easy is that the Pacific RR *Reports* are studded with historical and analytical essays on the existing and the earlier situation, and with lovely, lovely reproductions of maps it would take you forever to find by yourself. You simply sit on your can, make notes, and thank God for a time when West Point was an educational institution.

But beyond that and to fill in the chinks and to render the authoritative Stegner judgment, well, son, those are tears of pity you see on my cheeks. You're going to wish you'd paid your tithes. You are going to live for a long time in the best collection of maps you can handily reach. The Bancroft, I'd guess. Nobody has done this work for you, you've got to do it map by map, hypothesis by hypothesis, correction by correction. Then after you're sure you've got it all worked out and know far more than anybody before you, you're going to wake up some dawn and say, oh, God, and traipse off to the War Department to look at their maps. After many days of frustration, you will inadvertently discover that their maps were transferred to the Library of Congress long ago. You go to the L of C to clean up in a few hours and find that they have had no funds to catalogue the Map Division since about 1890. They don't know what they've got but they're courteous people and quite willing to help you go through their stuff map by map. You do that for a year, during the course of which you run into a couple of dozen inserted but loose sheets saying that this map is somewhere else, they don't know where. Laying these end to end, you find that the maps they don't know are where are just precisely the ones you've got to find out about if you're to say anything to the point. You start looking for them and you keep on looking for them but never find them, not a damn one of them. So you go back home and finesse the whole play with one of those historians' sentences that hint you know this so well that you must assume the reader does too.

While you're in Washington you also wear yourself out at the Geological Survey and there you do get an occasional minute bit of dope. Won't help much but you feel so nice about it.

Well, so far as geographical knowledge is concerned, and maps, the L&C expedition is the beginning of knowledge. It did lay down the dope from Bismarck to the sea, a narrow zone but a long one, and the first knowl-

[1] Editor of *Woman's Day*. During the 1940s and early 1950s she was DeVoto's meal ticket —and mine.

edge. You read my last three chapters[2] and look at the maps reproduced in a pocket in the fourth volume of Coues and the four or five big ones that count in the Atlas volume of *Journals* and the one which the Yale Library published last year. Then you go back to your map collection and go through the geographies and atlases from 1806 to the Pacific RR surveys and sweat it out. . . . By this time you have learned that the maps are no damn index to knowledge—though, pitying my agonies, you realize they're a damn sight closer to being one in this period than back in the ages I had—but they are an index to mapping, which is what you want.

Pike unimportant, Long unimportant, so far as maps go but frightfully important for geographical misconceptions. No maps worth a damn came out of the fur trade period but your geographies and atlases show you what notions, right and wrong, spread out from the he-men to the thinkers. Nothing worth bothering about till the 1840s and you already know what counts from then on. Abert, Emory, Fremont, Stansbury, and I suddenly realize that that's all except the stuff you've already mentioned to me.

I don't know what you want on theory of mapping and U.S. practice east of the West. You probably have to know about Joseph Nicollet but that's easy. There certainly must be plenty of critical analysis in Powell himself and there's quite a bit in the *Reports*. I don't know a damn thing about conventions, etc., that you inquire so wistfully about. It wasn't my stuff and I never paid any attention to it when I was working on maps, and besides the maps I worked on were practically all pre-L&C. It's easy enough to pick up as you go, however.

Don't permit yourself to go chasing off in misconceptions beyond the thing immediately at hand. They fascinated me, I lost months on them, and they distort my book. Stick to your job and just say, Hell, most of what they thought they knew was screwy.

It's easy, my boy, it's just looking at maps for ten years.

Oh, and being wrong about them.

It's a fine, virgin field that nobody can help you with and you're privileged to do it all by yourself, decade by decade. I'll have lots to say when I see you and none of it will be worth listening to. . . .

Yeah, I know, I haven't said a useful word. But it's easy, you just look at maps, particularly the ones you can't locate.

Yrs,

[2] Of *The Course of Empire*, whose manuscript he had sent me.

TO WALLACE STEGNER

July 7, 1952

Dear Wally:

You must be going through some previously undramatized part of your adolescence. I don't know that I ever saw a worse attack of literary megrims. Why, you God-damned idiot, this is a distinguished book, a fascinating book, and a very much needed book. For Christ's sweet sake! Stop beating your breast and earn some writer's cramp. . . .

You have not only got to have the first two chapters, they could well be longer. I advise you to make the utmost possible use of Henry Adams. The contrast with Powell is a marvelous device: get the utmost out of it. Furthermore, everything you say about the background of deprivation here will earn you from ten to a thousand later on, so you can well afford to say some more if you feel like it. [Marginal note: Esp. the Arid Region.]

How long is a book? As long as necessary. Furthermore, you are writing for the reader of the book, not the buyer thereof. The buyer rests with God, he's outside your control. The difference in take between those who will buy the book if you write it the way you think is called for and those who will buy it if you write it with obeisance to what you consider their sales requirements is about four dollars, less taxes, and it's probably in your favor at that. *Never* be afraid of length, only of superfluity. Write at whatever length seems called for. Furthermore, trust your earliest, instinctive conception of this; the one that comes just after it is the one to suspect. . . .

From where I sit, I can see no arrangement of the second section anywhere near as effective as a topical one. You have now hooked your reader anyway, and he will keep going no matter what, or almost so. But, for God's sake, much of what you write in these chapters will be narrative anyway. Don't you tell those privileged to listen to you in class that there are various forms of narrative and that narrative effects are secured by various means? Profiles, character sketches, incidents, moments of emotion—you can't help using them all the time.

Write things the natural and logical way, for God's sake. You've already taken on the big dare; you can't do much to an interested reader that he hasn't already contracted to endure. You are by God going to tell him what you think he has to know—that's your end of the bargain. If it's a million words, or if it runs to analyzing the spectrum of Antares, who gives a damn? You can't and he won't.

322

From my point of view, you are just now getting around to the guts of the book. We want every damned inch of them. And I charge you by the maidenhead of the sainted Brigham's seventeenth wife to give us the *Report on the Lands of the Arid Region* in full. The expression I have just used is, in full.

Look, son, you are writing the book about the culture of the West and the basis of life and society in the West. What the hell do some expositions matter, or a few hundred thousand words.

And me, I don't know what the service of American culture may be, if writing this book isn't it.

Without permission from you I have made marks here and there on the typescript. None of my damned business to tell you how to write or what to do, but I had the ms. in my hand, didn't I?

One principle: when you've got a climax, make it a climax. No point in putting a silencer on the gun when you shoot a sheriff.

A much more useful principle. You know this stuff, we don't. It's your job to help out the reader by locating him in space and on the map wherever you can, which is oftener than you do by a good deal; and to constantly locate him in time, by heaving dates at him every couple of minutes; and to give him something to tie to in your allusions to other people, places, and events. You've got to keep saying, Now this is happening in 1492, in fact on October 12, and what I'm talking about in this aside happened in 1641, in a premature snowstorm; and Joe Doakes was the guy who pushed a peanut up Pike's Peak, that was in 1702 and he was lefthanded and beat his wife. Keep saying, Pissant Pass is due west of Concord, Middlesex County, Massachusetts, about six miles, take Highway 2 or the new bypass. Or, right now he's where the Union Pacific crosses Highway 30 four miles outside of Paradise Junction, there used to be a whorehouse there but now there's only a Socony station. Tell us where the Joe Doakes expedition went, and when, and why. A couple of sentences shining such lights on the margins and into the parentheses *always* pay dividends in the reader's comfort. Also, make a cross-reference to your own text whenever you get a chance to.

But Jesus! you're screwy. This is a swell book, there's nothing wrong with it, you've handled it marvelously well, you will continue to. Get in there and pitch.

Any questions?

I'll return the typescript as soon as I can find out how to wrap it. (Temperature today 102°, relative humidity, 109.)

I sent you my ms by express quite a while ago. Did it ever make port?

Don't be a damn fool, Wally. This is a fine book. Write it without qualms. If you want some qualms, go have a baby.

Yrs,

TO WALLACE STEGNER

March 14, 1953

Dear Wally:

I'm having lunch with Paul Brooks on Monday and will take him your ms. If he were your psychiatrist instead of your publisher, I would feel obligated to mention the symptoms of an unconscious drive to return to your vanished virginity. If the Literary Artists of Carmel had held a contest to determine Noblest Soul and God-damnedest most annoying way to put a ms together, you would have won it without raising a sweat by putting x pages in a ring binder with rings 2 millimeters larger than the punched holes, and by a refusal to number pages which makes it impossible to solve for x or to guess which goes where. It is known to you that I, unhappy one, am no Artist; it may well be that I have hashed your unnumbered pages beyond restoration, for since it was impossible to turn them on the rings I had to take them out of the binder. I trust God loves you for Helen Phillips won't when she reads copy, and I am resigned to seeing you any moment in *Partisan Review*. . . .

A reading of my own symptoms indicates that my unconscious believes your book without flaw and wants me to advise keeping it as is, without change. My detailed notes spilled over to a second (and numbered) page, where they extended to seven lines. This one I have, the first one I have lost. It makes no difference, they were exceedingly minute and I will get them next time through, for I trust you are going to let me see the final version or else the galleys—and will at that time supply the footnotes. (It is another proof that you love Beauty almost more than you can bear that there were no signposts by which I could perceive what you were surreptitiously disclosing, and for God's sake, I want to buy one of your Powell reports but have no number to order it by. Cite it forthwith by postcard, for I am going to Washington and Lowdermilk probably has it. Report of the Public Land Commission. Sure, I know I could look it up, and still more easily if you had tossed in some dates, as I once directed you to. But scholarship, I understand, is to save work for others.) I mean to say, none of my notes was more than microscopic, and I have read no other ms in the three generations of my servitude where I needed to make so few.

Since I talked to you by phone I have reread Part I, which I hadn't done then. It is the stamp of your book. I dislike talking in the idiom of the *Stanford Idle Hour*'s star reviewer, but you establish your authority on the first page, your attack is truly magnificent, and I know of no book anywhere that has more sweep and certainty in its opening chapters. It makes self-evident its own complete relevance and its finality. You must, of course, expect the customary dismay from the academics. It has not occurred to any of them that the stuff you work in is history, that history is so multiple or is to be found in such diverse and unfamiliar places, that these things existed, that light was to be had on anything by finding out about them, or that there was any area of history not covered by their lecture notes. You may not enjoy it; I do but I will also enjoy seeing them on your neck.

For that reason and much better ones, you are forthwith to change the title of your preface. You may call it a note of explanation, but delete apology. Delete too everything that sounds or looks like apology in the preface itself. You may be modest to me if you like but you may not be defensive to historians. Why should you be? You are setting quite a few of them up in business, for they will write books out of yours; you are doing them all a service by providing them with material, information, and ideas most relevant to their job, and greatly needed; for a few, and they the best, you are doing an inestimable service, you are showing them how to write about ideas, personalities, and events. The hell with apologizing to them.

The Powell-King-Adams tripod is terrific. For that reason, I want you to bring Adams in again at the end. In considerable detail—I mean, rather, turn the telescope back over the course of your book and contrast Adams and Powell again in terms of generalization about the half-century and the nation, the world too if you say so, and in the light of your book. I spoke to you about building up more of a climax in the last chapter. This may suggest to you how more of a climax can be built—I don't know. But to generalize retrospectively by way of Adams would give some additional appearance of unity, which the victim of multiplicity might enjoy.

Anyway, and apart from Adams, in that last chapter hit something hard. Slip your hands down to the end of the bat and swing. If no other way, what is rhetoric for?

I say again, and I'm not kidding: DATES. I want never to be in doubt what year this is. I want that even if I'm reading a sedate listing of the books in the Xenia Ohio Library in 1883, by which the senior Schlesinger is establishing the cultural index of America. I have damn well got to have it in a book which is carrying forward several developments at the same time and which is willing to leap back and forth in time as if that could be fun. It's simple enough, you simply write in: 1883. . . .

Which brings up your qualms about Part II. God knows I would never restrain a man from trying to make something better if he thought he could—that is, unless I suspected he had gone literary and entered a deep depression, or that his tinkering might mar a fine thing. . . . What's wrong with this stuff in your jaundiced, or rheumy, eye? It is not the 7th Cavalry riding down the Little Big Horn I grant you, but there is no reason why it need be. It has an absorption that will do quite as well as excitement, thank you. For that matter, I probably sat on the edge of my chair while reading it. Above all, son, it is *new* and it is *indispensable*. That is how Kitty Bowen would write that sentence and I want you to get the idea. You are out walking in the bright sun all by yourself here and history being what it is few of us ever get much of a chance to do that. Nothing whatever need be done to any of these sections. If you insist on doing something, lengthen them out. But if you think they are not utterly fascinating and rewarding, you are too screwy to be allowed outdoors. . . .

I think it's worth saying several times more that the General Land Office and the whole system of carving up the public domain were altogether corrupt. Incidentally, I was already writing the May Easy Chair[1] when your ms. came. All my instances but one are from your sources, not you. I'd forgotten about the miniature house but I decided you wouldn't mind if I stole it. The four quarter-sections at a time matter was, during my boyhood in Utah, widely attributed to Brigham. . . . It's astonishing how completely *Progress and Poverty* has vanished from my mind, though I was still fluent when I lectured at Harvard. I'm going to look it up; maybe you're forcing me to steal from you some more [. . . .]

That's all I've got to say at the moment. My lost notes are all [. . . .] piddling. You have made several incautious [. . . .] statements about Indians. I don't remember what they are but I'll nail them the next time through. I hope you realize that after your book ends Morgan is not so hellish right about the Iroquois. He looks at the Long House and sees the Senate or the Roman Republic, the way the Santa Fe poets see the Holy Ghost immanent in Pueblo head lice. There were some differences, even juridical and philosophical differences, between Rome and the Long House. But, as I say, that all comes out after your book.

I am not given to transports about books, especially books my friends write. But I say in all soberness that this is a book of remarkable distinction, originality, and importance, and that you have brought it off with tremendous eclat. It is a book that will produce dozens of others. Anyone who cares about the American experience, anyone who knows or wants to know what it is, anyone who wants to understand us will be in your debt from now on. It has stirred and delighted me and made me humble and grateful. And glad that I know you. Now go out and mourn and shiver.

Yrs,

[1] A caustic résumé of historic land frauds, entitled "The Sturdy Corporate Homesteader," *Harper's*, May 1953.

EIGHT
The Nature and Nurture of Fiction

To Hans Zinsser, 1934
To Elizabeth Page, January (?) 1937
To Lawrence Kubie, May 2, 1949
To Lawrence Kubie, October 2, 1949

DeVoto belonged to a generation of writers that, by and large, and with an occasional exception such as Hemingway, learned its craft in the universities. A surprising number of them, like DeVoto himself, learned it at Harvard, from the same teachers who were DeVoto's mentors and friends: Byron Hurlbut, Charles Townsend Copeland, and LeBaron Russell Briggs. It was a generation that revolutionized fictional technique in America and revolutionized poetry in the English-speaking world, and it was self-conscious about its intentions and its methods in ways that could only have been learned from schoolteachers. Many of its members became teachers themselves, completing the shift that literature had already begun to make from the newspaper offices to the campuses.

Because DeVoto began as a teacher, and taught for five years at Northwestern and seven at Harvard, and for more than a dozen summer sessions at the Breadloaf Writers' Conference, he was as self-conscious as any of his contemporaries about craft, though his craft was never "experimental" or "modern" in any significant way. His drastic independence and his skepticism kept him from adopting the imitations that so often pass for innovation, and the commercial necessities under which he practiced his trade of essayist, short story writer, novelist, reviewer, historian, and cultural critic gave a hard-boiled pragmatism to his own writing and to his teaching. Whatever you could get away with was right, but your obligation as a writer was not to your own vanity or any ideal of "expression." Your obligation was to your reader; the purpose of writing was communication, and in communication the tried ways were generally the best. Experiments were best made by those who knew how.

Much sound practical advice, little that altered, or tried to alter, the techniques of fiction. It was only in history that DeVoto was truly an innovator, and he was an innovator there by applying to the writing of history the sharp impressionism, the sensuous evocativeness, the limited point of view, the distortions of chronology, and the metaphorical sampling techniques that had already remade the art of the novel.

But the whys of writing were another matter. If DeVoto did not have a prescribed method for fiction, he did have a theory of it. His preoccupation was the buried impulses from which fiction and poetry appear to arise, what happens in the caverns of the soul, why literature seems so often to derive from a compulsion and why and how it manages to transcend the compulsive, how far a writer is a creator and how much he is merely the stylus of his own neuroses. He thought he knew the psychological depths from which serious writing derived, he knew the practicalities of the literary profession in a half dozen capacities, and he was always willing to instruct the young or unpracticed or daunted in either mystery, or to defend his theories and the lessons of his experience against anybody.

It has not seemed necessary to include here more than one of the many patient letters to students or colleagues in which DeVoto instructed them in craft or soothed their panics. Several letters of that kind may be seen in the section on the writing of history. More important, in my judgment, are such letters as those to Hans Zinsser and Lawrence Kubie, in which DeVoto defended his theories and argued against what to him were heresies. One feels a certain desperation in some of these arguments; his positions were positions of safety, and he dared not abandon them except for sorties and counterattacks. Ultimately, despite his emphasis on the subconscious wells of literature, what he believed in was control. It was one of the magics by which one held off dread and the dark. Art, he said in more than one context and more than one way, is man determined to die sane. It is therefore, while constantly subject to judgment, never to be interfered with from without by censors, fashions, or canons of taste. The position is elaborated at length in *The World of Fiction.*

TO HANS ZINSSER

*It is not clear whether this letter is a reply to
a Zinsser letter, to Zinsser's criticisms
expressed in conversation, to Zinsser's
imaginary dialogue with DeVoto in the
opening chapters of* Rats, Lice, and
History *(then in manuscript), or to all
three. The occasion was the publication of
DeVoto's fourth novel,* We Accept with
Pleasure, *which contains a character, Gage
Ewing, modeled partly on Zinsser. Zinsser
objected to some of the words and opinions
put into this fictional bacteriologist's mouth.
The apparent vehemence of his objections,
as well as the vigor of DeVoto's reply,
should mislead no one: they were both
vigorous and opinionated men, and the best
of friends.*

[1934]

Dear Hans:

It is the old debate and it will never be settled this side of the grave. I
have no hope that this chapter of the continuation will convert you, any
more than its predecessors have done, but I have never been able to deny
myself the obligation of defending my profession, and its standards, from
you and all other Goths. Only, with that obligation, I note an increasing
anxiety in myself, a growing wonder why your intelligence, so emancipated
in all other fields, is able so willingly and so trustingly to shackle itself when
it enters this one. For, you must know, you think very badly indeed about
"good taste" in literature. And you do shackle yourself. In your present
chapter you do some picturesque surgery on other critical ideas, and I enjoy
it and back you to the hilt, and yet far more can be said for Van Wyck
Brooks's imperatives of criticism, to mention only one critic you go after,
than for the imperative of good taste.

I shrink from pointing out the obvious to you, of all people. And yet you seem to forget that "good taste" is one of those subjective phrases which embody sentiments that differ from person to person, and that my good taste may be, and in fact has proved to be, your poison, and that not even God can say that my good taste is better than yours or worse. What good taste, which one of several contemporary hundreds, would you ask me to conform to in my book? Yours? That would be an egoism too egregious for you to commit in any other form. Dr. Conrad's? Henderson's? Judge Grant's? Cardinal O'Connell's? Proust's? Joyce's? Dexter Perkins's? That would, any one of them, be a particularization in grotesque dis-accord with all the others. But, you say, you mean the canons of literary good taste formulated long ago and adhered to throughout the ages. But of course you don't, for there aren't any. The canons of taste, in literature as in cosmetics, hats, morals and political dogma, are mere fashions of different groups representing different sentiments and always at war with each other. So that, at only one remove, you do ask me to observe the subjective canons of your own taste. Meaning: you have been taught to believe that some subjects, and, what seems to me much worse, some words, are to be avoided in fiction. And meaning, further, I insist, that, when you get out of the laboratory and into the easy chair, you lose sight of facts and concern yourself with words. You let the genteel tradition form your conclusions for you.

Of course, what I have said up to now is merely sociology. The mere matter of good taste, in that sense, doesn't concern me—meaning me as a writer, now, and not as a friend answering your complaint. When we get out of sociology into literature, when I become an apotheosized writer defending my profession against you, as the concentrate of critics (you are, you know, practicing literary criticism when you ask me to conform to a principle of literary good taste)—the argument gets to much sterner ground. For, it seems to me, you miss the very essence of the problem, and I'm damned if I can see why you do. Honestly, I can't. For you must know that the only canons which a writer of fiction can accept are precisely the ones that govern the laboratory scientist. How, for God's sake, does good taste determine the conduct of your experiments in typhus? Good taste in experiment would be as meaningless as to speak of a bacteriological investigation in the key of C-minor. A meaningless term—exactly that, a term without meaning, as who should speak of a yellow and blue earthquake or a chord of music that turned litmus paper. Meaningless—and as irrelevant as to determine your achievements as an investigator by the cut of your suit or the color of your laboratory apron. If a man came into your laboratory and exhorted you to investigate syphilis or herpes according to the canons of good taste you would first tell him that he was talking nonsense and then order him out of the room for his presumption and impudence.

Well, consider that the writer of fiction is quite as serious, quite as conscientious, and quite as whole-heartedly a worker toward truth as the laboratory bacteriologist. Don't commit the elementary and unjustifiable mistake of thinking that he does anything by chance or for the sake of fashion or applause or sensation or scandal. Don't, above all, think that he is ever unaware of what he is doing, or does anything idly. If he is a serious artist—and I speak of no other, as you would not use the word scientist to describe a dilettante or a faker—then every scene he imagines and every word he writes it with is a deliberate step toward a deliberate end. It is, too, the choice of his skill, of his mastery. Every step that you take in a scientific investigation is the deliberate use of your tools, whose use you have mastered, for a chosen end. You know that and you rightly require me, the layman, to understand that when I am trying to understand you. You would dismiss as preposterous any idea of mine that failed to take that knowledge and that freedom into account. You would blast me to hell if I tried to limit either your skill or your freedom. If the lay world tried to impose such a limitation on you, you would cheerfully devote the rest of your life to fighting it . . . Be so good, then, as to credit the novelist with the same maturity of skill and knowledge—and refrain from imposing limitations of him. Good taste—hell! Fiction knows no such thing as good taste. Its fidelity is much, much sterner than that. A novelist is faithful to human nature, to human behavior, to human emotion, to human experience—and to the art of communicating them to others. It [sic] is faithful to character, to the truth as the novelist sees it, and to the communication of character. And it is faithful to nothing else. I exhaust my skill, I rack myself with torments no genuinely sane person would endure, I tear my bowels out—trying to render human experience as I see it. And then you bid me refrain from certain words and certain scenes that help me fulfill my purpose! Christ almighty—it's as if you told me never to grow a mustache while writing a novel, or to write it on blue paper only, or to make sure that I fasted and went to communion once a week during the act of composition. I tell you that no novelist worth a damn can listen to such irrelevancies. If he could, he wouldn't be worth a damn and wouldn't be a novelist. His job is his master and his criterion, and he can acknowledge no other. When you tell him to use good taste in his material and vocabulary—when a Humanist tells him to observe decorum, when a class-struggle critic tells him to orient himself by the proletarian values, when a Brooks or Mumford tells him to govern himself according to the canons of the eidolon-artist—the only possible answer is to hell with you. To hell with you for this simple and adequate reason: this is my job and nothing shall stand in the way of my doing it. What can stand in the way of your doing a research? Only the limitations of the search itself, the conditions imposed by the material. Only that can stand in my way when I'm writing a novel. If I tell you to observe decorum or good taste or the eidolon-scientist when you are working in the laboratory, what do you do? You laugh at me as a fool or you attack me as a public enemy. Well, you must realize that the writing of fiction is quite as serious a job.

You can, of course, tell me that you don't like my stuff, or that such scenes and words offend or disgust you. That is something very different. The answer to that is, I'm sorry, and it's too bad, but it can't be helped. In the nature of things, the job I set out to do must offend and disgust some people, weary others, leave still others cold. I realize that before I begin—but should the realization affect my professional conduct? I choose to do my job, and I must acknowledge no obligation except those the job creates. And there is something more than that. Is it relevant to your experiments that phases of them offend me? Hardly. The sight of a laboratory animal in pain may give me pain, infected flesh may disgust me, acquaintance with the stigmata of the disease you are studying may give me an accessory disgust. That is nothing to you. You have chosen to do your job, and how it affect[s] me is irrelevant. Except that, quite rightly, you may bid me overcome my disgust and repress my queasiness and sentimental pain, for this job is an effort toward truth, it is an attempt to push the frontier of the known farther than it has been, and as such it is entitled to my respect, as such it has a dignity that transcends the stink and mess and dumb suffering, as such it is beautiful. You may say to me, if you cannot accept the means, then be content to do without the end —if you have not stomach for the method of science, then do not try to understand it and give up the presumption of passing judgment on it. I too. A novelist's effort to render human experience in fiction is entitled to your respect, it is an effort toward truth, and if you cannot stomach its means then be content to do without its end and give up the presumption of judging it. For, be assured, it is not fiction unless it is true to itself, and it cannot be true to itself if it accepts arbitrary canons, yours or anyone else's, from without.

This from me, as novelist, to you as obscurantist imposer of good taste. That is the only dogma of literature I should be willing to sign my name to. It has little reference to my book. Except this: that if I were to change the book, now that I have seen it in type, I should change, not the vocabulary but the insufficiencies. I would try to make it better, as God knows it could easily be, but I would not alter the things you object to. It is your privilege to like or dislike what I have done in it, but it is my obligation to do it as well as I know how, and I've done that.

As I say, what puzzles me is the fact that you know all this. It is all implicit in your first chapter. It is certainly explicit in a hundred things you have said to me, and yet you always innocently walk into this confusion when the topic shows up. It seems to me that this is a curious island in your mind. At this one point you cease being a scientist, a worker in the natural history of the world, which is precisely what a novelist is, and become—well, what? A member of a congregation, a clubman, a phrase-idolater, God help us all, even a literary critic. Well, never say that I have not tried to save your soul. I have wrestled with it in prayer God knows how often. This is another chapter in that prayer, certainly not the last one.

Christ, man, you know all this when you pick up a pen. You feel it in the very characters you write. Well, trust the pen. It's wiser than your canons of criticism . . . As for that passage in your article you regret, balls. It's good stuff, and you know it is. I assure you that if I had written it I should be swathed in an impenetrable content and I should no more think of it as bad taste than as helium or quartz. It isn't. And that's all there is to it—it isn't quartz, it isn't taste of any kind, it's something much finer, it's literature.

TO ELIZABETH PAGE

January[?] 1937

Dear Miss Page:

I haven't any comfort for you, and no one can have. You are obviously down with the green sickness of a first novel. My own first is so far behind me that I can hardly even sympathize with the symptoms. I burned it up,[1] though offered publication, and it cannot delight you that I now wish I had also burned up its successor, which was published.

What you are asking for now is an assurance and skill you can't possibly get without the long series of mistakes that writing a number of novels implies. You will not be able to judge your material and methods by any way except trial and error until you have made a sufficient number of errors. You learn to write novels the way you learn to do anything else, by doing it wrong until you can do it right. You keep falling off a bicycle until your muscles have learned how to keep you on. After you've written a novel you know what is wrong with it. Many of the defects you can put right by rewriting. But mostly no one has enough guts to rewrite entirely. And besides you probably can't see the worst defects till a couple of years later.

I can only tell you to write your story as you see it and leave significance to God. Probably it won't have much significance anyway. How many novels do? If it's about genuinely felt characters genuinely represented, that's enough for anyone. It certainly ought to be enough for any first novel, unless you've taken infection from Thomas Wolfe.

I'd scrutinize with the greatest suspicion any passage that I thought was pretty damn good.

The pace question is easy: you pace any given passage according to its

[1] He didn't. It is among his papers, entitled *Cock Crow*.

content and its relation to the whole. That is to say, you write when you've got something to write, and stop writing when you're done with it. You say as little as possible, and, having said it, you cut it down to half. Then when you revise, you leave it out entirely. Or all but a couple of sentences. The way to write a novel is to leave things out. Patricia gets four pages because as you first saw the scene it was the whole book and you allotted it three hundred and fifty pages. After it's been out a month you see she should have got a page and a half. Or half a page.

All your descriptions are wrong. All your analyses and explanations are wrong. Practically everything your characters think should be left out. A third of what they do and a full half of what they say ought to go too. You'll see that too when you've done your third novel.

Throw away your three chapters and start over. Start about where your tenth chapter was to start. But first burn up all your notes. Then write your story as you see it. Forget about significance, forget about thesis and point, forget about yourself. Write the story. Write about a tenth of it and suggest the rest exclusively by means of that tenth. And write it in motion and emotion. When it's moving in time or space or in the way someone feels about what's going on, everything is okay. When it isn't, no matter how good the thing at hand seems, it's fatally wrong.

Yours,

TO LAWRENCE KUBIE

When DeVoto moved from Cambridge to take over the Saturday Review of Literature *in the fall of 1936, he was still having sessions with his analyst, William Barrett. Barrett passed him on to Lawrence Kubie, the distinguished analyst who was as interested as DeVoto himself in the psychological bases of art and literature. That first medical relationship developed later into a long-distance friendship and a running argument, DeVoto insisting that Kubie wanted art to be simply therapy, a means of increasing the conscious control of the writer/patient. Kubie denied the charge, and denied it till his death; it remained a*

*cause of roughened feelings between them.
When DeVoto began to gather together his
writings on the subject and weave them into
the coherent exposition of* The World of
Fiction *in the spring of 1949, he sent
sections of the book to Kubie for comment,
and the debate began all over again. The
Easy Chair mentioned is probably that of
September 1948, on Freud and W. H.
Auden.*

May 2, 1949

Dear Larry:

This is under the handicap that Tola,[1] with whom I am also discussing my proposed chapter on art versus psychiatry, has the original Easy Chair at the moment. Let me therefore make some random remarks about your letter and postpone a regular discussion until I have the Easy Chair back, or better still, until you and I can spend an evening discussing the problem at length, which I hope may be soon. I am going to Washington tomorrow and may stop off in New York on Saturday to discuss another chapter in the book with Garrett Mattingly. If I thought there was any chance of your being back from New Haven in time and having some free time on Sunday, I would stay over Sunday too.

When I wrote the Easy Chair I thought it clear that at precisely the point you name I stopped talking about your article and your ideas and went on to speak more generally of attitudes I had observed here and there in the psychiatric literature at large. I was not identifying you and psychiatry and certainly did not mean to imply that you specifically had asked art to be psychiatry—though I think that in a way and to some degree you sometimes do, even in your letter. A number of points made in the literature of psychiatry seem to me to ask art to be in some part psychiatry or to reproach it for not being. Whether or not the writers are aware of what they say, there is a sufficiently large number to justify what I said. When I come to write that chapter in my book, I will take care to cite these points and of course take care not to associate you with them.

I agree with a good many things you say in your letter but I disagree with others. You are certainly right in believing that most novelists (though I do not think all) who try to use a conscious knowledge of, say, psycho-

[1] Beata (Tola) Rank, former wife of Otto Rank, and herself an analyst. There is some question whether DeVoto was ever her patient—Dr. Gregory Rochlin, a close friend, believes he was; Avis DeVoto insists he was not ("And I ought to know, I paid the bills"). But there is no question that they discussed literature and psychiatry in many intense sessions. DeVoto dedicated *The World of Fiction* to her.

analysis in presenting the experience of imaginary characters make a mess of it. Usually it is, as you say, the artist who faithfully presents symbolic phantasies that renders fiction's best account of unconscious forces. Dostoevski, for example, was certainly not trying to apply Freud and neither was Proust, though both rendered a perfectly acceptable analytical account of the unconscious. On the other hand, I think Joyce's account in *Ulysses* was just as valid and he certainly was consciously using analytical theories. But I said in my Easy Chair and have several times said elsewhere that though possibly analytical theories might make a novelist better able to understand himself, they were unlikely to be of help and very likely to be harmful to him when he came to write novels.

I agree with you in part about cheap and vulgar art but only in part. Let us make it, however, humble or naive art as opposed to more sophisticated or higher forms of art. There are plenty of valid and very moving symbols and experiences in unsophisticated art, and that fact is fundamental in my theory and I have variously elaborated on it in the past and will do so at length in this book. But certainly art is "cheap and vulgar" precisely when it is false, unreal, and misrepresentative of experience. Was not precisely that the point you made against the movies? In my Easy Chair I accepted that point and went on to say that it was possible for a person to take over even the falsity and vulgarity and cheapness of the movies because the outline phantasy— what your profession calls the unconscious phantasy—might be welcomed with thanksgiving in spite of them, not because of them.

Go back to the fourth paragraph of your letter. You say that "the artist should not at least give false answers." The utmost we can ask of an artist or anyone else is that he give us answers as true as he is able to. Something of what you imply here is implicit in a totally different problem discussed in my book. This morning I wrote a passage naming Frances Perkins, Plato, and various literary critics as well as one point of view of psychiatry as deprecating fiction on the ground that it might give readers false ideas about life or confirm, or at least strengthen, unreal phantasies. I wrote, "The reader of novels, I judge, has got to take his chances, to run the risk. Apart from fiction he is used to it. He lives in and is forced to accommodate himself to a world where the realities are incorrectly reported to him by every kind of specialist he must depend on. He must make his way as best he can among the errors of, say, dentists and economists. Not all that philosophers and literary critics have said about life has turned out in the end to be true, and we may guess that an occasional psychiatrist has been wrong in his understanding of human experience."

I would make the further point that even false and dangerous private phantasies may perhaps be safely discharged by the reading of fiction and that certainly they can be so ordered in fiction that they will lose some of their potential danger. This is not the place to elaborate that point, however, but look again at "art should not perpetuate flagrant error." When you come right down to it, who says that it should not and by what authority? Are you not here in at least a slight degree yourself asking art to be psychiatry?

The heaviest point in your letter is the one in the longest paragraph on page two. This is one I will want to talk out with you even more thoroughly than our habitual problem of free will. In the last sentence of this paragraph it seems to me you are making an assumption that I cannot accept, and in the sentence second before it I find myself unable to believe that the arts do in fact increase the area of unconscious control. Here your Talmud appears to me to be at variance with the Scriptures, and I hold with *Civilization and Its Discontents* that not only may art serve the vital psychological function of giving mankind the pleasure by which alone it is enabled to survive in a world organized to make pleasure all but impossible for it, but also that art may be a return to reality, which psychologically is more important still.

There are a good many other points I want to take up with you but it seems idle to try to do so in the fragmentary method of correspondence. We had better get together when we can. I hope you will not mind if without ascribing them to you I state some of the relevant ideas of yours with which I disagree and then proceed to answer them as well as I can.

Yours,

TO LAWRENCE KUBIE

October 2, 1949

Dear Larry:

I don't know Cousins but he makes controversy the pivot of the SRL and I imagine that he'll take your piece[1] on its controversial value alone, whether or not he understands it or thinks it's sound. You'll find yourself shot at from all angles and you won't get much space to reply; drama critics are the most vocal and belligerent of literary critics and they have more spare time than the rest of us and like to use it up arguing. If Cousins doesn't take the piece, I can't predict how *Harper's* will feel about it. The boys are very little interested in literary criticism, which, of course, is what the piece is. The only way to find out is to send it in, but remember that a magazine like *Harper's* has its own ideas about where it wants to go and by what avenues. You know Kay Jackson:[2] send it to her.

[1] An essay on psychiatric aspects of Arthur Miller's *Death of a Salesman*.
[2] Katherine Gauss Jackson, daughter of Dean Christian Gauss, of Princeton, and for many years fiction editor of *Harper's*.

You've got me over a barrel. I spent the whole evening last night writing you a long letter about your piece and about your literary ideas, which it merely applies to a specific case. I'm not going to send it to you. I can't change your ideas. You get sore when I disagree with you. And you're in an unassailable position; anybody who stands on your assumptions can't be wrong. As I said in my letter, what the analyst says is objective, based on reality, and carefully arrived at step by step in a rigorous process of establishing the proof, but what anyone who disagrees with him says is subjective, the outcome of his own unconscious necessities. Even what I say here will turn out to be distorted by my feelings about my father and brother projected on you, and therefore wrong, and therefore to be disregarded. That's a very gratifying position to be in, logically. But I don't know how much light there is in it for the rest of us, and you crusade about literature so tirelessly and even so violently that you must want to bring us light. The trouble is that we've got to get light purely on your terms, which are that we're just wrong. You say in this piece that if writers will go through a ritual which is in accord with psychiatric principles—but inconceivable in the creative process so far as I know anything about that process—then "the creative artist of the future" may be brought "to a maturity which he has almost never attained in the past." You see, you wave away practically all the literature there is. "Almost never"—that's stronger than those of us who work with literature in its own terms can grant. It seems to me, impersonally it must seem to nearly anyone, that anything of such persistence as the writing and reading of literature can't be so arbitrarily dismissed, that your conception of "the mature artist" has something very wrong with it, something fatally out of accord with the realities. You wrote to me last spring, "I feel about the arts much as I feel about religion; namely, that they have all tried magnificently and failed dismally." Actually what that says is that the arts have failed to satisfy your specifications, which is, from an impersonal point of view, pretty arrogant. But from where I sit it's worse than arrogant, it's wrong. Your specifications leave out most of what the arts—let's make it merely literature—most of what literature actually is, most of what it does, most of what it means. You are quite free to be dissatisfied with literature and to reject it, but I don't think that you are free to extend your dissatisfaction and rejection into a set of imperatives: literature must be thus and so or it will be wrong, weak, futile, trivial, or dangerous. I simply do not believe there are imperatives that literature has to obey, yours or anyone else's. I don't think you can be in the position of telling even one writer what he must write and how he must write it, still less set metes and bounds for all writers on penalty of failure.

Your literary ideas are narrow and curiously puritanical. You are one more literary critic with a system. The system fits here and there, most systems do, but in the main it doesn't touch literature at all. It ignores too much. I think it is misconceived and wrong, it simply is not applicable and will not work.

I haven't seen *Death of a Salesman*. I can't talk about it specifically. But what you say about it is of one piece with what you've been saying to me about literature in general and, from my point of view, there are fatal flaws in that. Most of us do not expect from the theater what you ask an ephemeral piece of entertainment to have—and would not, as you do, go gunning for field mice with such heavy armament. Most of us do not expect the theater to have profound or accurate ideas about life more than once a generation at the outside. Factually, historically, and we therefore say essentially, the theater has another function, several other functions in fact, and in the main is devoted to entirely different ends. Essentially it is wholly different from what you require it to be. In four hundred years it has changed only on the surface—neither history nor literature will accommodate itself to the neat chronological and ideological scheme you express two-thirds the way down your first page. And in four hundred years there have been hardly twenty-five plays in all the literatures of the world to which your tests and theses can be applied. You are in the position—aren't you—of saying that all the thousands of other plays were dire, worthless, heretical, and against God. Because against your ideas of what they ought to be. Well, is that true? Isn't it at least possible that your ideas leave entirely out of account something about the theater that is all-important? Something that literature, and those who read it, have to have. Something that is not necessarily wrong and dangerous but merely outside your theses.

On page 3 you say that the critics are wrong about the play. On page 4 you say that the author does not understand what he has written, and you repeat this several times as you go on. On page 6 you begin to tell him that he should have written it differently. ("Indeed it is to be regretted . . ." and "it could not have failed to enrich the play . . .") Before you've finished you are telling him that he should have written something else instead. And on page 5 the audience is misled by the surface drama—doesn't understand.

What happens if he, the audience, and I question your authority? Actually, you have only moved in a circle: the play does not measure up to your imperatives about literature, whereas it would have done so if it had been written in accord with them, and a play that is written in accord with them will measure up to them. And how do you know, and by what authority do you speak? You aren't an artist, you are only an amateur and occasional critic, as a student of literature you are a latecomer who works at the job only infrequently. And this suggests that possibly you have missed a fundamentally important point. It may be that what the play meant, and what the audience got from it, was something entirely different from and unrelated to the things you assail it for not having. It's possible that, in this play and in general, the theater serves a function entirely different from the one you arbitrarily require it to have, unrelated to it, and entirely valid, even entirely good. It may be that your imperatives have no force. It may be that you fail to understand what the theater is.

The cornerstone of your theory is expressed in the first two sentences of your piece, though you've expressed it better in letters to me. And I can't accept it. There is a central fallacy in what you say and, quite apart from the fallacy, the theory is for the most part irrelevant to literature. A great part of the great literature of the world has nothing to do with extending the "area of behavior which is determined by conscious psychological processes." Nothing whatever: It cannot be discussed in relation to that idea, and yet it has a great direct bearing on "human wisdom, dignity, and freedom" and for all I know may be "a force for growth." And there is no need for literature to be great anyway; on many levels, in many ways, it ministers to the human mind and the human spirit without at any point coming under the test you here set forth. Moreover, the fact that it does not increase the area of conscious control of behavior does not mean that it therefore "expands the darker empire of unconscious control." I would be very hard to convince that any literature ever does that or can do it, for reasons which I have spent forty thousand words explaining in my book, and I am as sure as it's safe to be about anything, though far less sure than you are about literature, that the great mass of literature, good, indifferent, and bad, hasn't anything to do with expanding that dark empire—is entirely incommensurable with your idea. Finally, the literature which, by deduction, I assume you believe does expand it performs, as I see it, quite the opposite function: it immunizes against that dark empire, if you'll accept the figure.

But the point is, your theses and requirements are not only inadequate but misconceived. Literature works to an entirely different end from the one you are trying to enforce on it. If you want to say that you don't like literature or respect it, that for the most part it bores you stiff, and to hell with it—all right, that's an intelligible and respectable point of view. But you can't legislate for it, and you cannot wave it away as dangerous for others. For you don't understand it and your imperatives are unrealistic. It serves purposes and functions which you entirely disregard, but which cannot be disregarded in the study of literature or in any judgment passed on it that I can deal with seriously. Most of the area literature covers is outside and beyond the goals you set for it. You cannot limit it to your ideas about it, for it simply is not that way or for those purposes or to those ends, and your objections are not in point.

I said above that your literary ideas are curiously puritanical, and it's striking how often, when I've been reading them, Cromwell has come to my mind, for you go after literature much the way he went after the enemies of God and the truth. Even so, I have several times wanted to quote you a solemn thing he said to his own Parliament, My brethren, by the bowels of Christ I beseech you, bethink you you may be mistaken. Bethink you. You are too damn sure and you are extending out of your own field ideas proper to that field but of very doubtful, and as yet wholly unestablished, application in a field which you don't know a hell of a lot about and which, by your own statement, you don't much respect or often inquire into. "I find it difficult to read most novels," you once wrote me. How much time have you spent thinking about them from any but a psychiatric point of view? How sure can you be that a psychiatric point of view is the right, or even a right, one from which to issue to literature a manifesto and a test oath? I say there is more to literature than you suppose.

I don't, I repeat, expect this to change your views in any particular, but only to make you mad. You were pretty damn mad when you last wrote to me, mad enough to make me wonder if it might not be okay for me to take a logically unassailable position and say that your ideas were determined by your unconscious needs. I argued the whole thing out with Tola listening impassively. When I came to the art-and-psychiatry chapter of my book, I wrote it as a kind of personal issue between you and me. Then I said, the hell with it, this is idiotic, and rewrote the chapter so that it leaves that issue out entirely and, I believe, fully represents the legitimate psychiatric approach to literature. I never answered your letter for I didn't know how to without taking issue with your ideas. But I can't see that it's wrong to disagree with you. You advocate your ideas with complete assurance and self-confidence. They are certain to meet opposition and I can't see why, if I don't accept them, I shouldn't say so.

Yours,

NINE
Conservation and the Public Domain

To Struthers Burt, March 2, 1948
To William Sloane, May 8, 1948
To Harold Stassen, June 10, 1948
To Russell Thorpe, January 12, 1949
To a Mr. Foraker, July 5, 1949
To General Samuel Davis Sturgis, Jr., May 23, 1950
To Senator Mike Mansfield, August 1, 1950
To the editor of the Denver *Post*, August 1, 1950
To General Samuel Davis Sturgis, Jr., September 14, 1950
To Adlai Stevenson, July 30, 1952
To Garrett Mattingly, October 17, 1952
To the editor of the Denver *Post*, November 11, 1952
To Adlai Stevenson, May 19, 1954
To Adlai Stevenson, June 11, 1954
To Adlai Stevenson, August 24, 1954
To Adlai Stevenson, August 29, 1954
To Raymond Moley, February 8, 1955
To a Mr. Henry, June 15, 1955

When he came back from an extended summer tour of the West in September 1946, DeVoto was a confirmed and militant conservationist. In particular, he was disturbed by the efforts of resource interests, especially the stockmen's associations, to gain control of the public domain by having large parts of it removed from federal supervision and transferred or sold to the states. He opened his campaign in the January 1947 *Harper's* with an article, "The West against Itself," and an Easy Chair on the historical backgrounds of overgrazing and sheet erosion. That campaign he continued, now and then shifting his targets but in general concentrating on the public lands, until he died. He acquired many allies along the way. One of these was Struthers Burt, of Jackson Hole, a member of the Dude Ranchers' Association and an opponent of the stockmen's "landgrab." Another was Charles Moore, of Dubois, Wyoming, the president of the Dude Ranchers' Association. Others were Arthur Carhart, of Denver, and Joseph Kinsey Howard, of Missoula. Various conservation organizations, particularly the Izaak Walton League and the Wilderness Society, and various government bureaus, especially the Forest Service and the National Park Service, found in DeVoto a highly vocal champion. Moreover, he had a monthly forum, the Easy Chair of *Harper's Magazine*, the oldest department in American journalism and in his hands one of the liveliest and most influential. In the years before conservation and environmental concern became a mass movement and a shibboleth, the Easy Chair was its stoutest champion. Without it, the effort to preserve in the public interest the grass, timber, and scenery of the West would have been very much weaker and less effective.

In the volume *The Easy Chair*, published just before his death in 1955, DeVoto collected some of his conservation polemics under the rubric "Treatise on a Function of Journalism." It was a function and a public service of which he was justifiably proud; and after his death it was to DeVoto the conservationist that the Forest Service and other friends erected a memorial plaque in a cedar grove on the Lochsa, on the trail followed by Lewis and Clark.

TO STRUTHERS BURT

March 2, 1948

Dear Struthers:

Well, I might by now put in a kick about Mr. Moore, for he hasn't acknowledged either the *Harper's* or the book I sent him, but I won't, I'll probably apply to him for more dope. If you listen late at night—in that springtime wonderland of yours where doubtless the cottonwoods are budding and you've cut your first alfalfa, whereas we are at this moment finishing our eleventh foot of snow of this winter—you will hear an odd, steady sound. That is me boiling. I don't know when I came to a boil or just why but I suddenly realized that it had happened. I've just been knocking up practice flies in this game so far. Now I'm coming up to bat. Give me some offstage noises for I'm in the saddle again, off the reservation, and out for blood. Somehow I seem to have got mad.

I am going to do another full length piece for *Harper's* and support it with frequent Easy Chairs. I am doing a slight but useful piece for *Look*. I have arranged to do a piece for *'48*. I'm going to see if I can do a piece for *Fortune*. I am prodding the *Atlantic* to take a couple of pieces by Carhart. I am going to Washington as soon as I can—the end of the month, probably —and see what I can learn and stir up there. (Krug[1] has put me on the advisory board of the Parks, so that I have a slight official standing.) I'm going to work on Elmer Davis, an old friend of mine, and Joe Alsop, a friend and former student, and see if I can get them to deliver an occasional blast and get them to put me in touch with other columnists and radio commentators and work out on them. I'm going to see if I can lay a pipeline to Congress. I figure that this business is a set-up for any young Eastern Democrat who will take it up. He can make quite a national name for himself at no risk whatever in his local district.[2] I am going to confer with everybody I can think of—all suggestions gratefully received—and I'm going to land an article everywhere I can. Also a slug.

Sit down and write me the full extent of your suspicions, whether you've got any legally acceptable evidence for them or not. I'd like to know just

[1] Julius Albert Krug, Secretary of the Interior.
[2] From 1952 on, DeVoto gave this notion applied leverage by becoming a conservation adviser and speech writer for Adlai Stevenson.

349

what the largest outline you've got in mind is. Also, name names to me. Tell me everybody you think is in it, all the big bastards, all the little sons of bitches, and so far as you can allocate their parts and proportions. Suggest tactics to me. Give me themes and openings. Tell me what to read (I read all the hearings, all the Izaak Walton League stuff, all that sort of thing anyway), what to meditate on, what to look for. R'ar back and let fly at me.

Do all this in the shade of your cottonwoods, with your shirt unbuttoned and a cooling drink at hand. And maybe you better start raising funds for the Yankees, for this remains the year with two winters, one on top of the other. I am not kidding above. As of this morning we were ten feet two inches of snow so far, and today's fall will be more than eight inches when it ends. If, that is, it does end. My God, you thin-blooded, enervated Westerners have it soft. The Old Farmer's Almanac says snow in July. It's a lead-pipe cinch. However, frontier life is my great subject and I never knew before how close kin I am to Jonathan Carver. Good luck and good haying to you—let's hear from you.

Yours,

TO WILLIAM SLOANE

May 8, 1948

Dear Bill:

Thanks for your pleasant words about me and the late Mr. Pulitzer.[1] Let us, however, repair to the nearest bar or house of worship and recall the turkeys that have received this award and thereafter go about our business invigorated by a genuine respect for $400 cash money.

Since I saw you—alas, not long enough—I have been in so many places and talked Vogt's book[2] to so many people that you and I will have to do some bookkeeping. Vogt himself turned up at a cocktail party at Elmer Davis'. Elmer was reading and being depressed by *Our Plundered Planet*[3] and I told him it was merely milk for babies. Will you send him a copy or shall I? At the same party I braced Walter Lippmann with the usual result. For twenty-five years I have suffered from oxygen deficiency whenever I have tried to reach the altitudes at which he lives and thinks. I plugged Vogt to him for half an hour but I doubt if Vogt can be reduced to generalizations sufficiently noble and profound for that great mind and I will be good god-

[1] DeVoto had just won the Pulitzer Prize in history for *Across the Wide Missouri*.
[2] William Vogt, *The Road to Survival*, which William Sloane Associates was about to publish.
[3] By Fairfield Osborn.

damned if I will waste one of my copies on him. Marquis Childs was also there and I gave him the same treatment to far better affect. Immediately after the political conventions he is going west to look over my private battleground and will write several columns, perhaps more than several, in the same crusade. Unquestionably he can and will use Vogt. Will you send him a copy or shall I?

I also did my stuff to Mrs. Gifford Pinchot, 1615 Rhode Island Avenue, N.W. She is a marvelous woman and she sits there with not only all conservation but all social and political Washington streaming through her house. A copy there is almost equivalent to one on the President's desk. Will you supply it or shall I?

I went through my routine elsewhere in Washington and St. Louis but that is bread on the waters stuff and need not be entered on our ledger. I enormously enjoyed meeting Vogt. His talk was fascinating and eased my own inquiries considerably. I am sorry I did not get a chance to look at his pictures but that will have to go over. I note one potential danger, however. He has been heavily semanticized and talks about Korzybski in tones I reserve for I'll be damned if I will tell you whom.

There are now three classes of Harvard professors, those who have joined Avis' crusade, the dead, and a few in headlong flight whom she will axe before the weekend. I think you had better come up here and watch her in action. You will have no qualms about our national strength in any future unpleasantness with Russia.

Yours,

TO HAROLD STASSEN

The Easy Chair of May 1948 was an enthusiastic review of the re-issue of Gifford Pinchot's autobiography, Breaking New Ground. *In it, DeVoto had named Harold Stassen as one of the politicians who were playing the stockmen's and lumbermen's game for political advantage. The letter below is in response to Stassen's protest.*

June 10, 1948

Dear Mr. Stassen:

Your letter was sent to *Harper's Bazaar,* not *Harper's Magazine.* Hence my delay in answering it.

If I have misunderstood and misrepresented your position, I shall be glad to retract my statements in the same place they were made at the earliest date possible. In an article which will be published in the July *Harper's* I am saying, though in only a single sentence, that you have called for a "major revision of public lands policy" and that this demand lines you up with the pressure groups which for years have been trying to make inroads on the public lands.

During your February trip west the New York papers, reporting your speech at Spokane and another one (I think in Montana, but as I sent my clippings to one of the conservation organizations I cannot check my memory), quoted you as saying a number of things that were alarming to a conservationist. They quoted you directly as saying "There is too much public land now" and indirectly as saying that no more should be acquired. Since small areas of privately owned land must be acquired if western watersheds are to be protected, and large areas of cut-over timber land still in private hands or forfeited to the states for taxes not only must be but certainly are going to be acquired for reforestation, and since various other land-acquisition steps are integral parts of conservation measures now in operation and others that are planned, which are supported not only by conservationists but by conservation-minded industries—the indirect quotation was sufficiently disturbing. The direct quotation, however, used language which anyone who is familiar with the pressure group of stockgrowers would recognize as identical with the language that group customarily use. I recognized the identity of language, though I also recognized that it might have been purely by chance. But the "too much public lands" line, even if used by chance, is one that could open all the public reserves to the special private interests that want to get hold of them.

I did not care to trust to newspaper accounts, and you will note that in my *Harper's* piece I did not allude to the subject mentioned in the above paragraph. I tried to get copies of your speeches from your headquarters in both Minneapolis and New York. Neither headquarters could supply me with the speeches. Both sent me a release dated Spokane, February 19, summarizing your speech of February 18, and one sent me a somewhat longer release. I sent the latter and one copy of the former, together with my clippings, to a conservation organization, as I have said above, and so I can speak here only of the former. It is, however, the one on which I based what I said in *Harper's*.

What I object to in that release is that it exactly parallels the propaganda tirelessly turned out by various special interests whose objective is to get hold of all natural resources now held in public reserves, and comes to exactly the same conclusions, and makes exactly the same recommendations. You do not want instruction from me here. But let me say that this entire question is wholly familiar to me and that for two years I have been working hard to defeat the assault on the public reserves which, in my opinion, your release of February 19 vigorously supports.

As a historian I can tell you that this assault has been going on ever since the first public reserves were made in the 1880s, and that all the arguments which those who are trying to make another landgrab now use were used by the opponents of reserves then and have been used every year since then by special interests that stood, and stand, to profit from the distribution of publicly owned natural resources to private exploitation. As one who has taken part in the fight, I can tell you that one campaign in the general attack on the public lands has already succeeded. At present, the big cattlemen and the big sheepmen, with their press, their two national associations, the four most powerful state associations, and their lobbyists are carrying the ball, though they are receiving the support of other special interests that will profit if they win. Well, the Grazing Service, of the Department of the Interior, was originally set up in response to stockgrowers' own demands for arbitration and regulation and protection. But it took too seriously a duty with which Congress had charged it, that of protecting and repairing the grazing ranges under its jurisdiction, the public domain organized under the Taylor Act. So the pressure group began, in 1941, to try to paralyze or destroy it—using, with others, arguments to which your release gives strong if unintended support. In 1946 they succeeded. The Grazing Service, always tolerably subservient to stockgrowers' interests, is now unable to regulate grazing at all. As a result, the Taylor Act lands, enormous parts of which were in dreadfully bad shape when they were turned over to it, are now in far worse shape. Vast areas are destroyed beyond any possibility that they can ever be restored. Even vaster areas are approaching that condition under the unregulated, the totally criminal overgrazing they had been subjected to. An enormous amount of wealth that belonged to the future has been lost forever, an enormous additional amount is going to be. That wealth belonged to the people of the United States, whose lessees only the people who destroyed it were. And, of course, the reduced carrying capacity of the Taylor Act lands has made all the more intense the single-minded efforts of these groups, who see no other possible use for any land that can be grazed at all, to get hold of such grazing land as there may be in the national forests, the national parks, and all other public reserves.

The next step in a quite open plan of attack on the public land is to weaken, intimidate, discredit, and so far as possible bind and supersede the Forest Service. It has been made repeatedly. It was stopped in 1946 and again in 1947 and will be stopped this year. But it is steadily under way and less than two weeks ago Congressman Barrett of Wyoming, the usual spokesman of the attack in the House, introduced a resolution which would make the annual campaign even more flagrant and crooked than it has been so far. He and various others carried on the attack before the House Committee on

Appropriations. Week by week the pressure group press in the West carries it on in the familiar ways, making the familiar demands. General Hurley is campaigning for the Senate with the attack basic in his platform. And so on. You can read a summary in my article in the July *Harper's*.[1] As I say, it will be stopped this year. But there will be no point in stopping it if an administration pledged to the third paragraph of your February release, or even remotely sympathetic with that paragraph, comes into office.

Also, if Richard Neuberger's dispatch in *Nation* of May 22 is correct, I must call your attention to something else. He says that you joined Governor Dewey (I myself know nothing to that effect) in saying that "Western resources should be in the hands of people who live in the West." The federal government has charge of no Western resources. All the natural resources it has charge of are national: they belong to the country as a whole. I hope that you did not join Governor Dewey's dangerous "carpetbagger" idea, though I am very sure that some of your Western local managers urged you to, and I know some of the men who put pressure on them. It is a highly dangerous idea, and it is one which has been repeatedly used in the propaganda campaign. There are plenty of Westerners who would make excellent Secretaries of Agriculture and the Interior. There has seldom been a better Secretary of Agriculture than Clint Anderson. But residence in the West is not a necessary qualification: Harold Ickes was as good a Secretary of the Interior as we have ever had and Cap Krug has maintained the same standard, and neither is a Westerner. But those two Cabinet posts are pivotal in the protection of the publicly-owned resources and there are other Westerners who are running and being run for them with the deliberate and sometimes avowed purpose of reducing, impairing, and eventually obliterating the public lands. All conservationists know of some of these candidacies; there are probably others we don't know about. If you or any Republican is elected in November, it will be our immediate duty to raise an uproar against the appointment to those offices of men who believe in and would support special interests as against public interests in the public lands and other publicly owned natural resources. Plans that would make Albert Fall[2] seem like a smalltown piker are already developed, engineered, and waiting for the right men in the right places to put them into effect. Your release of February 19, whether or not you intended it to, makes a play for the support of interests that have interpreted it as such a play, or at least as evidencing a sympathetic state of mind. If you are elected President, you will be expected to pay for the support attracted by that statement. You will be expected to pay for it by naming the right men to the right positions—and by implementing your demand for "a major revision of public lands policy."

No major revision of public lands *policy* is possible except one which

[1] "Sacred Cows and Public Lands."
[2] Secretary of the Interior during the Teapot Dome scandal.

would weaken and eventually destroy all the conservation measures that have been put into effect in the last sixty years. The repeated demands of various interests, notably the stockgrowers' pressure group (which is only a small percentage, though a powerful one, of Western stockgrowers) and the power companies, for such a commission as you propose represents a very deadly intention to destroy as much of them as may be possible. You must know—if you do not, then you certainly ought to know—that the language of your last two paragraphs repeats word for word the infinitely repeated demands of just those people, with just that end in view. You must know, or if you do not you should have informed yourself before saying anything, that the opportunity created by the appointment of such a commission would be the one which the enemies of the public lands policy of the United States have periodically striven to bring about every few years since 1905, and in the last decade have never stopped trying to bring about. You must know, or if you don't then any conservationist can show you a ton of evidence, that the agitation for such a commission is an agitation to have that commission composed of, in a word, Alber Fall. You must know that, though (as any conservationist will be the first to assert) effective coordination of existing conservation bureaus and consolidation of some of them is absolutely necessary, there is no question about policy, except in the minds of anti-conservationists. You must know that the Hoover committee on the reorganization of the executive is working out plans for such cooperation and consolidation now, that such measures as the Hope Bill are designed to effect it, that there are many similar public-spirited efforts under way—and that all these deliberately and with the greatest care detour such a commission as you propose, for they know what it means. You must know that practically every expert in the management of natural resources is against such a commission. You must know that the first sentence of your third paragraph, dealing with the problem of increasing population in the West, is, when it is joined to the demand for such a commission, a complete concession to the enemies of conservation. For the master condition of life in the West, the limiting factor in population increase and the base to which all commercial and industrial expansion is anchored, is the water supply. The master condition not only of any future developments in the West but of the maintenance and safeguarding of what exists there now, is the development and conservation of water production. Water, which is rigidly limited by the geography and climate, is incomparably more important than all other natural resources in the West put together. But all the fundamental watersheds of the West are in public lands, Taylor Act lands, the national parks, especially the national forests, and in small degree certain other public reservations. All suggestions so far made in the West or elsewhere for a change in the policy or the administration of the public lands or the government bureaus in charge of them would have the effect of impairing and eventually ruining the watersheds—which means an absolute end to the growth of the West and its eventual bankruptcy, which the United States at large cannot afford. When you support, however inadvertently, a quite open attempt on the public lands, in the exact language used by its acknowledged leaders, you are giving formidable support to efforts which I and people of like mind hold to be the efforts of enemies of the public.

The statements of fact I have made so far are incontrovertible—they are proved and most of them are acknowledged as fact by the people I have been talking about. It is open and proved knowledge that a program for first a very serious curtailment and eventually complete liquidation of the publicly owned resources of the United States has been drawn up and is being furthered by well organized, well financed, very expert groups. At the moment, as I have tiresomely repeated in many articles, the stockgrowers' pressure group is the one that is working in public. It intends—and no week passes without this being acknowledged in the West—first to get control of administration of the Taylor Act grazing lands, and then to turn them over first to State ownership and eventually to private ownership, with the present holders of permits being guaranteed the right to buy what they want, at prices set by themselves, to the exclusion of anyone else who may want either to lease or to buy, and to the exclusion of all other uses of the land. The next step is to do exactly the same things with about eighty percent of the national forest land, and with such parts of the national parks and national monuments as contain grazing land—and remember that the national parks not only were set aside as scenic and recreation treasuries for the people of the United States as a whole, but also are the only possible laboratories for studies in ecology on which the future determination of much land-use policy must be based. There, so far, the stockgrowers' pressure group rests. But part of the timber industry and practically all the power industry already go farther than that, and the rest of the forests and all the public power reserves are in danger—and if a precedent is set by altering the policy or the administration of grazing lands, the forests, and the national parks, there can be no saving the rest. Water interests and oil interests have not yet shown their hands— but the public lands of the United States contain large areas extremely important to both. And we do remember Teapot Dome—and have lately had the coastal oil lands shoved in our faces.

So you force on me and people who think as I do—we are of all parties and most political and economic points of view—a dilemma that gives us no comfort. Either you know these things, as nearly everyone does, and have given them the support of a man who intends to be President of the United States if he can make the grade, or else you don't know them and are running for the Presidential nomination and committing yourself in ignorance of them. In either case, conservationists must speak out.

Several parts of your Omaha speech of March 24 bear on this question.

But it seems to me contradictory in some places and in some others vague and I will not go into it here. But if I apply my usual touchstone to it, I find at least potentially the same sentiments that I believe I find in what seems to me your support of the land grab. The question of river valley authorities is to be fought out in open debate, by all the methods of political democracy, and though I am opposed to what I take to be your ideas I find nothing in them that is special pleading. But in what you say, and especially in what you do not say, about reclamation, you seem to be again supporting the enemy. Reclamation and irrigation are the great sacred cow of the West and, like every Presidential candidate I can remember, you are altogether un-critical of them. But being uncritical is to support the enemy. From the point of view of the values which I believe I represent, the first duty of any candidate (or President) who believes in conservation and in the use for the general public good of the publicly owned natural resources is to in-quire into them very critically indeed. To inquire into reclamation and ir-rigation, and especially the Bureau of Reclamation, the Army Engineers, the projects they have already settled on, and those they are planning. To in-quire with an eye to determining whether or not they are uneconomic. This is not the place to argue the question, I merely submit it to you as a corner-stone of conservation thinking. And I call to your attention one final fact: that the increase of the 1948 appropriations of the Army Engineers over their 1947 appropriation, merely the increase, not the total appropriation, was greater than the budgets of all conservation bureaus and departments of the government put together. This also is a key fact in the question with which your release of February deals.

Sincerely yours,

TO RUSSELL THORPE
Secretary, Wyoming Stock-Growers' Association

The Subcommittee on Public Lands of the
House Interior and Insular Affairs
Committee held hearings throughout the
West during the summer of 1947, for the
ostensible purpose of examining into
Forest Service management of range lands,
but clearly for the covert purpose of
discrediting the Forest Service. Chairman
Barrett, of Wyoming, systematically favored

*the stockmen's witnesses and discriminated
against the opposition. The proceedings
were in fact so blatant that most of the
press and public ended by disbelieving
the committee's findings. DeVoto, as his
letter indicates, was not invited to attend
or to testify; but he and other
conservationists were publicly vilified in
the meetings at Rawlins. The Hanson
article was evidently a follow-up of that
campaign to discredit the stockmen's critics.*

January 12, 1949

Dear Mr. Thorpe:

A mimeographed bulletin of the Wyoming Stock-Growers' Association called "Cow Country," dated Cheyenne, Wyoming, December 18, 1948, reprints all or a large part of an article by Mr. Dan Hanson originally published in the Wyoming *Eagle*. Several statements made about me in "Cow Country" by Mr. Hanson are false, defamatory, and libelous.

Mr. Hanson says under your imprint that I was invited to appear at the meetings of the Barrett Committee. This is not true. Will you please publish a correction? Do you care to retract Mr. Hanson's statement that I have published falsehoods and his insinuations that I am a Communist or employ tactics of the Communists? If you do not care to retract them, do you choose to stand on them and have them tested legally?

Sincerely yours,

TO A MR. FORAKER

July 5, 1949

Dear Mr. Foraker:

To begin with, western cattlemen did not lose anywhere near as much stock last winter as for propaganda and subsidy purposes they claim they did. Furthermore, most of those they lost would have been saved if the western cattle business in general were conducted on any level above imbecility and with any system more modern than that of Abel. The overall trouble with the livestock business out west is that it is antiquated in method and almost inconceivably stupid in conduct.

There is no need for a strain of beef cattle more resistant to winter. The answer to the absurd western system has already been worked out in Texas and other places where a minimum of brains is used. This is home ranching, home feeding, and breeding for increased production of beef per unit. Such western cattlemen as can read and sign their names are coming to see this. The rest will eventually be forced out of business if we begin to cut down their subsidies. When beef are raised and fed on the home ranch there is no problem.

There is no problem about grass either except to keep cattle off it long enough for it to come back. Scores of grasses perfectly capable of restoring the range and holding the soil down have been developed and are now in use. Cattle owners will not submit to regulation that will enable them to get a foothold, however, and Congress will not provide funds for the extensive and expensive reseeding that must be done. The native bunch grasses were good enough for buffalo and would be good enough for beef cattle if their owners did not insist on feeding ten where nature has supplied grass for only one.

I don't think there is any future for the musk ox in the United States. It would be simpler, less expensive, and more hopeful to shoot cattlemen.

Sincerely yours,

TO GENERAL SAMUEL DAVIS STURGIS, JR.

In May 1950 DeVoto spent several weeks touring the Missouri River from headwaters to mouth. His companions were William Lederer, author of All the Ships at Sea *and (later) coauthor of* The Ugly American, *and A. B. Guthrie, the author of* The Big Sky. *His hosts were the Army Engineers. His transportation, courtesy Lederer, who was then a Commander in the Navy, was by Navy plane part of the way and by Engineers' plane, boat, and car the rest of it. He went as a critic of the Engineers' plans for control of the Missouri and indeed of all Missouri River plans, and he maintained his critical attitude during the tour and afterward. But he did not let disagreement interfere with his good time. He enjoyed the company and the country and the arguments, and some Engineers'*

*PR man made sure that he would not
forget them. Among his papers is a pack of
snapshots an inch thick, showing him and
Brigadier General Sturgis with highballs
in hand and shirts unbuttoned and fingers
raised in adjuration or rebuttal.*

May 23, 1950

Dear General Sturgis:

I have asked Bill Lederer to let me know the proper way of expressing my thanks to you and the Engineers for their magnificent treatment of us, and in due time I will do so according to protocol. Meanwhile, I want to tell you how very good it was to meet you and talk with you and how deeply I appreciate the entire trip. It was, of course, inestimably valuable to me as a historian. It will directly affect my Lewis and Clark book, making it better than it otherwise would have been, and it will influence everything else I may write about the West hereafter. I have an insight into my professional problems that I could not possibly have got without it, and for this I cannot thank you enough.

I returned from the trip deeply impressed by the ingenuity, efficiency, loyalty, and *esprit de corps* of the Engineers. No one can see those vast projects in construction without great exhilaration and inspiration. The success of your projects in their own terms is unquestionable and I will gladly bear my testimony to that effect. About the problems of national policy, however, I remain unconvinced. Above the level of constructing to a specific end there does not seem to be either in the Corps of Engineers or outside it any board, commission, or committee charged with the duty of criticizing these vast plans in terms of the social good of the whole nation, or, indeed, in terms of eventual, practical, as distinguished from theoretical, overall results. This lack troubles me since the plans are so vast and the ends in view so hard to express. I shall probably be writing about this question sooner or later though I do not foresee where. If when I do I find myself differing from what I take to be the values served by the Engineers, it will be with no lack of respect or admiration for their brilliance in executing the jobs given them to do.

Nothing would please me more than to get a chance to discuss these weighty matters with you at length—except a chance merely to sit around and yarn with you with our collars unbuttoned and highballs in hand. I hope I may have a chance to do both. Meanwhile, to show you the perils you run when you associate with writers I am sending you a book of which I can say that it has the solid merit of containing no statistics, or at least none that I can understand.

Sincerely yours,

TO SENATOR MIKE MANSFIELD

August 1, 1950

My dear Mr. Mansfield:

This is comment on your letter of July 24th to the editor of the *Saturday Evening Post*.[1]

I expressed a suspicion that the Army Engineers had brought pressure to bear on you for the revival of the Glacier View Dam and I, of course, accept your statement that they have not. I suspect, however, that they have conducted an agitation among your constituents, who have thereupon brought pressure to bear on you.

Who is to determine when "beneficial uses of water resources," as conceived by the Engineers, is in conflict with interest in the preservation untouched of the National Parks and the policy in regard to them which Congress has maintained from the beginning up to now? The Glacier View Dam has not been approved by the Department of the Interior. On April 6, 1949, Secretary Krug wrote you personally that he believed the dam was not justified and that he would continue to oppose it. Is not your bill precisely what I called it, an attempt to make an end run around an established position?

In the letter I have just mentioned, Secretary Krug told you "approximately 19,840 acres" within the Park boundaries which Congress established would be flooded by the dam. That is not 12,000 acres as your letter says.

What you say about the character of the country agrees very closely with what the Engineers say. What you say about the timber entirely disregards the surveys conducted by the National Park Service. Secretary Krug told you in the letter I have quoted that 8,000 acres of virgin forest would be destroyed. In a letter to Secretary Royall of December 3, 1948, he said in addition "it would kill a considerable area of the finest Ponderosa pine forest found in the Northern Rocky Mountains." Unquestionably you have seen this letter. What you say to Mr. Hibbs[2] about the effect of the dam on wild life entirely disregards what Secretary Krug wrote you and disregards also the full report on this matter made by the National Park Service after consider-

---

[1] Senator Mansfield had written to the *Post* protesting DeVoto's article, "Shall We Let Them Ruin Our National Parks?" an exposé of the plans of both the Army Engineers and the Bureau of Reclamation to build dams within national park areas. At issue in Mansfield's case was the proposed Glacier View Dam in Glacier National Park, which a Mansfield-backed bill would have authorized.

[2] Ben Hibbs, editor of the *Saturday Evening Post*.

able study, which again you have unquestionably seen. What you say is not only contrary to the facts but exceedingly disingenuous. You also ignore the extremely important point made in my article about the balance of nature. This point is covered by specific reports on Glacier National Park and by many scientific studies which in my opinion, you are not entitled as a public servant to disregard. Your letter to Mr. Hibbs is also disingenuous and at variance with the facts when you dismiss the question of the damage to scenery.

There is no point in going into the history of the controversy about Glacier View Dam. I know it thoroughly and so do you. There is no point either in going into the merits of the controversy. Very formidable expert engineering and economic opinion takes issue with the Engineers' point of view which you expressed. It is enough that the Department of the Interior found against the dam, that the Engineers formally agreed not to build it, that conservationists and the general public rested on that agreement, and that your bill is an effort both to break established precedent and to undermine a position officially agreed to by all parties.

I am entirely familiar with Glacier National Park and with the proposed site of Glacier View Dam. I have visited them often and have probably been at the site more recently than you have. I have also talked to many Montanans who oppose the dam.

Your final statement that "man, animals, natural curiosities and timber can and will be benefited by the construction of Glacier View Dam" is simple nonsense, unworthy of you.

Sincerely yours,

TO THE EDITOR OF THE DENVER *POST*

August 1, 1950

As a native Westerner from Roseville, Illinois, do you read the texts you quote, misunderstand them, or merely misrepresent them? The point of my *Saturday Evening Post* article was entirely different from what you tell your readers it is. My point was that all the values which the Bureau of Reclamation alleges will be derived from the still illegal Split Mountain and Echo Park dams[1] could be secured by dams built outside Dinosaur National Monument. Now that I have explained what you were supposed to have read, please inform your readers.

[1] Dams proposed within Dinosaur National Monument as elements of the Upper Colorado River Storage Project. Fought first by DeVoto and then by a united conservation movement, both dams were forced out of the project plan in conservation's first great victory, in 1956.

And how good reporters do you hire? If you did not have one at the public hearing, surely the transcripts of it are available in Denver. But what passes as information in your editorial of July 22 is so close to the propaganda currently issuing from the office of Mr. John Geoffrey Will that I judge your legman got it from one of Mr. Will's handouts. It is pretty frail information. Thus, the evaporation loss is not "an additional 300,000 acre-feet of water a year," as you say, but, if the Bureau of Reclamation's own figures are correct, 89,000 acre-feet. You perceive there is a difference. Again, there is nothing in the Federal Power Act, the Federal Water Power Act, or any other act, including the Proclamation that established Dinosaur National Monument, that permits, or without an Act of Congress which would reverse long-established policy could permit, the construction in question. If there were, why would not the Bureau of Reclamation simply go ahead and build the dams? And why not have your reporters and editorial writers read the laws?

You bet your life the West has got to save water. Repulsive émigré that I am, I understand that necessity better than, apparently, the *Post* does. I suggest that one excellent way to save water is to scrutinize and criticize ill-considered, hastily adopted, and openly doubtful development programs.

And another thing. It is certainly Colorado's privilege to develop and save Colorado's water for use by Los Angeles, but just how bright is it?

You are certainly right when you say that "us natives" can do what you like with your scenery. But the National Parks and Monuments happen not to be your scenery. They are our scenery. They do not belong to Colorado or to the West, they belong to the people of the United States, including the miserable unfortunates who have to live east of the Allegheny hillocks. And, podner, as one Westerner to another, let me give you one small piece of advice before you start shooting again. Don't shoot those unfortunates too loudly or too obnoxiously. You might make them so mad that they would stop paying for your water developments.

TO GENERAL SAMUEL DAVIS STURGIS, JR.

September 14, 1950

Dear General Sturgis:

Could be the hazards of war will operate just that way. Bill Lederer has just left here after a two days stay. He is back from a month in Korea and he is trying to pressure me into going there. Decision postponed, pending the outcome of an attack which I diagnose as advanced senility. If it doesn't prove terminal, maybe I will go.

I must tell you of Bill's latest triumph. As you know, he is as expert a promoter as can be found operating anywhere, if not the winner by a Mormon block, which I personally believe he is [. . . .] Well, as you probably know, the Nieman Foundation at Harvard was established to "improve the standards of the press." Every year it selects from eight to twelve working newspapermen, gets their papers to give them a year's leave of absence and to guarantee that it will take them back at the end, brings them here and pays them the same salary they get from the papers, and opens everything at Harvard to them, to study whatever they may choose to. It is as pleasant a thing as can happen to a young or even a middle-aged newspaperman. (As I have conscientiously pointed out elsewhere, it improved the standards of journalism by getting Bud Guthrie out of journalism, for during his year here he wrote *The Big Sky*.) Just how you improve the standards of journalism by binding a working Commander of the Navy here I don't see, but Bill has fixed it up. He has persuaded the Foundation, which under the terms of the bequest could not possibly make a Fellow of him or pay him a dime, to make him an unpaid and unofficial member of this year's group, and he has got the Navy to assign him here on duty, to spend a year studying at Harvard—studying whatever he may want to. I call it a masterpiece.

Have you thought that we might sell seats to our match? Then if it looks like a good thing we could take it on tour.

As a preliminary form of my philosophical question, try this. (It's several questions but they're clearer if you take them that way than if you combine them in one, as they can be combined.) I grant that the healthy and profitable development of any section of the country is healthy and profitable for the country as a whole. I grant that the expenditure of federal funds in large sums (in the West, I mean here) is advisable if it results in a rise in the national income at even the most conservative return on the capital investment. I grant (though probably someone who is not a New Dealer won't, and probably plenty of New Dealers who are not Westerners, as I am) that it is equitable and proper to spend in the West beyond the point of return on the investment, considering how inequitably the West has been exploited by the other sections and considering further that up to a point the nation will profit from the greater availability, or utilizability, of the West's resources. (The second point could perhaps be somewhat defined by some kind of overall cost-accounting; the first point couldn't be determined by any means, since it is subjective, and let's not befog the issue by trying to say how far "beyond" I'd be willing to go. Well, grant all that. Now, we have some pretty vague terms here already, "healthy" and "profitable" in my first concession, for instance. So far nobody has even tried to define them. Well, how far is it nationally desirable to spend money on which the return will not be adequate? Should the people of all sections be taxed to build in the West projects from which only the West will benefit and which will never repay the investment? Should they be taxed to pay for projects of which the outcome is doubtful, theoretical, or in sound, if opposing, opinion wasteful or likely to fail? How much of a sectional project, whose outcome is theoretical but which in any event will never repay its cost, should be a charge against the people of the U.S. as a whole? If a sectional project is in conflict with a national interest should it be built? Who should determine?

And so on. For, you see, what I am really saying is that the national interest is not sufficiently represented against the sectional and local interests, and that there is no way, no effective way, of bringing criticism to bear on these projects. It is quite true that public hearings are held. But, against the effective organization of the local interests, well prepared, coached, disciplined, fully informed, there is only the weak and usually belated opposition of a few conservation organizations, whose membership is small, whose voice is feeble, and whose treasure is almost non-existent. Outside the West, most American citizens do not even know that these projects are being built, still less what they imply in money, taxes, real and imaginary benefits, and possibility of success or failure. Certainly I, as a citizen of Massachusetts, could travel to Kalispell, Montana, and formally protest the erection of Glacier View Dam—if I knew a hearing were going to be held, if I could afford an expert study of the engineering, political, economic, and social problems connected with the dam, and if I could afford to go. How many do? I dare say not a hundred citizens of Massachusetts know that they are helping to pay for Hungry Horse. But they participate in the decision by way of their Representatives? No, I'm sorry. That is the seamiest side of our political life. If Joe Kennedy,[1] my Representative, voted for Hungry Horse, he did so without any knowledge of it, without attending any public hearing, without any expert opinion, but merely as part of the logrolling for the annual pork, so that he could bring back a nice job of dredging the entrance of Mystic River so that a half dozen lobstermen and twenty-five owners of small pleasure boats could get into it more easily. That the Rivers and Harbors Congress should exist at all is a scandal, in my opinion, but so long as it exists and carries out its activities, it's idle and fallacious to talk about either the will of Congress or the pressure of public opinion in these matters. . . . My second point is the inability of the public to bring detached, expert opinion to bear on these projects, whether it supports them or finds against them. Take the Pick-Sloan Plan. Its soundness has been challenged by the MVA committee, the Task Force Report on Natural Resources of the Hoover Commission, and Morris Cooke's associates in "The Big Missouri." Within the month it has been challenged again in a report called "National Water Policy," issued by the Water Policy Panel of the Engineers Joint Council, which has the highest possible professional standing. All of these, with what they take to be due cause and after long study, criticize the Pick-Sloan Plan as in

[1] Slip of the pen. He means John F.

some degree, perhaps a high degree, uneconomic, wasteful, contradictory, hastily planned, in part unjustified, in part unjustifiable—and so on. These are, from my point of view and I think from the point of view of the public, very serious charges, so serious as at least to suggest that work ought to be halted where it now stands and the entire development restudied. That may or may not be true, but assume for the moment that it is true. Well, there is simply no way of making this criticism effective. If the public interest is endangered, there is simply no way of taking action to prevent the danger.

And that is the sum of what I am talking about.

For myself, I have been reluctantly forced into a position which I admit has specific dangers of its own: I side with the Hoover Commission and Senator Douglas in a belief that there should be a commission before which every federal construction project would have to be cleared before you people or anyone else could build it. The make-up and powers of such a commission are adequately described in the Commission's recommendations and the Senator's new bill. I do not like the idea of such boards but I see no other way to deliver either you or the people of the United States from the mess of political pressures in which you, as a public agency, are all enmeshed with the distribution of Congressional pork, paid for by me. If such a board existed now we would certainly not be going to spend a billion dollars, give or take a quarter of a billion, for the Central Arizona Project. And if you have a good word, even one good word, to say for that project, then you are the first person outside the state of Arizona and the first engineer outside the Bureau of Reclamation I have known to speak one in its favor.

Well, that's the general direction I shoot in. On the other hand, do not confuse me with the muzzy and evangelical minds with whom I am forced to form combinations [. . . .] God save us from our friends.

You see, you allege as a virtue what I allege to be a weakness, that the Engineers are public servants to carry out the will of the people, not to determine what is best for them. It seems to me that the people must determine for themselves in some other way than is now open to them. For actually you are not the servants of the public but an agent of Congressional will —that is of political horsetrading and vote-swapping, local pressures, lobbying, and bargaining. Yours not to question why. But someone must question why. I told you in *Harper's* you must study philosophy. . . . It is only part of the larger question, of the technologist let loose in a world which has not yet learned to constrain him, and I go now to set Norbert Wiener right.

We have not yet more than glanced at a promising solution for both the public and the Engineers, that at what can only be called fire-sale rates my services are always available for the solution of any problems whatsoever.

I will meet you at Phillippi, if that's the way it's spelled. And, I hope, soon.

Yours,

TO ADLAI STEVENSON

---

*Early in 1952, DeVoto had a telephone call
from his former Northwestern student,
George Ball. Ball, a close friend of Adlai
Stevenson's, was conducting, as he said, a
"cabal" to persuade Stevenson to run for the
Presidency, and he had been urged by
Arthur Schlesinger, Jr., to enlist DeVoto in
the effort. He got DeVoto to New York,
renewed a friendship that had been close
and warm in Evanston, took DeVoto to
Springfield to visit with Stevenson for
several days, and thereby promoted a
friendship equally close and warm between
his old Freshman English instructor and his
chosen candidate. DeVoto's Easy Chair for
April, selecting Stevenson as the logical
choice of the independent voter, scooped
the press of the country. The letter below
was written on the occasion of Stevenson's
announced decision to run, a decision finally
made almost four months after publication
of DeVoto's Easy Chair, and almost six
months after his having written it.*

July 30, 1952

Dear Adlai:

I give myself the satisfaction of so addressing you till I have to call you
Mr. President.

Doubtless my wire got lost among the hundreds of thousands and
doubtless this will too. I hope some one sees it who will record somewhere
my hope that between now and November you will find occasion for me to
throw a handful of commas and adjectives in some direction on your behalf
or on behalf of someone who you think needs them. If so, I will drop everything else at once.

I don't know how you feel but I feel that the United States is immensely
better off and the future looks a lot better because you have taken the plunge.

I don't know anyone who doesn't feel the same. It's magnificent, and you'll win in a walk.

I know that you are much in touch with Oscar Chapman.[1] That doesn't mean that there aren't other points of view, especially about the public lands. I'd like to write a brief for you on the conservation and public lands planks in the Republican platform. Have someone let me know whom to send it to and when.

It's wonderful. And I hope you can find some use for me.

Sincerely yours,

TO GARRETT MATTINGLY

October 17, 1952

Dear Mat:

The Houghton Mifflin editors are as usual today, scattered over New England and the moose moors of Canada. That would be as usual favorable, except that an epidemic seems to have hit the shop and none of the secretaries who run the place are there. But I finally located Lovell Thompson, banding birds in Ipswich Bay if I got the directions, and he thinks the Cape notion is wonderful. Makes everybody's costs cheaper, quoth he, and let's go from there, but also hold everything till Paul Brooks returns from whatever identification with Thoreau he is currently engaged in, when he will communicate with me. I will duly pass on the resulting truths to you. Meanwhile, go ahead and do what you damn well want to [. . . .]

The first third of the St. Louis speech was me, as you doubtless got when the Governor committed anticipatory plagiarism of my book. The waste of 75,000 bucks and an irrecoverable evening in the Mormon Tabernacle is to be explained by the absence of Dave Bell, who really heads the bureau in Springfield and who took to a hospital bed for several days, and of Arthur Schlesinger who had to put out some fire in Hollywood. The only flaw I have perceived in our candidate, a dismaying one I confess, is his falling for Herbert Agar's prose. It would not have happened if Bell or Arthur had been on the job, and if I had known that Herbert was in town I would have flown out and run a power play over him, but maybe the loss is not fatal. As a matter of fact, last night's speech on Korea has cured the megrims I have been in for some time. It was a ground-gainer beyond any question, and while the spell was still on me I thought it was touchdown and game.

I trust you have observed the presence of Elmer Davis in our backfield.

[1] Then Secretary of the Interior.

He has lately been terrific. If you don't tune in at 7:15, for God's sake form the habit.

Meanwhile I may have really done some good. I have spent ten days and God knows how much of the National Committee's money for tolls arguing a) that the Governor could by no means escape from the obligation of challenging Eisenhower's competence to be President on the ground that he is ignorant of the structure, functions, and mechanisms of the federal government, and b) that, besides the obligation, it was a ground-gaining thing to do. I finally wrote out pages and pages of things to say and the word today is that the boys have bought it. They don't know whether, or how far, they can convince the Governor, who tends to think we should not do such things—yes, I said, but he's a pro, he'll find himself convincing himself—but they are tentatively scheduling it for Tuesday's fireside.

I'm to join the campaign train—there's to be one at last—but whether I'm to go to Springfield and travel all the way or go to New York and board it there does not yet appear. If it turns out to be the latter, I'll come ahead of time and see you.

Yrs,

TO THE EDITOR OF THE DENVER *POST*

November 11, 1952

In the *Post* for October 30, 1952, Mr. Farrington R. Carpenter[1] says of me: "I do not know whether a clique in the Forest Service pays Mr. De-Voto for the disservice he does that fine organization by distorting the facts," etc.—continuing in Mr. Carpenter's well known vein of fact-distortion. The phraseology of this insinuation shows that Mr. Carpenter does know the truth and is being careful to avoid making a libelous accusation while getting the effect of one.

Mr. Carpenter knows very well that the Forest Service has never paid me a cent for anything I have written about it and that there is no way in which it could pay me. It is quite true that, as he goes on to say, the Forest Service has at times provided transportation for me, in planes as he notes and in automobiles and on horseback as he might well have added. I venture to guess that it has done the same for him; I do not understand how, otherwise, he could acquire the knowledge of the Service's field operations that he professes to have.

As a working journalist I frequently write about conservation subjects. It

[1] Lobbyist for the stockmen's associations.

is not only the policy but the duty of the Service to facilitate the inquiries of journalists and indeed of all other seriously interested citizens. As Mr. Carpenter, again, knows very well this is the policy and the duty of all government bureaus. Two years ago the Army Engineers transported me about their projects for three weeks by plane, automobile, and boat, piling up in a single trip a distance much greater than the total which the Forest Service has transported me in all the years I have been writing about it. The Engineers did this in the full knowledge that I was opposed to the projects they were showing me and was gathering material for criticism of them. Like the Engineers, the Forest Service would prefer informed criticism to ignorant criticism, and Mr. Carpenter can count on its showing him any of its operations he may care to see. Or would greater knowledge impair the effectiveness of the attacks he makes on it, for which presumably his clients pay him agreeable fees?

I am surprised that the *Post* opened its guest editorial columns to such abuse as Mr. Carpenter's article about me. If it will give me an opportunity to reply in kind, I will guarantee to be more pointed than he and equally successful in avoiding libel.

Sincerely yours,

TO ADLAI STEVENSON

The inclosure mentioned below was a gloomy piece called "Conservation, Down and on the Way Out." It was the basis for an extended briefing which DeVoto and his Forest Service friends gave Stevenson when they got him off in the forest outside of Missoula in the summer of 1954.

May 19, 1954

Dear Adlai:

I send you the inclosure at Arthur Schlesinger's instigation. It is to be the lead article of the August *Harper's*, which appears at the end of July. Probably Jack Fischer will change the title, a working definition of an editor being a person who changes titles, and I don't guarantee that he won't cut it to make space for it's overlong, though there's nothing in it I want left out.

The piece is the first effort anyone has made to put together the various parts of what amounts to an assault on the publicly owned resources along the whole length of the front. Since the various items have been carried out in various ways, in different branches of the government, a step at a time, and with varying degrees of pressure, hardly anyone has realized how drastic and dangerous an assault it is. I am dead sure that it offers the Democratic Party a brilliant opportunity in November and two years from now. We can carry the West on it. Added to farm prices, the rolling readjustment, and the mess in Washington, it ought to be pretty important outside the West as well.

Arthur tells me that you're going west and on to Alaska. This is good news in a number of ways, most of all in that it shows you have recovered from the ailment you shared with Samuel Pepys. I wonder if you are going to commemorate every anniversary of being cut for the stone, as Pepys did. I wish you increasing strength and a bland diet.

It's good news too in that there's some work for the gospel to be done out west. I assume you're going to see Dick Neuberger.[1] Are you going to stop off on the way to Oregon, and how much time are you going to have? I wish to God I could be with you and bore hell out of you expounding my notions. Since I'm not to be, let me say that I hope you will see Lee Metcalf in Helena, if Congress has adjourned. He has done a remarkable job in his first term and he's a comer.

What I would most like to have you do, however, if it's humanly possible, is to stop off somewhere and look at some of the typical workings of a national forest. The national forests are not only the basis of conservation, they are the foundation on which the future growth and prosperity of the West depends. If you spend even one day in one under the right auspices it would be a big thing for the country. I suppose Dick will introduce Lyle Watts to you, the retired chief of the Forest Service who is taking a part in his campaign, and Portland is a regional headquarters of the Service. But that's outside the arid country, which is the core of the problem. There are regional headquarters at Denver, Ogden, and Missoula. Is there any chance at all that you can go out into the field for a day from any of them?

I know that everybody on God's earth is pressing advice on you and making demands on your time. But there is no bigger domestic problem than this one and no brighter opportunity for the Democrats. And nothing that is more dangerously misconceived by people outside the West.

It's good to be in touch with you even by correspondence. I hope that sometime we can have an unhurried hour together.

Yours,

[1] Richard Neuberger, then a journalist, later United States Senator from Oregon.

TO ADLAI STEVENSON

June 11, 1954

Dear Adlai,

I was glad to get your letter and its assurance that you thought favorably of seeing some exhibits of forestry in the interior, arid West. Arthur Schlesinger now brings me your weekend declaration that you wouldn't mind having me along. There is nothing I'd like better.

I am going to go west for a couple of weeks, anyway, and I can adjust my movements to your schedule. I want to go to Grand Coulee Dam for a couple of days and to spend a week or so going over once more some really dramatic conservation stuff in Utah—all this for the sake of the book I began writing a little while back.[1] I can do all of it before your trip to Missoula, that being the place your letter said would be most convenient for you, or all of it after you have finished there, or part of it before and the rest afterward.

If you can tell me now roughly, within a week or ten days say, when you can show up at Missoula, I'll go about making the arrangements. These have to be made with a little care, as I had better explain.

As you know, the Forest Service is under attack from various interests, notably the Western stock associations and their much more important ally, the U. S. Chamber of Commerce. They would dearly love to catch the Service playing politics and they would be ravished with joy if they could catch me mixed up in it, since I have been battling them on behalf of the Service for nearly ten years. What I want the Service to do is to line up a trip, a two-day trip if you can spare that much time, that will show you examples of the most important problems it has to deal with and the ways in which it is dealing with them. It is duty bound to show these things to any citizen who is interested in them. But in the circumstances we must be scrupulous to avoid the appearance of collusion and to receive nothing from the Service that anyone is not openly entitled to receive. For instance, in Missoula we had better rent our own car and travel in it, so that it cannot be alleged that Adlai Stevenson or that bastard DeVoto used government gasoline paid for by the taxpayer in their low plot to pile up political ammunition.

If you agree, I will draft a letter from you to Region One of the Forest Service, at Missoula, saying that you hope to take advantage of your Western trip to learn as much as you can about the problems of the West, and that while you are in Missoula you would like them to show you typical problems

---

[1] Entitled *Western Paradox*, it was completed only in rough first draft at the time of DeVoto's death in November 1955, and was never published.

of erosion, watershed management, fire control, and the like. Then you can have it typed on your letterhead, sign it, and depart with a tranquil heart. Anyone is entitled to ask for this, there can be no accusation or come-back, and the Service will be in the clear.

I'll take it from here. I'll write my pals in Region One and tell them what we want to see and have them work out as comprehensive and as vivid a display as possible. They'll love it.

I'll love it too. I can't imagine anything better than being with you in such circumstances. I hope that you will be able to do it.

I take it that Bill Blair and two of your boys will be with you. Anyone else? Trip can be arranged for any number and no need to specify now.

Sincerely yours,

TO ADLAI STEVENSON

August 24, 1954

Dear Adlai:

The press accounts of your bout with the lightning[1] scared me badly. Carol's[2] account scared me worse. I can only conclude that providence designs you to be President, which is where I came in early in 1952.

I am pretty much beat up after the Utah and Colorado portions of my trip and am going to Williamstown with Avis for two or three days of rest, tomorrow morning. When I get back I will compose some paragraphs for you about the foothill lands—the lands above irrigation and below the forests. They are the critical area of the West, and those that you saw are in almost incomparably better condition than those farther to the south. As for the dry-farmed wheat, I don't know that there is or ever will be an answer except our traditional one; let the bastards clean up big in the wet years and the high market, then bail them out when the market breaks and the dry years come. But wheat is only a minute fraction of the foothill area, and for the rest of it there is an answer, or could be one. Which is what I'll write you about.

I hope that it will be possible to spend an evening with you, or an afternoon, or part of one or the other, at some time during the next few months. My schedule is almost as crowded as yours but I'll grab any chance you may get. I have some notions about what the U.S. had better do about its West, and what it therefore behooves Democrats to advocate.

[1] Stevenson's plane was struck by lightning on its way back from Montana.
[2] Carol Evans, Stevenson's secretary.

I never had a better time in my life than those few days in Missoula. I'd like to do it all over again. If you ever want a trout or a Douglas fir, yell and I'll come running.

I have other thoughts of dignity and moment to communicate to you but they can slide for the moment.

Yours,

TO ADLAI STEVENSON

August 29, 1954

Dear Adlai:

You asked for a few paragraphs. You get six pages.[1] It's a dirty trick but if I do say so, I think they're worth reading. I think I've tied this one up and in half an hour you get the basis of a big problem.

The further point is that this problem dovetails with all the other basic problems of the West and cannot really be separated from them. There is no greater domestic need than a comprehensive program for the West. We need bold and imaginative thinking about resources, thinking on a large scale, and most of all new thinking. Conservation thinking suffers from repetitiousness, hidebound tradition, and an inability to realize that the world of 1950 frequently requires different answers from those that were satisfactory in 1900. If the Democratic Party could work out a resources policy that would safeguard the tested principles and preserve the gains made up to now, and that at the same time would dare to look forward to the needs of the next fifty years, it could get and hold the West indefinitely. We need a mid-twentieth century Pinchot.

If you make use of any of the stuff herein, better say tentatively and gradually what I say flatly.

Mostly because I was with you and my *Harper's* piece[2] had made me hot, the Department of Agriculture is suspicious of your Missoula visit. Better therefore not mention the Forest Service directly if you make any challenging remarks.

One of these days I'll challenge the theory and expenditures of Reclamation for you.

Sincerely yours,

[1] Accompanying this letter is a careful six-page summary of conservation and resource problems in the West.
[2] "Conservation, Down and on the Way Out."

TO RAYMOND MOLEY

February 8, 1955

Dear Mr. Moley:

I will not be able till later in the week to get an evening to read your book[1] with the care it must have. I thank you for sending it to me. It comes at a most convenient time, for I am approaching a chapter that deals with its subject in a book which I am, rather episodically, writing about the West.

I have indeed admired what you have written about reclamation in *Newsweek* and have agreed with most of it. Some parts of your argument, however, I do not accept. Let me try to outline briefly the point of view I will be bringing to bear on your book.

I do not think that any further reclamation of arid land can be justified, now or so far as I am able to look ahead, which may not be very far, and when more cropland is needed I think it would be far better and cheaper to restore deteriorated land in the South and Midwest. I think it of the utmost importance that the costs of current and proposed reclamation projects, and the disguises behind which they are hidden, be effectively and tirelessly publicized. (And with them the capriciousness, arbitrariness, and changeability of the Bureau of Reclamation and the Corps of Engineers.) In particular, I want to see both the costs and the details of the Upper Colorado Storage Project first determined—for I doubt if the Bureau has any useful idea of what they will be—and then held up to the public view in the brightest light. Beyond this, I regard the Colorado River Compact as unrealistic, unworkable, legalistic, and dangerous; I think it should be abrogated. I would not object to repealing the 160-acre limitation.[2]

I assume that you more or less agree with the foregoing. But there are certain considerations which, I think, you either disregard or refuse to accept.

One is the simple fact of political necessity. It seems to me certain that the arid states are going to get additional water development and that the federal government is going to pay for part of it. Neither political party will ever dare, I think, to shut up the reclamation shop; the most we can hope for

---

[1] It is not clear what this book could be unless an early manuscript version of "The Upper Colorado Reclamation Project: con by Raymond Moley, pro by Arthur Watkins" (Washington, D.C., 1956).

[2] The clause in the Newlands Act that restricts beneficiaries under reclamation dams to the water which will serve 160 acres.

is that the wilder projects will be voted down and that the taxpayer at large will be assessed a smaller percentage of the costs of the others than he now pays. Only California, I think, is capable of paying the full cost of the water it needs, a lot of water it will get is not its own, and it will have to buy it by supporting the demands of the other states. (Also, I cannot imagine assumption of the Central Valley Project by California; it would produce something pretty close to civil war.) Furthermore, I am willing to accept some degree of subsidy as beneficial to our economy and society as a whole. The West always has been kept solvent by various kinds of federal payments, I think it will always have to be, and reclamation projects of a reasonable kind, if there is such a kind, are an acceptable form of subsidy. Its wealth is raw material which is processed and fabricated elsewhere and in effect it is forced to export capital. The rest of the country can profitably pay a tax to replace what is exported, and at least in theory reclamation projects have the virtue that they help to reduce both the export and the tax. This does not make fiscal sense but neither do a lot of other artificial adjustments, both public and private, in the economy.

I believe, as you do not, in the necessity of a federal power program. For one thing, it is the only effective way of regulating utility companies, whose inherent tendency to abuse their natural monopoly is a matter of record. Primarily for this reason, I support the plans for the development of the Columbia basin.[8] I have never supported a Columbia Valley Authority but I think that the existing plans make sense, as those for the Missouri basin and especially for the Colorado basin do not. They are an integration; the Columbia basin lends itself to integrated development; God was in an engineering phase when he created it. If a thorough-going re-examination of the plans would improve them, fine, I'm all for it. I would be especially glad to have the hidden subsidies of reclamation highlighted. In effect, what would follow would be less reclamation in the plans and more power, both highly desirable from my point of view. I do not believe that the planned development is an injustice to the utility companies, quite the contrary, it does a lot for them. Look at Cabinet Gorge, for instance.

I believe that, in this area at least, the concept of multiple purpose is sound. In some cases it has not been soundly applied and in some it has been dishonestly applied, but those facts seem to me to call for applying it soundly, not abandoning it. And as one who saw Vanport and has seen other desolating floods, I support the flood-control component. It is not the answer to floods but it is part of the answer.

Frankly, I think that both the Bureau and the Corps are intolerably irresponsible, arrogant, and in their public statements and backstage dealings dishonest. I do not know how their power can be limited or broken but I am

[8] The date is 1940.

sure that it ought to be. I will support any measure that seems likely to make them operate in the open and to enable us to hold them to genuine studies, calculations, and estimates.

As a Westerner, I toss a couple of general questions at you. With the example of Montana before us, is it safe to let any Western state come even partly under the control of any kind of monopoly enterprise? And: What is a Western state to do as it approaches equilibrium with its aridity? The answer to the last question is simple and clear enough when you consider Nevada, and not much harder when you consider Wyoming. But what about Utah and Idaho? For that matter, what about New Mexico and South Dakota?

I have dictated all this hurriedly and it probably does not much illuminate my point of view. I will say it better in my book. I hope, however, that it indicates to you that I expect to be on your side through much of the battle that is ahead of us, though I expect also to be sometimes opposed to you.

Sincerely yours,

TO A MR. HENRY

June 15, 1955

Dear Mr. Henry:

Harper's has sent me your infuriated and sophomoric letter.[1]

I did not call you a liar. Till I saw your letter, I had never heard of you. If you want further comment from me, here it is.

I suppose that there is a distinction between a person who utters untruths in his own person and in his own interest, and one who utters them professionally on behalf of a client. But whatever the distinction may be, if you wrote the Rayonier ad in question, then you wrote what comes under the dictionary definition.

Webster's New International Dictionary, page 1426, "*lie*, a falsehood uttered or acted for the purpose of deception; an intentional act or statement of an untruth designed to mislead another." The third and fifth paragraphs of your ad fit that definition exactly; so does the statement that Olympic National Park is "practically impenetrable." In addition, the entire ad is intentionally designed to mislead; constructively, it is a lie.

You know that the timber in the national parks is managed in accordance with the basic law under which the national parks are operated, and that Congress after Congress has continued that law in force ever since the

[1] In response to some DeVoto comments on a Rayonier advertisement.

377

establishment of the first park. I understand your ad to be part of an effort to get the law governing the national parks changed and to put the timber in them on the same basis as the timber in the national forests, or perhaps the timber in privately owned forests. That effort has been going on for many years; there is nothing new or original in your misrepresentations or in the newspaper clipping you send me.

I should have supposed that you were accustomed to being called when your profession required you to enter fields of public interest and public controversy. Rayonier is entitled to hire you to make such statements as you did and you are entitled to make them, so long at least as the present standards of truth in advertising prevail. But also I have been challenging such statements and opposing such efforts for a long time, and I expect to go on doing so. People of greater importance and, I dare say, greater sagacity than you have not succeeded in stopping me, and I am not stampeded by your threat to come to Boston and punch me in the nose. We have sophomores here too and if you insist on behaving like one, you will end in jail.

Yours truly,

INDEX

Index

Blakelock, 144
Bliss, 79
Bodmer, Johann Jakob, 141, 146, 150, 151, 299
Boggs, Lillburn, 267
Book-of-the-Month Club, 208, 209, 216, 227–29
Boston *Globe* (newspaper), 237
Boston *Herald* (newspaper), 155, 157, 159–60, 189
Boston *Post* (newspaper), 189
Bowen, Catherine Drinker, 28, 212, 249, 261, 326
  adviser to, 310
  letters to
    on education, 33, 48–50
    on Mark Twain Estate, 55, 67
    on writing of history, 285–86
Boyd, Julian, 271
Breadloaf Writers' Conference, 201, 207, 285, 329
  advice to former student of, 112–14
  as best club, 51, 246–48
  Frost and, 51, 103, 120–21, 246
Breaking New Ground (Pinchot), 351
Brebner, John B., 301, 305
Breed, Elaine, 94–95
Brendan, Saint, 290–92
Bricker, John W., 196
Bridgman, Pete, 30, 128
Briggs, Dean LeBaron Russell, 3, 5, 8, 9, 53, 329
Briggs, William, Mark Twain Estate and, 55, 78
  letters on, 73–74, 84–85, 99–102
Brigham, 290
Brinton, Crane, 210, 211
Brodie, Fawn M., 274–77, 280–81
Brook Farm, 108, 110
Brooklyn Museum, 140
Brooks, Paul, 199, 235–36, 311, 324, 368
Brooks, Van Wyck, vii, 136n, 283n
  characterized, 130
  feud with, xiii, 25, 57, 67, 87–88, 105
    Brooks's psychoanalytical method attacked, 62
    propagation of errors blamed on Brooks, 61, 63, 68
    subjective interpretation of facts criticized, 67
  friends of, 124
  health problems of, 127–28
  letters to, 103, 121–23
  and nature of fiction, 331, 333
Brownell, Herbert, 196
Brownson, Orestes Augustus, 109

Brown University, 39
Bryan, William Jennings, 17, 169
Bryant, William Cullen, 292
Buck, Paul, 263, 271
Buckle, Henry Thomas, 66
Bulletin of the Brooklyn Museum, 144, 146
Bureau of Reclamation, 362, 363, 366, 376
Burke, Miss, 1, 3, 27–33, 295
Burnside, Gen. Ambrose, 166
Burpee, Laurence J., 301, 302, 304
Burt, Mr., 199, 250–54
Bushnell, David I., Jr., 146
Business civilization, 117–19

Cabeza de Vaca, Álvar Núñez, 293
Cable, George Washington, 22, 232
Cahill, Holger, 105, 140, 141, 143–44
Cambridge, Mass., 8
Canada, 194
Canby, Amy, 227
Canby, Henry Seidel, 12, 132, 133, 203–7, 226, 245
  letters to, 199
    on selection of *The Year of Decision: 1846*, 227–29
    on writing for *Saturday Review*'s 25th anniversary, 242
    and reviewing *The Story of a Novel*, 252
Cane, Melville, 131
Capote, Truman, 313
Carhart, Arthur, 347, 349
Carnegie, Andrew, 77, 83, 94
Carpenter, Farrington R., 369–70
Cartier, Jacques, 285
Carver, Jonathan, 301, 350
"Case of the Censorious Congressman, The" (DeVoto), 189–90
Cathcart, Noble, 225–26
Cather, Willa Sibert, 22
Catherine of Aragon (Queen of Henry VIII of England), 28
Catholicism, 150
Catlin, George, 140–52, 299
Celler, Emanuel, 155, 189–92
Censorship
  book, 160–61
    Strange Fruit, 134, 157, 172–73, 187, 271
  of war news, 155, 162, 164–72
"Centennial of Mormonism, The" (DeVoto), 108
Central Arizona Project, 366
Central Intelligence Agency (CIA), 196
Central Valley Project, 376

DATE DUE
